Congress Reconsidered

Second Edition

Politics and Public Policy Series

Advisory Editor

Robert L. Peabody

Johns Hopkins University

Congress Reconsidered

Second Edition

edited by

Lawrence C. Dodd
Indiana University

and

Bruce I. Oppenheimer
University of Houston

Congressional Quarterly Press
a division of
CONGRESSIONAL QUARTERLY INC.
1414 22nd Street N.W., Washington, D.C. 20037

Copyright Acknowledgments

"Executive-Congressional Conflict in Foreign Policy: Explaining It; Coping With It," by I. M. Destler. Copyright © 1981 by The Carnegie Endowment for International Peace.

"Congress, the President, and the Crisis of Competence in Government," by James L. Sundquist, has been condensed, with minor modifications, from the author's chapter in *Setting National Priorities: Agenda for the 1980s,* edited by Joseph Pechman. Copyright © 1980 by The Brookings Institution. Used by permission of The Brookings Institution.

Cover Photo: William Tucker/Uniphoto
Cover Design: Richard Pottern

Printed in the United States of America

Library of Congress Cataloging in Publication Data

Main entry under title:

Congress reconsidered.

    Bibliography: p.
    Includes index.
    1. United States. Congress — Addresses, essays, lectures. I. Dodd, Lawrence C., 1946- II. Oppenheimer, Bruce Ian.
JK 1061.C587   1981   328.73   80-39915
ISBN 0-87187-162-9

Preface

The four years since the initial publication of *Congress Reconsidered* have demonstrated that the congressional changes under way in the early and mid-1970s were not insignificant or transient departures from "normal" patterns of congressional organization and procedure. Instead, these changes have become an accepted part of congressional life and have produced distinctly new forms of organization, policy-making, and legislative-executive relations. Moreover, the intervening years have seen further organizational reform, departures from traditional patterns of congressional elections and member retirement, and, most recently, a change in party dominance in Congress.

The purpose of the second edition of *Congress Reconsidered* is to examine the factors that will influence Congress in the 1980s. We have approached this edition somewhat differently from the first. There we sought to document as extensively as possible the immediate changes taking place. This edition, too, is concerned with organizational change, but it also includes essays that trace the effects of electoral, organizational, and membership change on the behavior of members, the policy process, legislative voting, and congressional-executive relations. In addition, greater attention has been given to the broader environmental, historical, and theoretical perspectives of Congress.

In order to meet these goals, substantial changes in the second edition have been made. Thirteen essays are new, and the other five have been revised to incorporate events since 1977. The first three chapters in Part I, Patterns and Dynamics of Congressional Change, are overview essays on the Senate, House, and congressional elections; they present new and updated materials essential to an integrated understanding of the modern Congress. Chapter 4 examines increases in voluntary congressional retirement, linking them to the organizational demands of the contemporary Congress. The different dynamics of committee reorganization efforts in the House and Senate are compared in Chapter 5.

The essays in Part II, Congressional Processes and Institutions, take a close look at the internal workings of Congress. Chapter 6 focuses on the primary force for congressional centralization — party leadership. Recent party leaders in the House are introduced and possible changes in the leadership of both parties are discussed. In Chapter 7 the author explains how committees and subcommittees affect the "capacities, disabilities, and biases" of congressional policymaking. Chapter 8 treats the history and significance of the Conservative Coalition, and Chapter 9 examines the proliferation of nonofficial groups in Congress. The Congressional Black Caucus, the Northeast-Midwest Congressional Coalition, and the New Members' Caucus are described in detail. Chapter 10 examines changes in congressional voting patterns from 1925 to 1978, particularly in the political agenda, policy outputs, and voting alignments. This section concludes with a re-examination of the congressional budget process — how it operates and its impact on congressional behavior and spending policies.

Part III, Congress, the Executive, and Public Policy, shifts attention from organization, procedure, and voting coalitions to analysis of domestic and foreign policy processes and congressional-executive relations. Chapter 12 examines how the reforms of the 1970s created new capacities for democratic obstructionism throughout the congressional process. Using domestic energy legislation as a primary focus, the author explains why it took Congress so long to enact energy legislation and evaluates the costs of delay. Chapter 13, a study of congressional-executive conflict in foreign policy, describes Congress's efforts after Vietnam to reassert itself in foreign policymaking and suggests various ways of coping with the conflict that resulted. The final two essays in Part III concern relations between Congress and the federal bureaucracy. Chapter 14 examines Congress's oversight responsibilities and the likelihood of improved oversight. Chapter 15 takes a provocative look at the unwillingness of Congress and the inability of the president to control the federal bureaucracy in a coordinated fashion.

The three essays comprising Part IV, Congress in the 1980s, attempt to place congressional change and performance in a broader context. One views changes in Congress as part of an ineffective response to the crisis of competence in government; one approaches congressional change from a marxist perspective; and one argues that Congress is being shaped by the post-industrial world of scarcity and international volatility in which we live. The crisis of competence in government and the built-in structural and institutional problems at its root are discussed in Chapter 16. In contrast, Chapter 17 views congressional change and the lapses of congressional performance as the result of traditional political approaches to economic problems inherent in the later stages of capitalist economics. In the final essay, the author contends that Congress has entered a new era of electoral vulnerability in which institutional incapacity to organize effectively and solve pressing economic and social problems will produce increased member turnover, congressional immobilism, a renewed growth of executive imperialism, and a decline in public support not only of Congress but also of its members. The author suggests that this crisis of congressional legitimation can be averted primarily through constitutional revision.

All of these essays, of course, must be approached in light of recent election trends, especially the Republican capture of the Senate and the presidency in 1980. The prologue to this book analyzes these election results in an effort to understand the effect that they will have on the organization and operation of Congress in the eighties. In particular, it focuses on the capacity of Congress under divided party control to operate effectively.

For help in the preparation of this book, there are many people we would like to thank. First are the contributors. They have willingly revised their drafts, been prompt in meeting the various deadlines we have set, and produced what we consider to be exceedingly fine essays. It would be difficult to find a more cooperative group of scholars.

In addition, there are a number of individuals who in various direct and indirect ways — some knowingly and others unknowingly — assisted us, including James Anderson, David Brady, Joe Cooper, Cheryl Dodd, Michael Dodd, John Ellwood, Robert Erikson, Edward Harpham, Malcolm Jewell, Tom Mann, Richard Murray, Robert Peabody, Leroy Rieselbach, Catherine Rudder, Alan Stone, and Terry Sullivan.

The resources provided us by our respective departments at the University of Houston, Indiana University, and the University of Texas-Austin and the assistance and support of our colleagues in these departments are greatly appreciated. Bruce Oppenheimer wishes to thank people who assisted him during various research trips to Washington, in particular Representatives Richard Bolling and Gillis Long, and their staffs, as well as the staff of the House Rules Committee. Especially during final preparation of the book, both of us were a substantial imposition on the play routines of Christopher and

Meredith Dodd and on Cheryl's patience. Their presence made work on the book a more enjoyable experience for us, and we greatly appreciate their tolerance.

We also owe a lasting debt to the American Political Science Association Congressional Fellowship Program. Our experience as Congressional Fellows from 1974 to 1975 provided the prime stimulus for *Congress Reconsidered* and served as the starting point for our collaborative efforts.

Of great importance to the success of this edition have been the efforts of the editor at Congressional Quarterly, Jean Woy. From the interest she demonstrated in persuading us to publish this edition with CQ, to her concern with overall style and content, to her attention to the numerous important details, Jean has been tops. At every step she has been willing to listen and discuss our ideas no matter how outrageous they might have seemed at first. In addition, working with Barbara de Boinville, who managed the production of the book, has been equally superb. We could not have asked for a better and more professional relationship than we have had with the editorial staff at Congressional Quarterly.

Finally, we must note that as Congress has changed, so have we. Oppenheimer has moved from the snowbelt to the sunbelt, and Dodd just the reverse. But unlike Congress in recent years, stability seems to be our forte. Dodd remains Texan at heart and 5'7" in stature. Oppenheimer, 6'6" and Texan in stature, remains an unreconstructed Yankee. Despite these differences, though, we are still able to see eye to eye. And as with the first edition, we must each acknowledge his tremendous debt to the other. From start to finish this has been a joint project with equally shared tasks. The experience continues to underscore for us both the personal joys and friendship that can derive from such a truly cooperative intellectual venture.

L.C.D.
B.I.O.

Contents

Electoral Upheaval and Congressional Change: A Prologue to the 1980s

Lawrence C. Dodd and Bruce I. Oppenheimer

The 1980 election serves as a dramatic prologue to the study of Congress during the coming decade. The Republican party won control of the Senate for the first time since 1953, confronting the nation with divided party control of Congress, which it had not seen in 50 years. As the 97th Congress convened, the Republicans held a 53-47 seat edge in the Senate, and in the House the Democrats' margin of control was substantially reduced. Now only 26 members short of a majority, Republicans hope to take control of the House after the 1982 elections. In the interim, House Republicans, in league with conservative Democrats, may be capable of dominating House policy decisions.

The electoral landslide of Ronald Reagan and Republican gains in Congress offer to conservatives their first full-fledged opportunity to govern since the presidency of Herbert Hoover. Some commentators predict that the age of postwar liberalism has ended. Most of the postwar leaders of the liberal movement in the Senate — Birch Bayh, Frank Church, Hubert Humphrey, Warren Magnuson, Mike Mansfield, George McGovern, Lee Metcalf, Walter Mondale, Edmund Muskie, Gaylord Nelson — are gone, as are many liberal leaders in the House. Those who remain in Congress face a far less promising electoral and organizational future than they did in 1974.

Recent election results raise questions about the advantages of incumbency, particularly in the Senate. In the 1976, 1978, and 1980 elections, only 60 percent of Senate incumbents were victorious, a dramatic decline from the 80 percent victory rate enjoyed by senators during most of the period since World War II.[1] House incumbents have continued to win re-election at the 90 percent rate of the preceding postwar years; 90.4 percent of the 398 incumbents seeking re-election in 1980 were victorious.[2] However, the 1980 elections witnessed the defeat of numerous influential and previously "safe" House Democratic incumbents, including Ways and Means Committee Chairman Al Ullman (Ore.) and House Majority Whip John Brademas (Ind.). Scholars must now consider why electoral vulnerability has increased in the Senate, and whether it will spread to the House.

In this prologue we will trace the broad contours of the electoral changes that appear under way and offer initial speculations about the capacity of the Congress under divided party control to function effectively.

THE SENATE ELECTIONS

The nature of the partisan shift that occurred in the Senate is presented in Table 1. In the aggregate, the Democrats fell from a high of 62 members in the 95th Congress (1977-78) to 47 seats in the 97th (1981-82), and Republicans rose from 38 to 53 seats. In the 95th Congress, the Democrats were the Senate majority party in the East, Midwest, and South and were tied with Republicans for control of the Senate seats in the West. After the 1980 elections, the Democrats had fallen to minority status in the Midwest and West and retained narrower majorities in the East and South.[3]

Why, after more than a quarter century as the minority party, were Republicans suddenly able to generate a Senate majority? A combination of factors appears to have been at work. In the 1978 and 1980 elections, Democratic incumbents were linked by Republican challengers to the poor performance of the nation's economy under a Democratic president. In particular, the recession of 1980, coming as it did late in the election year, caused serious economic problems among traditionally Democratic voters such as blue collar workers. Early survey analysis suggests that turnout among these voters was lower than in the past and that those who went to the polls voted Republican in larger percentages than usual.[4]

The rejection of President Carter meant that most Democratic candidates had to run substantially ahead of the party's standard-bearer in order to win. The problem created for incumbents is illustrated dramatically when one compares their vote totals to those of President Carter in their states. In Idaho, for example, Frank Church received nearly twice as many votes as Carter and lost the election by less

Table 1 The Partisan Distribution of Senate Seats, 1977-1981, and Contested Seats, 1982

Congress	East	Midwest	South	West	Total
95th (All Seats)					
Democrats	14	16	19	13	62
Republicans	10	8	7	13	38
97th (All Seats)					
Democrats	13	10	15	9	47
Republicans	11	14	11	17	53
98th (Seats Open for Contests)					
Democrats	6	5	5	5	21
Republicans	5	3	0	4	12

NOTE: *East:* Conn., Del., Maine, Md., Mass., N.H., N.J., N.Y., Pa., R.I., Vt., W.Va. *Midwest:* Ill., Ind., Iowa, Kans., Mich., Minn., Mo., Nebr., N.D., Ohio, S.D., Wis. *South:* Ala., Ark., Fla., Ga., Ky., La., Miss., N.C., Okla., S.C., Tenn., Tex., Va. *West:* Alaska, Ariz., Calif., Colo., Hawaii, Idaho, Mont., Nev., N.M., Ore., Utah, Wash., Wyo.

than 4500 votes. Likewise, defeated incumbents such as John Culver, Birch Bayh, George McGovern, and Gaylord Nelson all ran well ahead of Carter. Even the losing Democratic challenger to Barry Goldwater in Arizona received over 50 percent more votes than the president.

Figures such as these suggest that it required substantial ticket splitting and strong independent Senate campaigns for Democratic senatorial candidates to survive the Carter defeat. Senators from traditionally Republican states (such as Bayh, McGovern, and Church) were particularly vulnerable to both the partisan swing produced by Reagan's defeat of Carter and to charges that they were out of step with the mainstream politics of their state.

From an interest group perspective, many Republican candidates were assisted by conservative political groups such as the National Conservative Political Action Committee (NCPAC) and the Moral Majority. Not only did these groups provide considerable financial backing for conservative candidates, but they also organized extensive media campaigns against liberal senators. These efforts, in conjunction with voter turnout campaigns among fundamentalist religious organizations, may have contributed to the troubles of the incumbent Democratic senators. They also may have helped return Senate elections in the South to a pattern of two-party competitiveness. This pattern, which had emerged in the 1960s, was disrupted by Watergate and Carter's election in 1976. Now, however, the days of uncontested and noncompetitive Democratic Senate seats in the South appear to be over.

Finally, one must consider the role of the National Republican Senatorial Committee, which took advantage of a special provision in the campaign financing laws. Between January 1, 1979, and September 30, 1980, the committee raised more than $10 million, which it distributed to Republican challengers as well as incumbents. By comparison, its Democratic counterpart raised less than $500,000 in the same time period.[5]

Taken together, these various factors resulted in vulnerable Democratic incumbents faced by aggressive challengers and well-financed campaigns. Moreover, it is possible that in the 1982 elections the Republicans will maintain and perhaps increase the size of their majority. As Table 1 shows, of the 33 Senate seats to be contested, the Democrats currently hold 21, and the Republicans hold 12.

Whereas relatively few Republican incumbents appear very vulnerable in 1982, several Democratic incumbents are from traditionally Republican seats. Quentin Burdick of North Dakota, Dennis DeConcini of Arizona, and Edward Zorinsky of Nebraska can expect a tough fight. Others may not run for re-election, which opens their seats for strong two-party contests independent of incumbent advantages. These Democratic seats are already being targeted as are those held by liberal Democratic senators such as Edward Kennedy of Massachusetts, Daniel Moynihan of New York, Donald Riegle of Michigan, and William Proxmire of Wisconsin. Failures of a Republican administration could cost the Republicans their Senate majority in 1982, but barring scandal, deeper economic crisis, or foreign policy disaster, the statistical odds favor Republican retention of Senate control through the 98th Congress.

In conclusion it is interesting to note that during the last three decades the Senate became an incubator for presidential candidates.[6] But today Senate seats, once relatively safe, are less secure, and the job of being a senator has become more time-consuming. It is no accident that Carter and Reagan ran for the presidency as former undefeated governors. With the development of revenue sharing and other programs designed to return federal tax dollars to states and localities, governors have been relieved of some of the burdens of state taxation and fiscal management and have improved their electoral security and popularity. It would not be surprising to see a continued shift away from the Senate and toward the statehouse as the prime presidential recruitment ground.

THE HOUSE ELECTIONS

Table 2 compares the partisan distribution of House seats in the 95th and 97th Congresses. In the 1980 elections, the Democrats suffered a net loss of 49 seats, and the Republicans gained seats in every region of the country. Although the Democrats still hold

Table 2 The Partisan Distribution of House Seats, 1977-1981

Congress	East	Midwest	South	West	Total
95th					
Democrats	82	68	91	51	292
Republicans	35	53	30	25	143
97th					
Democrats	68	58	78	39	243
Republicans	49	63	43	37	192
Net Republican Gain	14	10	13	12	49

NOTE: The regional categories are the same as for Table 1.

a substantial majority of House seats in the East and South and a very narrow majority in the West, the Republicans now possess a majority of Midwest seats.

Clearly, these partisan shifts are less extensive than those in the Senate, in part because House members tend to represent smaller, more homogeneous districts. They are able to serve their constituents in a more personalized fashion, which helps to insulate them from national partisan swings. House seats continue to be overwhelmingly "safe" for incumbents, with 72.4 percent of House incumbents who ran in the 1980 general election winning re-election with at least 60 percent of the two-party vote. This percentage is consistent with those that have characterized House elections in the 1960s and 1970s.

These aggregate statistics, however, may understate the potential competitiveness of House races and the vulnerability of House members. Of 29 incumbents defeated in 1980 who had served at least one full term, 14 received more than 60 percent of the vote in the 1978 general election, and thus could be considered as occupying safe seats going into the 1980 contest. In its description of Ways and Means Chairman Al Ullman and his Oregon district, for example, the *1980 Almanac of American Politics* maintained, "...Ullman is in no danger of losing the Ways and Means Chair, nor does he appear to face any significant political difficulty in his home district. He is solidly entrenched in east Oregon, and the Second District as a whole seems pleased to have such an important Congressman."[7] Yet Ullman, after winning the two previous elections with 72 and 69 percent of the vote, lost his re-election bid in 1980, receiving only 47 percent of the two-party vote.

A second case in point is the experience of Bob Eckhardt of Texas, who won the general elections by safe margins throughout the 1970s despite strong challenges and the 1972 Nixon landslide. In 1980, however, the Republican party and conservative interest groups targeted Eckhardt for defeat, in part because the liberal south-westerner was to inherit the chair of the important Energy and Power Subcommittee of the House Interstate and Foreign Commerce Committee.[8] Similarly seasoned Democratic incumbents — Lionel Van Deerlin (Calif.), Lester Wolff (N.Y.), Richardson Preyer (N.C.), and Mike McCormack (Wash.) — won election in 1978 with over 60 percent of the two-party vote only to face defeat in 1980. The unexpected defeat, of such long-term "safe" incumbents in the 1980 election, together with retirement of others, produced a drop in House careerists (those members serving at least 10 or more terms) to 10.8 percent of the membership of the 97th Congress, the lowest point since 1953.[9]

These examples certainly do not negate the advantages of incumbency in the House. Democratic House members completing their first full term again experienced what Cover and Mayhew describe as "sophomore surge."[10] These 27 Democrats, who ran with Republican opposition both in 1978 and 1980, won on the average by 6.3 percent more in 1980 than in 1978. Twenty-one of the 27 ran stronger in 1980 than they had in 1978. Despite the advantages that may accrue to incumbents, however, incumbency can be a liability when exploited by an aggressive opponent. Well-financed campaigns targeting incumbents in seemingly safe districts may prove successful in the House as well as in the Senate.

In 1982, Republicans and conservative interest groups will probably expand their targeting of Democratic House seats for defeat. If they succeed, they may prove false the rule that the party of an incumbent president, especially a president elected by many "defectors" from their normal party affiliation, loses seats in the midterm election.[11] The Republicans won a number of such seats this year by narrow margins. Moreover, Democratic incumbents who won in 1980, albeit by narrow margins in some cases, have shown a capacity to survive the Republican swing under very adverse conditions.

Projections for the 1982 elections are also complicated by two additional factors, *redistricting* and *turnout*. Congressional redistricting following the 1980 census could benefit Republicans by expanding the number of conservative suburban seats in the South and West and by decreasing inner city Democratic seats in the Northeast. Moreover, Democrats have had difficulty in recent years in getting traditionally Democratic voters to the polls, especially in off-year elections. Should this pattern continue, off-year gains for the Democrats as the opposition party may not materialize. On the other hand, the Democratic party and their traditional supporters may be able to improve turnout by focusing on the record of a conservative Republican administration.

GOVERNING IN THE 97TH CONGRESS

Not since 1931 has the country faced divided party control of Congress. Given the limited modern experience, it is difficult to assess exactly how well Congress will operate under such conditions. Here we offer a few initial observations.

The Senate

Majority party status carries with it primary responsibility for the functioning of the Senate. At a committee and subcommittee level, Republicans must chair meetings, establish the agenda, and schedule hearings. They will have increased responsibility for committee staff management and for managing major pieces of legislation through committee as well as on the floor. On the floor, the Republican leadership and bill managers will now have primary responsibility for scheduling legislation, building coalitions that support rather than simply oppose legislation, fending off amendments offered by recalcitrant members of their own party as well as from minority Democrats, and ending filibusters — all responsibilities that they and their staffs have little experience handling. Except for Strom Thurmond, who was then a Democrat, no current Republican senator served in that body in the 83rd Congress when the party last controlled the Senate.

One problem Republicans may face in fulfilling their responsibilities, aside from inexperience, is that their floor leaders and committee chairs are ideologically more heterogeneous, and in some cases considerably more moderate, than the rank-and-file Republican senators. Appropriations Chairman Mark Hatfield (Ore.) and Foreign Relations Chairman Charles Percy (Ill.) have received ADA scores that averaged above 50 percent in recent years, well toward the liberal end of the ADA spectrum. By contrast, other key chairs, such as Thurmond (S.C.) of Judiciary, Jesse Helms (N.C.) of Agriculture, and Orrin Hatch (Utah) of Labor and Human Resources, have ADA scores that rarely rise above the single-digit range.

Moreover, Majority Leader Howard Baker, a moderate conservative, was considered the prime moderate candidate in the party when he ran for the Republican presidential nomination in 1980 and was outflanked on the left by only John Anderson. Thus, while the moderate to liberal side of the Republican party in the Senate has been diminished in recent years, the party remains somewhat ideologically diverse. The largely conservative junior Republican senators may find their policy goals frustrated in certain committees, and they may become disaffected from some key Republican leaders.

Two factors could help the Republicans offset their problems of inexperience in institutional management and membership heterogeneity. The first is their incentive to act in a quick and cohesive manner to take firm hold of the Senate. Frustrated by years in the minority, Republicans are anxious to generate a positive image of Republican governing capacity that can be exploited to sustain voter support.

The second factor is the recent use of the National Republican Senatorial Committee as a major financial contributor. Republican party leaders may now be able to use past contributions and promises of future ones to nurture party loyalty among their colleagues. However, as every Majority Leader since Lyndon Johnson has discovered, an increasingly decentralized and permeable structure of Senate decisionmaking increases the opportunity for policy obstructionism by disaffected senators and tends to produce policy immobilism on major, controversial policy initiatives.

The success of the Republican leadership thus will depend in part on the actions of the minority Democratic senators. The Republicans will often need to attract Democratic support to enact legislation in a number of policy areas. It will be interesting to see whether Democrats, now in the minority, choose to use the tools of obstructionism available in the Senate that Republicans have used in the past. In addition, the ability of Senate Republican leaders to pass legislation the Reagan administration favors depends on their ability to work with the House.

The House

On the surface, it would seem that one could add the number of Republicans to the number of Southern Democrats and conclude, as one could in the 1950s, that there is a conservative majority in the House. However, Southern Democrats are no longer uniformly conservative. Many are quite moderate, and some conservative voting scores belie the extensive unseen support Southern Democrats provide for Democratic party positions. Moreover, many of the Southern Democrats depend on the support of blacks, unions, and other liberal groups of voters. Unlike Southern Democrats of an earlier vintage, they may oppose, or simply be unable to support, the programs espoused by a conservative Republican president.

Will the Republicans in the House be able to provide the Reagan administration a strong base from which to build majority coalitions in the House? Their success depends on several factors. First, to attract the 20 to 40 Democratic votes they will need, they probably will be forced to support slightly more moderate stands than the Republican Conference would ideally choose. Second, they must learn to use the resources of the presidency to win Democratic converts without offending fellow Republicans. Third, they will have to overcome certain organizational advantages that rest with the majority party in the House.

As the majority party, Democrats in the House will control committees and subcommittees, policy agendas, and procedures and scheduling. If used effectively, these advantages can be employed to put forward, and pass through the House, Democratic policy alternatives to those of the Reagan administration; to develop policy compromises with Republicans; or to delay, obstruct, and defeat Republican proposals.

No doubt the Democrats will follow each of these approaches at some time and on some issues. However, if the Reagan administration successfully steers conservative policies through the Senate (certainly not an easy task), the House Democratic leadership may find itself facing very difficult strategic choices. To acquiesce to, or compromise with, conservative Republican proposals may effectively cripple programs to which the Democratic party has had a longstanding commitment. However, to simply obstruct the Republican proposals leaves the Democratic majority in the House open, as the only holdout to a Republican president and Senate, to being made the scapegoat for policy failures of the Reagan administration. The House Democrats thus walk a tightrope as they attempt to combine their party role as loyal opposition with their institutional responsibility for legislative policymaking.

CONCLUSION

We have presented several perspectives from which to assess the nature of the electoral upheaval of recent years and its effects on the operation of Congress. Left to be determined is whether we are observing a major political realignment, merely a short-term electoral aberration, or movement into a long-term era of incumbent vulnerability and electoral volatility. Reagan's landslide victory and the Republican sweep of the Senate create the potential for realignment. Yet one would expect the emergence of a realignment to be visible first in the House where its members are elected every two years. Precisely the reverse has happened. Perhaps incumbent House members today possess the resources, including relatively homogeneous districts, to delay the electoral impact of a realignment or, alternatively, to cushion the effects of electoral protests.[12]

Public opinion polls indicate little change between 1976 and 1980 in positions held among the public on major issues, in partisan identification, or in ideological self-rating. These results suggest that the 1980 election is not in itself a realigning election. Yet certainly Reagan administration success in dealing with economic, energy, and foreign policy problems could solidify the partisan gains of 1978 and 1980 and activate a long-term partisan realignment.

On the other hand, Republican failure to resolve the pressing domestic and international policy dilemmas that gave rise to the Republican victories may result in continued frustration among voters and continued defeat of incumbents. Such an occurrence would lend support to the view that the country is moving into an era in which complex and somewhat unmanageable policy problems create electoral conditions in which incumbency can be a disadvantage to presidents, senators, and even to members of the House. This perspective would suggest the continuance in the Senate and expansion to the House of incumbent vulnerability and electoral volatility. If this were to occur, the electoral upheavals of the last two congressional elections would be symptomatic of a fundamental change in the nature of congressional elections, with significant implications for the operation of Congress.

NOTES

1. Warren Lee Kostroski, "Party and Incumbency in Postwar Senate Elections: Trends, Patterns, and Models," *American Political Science Review* 68 (1973): 1213.
2. Ibid.; Charles O. Jones, *Every Second Year* (Washington, D.C., The Brookings Institution, 1968), p. 68.
3. For a more extensive discussion of changes in the regional basis of partisan strength in the Senate and House, see William J. Keefe and Morris S. Ogul, *The Legislative Process: Congress and the States* (Englewood Cliffs, N. J.: Prentice-Hall, 1981), pp. 99-104.
4. See, for example, Adam Clymer, "Poll Shows Iran and Economy Hurt Carter Among Late-Shifting Voters," *New York Times,* November 16, 1980, pp. 1, 19.
5. *Congressional Quarterly Weekly Report,* November 1, 1980, pp. 32-38.
6. See Norman J. Ornstein, Robert L. Peabody, and David W. Rohde, "The Contemporary Senate: Into the 1980s," in this volume.
7. Michael Barone, Grant Ujifusa, and Douglas Matthews, *The Almanac of American Politics, 1980* (New York: E. P. Dutton, 1979), p. 735.
8. Robert Sherrill, "A Texan vs. Big Oil," *New York Times Magazine,* October 12, 1980, p. 42.
9. Charles S. Bullock, III, "House Careerists: Changing Patterns of Longevity and Attrition," *American Political Science Review* 66 (1972): 1265.
10. See Albert D. Cover and David R. Mayhew, "Congressional Dynamics and the Decline of Competitive Congressional Elections," in this volume.
11. Keefe and Ogul, *Legislative Process,* p. 106; and Barbara Hinckley, *Stability and Change in Congress* (New York: Harper & Row, 1978), pp. 17-22.
12. William J. Crotty and Gary C. Jacobson, *American Parties in Decline* (Boston: Little, Brown & Co., 1980), pp. 194-198.

I

Patterns and Dynamics
of
Congressional Change

1

The Contemporary Senate: Into the 1980s

Norman J. Ornstein, Robert L. Peabody,
and David W. Rohde

Few political institutions have captured the attention of the American public as the United States Senate has. From televised hearings on crime, communism, and Watergate, from media coverage of Senate-based presidential contenders, and from movies like *Mr. Smith Goes to Washington* and *Advise and Consent,* the public is much more aware of the Senate than it is of "the other body," the House of Representatives. Curiously, though, the public's awareness of the Senate has not been matched by a comprehensive and systematic analysis of how the Senate operates and how senators behave. We know a lot about the Senate of the 1950s, thanks primarily to the efforts of two outstanding political scientists, Ralph K. Huitt and Donald R. Matthews.[1] But, like the rest of the American political system, the Senate has changed considerably in the past two decades — in the nature of its membership, in its formal and informal leadership, in its internal processes and structures, and in its policy directions. This essay attempts to show how the Senate has changed, to what extent it has remained relatively stable, and why.

THE MEMBERSHIP

It will come as no surprise that the membership of the Senate has changed substantially since the mid-1950s. Only 10 of the senators serving in the 96th Congress (1979-80) were also members of the 85th Congress (1957-58). The change, however, has meant more than simply substituting one member for another. With respect to a variety of criteria and categories, different kinds of senators have replaced those who served earlier, and this has had an effect on the operation of the Senate and on the policies it has produced. We will consider three aspects of this change: partisan division, ideology, and sectional party affiliation.

The most obvious of the changes has been in party affiliation of the membership. From the end of World War II through most of the 1950s, the partisan division of the Senate was unusually close; neither party ever controlled the body by more than a few votes. However, in the election of 1958, the Democratic membership of the Senate jumped from 49 to 64 seats. Through the 1970s, the number of Democrats was usually in the sixties. In the 94th and 95th Congresses, Democrats held 62 seats, and in the 96th they had 59. But 1981 brought a stunning reversal, as Democrats saw their two decades of dominance transformed into a narrow Republican majority.

A second aspect of change relates to the regional character of the two parties. Through the 1950s Democratic membership was concentrated in the South and West, while Republicans came primarily from the East and Midwest. For example, in 1957 the Democrats held every Senate seat from the South and 13 of the 22 seats from the West, but they had only 5 of 20 eastern seats and 3 of the 22 midwestern seats. By the 1970s, however, these regional patterns had changed markedly. In the 96th Congress the Democrats held majorities in every region except the West (where Republicans held 14 of 26 seats), including 11 of 20 in the East and 13 of 22 in the Midwest. These dramatic gains by Democrats were offset somewhat by losses in the South. In 1979 the Democrats held 16 of 22 southern seats.

These two changes — the increase in the number of Democrats and the altered regional character of the parties — have combined to alter substantially the relative power of various groups within the Senate. Until the 1960s Southern Democrats dominated the Democratic party in the Senate, and through that dominance and frequent alliance with conservative Republican members, they were able to control the Senate. With the narrow partisan division of the 1950s, southerners accounted for more than 40 percent of the Democratic membership. With the large influx of Northern Democrats after the 1958 election, the percentage fell to 34. This was followed by a fairly continuous decline as the Republicans began winning seats in the South. In 1979 southerners accounted for only 27 percent of Senate Democrats.

The partisan and regional changes in the Senate contributed to changes in the ideological character of the membership. Table 1-1 shows the proportions of liberals, moderates, and conservatives among various groups of senators in 1957-58, in 1975, and in 1979.

Democrats in the 85th Congress were divided almost evenly between liberals and conservatives, whereas the Republicans were overwhelmingly conservative. This produced a conservative majority in the Senate in 1957-58. The subsequent sharp increase in the number of Democrats and almost matching decline in the number of Republicans produced a liberal plurality by 1975.

It should also be noted from the table that not all of the ideological change was due to these numerical shifts. The makeup of various subgroups in the Senate had also shifted. For example, in the 85th Congress, while Northern and Southern Democrats had their distinct ideological character, there was also substantial heterogeneity within each group. By the 94th Congress this was no longer true; there were no northern conservatives and no southern liberals, and the

Table 1-1 Ideological Divisions in the Senate, 85th Congress (1957-1958) and the 1st Sessions of the 94th Congress (1975) and 96th Congress (1979)

	Northern Democrats	Southern Democrats	All Democrats	Republicans	All Members
85th Congress (1957-58)	*(N=27)*	*(N=22)*	*(N=49)*	*(N=47)*	*(N=96)*
Liberals	67%	9%	41%	2%	22%
Moderates	19	27	22	26	24
Conservatives	15	64	37	72	54
94th Congress (1975)	*(N=46)*	*(N=16)*	*(N=62)*	*N=38)*	*(N=100)*
Liberals	85%	—	63%	16%	45%
Moderates	15	19%	16	26	20
Conservatives	—	81	21	58	35
96th Congress (1979)	*(N=43)*	*(N=16)*	*(N=59)*	*(N=41)*	*(N=100)*
Liberals	58%	—	42%	7%	28%
Moderates	37	31%	36	32	34
Conservatives	5	69	22	61	38

NOTE: The classification is based on a variation of the conservative coalition support score published annually by Congressional Quarterly. The support score of a member was divided by the sum of his support and opposition scores, which removes the effect of absences. Members whose scores were 0-30 were classified as liberals, 31-70 as moderates, and 71-100 as conservatives. The number of persons used to compute each percentage is shown in parentheses at the top of each column. The scores for 1957-58 were calculated from the appropriate roll calls listed in the *Congressional Quarterly Almanac* for those years. The scores for 1975 were taken from the *Congressional Quarterly Weekly Report*, January 24, 1976, p. 174; and the 1979 scores from *Congressional Quarterly Weekly Report*, January 26, 1980, p. 198.

proportion of moderates in each group had also declined. Moreover, over the same period the Republicans in the Senate became considerably more heterogeneous.

In the 96th Congress these trends began to reverse, particularly among Northern Democrats. Due to the election of a substantial number of conservative Northern Democrats — J. Jones Exon and Edward Zorinsky of Nebraska, Dennis DeConcini of Arizona, and David Boren of Oklahoma — and the shift to a more conservative voting pattern by a number of senior senators, this party group became much more heterogeneous ideologically. Thus, overall, the Senate in the 96th Congress stood about midway between the 85th and the 94th ideologically, but with a stronger moderate group. The major difference from the earlier period, however, is that the more conservative members now tend to be found among the junior members.

With the 1980 election, a large and mainly conservative class of freshmen, including 16 Republicans, entered the Senate. For the first time since 1954, the institution was controlled by the Republicans. The Senate in the 97th Congress will be at least as conservative, overall, as the 1957 Senate, but what will really determine the shape of the decade will be the 1982 off-year and 1984 presidential elections. The Senate in the 1970s and in 1980 was quite a different institution from the Senate of the 1950s. The key aspects of change from the 1950s up to the landmark 1980 election are discussed below.

NORMS AND RULES

The Senate is a decisionmaking institution, and as such it has a set of formal rules that regulate its operations. It is also a group of individuals, and "just as any other group of human beings, [it] has its unwritten rules of the game, its norms of conduct, its approved manner of behavior." [2] The Senate has both formal and informal rules, and while there has been a great deal of continuity in both categories during the past two decades, there have also been some significant changes.

The unwritten rules or norms of the Senate are patterns of behavior senators think other senators should follow. Many members share similar expectations about how a senator ought or ought not to behave. In his study of the Senate in the mid-1950s, Donald Matthews cited six norms or "folkways": legislative work, specialization, courtesy, reciprocity, institutional patriotism, and apprenticeship.

The first norm required that members devote a major portion of their time to their legislative duties in committee and on the floor and not seek personal publicity at the expense of these legislative obligations. Second, a senator was expected to concentrate on matters pertaining to committee business or directly affecting constituents.

The third norm — courtesy — required that the political conflicts within the Senate should not become personal conflicts. References to colleagues in legislative situations should be formal and indirect, and personal attacks were deemed unacceptable. Reciprocity, the fourth folkway, meant that members were expected to help colleagues whenever possible and to avoid pressing their formal powers too far (for example, by systematically objecting to unanimous consent agreements). A member was to understand and appreciate the problems of Senate colleagues and to keep bargains once they were struck. The fifth norm of institutional patriotism required that a member protect the Senate as an institution, avoiding behavior that would bring it or its members into disrepute. Finally, new senators were expected to serve a period of apprenticeship. A freshman senator, it was felt, should wait a substantial amount of time before participating fully in the work of the Senate. During this time freshmen were expected to learn about the Senate and seek the advice of senior members.

Many of these folkways provide substantial benefits to the collective membership, and it is not surprising that most of them are still recognized in the Senate today. The norms of legislative work and specialization clearly persist. The Senate, like the House, is characterized by division of labor through the committee system. This system allocates legislative responsibilities to members, and these responsibilities have grown substantially since the 1950s. The Senate's ability to make policy and function effectively depends in large measure upon each member living up to his or her individual responsibilities. The norms of legislative work and specialization express the expectations of members that each of them ought to do so.

The way to have influence in the Senate, according to one senator, was "just year after year of patience — willingness to carry at least your fair share of the work." Another said, on the same point, "I believe the principle could be stated very simply — that is, keep up with your work." When asked about specialization, a third senator commented:

> I believe that senators do specialize in their activities as far as their committee ... that doesn't mean that they can't learn a lot about other things ... but you are expected to know in greater detail and greater accuracy about the things that your committee has jurisdiction over. That is an obligation.[3]

While legislative work and specialization still exist as norms — as expectations — we should note that these norms are observed less frequently today than they were in the 1950s. The Senate today has become a veritable presidential breeding ground. Many members are absent from the Senate for extended periods of time to explore or promote presidential campaigns. To enhance their presidential possibilities, senators will often turn to the mass media, rather than to their committees or the floor, as a forum for their policy ideas. An increasing number of senators are involved in a wide spectrum of policy areas extending beyond their committee assignments.

The folkways of courtesy, reciprocity, and institutional patriotism continue almost unabated in the Senate. Courtesy permits political conflict to remain depersonalized, allowing yesterday's opponent to be tomorrow's ally. (As one Republican senator said, "It's the catalyst that maintains a semblance of order.") Reciprocity, and particularly its aspect of individual integrity, continues to be important in an institution that operates informally and in which virtually all agreements are oral. Finally, institutional patriotism tends to be reinforced by the increase in competition between Congress and the executive branch for control over foreign policy and the budget.

Five of the folkways that were operative in the Senate two decades ago still describe expected behavior within the body today. This is not true, however, of the sixth norm, apprenticeship. Unlike the other folkways, it is difficult to discern what benefits apprenticeship provided to the membership in general or collectively. As Matthews noted, apprenticeship had its roots very early in the Senate's history.[4] Nevertheless, the only group that could be seen to benefit from the observance of this norm by the 1950s were the senior conservatives in both parties who dominated the positions of power in the Senate at that time. Beginning with the 1958 election, more and more liberal Northern Democrats entered the Senate, and the conservative dominance began to break down.[5] Consequently, junior members had less incentive to observe the norm. Gradually, as these junior senators of the early 1960s became senior members, the expectations regarding the norm became less widely shared. Today, not only do junior members not want or feel the need to serve an apprenticeship, but the senior members do not expect them to do so, as these statements from senators indicate:

> All the communications suggest "get involved, offer amendments, make speeches. The Senate has changed, we're all equals, you should act accordingly." [A junior Democrat]

> Well, that [apprenticeship] doesn't exist at all in the Senate. The senior Senators have made that very clear, both Democrats and Republicans. [A junior Republican]

> We now hope and expect and encourage the younger guys to dive right into the middle of it. [A senior conservative Republican]

Thus, the Senate of the 1980s is a more egalitarian institution when considered along seniority lines than it used to be. Junior members now play an important role within the Senate, and this change in the informal rule structure of the body has contributed to several important changes in the formal rules.

For example, in 1970 a rule was adopted that limited members to service on only one of the Senate's four most prestigious committees: Appropriations, Armed Services, Finance, and Foreign Relations. This new rule prevented senior members from monopolizing these important committee posts and facilitated the appointment of relatively junior senators much earlier in their careers than would have been possible otherwise. In addition, both parties adopted rules limiting the role of seniority in the selection of committee chairmen. In 1973 the Republican Caucus agreed to a system whereby the Republican members of each committee would elect the ranking member. In 1975 the Democratic Caucus adopted a proposal by Senator Dick Clark of Iowa (who had served only two years in the Senate), which permitted secret ballot votes by the caucus on any committee chairman if one fifth of the Democratic senators requested it.

As junior members became more active, they began to feel more intensely the disparity of resources between themselves and the senior senators, particularly with regard to staff. Therefore, the junior members sponsored and aggressively pushed a resolution, S. Res. 60, which permitted them to hire additional legislative staff members to assist in their committee duties. The Senate adopted the resolution in June 1975.

A number of the reforms adopted by the Senate in the 1970s were not a direct consequence of the expanded role of newer senators vis-à-vis their more senior colleagues. Certainly the most publicized of these was the 1975 change in the Senate's rule for cutting off debate. Liberals had been seeking since the late 1950s to alter the rule that required the vote of two-thirds of the members present and voting to end a filibuster. The new provision required the affirmative vote of only three-fifths of the entire Senate membership. If most members voted, cloture (the process by which debate can be ended in the Senate, other than by unanimous consent) would be easier to achieve under the new rule.

A final set of reforms affected the openness of the Senate's conduct of its business. In 1975, almost three years after similar actions by the House, the Senate adopted rules that opened to the press and public most markup or bill-drafting sessions and conference committee meetings.

Thus, since the 1950s, junior members have come to play an increasingly important role in Senate activity, and the expectations of senior members have gradually adapted to these changes. Partially as a consequence of this, the Senate has altered a number of its formal rules. The overall effect of these changes is that the Senate of the 1980s — for both parties — is a much more egalitarian and open institution in which the ability to affect policy is less dependent on a senator's formal position or seniority.

LEADERSHIP

The evolution in Senate leadership patterns from the 1950s to the early 1980s has both contributed to and been reflective of changes in Senate membership, committee structure, norms, and rules. That such organizational variables should be closely related is hardly surprising. But if anything, the relatively small size of the Senate, the lengthy tenure of its membership, and its pervasive collegial atmosphere have all tended to reinforce these interconnected aspects with enhanced consequences for decentralizing and power-sharing trends in the Senate.

Our task of assessing Senate practices and modifications in majority and minority party leadership since the 1950s is facilitated by three factors. First, the writings of Ralph Huitt, Donald Matthews, and others have provided a refined portrait of Majority Leader Lyndon Johnson and a well-developed sense of what the Senate was like under his direction from 1955 to 1961.[6] Second, his successor, Mike Mansfield (D-Mont.), served an unprecedented 16 years as Majority Leader from 1961 until his retirement in 1976. For the first eight years Mansfield worked closely with Democratic presidents Kennedy and Johnson; for the remaining eight years Republican presidents Nixon and Ford were in the White House. Thus, Mansfield's tenure in office provided an unusually rich opportunity to analyze the role of a Majority Leader under both united and divided party control of the national government. Third, the retirements in 1976 of Mansfield and Hugh Scott (R-Pa.), the Minority Leader from 1969 to 1976, and a combination of other circumstances, resulted in the 95th Congress (1977-78) becoming a benchmark in party leadership changes.[7]

On January 4, 1977, Democrats elevated Robert C. Byrd of West Virginia, their party whip for the previous six years, to the position of floor leader. Not only had Byrd shifted from a conservative to a more moderate stance on most issues, but he had also demonstrated his parliamentary astuteness at managing the Senate's business. His principal opponent, Hubert Humphrey of Minnesota, also a former whip before he became vice president in 1965, never figured strongly in the contest. Indeed, he withdrew on the morning of the vote. Humphrey, who was in failing health, died of cancer a year later.

On the Republican side, however, there was a real struggle for the Minority Leader position. On the opening day of the contest for the slot, Robert Griffin (R-Mich.), the minority whip since 1969, was edged out by Howard Baker (R-Tenn.) by a slim 19-18 margin. Baker, a contender for the Republican presidential nomination in 1980, had challenged Scott twice previously but failed to win the position of Republican floor leader. Baker beat Griffin in 1977, not as a result of ideological differences, but because a majority of the incoming Republican freshmen became convinced that he would make a stronger external spokesman for their party.

The election of Democrat Jimmy Carter as president, if anything, helped Byrd's easy victory. An "outsider" president would be in greater need of Byrd's technical skills and workhorse qualities. GOP President Ford's loss, on the other hand, gravely weakened his fellow Michigander's chances of moving up in the Senate leadership.

Before briefly assessing the effectiveness of the new Senate floor leaders Byrd and Baker, we will provide some useful background information. From the early 1950s until 1977, only two Democrats — Lyndon Johnson and Mike Mansfield — served as floor leaders in the Senate. The Republicans, however, were led by four men — Robert Taft (R-Ohio, 1953), William Knowland (R-Calif., 1953-58), Everett Dirksen (R-Ill., 1959-69), and Hugh Scott (R-Pa., 1969-76). The Democrats dominated the Senate in the 1960s and 1970s, and for most of this period the Senate Republican leadership was quite decentralized. With the major exception of Dirksen, Republican leadership continued to be "more formalized, institutionalized, and decentralized" than its Democratic counterpart.[8]

From 1955 to 1976 the Democrats were led by men with starkly contrasting personalities and leadership styles.[9] Johnson sought to centralize control over organizational and policy decisions in himself. Mansfield's objective, on the other hand, was to serve the Senate, to create and maintain a body that "permitted individual, coequal senators the opportunity to conduct their affairs in whatever ways they deemed appropriate."[10] One Democrat who served with both men thus summarized their differences:

> Johnson was aggressive and Mansfield is more the organizer, manager. I think he senses his primary duty is to insure the Senate moves in the conduct of its business in the most orderly fashion that we can. The result of our actions, while I'm sure he feels strongly on a lot of issues, he leaves up to each individual. Lyndon Johnson wanted to influence the outcome of every decision — not just to insure that we acted, but acted in a certain way.[11]

What can be concluded about the relative success of Majority Leaders Johnson and Mansfield? In his study of the last two Congresses under Johnson's direction and the first two Congresses under Mansfield's direction, John Stewart concluded:

> Despite the dispersal of many tasks of party leadership and the generally permissive if not at times passive attitude displayed by the majority leader (Mansfield) in managing the legislative program, the senatorial party in the Eighty-seventh and Eighty-eighth Congresses [1961-64] functioned effectively, and its performance compared favorably with and often surpassed the record compiled by the Eighty-fifth and Eighty-sixth Congresses [1957-60] under the driving and centralized leadership of Lyndon Johnson.[12]

Although greater historical perspective is needed to evaluate fully the relative effectiveness of these two leaders, they clearly exemplify the wide range of styles, given different environmental settings, allowable in effective Senate leadership. Clearly, Mansfield's relaxed manner and his conscious attempts to bring junior members into Senate decisionmaking have contributed to the diffusion of power and the opening of procedures that have characterized the Senate in the 1970s. Byrd in the 95th and 96th Congress appeared to be borrowing techniques and strategies that seemed to work for his predecessors and fusing them with his own personality and sense of the Senate.

Robert Byrd was first elected to Congress as a member of the House of Representatives in 1952 and then in 1958 as a senator from West Virginia. Thus, he gained a firsthand knowledge of Johnson's leadership style and techniques. Moreover, Byrd had served under Mansfield's leadership for 10 years, first as secretary to the party conference and later as party whip. Given the enhanced independence of members and the breakdown of the apprenticeship norm, Byrd was well aware that he could not revert to a 1950s style of centralized command. Nor did he care to emulate many of Mansfield's more laissez faire tactics. The result has been a gradual consolidation of control over party instrumentalities such as the Policy Committee (which discusses issues and helps set the legislative agenda) and the Steering Committee (which makes committee assignments).

Byrd's relationships with the Carter White House were initially rather strained and testy. By the second session of the 95th Congress, however, the new Majority Leader had developed a reasonable working relationship with the new Democratic administration, especially on such important legislative items as the ratification of the Panama Canal treaties, the Revenue Act, and the energy programs. It would be premature to compare Byrd's record as Democratic Leader with either Johnson's or Mansfield's, but his dogged devotion to detail, his mastery of Senate rules, his willingness to confront but also to compromise with such key senators as Russell Long, Edmund Muskie, Republican Leader Baker, and even his old protagonist, Edward Kennedy, contributed to Byrd's reputation as an effective floor leader.

Until the stunning 1980 election, the Republicans had not been in the majority in the Senate since 1954. Unlike the Democratic party leadership, which is largely concentrated in the floor leader and whip, the Republicans elect different senators as floor leader, assistant floor leader or whip, chairman of the Republican Policy Committee, chairman of the Committee on Committees, and chairman of the Republican Conference. From the late 1950s through the 1960s, Everett Dirksen's leadership style more nearly approximated Johnson's, especially in terms of its centralizing tendencies. Scott, his successor, in keeping with the changing membership and power structure of both Senate parties, more closely paralleled Mansfield's lower-keyed, shared leadership style.[13] The more open and relaxed leadership of both Scott and Mansfield was an important factor in the Senate's movement toward an egalitarian, decentralized form of decisionmaking.

Just after Baker defeated Griffin in January 1977, he was asked what his relationship with incoming Democratic President Carter would be. The new Minority Leader replied that he "intended to hear him out" and act in the best interests of the country. "There is no longer a minority President, only a minority in Congress," he said. Following the Nixon and Ford presidencies, the Senate GOP leaders — Baker, newly elected whip Ted Stevens of Alaska, and holdover Policy Committee Chairman John Tower of Texas — had to shift their roles. No longer did they seek to pass a Republican president's programs or uphold his vetoes. Instead they became responsible for voicing GOP alternatives in cooperation with the Republican House leadership and the Republican National Committee.

Everett Dirksen, Baker's father-in-law, had been especially adept at maximizing the role of the minority party in the Senate. Depending upon the issues, he either thwarted or cooperated with Democratic presidents. Baker appears to be following in Dirksen's footsteps. Despite pressures from home, Baker supplied crucial support in favor of ratification of the Panama Canal treaties. He also played a critical role in support of Carter's Middle East jet package. When Baker decided to seek his party's presidential nomination in 1980, his ability as Minority Leader to carve out a middle ground on issues was even more severely tested.

COMMITTEES

From its earliest days, the U.S. Senate, like the House of Representatives, has used a division of labor into a committee system to organize its work. The committee system is the single most important feature affecting legislative outcomes in the Senate; not surprisingly, it has changed as other aspects of the Senate — workload, membership, power — have themselves been altered in the 1960s, 1970s, and 1980s.

Committee Assignments

Every senator is assigned to committees shortly after being sworn in. When a vacancy occurs on a more attractive committee, senators can and do switch assignments. The committee assignment process is crucial to the Senate because it often determines the policy orientation and activity of each committee. The Democratic and Republican parties handle their own members' assignments differently. Democrats use a 19-member Steering Committee chaired by the Majority Leader, while Republicans have a 13-member Committee on Committees with an elected chairman. In the 1940s and early 1950s committee assignments reflected the norm of apprenticeship: freshmen senators were assigned only to minor committees, and senior members dominated such prestigious committees as Foreign Relations, Appropriations, Finance, and Armed Services.

When Lyndon Johnson became Majority Leader in 1955, he changed these procedures by instituting the "Johnson Rule," which guaranteed every Democrat, no matter how junior, a major committee assignment. However, as we have noted, Johnson ran the Steering Committee as a one-man show, and he handed out choice assignments very selectively. Senior, more conservative members continued to dominate the most prestigious committees. Under Mike Mansfield, the Steering Committee operated more democratically, and assignments to all committees became more open to junior and liberal Democratic senators. This egalitarian pattern has continued under Robert Byrd, although not entirely without controversy. Soon after Byrd's election as Majority Leader in January 1977, junior liberal Democratic senators, led by John Culver (D-Iowa), forced an acrimonious debate in the Democratic Caucus to protest Byrd's choices to fill Steering Committee vacancies. The liberals won an agreement that future Steering Committee choices would be submitted in advance to the party membership.

In the 96th Congress junior members had far greater access to assignments on the four most important Senate committees than had previous congresses, as Table 1-2 indicates. Indeed, in the 96th Congress seven senators of varying ideological commitments (including liberal Bill Bradley, moderate David Durenberger, and conservative Malcolm Wallop) were assigned to the Finance Committee; four had

Table 1-2 Mean Seniority in Years at Time of Appointment to Prestigious Standing Committees

Committee	80th-84th Congresses*	94th Congress	96th Congress
Foreign Relations	8.1	4.0	3.5**
Appropriations	5.8	2.0	4.0
Finance	3.0	2.7	1.1
Armed Services	2.1	1.2	0.0

* Figures taken from Donald R. Matthews, *U.S. Senators and Their World* (New York: Vintage Books, 1960), p. 153.
** Before Sen. Edmund Muskie (D-Maine) left the Foreign Relations Committee on May 10, 1980, to become secretary of state, the mean seniority was 6.8. Muskie had 20 years seniority.

served in the Senate two years, and three had no previous service. Of the six new members on Armed Services (two Democrats and four Republicans), not one had previous Senate service. Gradually, the important Senate committees are beginning to reflect more accurately the Senate as a whole; in the process they have become more junior and more liberal.

For the past several decades committee chairmanships have been selected through the process of seniority, although this procedure has been somewhat modified, as we have noted. But because of the operation of the seniority system, the decline in the number of Southern Democrats in the Senate has been reflected only partially in committee chairmanships. In 1975 southerners accounted for only 26 percent of Senate Democrats; however, they comprised 39 percent of committee chairmanships, including the leadership of such powerful committees as Appropriations, Finance, Armed Services, Foreign Relations, and Judiciary. Nevertheless, northern liberals have made gains in the past few Congresses. By 1979 they controlled 10 of the 15 standing committee chairmanships, including Budget, Appropriations, Foreign Relations, Governmental Affairs, Human Resources, and Judiciary.

Committees and Workload

An ever-increasing workload has had a major impact on the Senate. There were five times as many roll call votes on the Senate floor in the 93rd Congress as there were in the 84th, and the more than 1,000 roll calls were accompanied by increases in the number of bills introduced and hearings held. In response to the increasing number and complexity of decisions senators had to make, the Senate expanded the committee system. In 1957 there were 15 standing committees with 118 subcommittees in the Senate. By 1975 there were 18 standing committees with 140 subcommittees; if special, select, and joint committees were included in the tally, it reached 31 committees and 174 subcommittees in all.

More importantly, perhaps, the Senate increased the sizes of many of its committees and subcommittees. Since the size of the Senate has increased by only four members since the admission to the union of Alaska and Hawaii in 1959, this meant more assignments for individual members. In 1957 each senator averaged 2.8 committee assignments and 6.3 subcommittee assignments, whereas by 1976 senators on the average served on 4 committees and 14 subcommittees.

Under pressure particularly from junior members, the Senate early in 1976 created the Temporary Select Committee to Study the Senate Committee System, a 12-member bipartisan panel, chaired by Senator Adlai E. Stevenson (D-Ill.). After holding extensive hearings, the committee reported in September 1976 a set of detailed rec-

ommendations for revision of the committee system. The recommendations were taken up by the Senate at the beginning of the 95th
Congress, and after lively debate in the Senate Rules Committee
and on the floor, a modified version of the Stevenson Committee
plan was adopted by the Senate on February 4, 1977. The plan,
S. Res. 4, cut back substantially the number of Senate committees.
Three standing committees and five select and joint panels were
eliminated. Several new committees — Energy and Natural Resources,
Environment and Public Works, Governmental Affairs, and Human
Resources — were also created. By placing strict limits on senators'
subcommittee assignments and chairmanships, S. Res. 4 resulted in
a dramatic drop in the number of subcommittees (from an overall
total of 174 to 110) and in the number of assignments (the average
dropped from 4 committees and 14 subcommittees to 3 committees
and 7.5 subcommittees).

Despite these improvements in the committee system, senators
continued to be spread thin with little time or attention to devote
to any individual area. To respond to this fragmentation, the Senate
in the 1970s had begun to expand professional staffs. We have already
mentioned S. Res. 60, a 1975 device to increase the number of legislative
assistants available to senators. Committee staffs have also grown,
from roughly 300 in the 85th Congress to well over 1,000 (including
both permanent and investigative staff) by the 95th. S. Res. 4 retarded
this growth only slightly.

The expansion of staffs has allowed senators to cope more easily
with their heavy workload and increased responsibilities. It has also
distributed Senate resources broadly to junior as well as senior members. In recent years staffs have been allocated increasingly through
subcommittees rather than full committees, which has accentuated
the spread of power to junior senators and has correspondingly reduced
the relative power of committee chairmen. Writing of the Senate
in the 1950s, Donald Matthews commented, "Within certain limits,
the [committee] chairman appoints and controls the committee staff."[14]
Today, however, far more staff are appointed by subcommittee chairmen than by committee chairmen. The ability of committee chairmen
to maintain monopoly control over expertise and to command un-
challenged loyalty from staff no longer exists. Expertise and staff
are now widely dispersed throughout the Senate. It will be interesting
to see if the accession to committee chairmanships in the 97th Congress
of such aggressive GOP conservatives as John Tower (Armed Services)
and Jake Garn (Banking) in time results in a greater consolidation
of power and initiative to full committees and their chairmen.

Along with expanding subcommittee chairmanships and expanding
staffs, committee deliberations have become more open in recent
years. All of these factors together have loosened the control that

committee leaders once maintained over their committee members. Junior senators now have subcommittee bases from which to challenge the policy recommendations of committee chairmen. Moreover, senators who do not serve on a committee will have enough access to information to enable them to offer successful amendments on the floor to the committee's bills. Thus, in recent years committees have become less cohesive internally, and their bills have been more open to challenge on the Senate floor. These trends have lessened the influence of committees and committee chairmen in the Senate. During the 1970s legislation in the Senate shifted from the committee rooms to the Senate floor, while the functions of agenda setting and legislative oversight moved from the committees to the subcommittees. Committees remain highly important; all legislation is referred to them, as are all executive and judicial nominations, and they retain the authority either to kill or to report out the bills and nominations. But the Senate is a more open, fluid, and decentralized body now than it was in the 1950s. Power, resources, and decisionmaking authority have become more diffuse. The combined impact of changes in membership, norms, leadership, workload, and committees have produced a markedly different Senate in the 1980s.

THE SENATE AS A PRESIDENTIAL INCUBATOR

So far we have focused mainly on internal changes in Senate structures and behavior. But the Senate has not operated in a vacuum; it has been greatly affected by trends in the society and in the broader political system, and it has in turn had its own impact on American politics. Nowhere is this more true than in the area of presidential nominations. Though senators actively contested for presidential nominations in past decades, in the period from 1960 to 1972 senators were dominant. During that 12-year span, the two parties relied exclusively upon either senators (Kennedy, Goldwater, and McGovern) or former senators who became vice-presidents (Nixon, Johnson, and Humphrey) before obtaining their party's presidential nod.

The primaries and general election of 1976 were surprising on several counts. Former Georgia governor Jimmy Carter swept through the Democratic primaries and beat a number of congressional contenders to secure a first ballot nomination and eventually win the presidency. President Gerald Ford, a former House Republican Minority Leader, won his party's nomination but lost the election to Carter. However, both parties followed the predominant post-World War II pattern of selecting senators for vice-presidential candidates: Walter Mondale (D-Minn.) and Robert Dole (R-Kan.). Senators also competed actively, albeit unsuccessfully, for the presidency in the 1980 primaries

— Howard Baker and Robert Dole for the Republican nomination and Edward Kennedy for the Democratic party choice.

There are numerous reasons for the string of successes by senatorial contenders from 1960 to 1972. The near revolutionary growth in media influence over politics, especially that of television, has focused public attention on Washington and on the Senate. Television has contributed to, and been affected by, the increasing nationalization of party politics. A national attentiveness to foreign affairs has heightened the importance of the Senate with its well-defined constitutional role in foreign policy.

As the Senate has opened up its proceedings, spread its resources, and decentralized its power, it has become more attractive to potential presidential contenders. Nearly one-third of the members of the Senate were formerly governors, who now receive much more public attention from their Washington base.

The effects upon the Senate of this remarkable presidential focus extend beyond those few legislators who obtain party nominations.[15] Many senators consider themselves presidential possibilities or are mentioned as such on television networks and in the polls. Senators tailor their behavior accordingly, spreading out their legislative interests beyond the concerns of their individual states, increasing their legislative activity and public visibility, and emphasizing media coverage over legislative craftsmanship. This preoccupation with presidential aspirations has contributed to violations of the norms of specialization and legislative work. It has also increased the pressure within the Senate to spread out resources and power to junior members.

CONCLUSION

As we have seen, the Senate has changed in varied and interrelated ways since the 1950s. The nature of the membership of the Senate, its internal norms and rules, its leadership styles and effects, its committees, and the role of the Senate as a breeding ground for presidential candidates have all evolved to make the Senate of the 1980s quite a different legislative institution.

The Senate has gone from close partisan balance to dominant Democratic party control to a narrow Republican majority. A powerful Southern Democratic wing, which once maintained great power through the seniority system and a coalition with like-minded Republicans, has gradually diminished in size and influence.[16] Liberal northeastern and midwestern Democratic senators, from the 1958 election through the mid-1970s, experienced a corresponding growth in numbers and power only to diminish in numbers and power in 1978 and 1980. Junior senators, once relegated to a position of apprenticeship and subservience, have found their importance enhanced in the contemporary Senate, even with the recent partisan and ideological shifts. With the active assistance of Majority Leader Mike Mansfield, and the compliance of his successors, Democrat Robert Byrd and Republican Howard Baker, junior senators have won access to prestigious committee assignments and to legislative staff resources. Thus, they have carved out for themselves a highly significant role in the legislative process.

Through these and other trends, the Senate has become more open, more decentralized, and more equal in its distribution of power. It has also become more overburdened with work. As senators' obligations and time commitments multiplied, their ability to deal with complex questions in an in-depth fashion diminished. The comprehensive committee system reorganization of 1977 helped the Senate to cope with these problems, as did the accession of more aggressive leaders, especially Democratic Leader Robert Byrd and Republican Leader Howard Baker. Changes continued in the 96th Congress. When it convened in 1979, 49 of the Senate's 100 members were in their first term and were eager to make reforms in the Senate's institutional structures and rules. A newly Republican Senate in 1981, with a full 54 of its members in their first terms, was also ready to transform the body. With electoral, ideological, and institutional trends all in flux, the one certainty is that the Senate of the mid-1980s will likely be as different from the Senate of today as today's is from the Senate of the 1950s.

NOTES

1. See the collection of articles by Huitt in *Congress: Two Decades of Analysis,* Ralph K. Huitt and Robert L. Peabody (New York: Harper & Row, 1969); and Donald R. Matthews, *U.S. Senators and Their World* (New York: Vintage Books, 1960).
2. Matthews, *U.S. Senators and Their World,* p. 92.
3. This article is part of a broader study of the Senate conducted since 1973 by the authors with the help of a grant from the Russell Sage Foundation. In addition to legislative and electoral data, our analysis is based upon more than 60 semistructured, taped interviews with incumbent and former senators from 1973 to 1979.
4. Matthews, *U.S. Senators and Their World,* pp. 116-117.
5. For a discussion of the changes during the 1960s, see Randall B. Ripley, *Power in the Senate* (New York: St. Martin's Press, 1969).
6. See also Rowland Evans and Robert Novak, *Lyndon B. Johnson: The Exercise of Power* (New York: New American Library, 1966); Randall B. Ripley, *Majority Party Leadership in Congress* (Boston: Little, Brown & Co., 1969); and John G. Stewart, "Two Strategies of Leadership: Johnson and Mansfield," in *Congressional Behavior,* ed. Nelson W. Polsby (New York: Random House, 1971), pp. 61-92.
7. Robert L. Peabody, *Leadership in Congress: Stability, Succession and Change* (Boston: Little, Brown & Co., 1976).

8. Matthews, *U.S. Senators and Their World,* p. 124.
9. Stewart, *Two Strategies of Leadership,* and Peabody, *Leadership in Congress,* pp. 333-345.
10. Stewart, *Two Strategies of Leadership,* p. 69.
11. Norman J. Ornstein, Robert L. Peabody, and David W. Rohde, "Political Change and Legislative Norms in the United States Senate" (A revised version of a paper delivered at the annual meeting of the American Political Science Association, Chicago, Illinois, August 29-September 2, 1974), p. 26.
12. Stewart, *Two Strategies of Leadership,* p. 87.
13. See Neil MacNeil, *Dirksen: Portrait of a Public Man* (New York: World Publications, 1970); Jean Torcom Cronin, "Minority Leadership in the United States Senate: The Role and Style of Everett Dirksen" (Ph.D. diss., Johns Hopkins University, 1973); and Charles O. Jones, *The Minority Party in Congress* (Boston: Little, Brown & Co., 1970).
14. Matthews, *U.S. Senators and Their World,* p. 160.
15. For an extended treatment of the causes and impact of the Senate's role in presidential nominations, see Robert L. Peabody, Norman J. Ornstein, and David W. Rohde, "The United States Senate as a Presidential Incubator: Many Are Called but Few Are Chosen," *Political Science Quarterly* 91 (Summer 1976): 237-258.
16. One should not conclude that southern conservatives are now powerless. They still retain several important committee chairmanships. Moreover, a single dedicated senator with knowledge of the rules can have a tremendous impact on the legislative process. The late Senator James Allen of Alabama was one whose use of the filibuster and other techniques of parliamentary procedure delayed, killed, or significantly changed several pieces of major legislation in the past few years.

2

The House in Transition: Change and Consolidation

Lawrence C. Dodd and Bruce I. Oppenheimer

The 1960s and 1970s were times of upheaval, reform, and consolidation for major American political and social institutions. Although most people view the House of Representatives as an institution that resists change,[1] it was far from immune during this period. The reform movement that struck the House was the most thoroughgoing since the one that occurred in 1910 when insurgent Republicans united with Democrats to strip the Speakership of its power and lay the foundation for committee government.[2] In some respects the reforms of the 1970s were designed to reassert an element of party government by returning some powers to the Speakership, to the party leadership in general, and to party organizations in the House. Other reforms, however, were oriented toward strengthening subcommittees in the House. In the midst of these various reforms, House members increased their independence and their capacity to resist party constraints.

Because of the multifaceted nature of change in the House during the 1970s, considerable tension exists today among advocates of party government, subcommittee government, and individual policy entrepreneurship. This tension builds an element of uncertainty and transience into the institution, a dynamic propensity toward continuing transformation in the actual distribution of power within the institution. In this essay we will describe the changes that occurred in the 1970s, evaluate the impact that they have had on power in the House, and suggest some political choices and challenges that we expect will characterize the House in the 1980s.

MEMBERSHIP CHANGE

In recent years the House has undergone significant membership turnover. At the start of the 92nd Congress, it could boast that a record 20 percent of its membership had been elected to at least 10 terms. But House "careerism," as Charles Bullock has called this condition, has declined significantly since then.[3] At the start of the 96th Congress, only 12.6 percent of House members met the 10-term criterion (the lowest since 1955), and projections indicate that it should continue to drop. As Figure 2-1 indicates, the drop in careerism has been accompanied by a growth in the number of new House members.[4] The 96th Congress had more junior House members (those elected to three or fewer terms) than any Congress since 1937.

Figure 2-1 House Service: New Members (Three or Fewer Terms) and Careerists (Ten or More Terms), 1911-1979

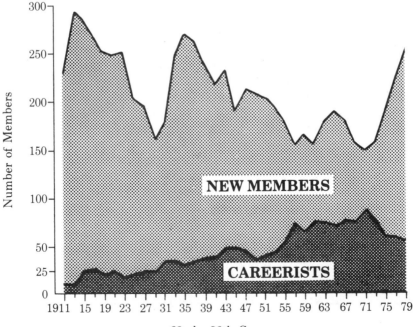

62nd - 96th Congresses

Voluntary Retirement Trend

This increase in membership turnover in the House is occurring for very different reasons than it has in past decades. In earlier decades electoral defeat was usually responsible for much of the turnover. But with the exception of the 1974 defeat of Republican incumbents in the "Watergate" aftermath, House turnover in the 1970s is a function of retirement. In 1974, 1976, and 1978 the House set new post-World War II records for retirement. In 1978, 49 members announced that they would not seek an additional term in the House. By comparison, only 19 incumbents were defeated in the general election and 4 others in primaries. And although one important study convincingly argues that incumbents are potentially quite vulnerable to electoral challenges, that potential has not been demonstrated.[5]

A variety of explanations has been offered for the increase in voluntary House retirements. They include: (1) improved pensions for retired members; (2) the more demanding nature of the job of a House member; (3) frustration over the difficulties the House has in making policy; (4) increased visibility of House members that improves their ability to seek other offices; (5) the end of the great liberal-conservative fight over such post-New Deal issues as civil rights and aid to education; (6) new House provisions limiting outside income, regulating campaigns, and requiring financial disclosure; and (7) change in the distribution of rewards for House service; those once given only to members with long tenure are available to many junior House members now. Retiring House members have generally cited one or more of these problems in explaining their exodus from the House. Although it is difficult to separate the public as opposed to the private reasons for retirement, it is fair to say that all of the above reasons have played a role.[6]

Whether members leave through retirement or defeat, of course, the result is in some ways the same. The House, criticized by Samuel Huntington in the 1960s for operating in isolation because it lacked "biennial infusion of new blood," received regular transfusions into the 1970s.[7] Change in House membership means more than just new blood replacing old, however. The partisan, ideological, and sectional makeup of the institution has changed as well as the age, sex, and racial composition of the membership.

History of Democratic Control

Since 1955, and with the exception of only four years since 1931, the Democrats have been the majority party in the House. The size of that majority has fluctuated during the past 25 years with as small as a 30-seat margin in the 84th and 85th Congresses that left control of the House in the hands of a conservative coalition of Republicans and Southern Democrats. Following the 1958 landslide election, the Democratic seat total increased from 234 to 283, but, as will be seen shortly, conservatives were still able to hold their own. Only after the 1964 Goldwater debacle that gave Democrats a 295-140 House majority in the 89th Congress were many of the liberal policies enacted in the Kennedy-Johnson legislative program.

After the 89th Congress, Republicans reasserted their strength, forcing liberal Democrats to focus on saving the policy initiatives of the 89th Congress. Democrats failed again to gain overwhelming control of the House until the 94th and 95th Congresses; Democrats elected 291 and 292 respectively to these, giving them a sizable margin of control. The success Democrats have had in holding their open seats in this period, together with their ability to maintain control of the traditionally Republican seats won in 1974, has allowed them to reach a high plateau of House control, surpassed in this century only by the New Deal Congresses of 1933-39.

Ideological Changes

The majority the Democrats built up in the late 1970s is important because of the nature of its ideological makeup, as well as its size, particularly when contrasted to Congresses in the early postwar years. Table 2-1 compares the ideological composition of the House during the first sessions of the 86th and 95th Congresses and provides some insights into the nature of the change.

First, although Northern Democrats in the 95th were not as exclusively "liberals" as they were in the 86th (68 versus 82 percent), the number of Northern Democratic liberals is nearly the same (135 versus 140) because their total number has increased from 171 to 198. More importantly, the combined total of liberals and moderates has increased from 163 to 193. These differences resulted from Democrats winning seats held by Republicans. Since the Republicans were overwhelmingly conservative, the effect was to make the House far more liberal. Second, there is a sizable decrease in the percentage of Southern Democrats classified as conservative and a corresponding increase in the moderate and liberal groupings of Southern Democrats between the two Congresses. Third, the Republicans, although fewer in number, remain very conservative.

Taken together, these changes indicate that the House is substantially more liberal than it was in the 86th Congress. True, the 95th and 96th Congresses are not as liberal as the 94th Congress, but conservatives no longer comprise a House majority as they did

Table 2-1 Ideological Divisions in the House, 86th Congress, 1st Session (1959) and 95th Congress, 1st Session (1977)

	Northern Democrats	Southern Democrats	All Democrats	Republicans	All Members
86th Congress, 1st Session	*(N=171)*	*(N=110)*	*(N=281)*	*(N=153)*	*(N=434)*
Liberals	82% (140)	2% (2)	51% (142)	4% (6)	34% (148)
Moderates	13 (23)	13 (14)	13 (37)	15 (23)	14 (60)
Conservatives	5 (8)	85 (94)	36 (102)	81 (124)	52 (226)
95th Congress, 1st Session	*(N=198)*	*(N=90)*	*(N=288)*	*N=146)*	*(N=434)*
Liberals	68% (135)	11% (10)	50% (145)	1% (2)	34% (147)
Moderates	29 (58)	31 (28)	30 (86)	20 (29)	26 (115)
Conservatives	3 (5)	58 (52)	20 (57)	79 (115)	40 (172)

NOTE: The classification is based on a variation of the conservative coalition support scores published annually by Congressional Quarterly. The support score of a member was divided by the sum of his support and opposition scores, which removes the effect of absences. Members whose scores were 0-30 were classified as liberals, 31-70 as moderates, and 71-100 as conservatives. The number of members used to compute each percentage is shown in parentheses at the top of each column.

in the 86th Congress. Instead, moderates hold the balance of power in the House, with this change resulting in large part from the growth of moderates and liberals among the Southern Democratic delegation. This moderation in Southern Democratic representation is an outgrowth from the implementation of the Voting Rights Act of 1965 and the resulting enfranchisement of black voters in the South. The change has further decreased the influence of conservatives within the House Democratic party.

Table 2-1 does not reveal a related change among southern House members. This is the growth in the number of Southern Republicans. In 1978, 31 Southern Republicans were elected to the House. Although this is a significant gain over the 7 Southern Republicans elected in 1960, it falls short of expectations Republicans had in the late 1960s and early 1970s. The growth in Southern Republican House membership leveled off in the early 1970s and actually declined slightly from a high of 34 in 1972.[8] In 1980, the growth of Republican House members resumed as nine new Republicans were elected from Virginia, North and South Carolina, Florida, and Texas. It should be noted that unlike their Southern Democrat colleagues, Southern Republican House members, with one exception, are uniformly conservative.[9]

Changes in Composition

There were other changes in House membership in the 1970s. It should not be surprising, given the high turnover rate, to find that the average age of House members dropped. At the start of the 94th Congress in 1975, the average age of a House member was less than 50 for the first time since World War II, and it has continued to decline in succeeding Congresses.

The racial and sexual composition of the House has also changed. In 1980 there were 17 black members of the House, compared to only 5 in 1962, and following reapportionment in 1982 blacks should gain additional seats in the House. Corresponding to the increased activity of women in politics, more women are also seeking House office. In the 1978 elections 46 women candidates received a major party nomination for a House seat. Only 16 were victorious, a net drop of 2 from the record 18 women members in the 94th and 95th Congresses.

Certainly these figures do not come close to being proportional to the size of these groups in the population, but, as with the growth of southern liberals, they do suggest trends toward membership diversification in the House. Moreover, they demonstrate how the House, with narrower, more homogeneous constituencies, has a better capacity than the Senate to include southern liberals, northern conservatives, blacks, and women in its membership. These changes in the House membership, especially the size and composition of the Democratic majority, the increase in member turnover, and the decrease in careerists, are essential to understanding the reforms and changes that have occurred in the operation of the House and assessing their significance.

RULES AND PROCEDURES

Since the House is a much larger institution than the Senate — 435 members as compared to 100 members — it must rely more on formal rules and explicit procedures than on norms. Norms do exist in the House: reciprocity, courtesy, hard work, expertise, and the most hallowed of all, seniority.[10] Nevertheless, the rules of the party caucuses, the rules of committees, and the rules of the House itself are primary guides to member behavior and are the centers of contention in struggles over power. Because there are so many new members in the House, it is difficult to socialize them rapidly to informal norms. As a result, formal rules have become even more important than they were in earlier decades; today formal rules are new members' primary guide to the legislative process in the House.

In response to the reforms of the 1970s, the rules of the 1980s are different from the rules that most new members read about in the 1950s, 1960s, and early 1970s.

Beginning of Reform Movement

The reform movement of the 1970s began in the late 1950s with the creation of the Democratic Study Group (DSG), an organization of Democratic liberals committed to liberal legislation and liberal control of the House.[11] Throughout the 1960s the group pushed for changes in House procedures and party practice. Liberals' efforts in the 1960s to bring about formal changes in House rules resulted in the 1970 Legislative Reorganization Act. That act, passed by a coalition of House Republicans in addition to liberal Democrats, primarily served to liberalize and formalize parliamentary procedure in committees and on the floor of the House.

During the late 1960s, just when these formal rules changes were approaching ratification, liberal Democrats fundamentally altered their strategy. Although they constituted the dominant faction of the House Democratic party in size, they did not dominate the positions of congressional power that are derived from party membership, particularly the assignments to the chairs of key committees. The formal changes in House rules could not alter the distribution of power positions because those positions derive from the majority party. Formal changes in rules also could not ensure the procedural protection of House liberals (or Republicans) because the only real way to enforce the changes was through discipline of committee chairs and party leaders within the majority party. Few mechanisms of party discipline existed to encourage committee leaders to abide by the changes.

Revitalization of the Democratic Caucus

In an effort to widen the focus of congressional reforms and make committee chairs follow rules changes, liberals shifted their attention to reforms of the House Democratic party itself. In January 1969 the Democratic Party Caucus, which had been dormant for most of the century, was revitalized by the passage of a rule stating that a caucus meeting could be held each month if 50 members demanded the meeting in writing. Utilizing the caucus, liberals throughout the early 1970s pushed for the creation of reform committees that would study the House and propose reforms of its structure and procedures.

Three reform committees were formed as a result of Democratic Caucus activity.[12] All were chaired by Representative Julia Butler Hansen (D-Wash.), and their proposals became known collectively as the Hansen Committee reforms. The proposals of Hansen I were debated and passed in January 1971, Hansen II in January 1973, and Hansen III in 1974. Another reform effort initiated by Speaker Carl Albert (D-Okla.) was the creation of a Select Committee on Committees headed by Representative Richard Bolling (D-Mo.). The Bolling Committee introduced its proposals in 1974, but they were defeated by the membership of the House, which chose instead to implement the proposals of Hansen III.[13]

Consequences of Reforms

These reform efforts had six particularly important consequences. First, they established a clear procedure whereby the Democratic Caucus could select committee chairs by secret ballot. This change in the traditional voting procedure provided a mechanism for defeating renominations of incumbent committee chairs, thereby bypassing the norm of committee seniority. Second, the reforms increased the number and strength of subcommittees. Third, in conjunction with these reform efforts the House moved to open to the public virtually all committee and subcommittee meetings. Fourth, the reforms increased the power of the Speaker of the House by giving him considerable control over the referral of legislation. A fifth change, which was not actually part of these caucus reforms but stemmed from the overall reform movement, was the creation in 1974 of a new congressional budget process and House Budget Committee.

Finally, the defeat of the Bolling Committee provisions restructuring committee jurisdictions left the maze of overlapping committee and subcommittee jurisdictions relatively untouched. In the 96th Congress the House created a new select committee on committees to review jurisdictions and procedures. Chaired by Jerry Patterson (D-Cal.), this new committee approached the reform process differently than the Bolling Committee, presenting reforms in a piecemeal rather than package form. Nevertheless, this approach also faced considerable opposition.

Despite these failures, other reforms of the post-1973 period did meet with some success. In the 94th Congress House Democrats refined the procedure for nominating committee chairs and voted down several incumbents. The caucus also adopted a rule requiring nominees for Appropriations subcommittee chairs to be approved by similar procedures. This rule, which seemed in order because Appropriations subcommittees are in many cases more powerful than other standing committees, was employed in the 95th Congress to deny a subcommittee position to a member who had been censured in the previous Congress for financial misconduct, Representative Robert Sikes (D-Fla.).

The Ethics Issue

The Sikes case, as well as the sex and public payroll scandals involving Wayne Hays (D-Ohio) and the probe of South Korean influence-peddling on Capitol Hill, focused attention on the inadequacy of House ethics provisions. During the 95th Congress the House, following the recommendations of the bipartisan Commission on Administrative Review chaired by David Obey (D-Wis.), adopted a new code of ethics. The code required annual financial disclosure by House members, officers, and professional staff; prohibited gifts that aggregate to $100 or more from a lobbyist or foreign national; prohibited unofficial office accounts; placed new restrictions on the use of the franking privilege; and limited members from receiving outside earned income in excess of 15 percent of their congressional salary.

This last provision was the most hotly debated. Some members claimed that it discriminated in favor of wealthier members since no restrictions were placed on unearned outside income from stocks, property, and other investments. Proponents claimed that there was no way the House could restrict unearned income and that the purpose of the provision was to limit the time members would devote to an outside job. Although the ethics code contained a sweetener in the form of an increase in office expenses, it was a bitter pill for a number of House members.

Among the reforms of the 1970s, the ethics code is one of the few that placed serious constraints on the new levels of independence House members had reached. Some members threatened to quit because of the limitations on outside income, and in several instances the ethics code contributed to the decision of members to retire. Since passage of the ethics code in 1977, financial misconduct and other wrongdoings continued to plague the House as seen in the scandals surrounding Daniel Flood (D-Pa.), Charles Diggs (D-Mich.), Charles Wilson (D-Calif.), and those involving other House members implicated in the FBI Abscam bribery investigation.

Summary

The ethics code was only one of numerous changes in the organizational structure and rules governing the House of Representatives that occurred in the 1970s. With the perspective the 1980s provide, it is possible to discern two definite trends in the reforms of the last decade. First, the reforms that occurred largely from 1970 to 1973 clearly served to decentralize power within committees. This first stage of reforms constituted a very real attempt to alter the House committee system. The second trend evident in these changes is a move toward centralization of certain powers in the party caucus, the Speaker, and a new budget committee. These reforms occurred largely after 1973. This stage of the reforms altered the role of the congressional parties, particularly the majority party, in the operations of the House. The overall nature and significance of these changes can best be seen by focusing separately on the committee and party systems in the House.

COMMITTEES

Party government began to decline in the early 1900s, and by the post-World War II era committee government dominated the House. The 1946 Legislative Reorganization Act contributed to the domination of the House by approximately 20 committee chairs. This era was characterized by brokerage politics in Congress — a politics in which committee chairs attempted to aggregate the numerous competing policy interests within their committee's jurisdictional domain through bargaining and compromise. The era was also characterized by a generally conservative bent to the policy process, since the norm of seniority tended to benefit conservative Democrats from safe one-party areas of the South.

As liberals began to dominate the Democratic party in the House during the 1950s and 1960s, opposition to the existing structure of committee government escalated. Aside from ideological considerations, the opposition was fueled by two environmental pressures on the House. First, the increase in both the number and complexity of federal concerns created the need for higher levels of legislative specialization, putting considerable pressure on the existing system and creating a demand for more meetings and investigations than could be handled easily by the standing committees. Second, the number of "careerists" in the House increased significantly. As a consequence, numerous seasoned members of Congress experienced in legislative life and capable of undertaking serious legislative work were frozen out of the legislative process because there were not enough committee chairs to go around.

As reformers in the 1950s and 1960s looked for ways to weaken the power of conservative chairs, increase the workload potential of the House, and provide the growing number of careerists access to legislative power, they turned their attention to the strengthening of subcommittees within the standing committees. Their efforts resulted in the reforms of the 1970s, which had two major dimensions: the rise of subcommittee government and the decline of committee chairs. It has also had consequences far beyond those ever envisioned by its creators.

The Rise of Subcommittee Government

During the early postwar years, most hearings, debates, and markup sessions were held at a committee level, and those that were not were subject to committee review and change. By the late 1970s most activity and authoritative decisions were at a subcommittee level.

Subcommittee government exists when the basic responsibility for the bulk of legislative activity (hearings, debates, legislative markups, that is, the basic writing of a bill) occurs, not at a meeting of an entire standing committee, but at a meeting of a smaller subcommittee of the standing committee. The decisions of the subcommittee are then viewed as the authoritative decisions — decisions that are altered by the standing committee only when the subcommittee is seriously divided or when it is viewed as highly unrepresentative of the full committee.

One indicator of the growth of subcommittees is in their number and staff. As Table 2-2 indicates, at the start of the 84th Congress (1955-56), when the Democrats began their current streak as the majority party in the House, there were 83 standing subcommittees in the House. By the 96th Congress there were 139. Moreover, the chair and ranking minority members of each subcommittee were entitled to appoint at least one professional staff member. By comparison, in the 86th Congress, the first time the *Congressional Staff Directory* was published, only 57 of the 113 subcommittees were shown to have their own staffs.

Not only have the number and staff of subcommittees grown, but they have become increasingly independent from the standing committees and committee chairs.[14] The Subcommittee Bill of Rights passed in 1973 as part of the Hansen Committee's reforms, and various other rules changes of the 1970s, moved the selection of subcommittee chairs away from the respective committee chairs and gave it to the full committee caucus of the majority party. This

Table 2-2 Standing Subcommittees in the House of Representatives*

84th Congress	83
86th Congress	113
88th Congress	105
90th Congress	108
92nd Congress	114
94th Congress	139
96th Congress	139

* Budget committee task forces are not included in the count.

arrangement enabled subcommittee chairs to develop personal constituencies and security independent of the full committee chairs.
Subcommittees also gained control over their own budget and staff,
and codified jurisdictions.

Finally, in an effort to spread subcommittee power more widely
and break the hold of committee chairs on subcommittees, the reforms
limited a member of the House to the chairmanship of only one
committee. This significantly increased the number of House members
who held a formal position in the committee system power structure.
As Table 2-3 indicates, 102 different individuals held a committee
or subcommittee chair in the 86th Congress. By the beginning of
the 96th Congress, the number had grown to 139. This increase is
all the more significant because the subcommittee positions held in
the 96th Congress carried with them greater formal authority than
those of the 1950s and 1960s.

With the rise of subcommittee government, committee decisionmaking responsibility flowed increasingly to subcommittees. One measure of this shift is the dramatic growth in the percentage of committee
hearings held in subcommittee rather than in the full committee.
During the late 1940s and early 1950s only 20 or 30 percent of committee
hearings occurred in subcommittees, whereas by the first session of
the 95th Congress, over 90 percent of all committee hearings took
place in subcommittees.[15] Also indicative of the growth in subcommittee
power is the increased number of floor managers for bills that are
subcommittee chairs. As late as 1970, this responsibility was the
exclusive province of committee chairs.

How then are subcommittee chairs selected since the rise of
subcommittee government? Under the Subcommittee Bill of Rights,
the majority members of each committee are allowed to bid in order
of seniority for subcommittee chairs. The member bidding for a subcommittee chair is then either elected or defeated by majority vote

Table 2-3   Distribution of Committee and Subcommittee Chairs

	Number of Standing Subcommittees	Number of Standing Committees	Number of Individuals Holding at Least One Chair
86th Congress	113	20	102
89th Congress	126	20	102
96th Congress	139	22	138

of the committee's Democratic members. If defeated, another member can then bid for the chair. In recent years there has been a number of particularly heated chairmanship contests. At the start of the 96th Congress, four senior members were defeated before the chair of a House Government Operations subcommittee was selected. Selection of a chair for the Health and Environment Subcommittee of the House Interstate and Foreign Commerce Committee was also controversial. A respected senior representative was defeated by a third-term member.

Some House members and observers criticize the selection process as a form of political cannibalism. Many of the challenges, they claim, are not based on merit but reflect instead the unrestrained ambitions of other members. The critics fear that the reactions to these contests may result in a return to strict seniority and that truly unworthy chairpersons will again be insulated from defeat.

The rise of subcommittee government, seen in these various quantitative indicators, is a qualitative change within the House. Basic legislative responsibility has shifted from approximately 20 standing committees to more than 160 committees and subcommittees. Today most legislation is actually drafted and reviewed in very small subgroups within Congress. The jurisdiction of the subgroups is much narrower than the jurisdiction of the parent committees. Because of the large number of subcommittees and committees that meets simultaneously in the House, and because of the press of other legislative business, often only a handful of members is present when a subcommittee meets, with primary responsibility falling on the subcommittee chair, the ranking minority member, and one or two other interested members. Since passage of sunshine legislation opening virtually all committee and subcommittee meetings to the press and the public, legislators are normally far outnumbered by lobbyists who are present to push their special programs and perspectives.

Once drafted in subcommittee, legislation goes for review to the standing committee, which acts as an appeals court where dissatisfied members can attempt to alter subcommittee decisions. Quite often legislation receives little meaningful alteration at a committee level and goes to the Rules Committee and the floor of the House for consideration largely as drafted in subcommittee.

The Decline of Committee Chairs

As subcommittees increased in importance during the postwar years, the power of committee chairs waned. This decline can be explained with the same general variables that account for the rise of subcommittees: the opposition of liberals to conservative dominance in the House, the increasing workload of committees that inhibited the ability of chairs to control all facets of policymaking, and the pressure from careerists within committees to democratize committee activity and spread responsibility. In the face of these pressures, throughout the late 1950s and 1960s the chair positions of individual committees were progressively weakened — often immediately following the retirement of a particularly influential or arbitrary chairperson.[16] For this reason, powerful committee chairs had already become an endangered species in the House by the 1970s. The systematic and formal diminishing of their power as a group, however, came with the reforms later in the decade.

The first formal crack in the armor of the chairs occurred when House liberals, after a series of reform efforts, established a procedure for the Democratic Caucus to elect standing committee chairs. It began with the adoption by the caucus of a Hansen Committee provision that allowed 10 members to demand a vote on a committee chair nomination, a procedure that clearly could threaten incumbent chairs. The threat was strengthened in 1973 when the caucus adopted the requirement of voting on every committee chair. Two years later, in the January 1975 meetings of the House Democratic Caucus, this rule was employed to defeat three sitting committee chairs in the bid for re-election. This "revolutionary" act went totally against the traditions of committee government and, by demonstrating the willingness of the majority caucus to discipline committee chairs, deprived them of their most potent weapon: their invulnerability to removal.

Changes in the procedures and traditions surrounding the selection of committee chairs, when combined with the other reforms of the early 1970s, clearly altered the status and authority of committee chairs. The chairs lost the right to determine the number, size, and majority party membership of subcommittees. They lost the power to appoint subcommittee chairs, to control referral of legislation to subcommittees, or to prevent their committees from meeting. Finally, as a result of the growth of subcommittee activity, many were forced to defer to their subcommittee chairs in the management of legislation.

It would be wrong to conclude from this analysis that committee chairs are devoid of power and that subcommittee government is all-encompassing. Despite the loss of formal powers, chairs generally remain influential. They still retain substantial control over the staff of the full committee and, to the degree that they do not abuse their powers, many maintain control over the agenda and the calling of meetings. Committee members still tend to defer to the judgment of the chair on questions about which the member is unfamiliar or undecided. Committee chairs who possess substantial policy expertise and/or political skill maintain the greatest influence potential. In fact, the recent decline in the number of careerists in the House means that many subcommittee chairs will be younger and relatively inexperienced individuals whom an astute and experienced committee chair can seek to control or constrain through use of greater knowledge and legislative skill.

Nevertheless, it is paradoxical that although the majority caucus now has the ability to select the individuals it feels are best qualified to head House committees, it has left those individuals with few sources of influence. The bulk of committee power has shifted to subcommittees and subcommittee chairs who, with the exception of the Appropriations Committee, are not selected by the full party caucus but rather by party caucuses within their committees. This shift toward subcommittee government, and the related weakening of the parent committees and committee chairs, are changing substantially the character of committee decisionmaking.[17]

Committee Decisionmaking

Historically, so long as the basic responsibility for decisionmaking rested at a committee level, the large number of interests that fell within the jurisdiction of a standing committee meant that committee decisionmaking tended toward brokerage politics. Thus a particularized interest group could not dominate committee policymaking. As Richard Fenno demonstrated in *Congressmen in Committees,* variation did exist in the heterogeneity of committees' jurisdictional environments, with more homogeneous environments producing committee decisionmaking more likely to be clientele-dominated.[18] Nevertheless, committee jurisdictions by their very nature tend to be fairly broad so that a narrow single-interest group could seldom dominate the general decisions of a committee.

The Rise of Single-Interest Groups. As power has shifted from committees to subcommittees, committee decisionmaking has moved to work groups with far more homogeneous environments. In other words, when one cuts a committee jurisdiction into a variety of segments and gives each subcommittee one segment to review, that segment will include within it a fewer number of policy concerns. Cutting a committee's jurisdiction into small pieces and placing real responsibility for decisions in the discrete subcommittees encourages particularized single-interest groups to disengage from umbrella lobby groups (that is, lobby groups that aggregate numerous interests in a policy domain into one lobby effort) and expend concentrated effort on the particular subcommittee determining the fate of their particularized interest. Concerned with only a few policy interests, these subcommittees are apt to become the captives of these clientele groups.

The move to subcommittee government thus has fueled the rise of single-interest groups in Congress and augmented the power of particularized lobby groups, increasing the probability of clientele dominance of congressional policymaking.

The rise of particularized single-interest groups affects not only the general pattern of decisionmaking, but also the nature of committee leadership and congressional careers. The era of committee government produced committee leaders who were basically brokers with broad policy interests. Within committees, individuals could specialize, but ultimately the decisive power to mold the overall pattern of a committee's decisions rested in the hands of the committee chair whose authority derived from responsibility over a broad range of policy jurisdictions. Because of the large number of interests within their authority, these committee chairs could maintain independence, if they so desired, from particularized, narrow interests and specific executive agencies.

Changes in Committee Leadership. With the shift of power to subcommittees and subcommittee chairs, and with subcommittees being the focus of a small number of particularized groups, the nature of committee leadership has changed. The power of subcommittee chairs rests not on their ability to balance numerous contending interests, but on their attention to a few particularized policy areas. As a result, there is considerable pressure for subcommittee chairs and members to be policy entrepreneurs who take a few narrow policy areas as their personal concerns, develop expertise in these areas, and build careers tied to narrow clientele groups.

Thus leadership within subcommittees is oriented less toward aggregating a broad range of interests and more toward articulating a few particularized interests. Over time, these subcommittee policy entrepreneurs are liable to identify their personal career interests with the success of their chosen clientele groups, becoming the captive of those interests psychologically as well as electorally. Moreover, the members of the subcommittees are not the only entrepreneurs. Subcommittee staff have a stake in developing activities for the members (hearings, legislation, amendments, speeches) as a way of proving their own worth and institutionalizing their positions.

Subcommittee members who wish to break out of the bind of particularized concerns must broaden the range of their policy interests and play a broader policy role. These efforts often produce a third pattern of change: the breakdown of jurisdictional alignments.

Committee Jurisdictions. As Fenno argues in *Congressmen in Committees,* House committee decisionmaking historically has tended to be "monolithic"; the committee given jurisdiction over a particular policy area guarded its authority in that area closely and opposed intervention by other committees. On the other hand, as Fenno points out, committee decisionmaking in the Senate was more permeable, with committees less jealous of their committee jurisdictions. This contrast existed largely because House members belonged to only one or two committees and were anxious to protect their power base, whereas senators, belonging to more committees and also having more national visibility, had a broader base of power and thus were less protective of their committee jurisdictions.

In many ways the rise of subcommittee government in the House creates a situation today somewhat analogous to the Senate described by Fenno. House members usually belong to a half dozen or more subcommittees. Since subcommittees are the real decision units in the House now, members have more diffuse loyalties. Unless a member is a subcommittee chair, he or she is normally torn between a number of different decision units and less tied to one subcommittee. Thus the desire to protect full committee jurisdictional boundaries that applied in an earlier era is less evident for most members except as it affects the jurisdiction of the subcommittees.

In addition, since most members today tend not to see the standing committees as the level at which they attain and exercise power, and since committee chairs lack the resources to protect committee jurisdictions that they once had, the capacity of committees to prevent encroachment on their jurisdictions by other committees has been considerably diminished. Moreover, the chaos created by the expansion of the number of House subcommittees makes it difficult to avoid overlapping jurisdictions. Finally, many current legislative issues cut across committee jurisdictions that have remained substantially unaltered since 1946. All of these factors orient the House today toward less monolithic committee decisionmaking. But the ultimate stimulus for a breakdown of committee jurisdictions is the motivation of the subcommittee chairs themselves.

At first glance it would appear that subcommittee chairs would be those most stringently committed to protecting the purity of committee and subcommittee jurisdictions. Since a House member can chair only one subcommittee, the power of subcommittee chairs seems tied closely to their subcommittee. Naturally, subcommittee chairs want to protect their jurisdictions. Thus, there is a pressure within a committee for subcommittees to honor each other's jurisdictional boundaries. Since subcommittee chairs are selected by the majority party caucus within a committee and can be disciplined if they fail to honor intracommittee and jurisdictional lines, such pressure has some success within committee. But control of jurisdictional raids into other standing committees' policy areas is another matter.

As noted earlier, subcommittee chairs who seek to avoid being the captive of a narrow clientele group within their own subcommittee have a very natural desire to broaden the range of policy concerns under their authority. One way to do so in the long run is to move up a subcommittee hierarchy using committee seniority as a means to claim the chairs of more important subcommittees with broader policy domains. But in the short run, subcommittee chairs follow a very different strategy. Since most subcommittee chair positions rest on a vote of their committee caucuses, subcommittee chairs who want to broaden their policy domains cross into the jurisdictional boundaries of other committees that have related policy concerns. These other committees have few mechanisms to protect themselves and are often unaware of the encroachment at the time because of the general confusion in the highly decentralized House.

A case in point is the postwar growth in the number of subcommittees from different committees that hold hearings on the same general policy areas and executive departments.[19] Committee jurisdictional lines thus appear to be breaking apart, and committee decisionmaking to be taking on the permeable characteristics of the Senate.

As a result of the growth in congressional decentralization in the House, the rise of House members as policy entrepreneurs, and the increasing permeability of House committee decisionmaking, the House during the postwar years looks more and more like the Senate. Because of the basic structural and environmental differences between the two bodies, as the House comes in some ways to resemble the Senate, the ultimate decision calculus of House members and the decision processes of the House are driven farther from that of the Senate.

In the Senate, decentralization spreads power among a relatively small number of members. Because the members serve constituencies that are normally quite heterogeneous (i.e., states), they necessarily must focus eventually, not on a few particularized interests, but on balancing a range of interests. In addition, because there are fewer senators, the spreading of power positions among the members of the majority party still leaves each senator with a wide range of policy jurisdictions. In other words, even with decentralization of power there is a natural tendency on the part of senators to think about balancing and compromising various interests. Thus, decentralization helps senators aggregate and balance interests by allowing them to become powerful in a number of different policy areas that are of particular concern to them and their states, giving them the expertise and authority necessary to convince the different forces that press on them of the need to compromise. The permeability of Senate committees largely serves to augment the role of individual senators as interest aggregators.

The effects of decentralization in the House are quite different. Decentralization spreads power among a much larger number of members in the House, members that have under their jurisdiction a small number of legitimate policy domains. (No member chairs more than one subcommittee.) The particularized and narrow focus of House members is reinforced by their service of relatively homogeneous constituencies. Since House members serve homogeneous constituencies, the permeability of House committees does not serve the same function that permeability serves in the Senate. Instead of allowing broadly oriented legislators to balance numerous contending forces, it adds to the chaos of the House and to competition among members for the support of particularized single-interest groups.

The age of strong standing committees in the House tended to force members at least to recognize the existence and relevance of contending forces within a general policy domain. The standing committees, in fact, were the main elements of interest aggregation and compromise in the postwar House. The move to subcommittee government considerably lessens the aggregating role of the standing committees. The growth in the permeability and irrelevance of committees' jurisdictions lessens even more the ability of a standing committee to aggregate interests in its policy domain.

Summary

It should be clear, then, that the rise of subcommittee government has altered considerably the character of House decisionmaking. This change has brought more members into the policy process, opened the possibility of policy innovations from a wider range of members, and probably increased legislative expertise in the House. But it has had its costs, too. Problems have been created that, if left unresolved, could cripple the legislative process in the House.

At its heart, subcommittee government creates a crisis of interest aggregation in the House. It largely removes committees as arenas in which interests will be compromised, brokered, and mediated. It has led to increased dominance of committee decisionmaking by clientele groups, particularly single-interest groups. If interests are to be checked and balanced, if the competing demands of different groups within a policy domain are to be weighed according to their relative merits, that action increasingly must occur, not within the committee system itself, but within the congressional parties and on the floor of the House. The responsibility for saving subcommittee government from itself — maintaining its benefits while offsetting its detriments — thus falls largely to the party and party leadership.

STRENGTHENING PARTY LEADERSHIP

Throughout most of the postwar years, political parties in Congress have been weak, ineffectual organizations.[20] Power in Congress has rested in the committees or, increasingly, in the subcommittees. Although the party caucuses nominally have had the power to organize committees and select committee chairs, the norm of congressional or state delegation seniority has dominated committee assignments (though not exclusively), while committee seniority has dominated the selection of committee chairs.

In reality, throughout much of the past four decades Congress has been governed by a conservative coalition composed of Southern Democrats and Republicans; their strength has been particularly evident on the most powerful committees such as Appropriations, Ways and Means, and Rules. The primary function of party leaders has been to assist in smoothing the flow of legislation and mediating conflict — not to provide policy leadership or coordination. The parties themselves — particularly the House Democratic party — have been loose coalitions of convenience, not programmatic or cohesive organizations dedicated to enacting a specified set of policies. As one observer has written, political parties in the postwar Congress have been in many ways "phantoms" of scholarly imagination that perhaps should be exorcised from attempts to explain congressional organization, behavior, and process.[21]

Many of the 1970s reforms addressed the weaknesses of House parties, and to a degree they reinvigorated the parties and presented them with new, expanded roles on the operation of the House. However, while the reform process did evidence a short-term emergence of party activism, it has not thus far produced an institutionalized form of party government. An examination of the Democratic Caucus and the party leadership will indicate why the reforms leave the House far short of the party government model.

The Party Caucus

One reason for the failure of party government to emerge vigorously from the reform era is that most of the reforms of the 1970s relied on the caucus as the focus of activity. Many of the recommendations of the Hansen Committee called for the further strengthening of the caucus. In particular, the provisions for the election of committee chairs by the caucus and the subsequent defeat of three incumbent chairs in the caucus at the start of the 94th Congress helped build a reputation for the caucus. Furthermore, the use of the caucus to direct Democratic members in particular standing committees to report certain legislation served to substantiate the notion of a powerful caucus. Republicans fueled the fire by claiming that "King Caucus" had returned and was infringing on the independence of Democratic members. Finally, the caucus chair in the 94th Congress, Phillip Burton (D-Calif.), used an active caucus to build his campaign for Majority Leader in the 95th Congress.[22]

As the 94th Congress progressed it became clear that although the caucus was far more active than in earlier years, its prowess had been exaggerated. Limits began to be placed on expansion of its power. Caucus meetings became more infrequent as the press of legislation increased. Those viewing Burton's activities in chairing the caucus as competing with rather than complementing the party leadership worked to defer activity away from the caucus. And in the 95th and 96th Congresses its main functions were organizational: voting on rules changes, approving committee chairs, and electing party leaders. With the exception of the Sikes case, which involved an Appropriations subcommittee chair, no chairs have been denied by the caucus. To the degree that the caucus remains active during a Congress, it does so through its Steering and Policy Committee, a group that is more an instrument of the Speaker than of the caucus.

The Speaker

Throughout most of the twentieth century, parties in the House have been unwilling to invest power in their party leaders. This reticence stems from early in the century when Speaker "Uncle Joe" Cannon used the considerable authority that the Speaker possessed at that time to dominate House proceedings and relegate most members to a relatively insignificant status. After the 1910 insurgency against Cannon stripped the Speakership of all of its major powers except the constitutional role as presiding officer, members guarded their personal prerogatives and committee power assiduously against usurpation by the Speaker. Although the 1946 Legislative Reorganization Act attempted to resolve many problems of committee government, it did not include reforms strengthening the Speakership or party leaders.

In the early 1970s liberals in the House were willing to turn to the Speakership for a variety of reasons. First, the Speaker was Carl Albert, a man who supported, or at least did not oppose, many of the reform efforts of the caucus, including the strengthening of subcommittees and personal prerogative of members on the floor. Albert had liberal leanings, at least for an Oklahoman. And because of his mild demeanor and consensual politics, he was not perceived by the members as a personal threat. A second factor, not to be underestimated, was the presence of Representative Richard Bolling

(D-Mo.), who strongly influenced reformers and Albert. Bolling is an individual who has studied the history and structure of the institution and developed reform proposals. As a result of his experience as a lieutenant to Speaker Rayburn and of his study of the House, Bolling has become a staunch supporter of a strong Speakership and strong party leadership. He has continually pushed his views, kept them alive, and added an element of legitimacy to them.

A third reason why House liberals in the 1970s looked to the Speaker for leadership was the existence of divided government and the presidency of Richard Nixon. As Nixon forced such issues as the Cambodia invasion and impoundment, Democrats needed some leadership and coherent strategy to thwart his efforts at undermining the role of Congress in public policy. A strong Speaker offered the possibility of leadership. Fourth, because the party caucus elected the Speaker by secret ballot, the Speaker should be more responsive to the caucus than committee chairs, protected by the seniority norm, had traditionally been. Finally, through procedural changes the party could strengthen the office of Speaker without investing in it all of the power Cannon had possessed. The three-day layover requirement governing consideration of conference reports and amendments, and electronic voting, limited the ability of the strengthened Speaker to control arbitrarily floor votes. In addition, the central power of the party could be divided between the Speaker and a Steering Committee in such a fashion as to keep the Speaker in bounds.

Reforms Strengthening Speaker. The move toward a strong Speakership came in two waves. First, the Hansen reforms of 1973 placed the Speaker, as well as the Majority Leader and caucus chair, on the Committee on Committees chaired by Wilbur Mills (D-Ark.), effectively curtailing his power. Simultaneously, they strengthened the Speaker, giving him a formal role in the selection of committee members and chairs. The 1973 reforms also replaced the dormant Steering Committee with a new Steering and Policy Committee consisting of 24 members: the Speaker, the Majority Leader, the chairman of the caucus, the majority whip, the chief deputy whip, the 3 deputy whips, 4 members appointed by the Speaker, and 12 members elected by regional caucuses within the House Democratic party. The role of the new committee was to help direct party strategy. The Speaker was made the chair of Steering and Policy and was given a dominant role in selecting its members. Not only would he appoint four members, but the five whips would also be indebted, since they are appointed by the Speaker in conjunction with the Majority Leader.

The second wave in strengthening the Speaker came at the end of 1974 and early 1975. The Hansen substitute for the Bolling plan gave the Speaker considerable control over the referral of bills. The early organizational caucuses of the 94th Congress further strengthened the Speaker by giving him the power to nominate the chair and Democratic members of the House Rules Committee, thus bringing that committee more clearly into the control of the Speaker and the party.[23] At the beginning of the 96th Congress, Speaker Tip O'Neill asserted this power when he refused to appoint Jerry Patterson (D-Calif.), the choice of California House Democrats to fill a Rules vacancy, and instead selected Anthony Beilenson, another Democratic representative from California.

Although the 1973 Hansen reforms made considerable headway in bolstering the power of the Speaker, 1975 brought even greater changes. The caucus in the 94th Congress took the Committee on Committees' power away from Ways and Means Democrats and placed it in the Steering and Policy Committee. This greatly increased the role of the party leadership, particularly the Speaker, in selecting committee members and committee chairs. Out of the committee of 24, the Speaker thus had 10 votes over which he should have considerable sway (his vote and those of his 4 appointees and the 5 whips).

Two other changes took place in the 1970s that served to strengthen the Speaker. First, increases in the financial and staff resources of the party whip office and in the number of whips appointed by the party leadership resulted in a stronger and more active whip system at the disposal of the party leadership in efforts to pass legislation.[24] Second, the creation of the new budgetary process provided mechanisms through which a skillful party leadership could control budgetary process and coordinate decisionmaking by House committees. The Speaker's potential control of the House budgetary process resulted from his appointment (in conjunction with the Senate's president pro tem) of the director of the Congressional Budget Office, the leadership's appointment of one of its lieutenants to the House Budget Committee, and the ability of the Speaker, as Steering and Policy chair, to oversee appointments of Democrats to the Budget Committee.

Consequences of Reforms. Taken together, all of these changes substantially increased the prerogatives of the Speaker. For the first time in decades, a Democratic Speaker now has a direct and significant role in committee nominations and the nominations of committee chairs. While he cannot make the decisions in a personal, arbitrary fashion (except in the case of Rules), the Speaker does chair the Committee on Committees and plays a dominant role in the selection of 9 of the other 23 members. Members of the party seeking committee positions or leadership roles now have far more reason to listen to and follow the Speaker than in the past, since this office, perhaps more than any other, is critical to successful candidacies.

Second, although the Speaker is not a member of the Rules Committee and does not chair it (as was the case in Cannon's day), the Speaker does choose the Democratic members of that committee, lessening thereby the likelihood that its Democratic members will delay or block the scheduling of legislation desired by the party leadership. Third, as chair of the revitalized Steering and Policy Committee, the Speaker now has greater legitimacy as a policy representative of the party and greater opportunity to fashion and direct the party's legislative program. Fourth, the Speaker has regained some of the ground lost by Cannon concerning control over the referral of bills. Fifth, the Democratic Speaker now has a strengthened whip system to use in passing Democratic legislation. Finally, the Steering and Policy Committee, together with the new budget process, provide tools that a Speaker can use to coordinate and direct major legislation.

Ironically, many of the recent reforms have created heightened expectations for leadership performance and resulted in members making new and increased demands on the leadership. However, the new powers are sufficiently modest that the expectations and demands are not easily satisfied, particularly in the context of decentralized, subcommittee government.

The one area in which the reforms of the 1970s do not seem significantly to have redressed the loss of ground after Cannon is the control of parliamentary procedures on the floor. Recorded votes on amendments and electronic voting (which has cut the time of roll call votes considerably and reduced leadership control over the pace of floor votes) have further reduced the Speaker's power as presiding officer and solidified the procedural protections of the average member. Nevertheless, the sum total of the changes constitutes a real resurgence of the Speakership and a move back toward the power of the era of Cannon from 1903-11. This movement is not uninhibited, however. It is constrained by the Subcommittee Bill of Rights and other rules changes that protect members' rights within committees and subcommittees, by the specification of fairly clear-cut procedural roles on the floor, and by the existence of the Steering and Policy Committee.

With the retirement of Carl Albert and the selection of Tip O'Neill as Speaker, the Democrats significantly strengthened the party leadership at the start of the 95th Congress. In personal terms, O'Neill is a more forceful, active, and visible leader than Albert. But perhaps more importantly, he is freer to use the substantive powers that were brought to the office during Albert's tenure than was Albert.

O'Neill's establishment of the Ad Hoc Select Committee on Energy, his setting of deadlines for the standing committees to report their pieces of the Carter energy program, and his work in holding enough House Democrats together to pass the program largely intact reinforced the notion that an era of strong party leadership had arrived. This optimism, however, proved premature. In fact, the leadership had to use its limited resources extensively to succeed with the energy package, and any of those resources once used was not easily replenished. Later in the 95th Congress when the leadership sought the support of Democratic members on other important legislation, some members warded off persuasive efforts with the reminder of support they had given earlier on the energy program.

Defeats of common situs picketing and the Obey Commission's recommendations on internal House administrative reform, as well as difficulties in holding House Democratic conferees together on the natural gas compromise, indicated that even with strong personal leaders, with increased substantive leadership powers, with a president of the same party, and with a two to one majority, the leadership could not overcome the independence of House members. Many problems still remained. The system of subcommittee government provided regular jurisdictional disputes — both real and contrived — and it was not feasible to create an ad hoc committee each time jurisdictions became entangled. Democrats on the Rules Committee, although generally supportive of the Speaker's wishes, balked occasionally. Members with their own fiefdoms were not only immune from leadership pressure but often possessed resources to attract the support of other members. Relations with the president did not always pay off, especially when issues like public works projects were involved. While the new leadership was more successful than its predecessors, it clearly lacked the recipe for party government; additional ingredients were still needed.

The Steering and Policy Committee

The key to closer party government may come from more active use of the Steering and Policy Committee. For party government to be successful, to endure, caucus members must recognize that a cooperative effort is needed to fashion a widely accepted set of policies and strategies. The Steering and Policy Committee — a small committee composed of the Speaker's appointees and members selected by regional caucuses — provides the best arena in which the spirit of party cooperation and a representative direction to party efforts can be fashioned, while at the same time constraining and guiding the Speaker.

Ideally, the Steering and Policy Committee will become a representative body that keeps the Speaker in touch with the general sentiments of the party, provides healthy debate and innovative direction on public policy, gives guidance to committees and subcommittees, and spurs the party leadership into an articulate, persuasive policy role that reflects the dominant sentiment of the party. But since its creation, the committee only occasionally has given evidence of an ability to perform these roles. Its activities in policy planning and direction have been limited. Aside from the creation in 1974 of the Task Force on the Economy, which made broad policy recommendations on energy and the economy early in 1975 and then dissolved, the activities of the Steering and Policy Committee have been limited for the most part to legislative strategy sessions and decisions on whether the party will take a position on legislation just prior to the legislation coming to the floor. Although the committee's role in making effective committee assignments is important, even here it can be challenged. For example, at the start of the 96th Congress, several of its assignment recommendations were contested in the caucus; in two cases the Steering and Policy Committee's choices were defeated. Nevertheless, there was some indication that O'Neill intended to expand the role of the Steering and Policy Committee. More direction might have been given to the party legislative program by paying more attention to long-range scheduling, and setting legislative priorities and goals for committees and subcommittees. These lofty goals for the Steering and Policy Committee seem to have been forgotten as the leadership found itself under the day-to-day press of legislation.

The potential success of the leadership in making the Steering and Policy Committee a more useful instrument and in moving the House toward any semblance of party government requires that it clean up the jurisdictional nightmare among House committees and subcommittees. The current structure of committees and subcommittees invites jurisdictional disputes from those who see their influence threatened and from those who realize such disputes can be used to delay and defeat legislation.

During the 94th and 95th Congresses the leadership relied on three primary weapons to confront jurisdictional disputes: the creation of ad hoc committees, the use of multiple referral of legislation combined with having the Rules Committee write complex rules of multiple committee floor management, and persuasion. None of these is a long-term solution, and each has its drawbacks. The first, as mentioned earlier, can only be used occasionally. The second reinforces committees' desires to make jurisdictional claims and continues the piecemeal approach to complex policy problems. And the third uses time, energy, and resources that might better be applied elsewhere. Not until the problem of overlapping committee jurisdictions is thoroughly addressed and resolved will the House leadership, no matter how skilled, be able to provide the institution with clear policy direction. One thing is certain, however. As the Bolling, and more modestly, the Patterson Committees discovered, rearranging and clarifying committee jurisdictions is no easy task. Too many members and special interest groups have developed substantial personal stakes in the current committee structure.

CONCLUSION

Today the House of Representatives is at a major turning point. As a result of the changes and reforms unleashed in the 1970s, the era of committee government dominated by conservative Southern Democrats is gone. In its place has come a liberal, reformed House in which power is shared by subcommittees, committees, and party leadership. This distribution of power among the distinct hierarchical levels of House organization is an uneasy arrangement. On the one hand, the career and power interests of individual members, together with specialized policy interests, generate support for a decentralized form of subcommittee government. On the other hand, subcommittee government lacks a means of generating support for interest aggregation and strong party leadership.

In the 1980s the House will have to confront the tensions between these counteracting tendencies, providing some institutionalization or resolution. Such a confrontation might end, of course, with a power structure and process much like the one that currently exists; such a resolution almost surely would require the emergence of new norms and structural/procedural supports that would rationalize and ameliorate the current tension, helping subcommittee government mesh more easily with party leadership. Alternatively, the House could slide decisively toward subcommittee government, react to the inadequacies of subcommittee government by implementing stronger party government, or return to a variant of committee government as a necessary compromise.

Many factors will influence the direction that the House takes. Chief among these are the quality and skill of party leaders, the role of the president in supporting party government, and the facility of subcommittee chairs at solidifying control of their policy arenas. Among all the various variables at work, however, one factor is probably overriding: the nature of membership change.

As the history of the House of Representatives demonstrates, turnover and careerism are critically important influences on internal organizational dynamics.[25] Depending on the nature of turnover in the 1980s, several alternate organizational paths may develop within the House. A return to low turnover and careerism probably would solidify and increase preoccupation of members with personal power prerogatives, thereby lending support to an institutionalization of sub-committee government and a renewed weakening of the party leadership. By contrast, significant turnover, combined with a continuing drop in the number of careerists, might fuel support for strengthening party leadership. Such support could come on several basis: the large number of new members could create such chaos that strong leadership would be needed simply to maintain order in the House; the loss of a large pool of truly experienced members might deprive the House of the type of membership needed to provide rigorous support for the existence of subcommittee government; and a large number of inexperienced members could provide a group from whom an astute Speaker might build a supporting coalition. The existence of moderate levels of turnover, by contrast, might tilt the House toward committee government, with too few experienced members for full-fledged sub-committee government to work, yet too many careerists for a willing reliance on strong party leadership.

It is, of course, difficult to predict the patterns of turnover and careerism in the 1980s. Much of the turnover in the last decade was voluntary in nature; many old-timers retired. With the coming of the 1980s, the large pool of careerists who fueled voluntary turnover particularly in the late 1970s is now largely gone. For voluntary turnover to continue, it must come increasingly from the newer members, members who may well have reason to leave more rapidly than their predecessors did at a similar career stage as these factors suggest: financial constraints of service, the greater rigors of the job, and a more rapid rise to power positions that can serve as vehicles for races for other offices.

Increased turnover could also come through defeat of incumbents. While the decline in competitiveness of congressional elections suggests that turnover probably will not occur because of defeat,[26] one might witness a reversal of this situation, at least temporarily, by a massive scandal, a new electoral realignment during a presidential election, the rise of single-interest groups, weariness with Democratic control, or fundamental campaign finance reform that improved the resources of challengers in congressional campaigns. Involuntary turnover is more likely to produce partisan or at least ideological change in the House than voluntary turnover, with incumbents beaten in primaries by ideological opponents or in general elections by partisan opponents.

If the electorate continues to operate by traditional dynamics, the experience in the House in the last sixty years suggests that we will witness in the 1980s neither high voluntary nor involuntary turnover, but rather a return to lower turnover and renewed careerism.[27] From this perspective, the turnover of the 1970s has served primarily to cleanse the House of an earlier generation and establish a new generation that now may stay for a significant length of time, attracted by the availability of power positions at a subcommittee level and buoyed by safe congressional seats. This vision of the future would suggest that the 1980s could conceivably witness quite a low turnover.

All three of these alternate models — high voluntary turnover, high involuntary turnover, or low turnover — have plausible supporting arguments. And it is possible to envision a number of permutations on them that would generate more complex dynamics. Whatever happens, it is clear that membership change in the 1980s is an important variable to watch as a key to the internal organizational dynamics of the House.

NOTES

1. For example, see Samuel P. Huntington, "Congressional Responses to the Twentieth Century," *The Congress and America's Future,* ed. David Truman (Englewood Cliffs, New Jersey: Prentice-Hall, 1973). For a more recent work that emphasizes the stability of Congress, see Barbara Hinckley, *Stability and Change in Congress* (New York: Harper & Row, 1971). For background on the House, see also George B. Galloway, *History of the House of Representatives* (New York: Thomas Y. Crowell Co., 1962); and Neil MacNeil, *Forge of Democracy: The House of Representatives* (New York: David McKay Co., 1963).
2. On the insurgency era, see Kenneth W. Hechler, *Insurgency: Personalities and Politics of the Taft Era* (New York: Columbia University Press, 1940); and John D. Baker, "The Character of the Congressional Revolution of 1910," *Journal of American History* 60 (1973): 679-691.
3. Charles S. Bullock, III, "House Careerists: Changing Patterns of Longevity and Attrition," *American Political Science Review* 66 (1972): 1295-1305. Bullock's operational definition of a House careerist is a member elected to 10 or more terms.
4. Much of the data on careerism was originally developed by Bullock with recent years updated here.
5. Thomas Mann, *Unsafe At Any Margin* (Washington, D.C.: American Enterprise Institute, 1978).
6. For an analysis of retirements, see Joseph Cooper and William West, "The Congressional Career in the 1970s," in this volume.
7. Huntington, "Congressional Responses," p. 9.
8. *1974 Congressional Quarterly Almanac* (Washington, D.C.: Congressional Quarterly, 1975), p. 855.
9. The Southern Republican moderate referred to is Representative John Buchanan (Ala.), who was defeated by a conservative challenger in the 1980 Republican primary.
10. See Herbert Asher, "The Learning of Legislative Norms," *American Political Science Review* 67 (1973): 499-513.

11. See Mark F. Ferber, "The Formation of the Democratic Study Group," in *Congressional Behavior,* ed. Nelson W. Polsby (New York: Random House, 1971), pp. 249-267; and Arthur G. Stevens, Jr., Arthur H. Miller, and Thomas E. Mann, "Mobilization of Liberal Strength in the House, 1955-1970: The Democratic Study Group," *American Political Science Review* 68 (1974): 667-681. For a discussion of the reform efforts in the House and the initial role of the DSG, see Norman J. Ornstein and David W. Rohde, "Congressional Reform and Political Parties in the U.S. House of Representatives," in *Parties and Elections in an Anti-Party Age,* ed. Jeff Fishel (Bloomington, Ind.: Indiana University Press, 1976).

12. For a more extensive chronological discussion of the reform processes, see Lawrence C. Dodd and Bruce I. Oppenheimer, "The House in Transition," in *Congress Reconsidered,* 1st ed., edited by Dodd and Oppenheimer (New York: Praeger Publishers, 1977), pp. 27-32; see also Norman J. Ornstein and David W. Rohde, "Congressional Reform and Political Parties in the U.S. House of Representatives," in *Congress Reconsidered,* 1st ed.; and Leroy N. Rieselbach, *Congressional Reform in the Seventies* (Morristown, New Jersey: General Learning Press, 1977).

13. For an excellent discussion of the Bolling Committee, see Roger H. Davidson, "Two Avenues of Change: House and Senate Committee Reorganization," in this volume; and Roger H. Davidson and Walter J. Oleszek, *Congress Against Itself* (Bloomington, Ind.: Indiana University Press, 1977).

14. See David W. Rohde, "Committee Reform in the House of Representatives and the Subcommittee Bill of Rights," *The Annals* 411 (January 1974): 39-47 and Norman J. Ornstein, "Causes and Consequences of Congressional Change: Subcommittee Reforms in the House of Representatives, 1970-1973," in *Congress in Change,* ed. Ornstein (New York: Praeger Publishers, 1975), pp. 88-114.

15. See Lawrence C. Dodd and George C. Shipley, "Patterns of Committee Surveillance in the House of Representatives" (Paper delivered at the annual meeting of the American Political Science Association, San Francisco, California, September 2-5, 1975); and David E. Price, "Congressional Committees in the Policy Process," in this volume.

16. See, for example, MacNeil, *Forge of Democracy,* pp. 161-170; and James T. Murphy, "The House Public Works Committee" (Ph.D. diss., University of Rochester, 1969).

17. For case studies that demonstrate the legislative impact of committee change, see Catherine E. Rudder, "Committee Reform and the Revenue Process," in *Congress Reconsidered,* 1st ed.; and Norman J. Ornstein and David W. Rohde, "Shifting Forces, Changing Rules, and Political Outcomes: The Impact of Congressional Change on Four House Committees," in *New Perspectives on the House of Representatives,* ed. Robert L. Peabody and Nelson W. Polsby, (Chicago: Rand McNally & Co., 1977). For a discussion of the impact of committee change on legislative oversight, see Lawrence C. Dodd and Richard L. Schott, *Congress and the Administrative State* (New York: John Wiley & Sons, 1979).

18. Richard F. Fenno, Jr., *Congressmen in Committees* (Boston: Little, Brown & Co., 1973).

19. For a study of committee hearings, see Lawrence C. Dodd, George C. Shipley, and Philip Diehl, "Patterns of Congressional Committee Surveillance, 1947-70" (Paper delivered at the annual meeting of the Midwest Political Science Association, Chicago, Illinois, April 1978).
20. See Robert L. Peabody, *Leadership in Congress: Stability, Succession and Change* (Boston: Little, Brown & Co., 1976), chap. 2.
21. David R. Mayhew, *Congress: The Electoral Connection* (New Haven: Yale University Press, 1974).
22. See Bruce I. Oppenheimer and Robert L. Peabody, "The House Majority Leadership Contest, 1976" (Paper delivered at the annual meeting of the American Political Science Association, Washington, D.C., September 1-4, 1977).
23. For a discussion of the Hansen substitute for the Bolling plan, see Davidson, "Two Avenues of Change." On the Rules Committee in earlier eras, see James A. Robinson, *The House Rules Committee* (Indianapolis: Bobbs-Merrill & Co., 1963); on the new Rules Committee, see Bruce I. Oppenheimer, "The Rules Committee: New Arm of Leadership in a Decentralized House," *Congress Reconsidered*, 1st ed., pp. 96-116.
24. On the whip system in an earlier era, see Randall B. Ripley, "The Party Whip Organizations in the U.S. House of Representatives," in *New Perspectives on the House of Representatives*, ed. Robert L. Peabody and Nelson W. Polsby (Chicago: Rand McNally & Co., 1969); on the new whip system, see Lawrence C. Dodd, "The Expanded Roles of the House Democratic Whip System: The 93rd and 94th Congresses," in *Capitol Studies*, forthcoming.
25. For various discussions that indicate a linkage, see Nelson W. Polsby, "Institutionalization in the U.S. House of Representatives," *American Political Science Review* 62 (1968): 144-168; H. Douglas Price, "Congress and the Evolution of Legislative 'Professionalism,'" in *Congress in Change*, pp. 2-23; H. Douglas Price, "Careers and Committees in the American Congress: The Problem of Structural Change," in *The History of Parliamentary Behavior* (Princeton, New Jersey: Princeton University Press, 1977); and Lawrence C. Dodd, "Congress and the Quest for Power," in *Congress Reconsidered*, 1st ed.
26. For discussions of decline in competitiveness, see David R. Mayhew, "Congressional Elections: The Case of the Vanishing Marginals," *Polity* 6 (1974): 295-317; Morris P. Fiorina, *Congress: Keystone of the Washington Establishment* (New Haven: Yale University Press, 1977); Albert D. Cover and David R. Mayhew, "Congressional Dynamics and the Decline of Competitive Congressional Elections," in this volume.
27. For a relevant discussion of the variables influencing turnover, see Morris P. Fiorina, David W. Rohde, and Peter Wissel, "Historical Change in House Turnover," in *Congress in Change*, pp. 24-57.

3

Congressional Dynamics and the Decline of Competitive Congressional Elections

Albert D. Cover and David R. Mayhew

In broad outline the last decade and a half of American politics has been a time of public discontent and a consequent search for new modes of public participation. Given the discontent and the search, the record of congressional elections in these years and since presents something of an anomaly. At the constituency level — on the House side anyway — elections to Congress have become less competitive. Fewer representatives have been winning their seats by narrow November margins, more by "safe" margins. Although a slow decline in House "marginality" has been visible throughout the twentieth century,[1] it was especially noticeable after the mid-1960s.

In this essay we present evidence on the decline in congressional marginality in the last decade and a half and explore some possible causes and implications of the decline. The change we discuss is a change in House elections, but we take some side glances at the Senate to suggest briefly what continuities and changes are evident in elections to that body. Our data cover the 1978, but not the 1980, elections.

EVIDENCE OF MARGINALITY DECLINE

The specific phenomenon of interest is that in recent general elections smaller proportions of House incumbents have been winning victories in the "marginal" range. No such trend is evident in elections for "open seats" — those 10 to 20 percent of contests each year that offer no incumbents on the November ballot.[2] In the following data analysis we shall confine our attention to elections with incumbents running. The decline in marginality appears regardless of what definition one chooses for "marginality." Winning with under 55 or under 60 percent of the vote is the customary choice. What makes marginality interesting, of course, is the presumption that members of Congress with close victories feel more vulnerable and are more vulnerable to electoral defeat.

Incumbents' Share of Major Party Vote

The decline in closely contested House seats is captured in the summary data presented in Table 3-1. Figures on the share of the major party vote won by incumbent House members running in elections between 1956 and 1978 are depicted. For each election year the table gives the proportion of all incumbent seats in which representatives gathered at least 60 percent of the district vote. (The complement of each listed percentage here is the proportion of incumbent seats in which members won with under 60 percent or lost.) One obvious point emerging from the table is that House incumbents have generally done quite well during this period; if we

Table 3-1   Decline in Marginality in House Elections, 1956-1978

Year	Proportion of Incumbents Winning at Least 60 Percent of the Major Party Vote	N
1956	59.1%	403
1958	63.1	390
1960	58.9	400
1962	63.6	376
1964	58.5	388
1966	67.7	401
1968	72.2	397
1970	77.3	389
1972	77.8	373
1974	66.4	383
1976	71.9	381
1978	78.0	377

SOURCE: Data for 1956-72 elections were taken from David R. Mayhew, "Congressional Elections: The Case of the Vanishing Marginals," *Polity* 6 (1974): 316-317. Data for the 1974 and 1976 elections were taken from the relevant editions of Richard Scammon's *America Votes* series. Data for 1978 were taken from *Congressional Quarterly Weekly Report*, November 11, 1978, pp. 3283-3290.

call a seat safe when the incumbent secures at least 60 percent of the vote, then at no point during this period have fewer than half the incumbents won by safe margins.

More important, however, is the changing proportion of safe House seats over time. Before 1966 about three-fifths of the seats were safe, but after the mid-1960s approximately three-fourths of the seats fell into that category. Even in the swing year 1974 about two-thirds of House incumbents won at the 60 percent level — a higher proportion than in any election from 1956 through 1964. The general trend is toward elevation of districts out of the marginal range.[3]

Table 3-2 presents comparable data on the proportion of safe seats for Senate incumbents. With only a third of the Senate coming up for election at any one time, we must aggregate Senate data over several elections to get enough observations for meaningful comparisons over time. For this reason the table is based on election triplets extending back to 1944.

The Senate pattern is different. The last column of percentages in Table 3-2 yields no important overall trend toward safeness in Senate elections with incumbents running, although the regional breakdowns in the other columns do show some change. Seat safeness in the old Confederacy has been eroding away (much more strikingly in Senate than in House elections), reaching a new low in 1978 when an identical one-third of Senate incumbents in *both* North and South won with over 60 percent of the vote. Meanwhile, more

Table 3-2 Changes in Marginality in Senate Elections by Region, 1944-1978

Election Triplets	Proportion of Incumbents Winning at Least 60 Percent of the Major Party Vote			
	South	*North*	*Total*	*N*
1944-48	100.0%	22.9%	39.3%	61
1950-54	100.0	18.3	35.5	76
1956-60	95.5	24.2	42.9	84
1962-66	70.0	36.4	44.2	86
1968-72	71.4	38.3	44.6	74
1974-78	57.1	37.5	41.4	70

SOURCE: A convenient compilation of data on Senate elections is *Guide to U.S. Elections* (Washington, D.C.: Congressional Quarterly, 1975), pp. 485-509. Congressional Quarterly election reports were used for the more recent elections. For the purposes of this table, senators appointed to the Senate are not considered incumbents in the elections just after appointment.

northern incumbents have been winning 60 percent or better of the vote — only about a fifth of them in decades just after World War II, but about three-eighths of them after 1960. Having so many north-erners run as well as William Proxmire (D-Wis.), Henry Jackson (D-Wash.), Ted Stevens (R-Alaska), and Edward Kennedy (D-Mass.) have usually done is a new development. Intriguingly, the jump upward in the northern series occurred in the 1960s — at about the same time the shift away from marginality appeared in the House data. Nevertheless, in the nation as a whole the South cancels out the North. The overall proportion of Senate incumbents winning at 60 percent or better has stayed at about two-fifths for four decades.

Frequency Distribution in House Elections

The House elections, which display clear evidence of change over time, merit closer analysis. Figure 3-1 gives snapshots of the 1972 and 1974 elections, showing what elections with eroded marginality have come to look like. For each election year we have sorted seats with incumbents running into classes based on the Democratic per-centage of the major party vote. This sorting creates for each year a frequency distribution that makes it readily apparent whether election contests tend to cluster in the competitive region, whether one party wins easily in all contests, or whether each party wins handily in some contests while running quite poorly in others.

The top of Figure 3-1 presents the frequency distribution based on 1972 House races involving incumbents. Note that all values to the left of the 50 percent mark record Republican victories in in-cumbent-held districts. Almost all of these were victories of Republican incumbents, but six were narrow victories of Republican challengers over Democratic incumbents. Similarly, the values recorded to the right of the 50 percent mark include three narrow victories by Demo-cratic challengers over Republican incumbents. The important message here is that the distribution has a gap in the middle — in roughly the marginal range. If we set aside the most heavily Democratic outcomes — those on the right edge of the figure in which Democratic incumbents faced no major party opponent in the general election — we see that the 1972 pattern is a bimodal one with a cluster of solid Republican districts on the left, a cluster of solid Democratic districts on the right, and the prominent gap in the competitive middle.

This bimodal pattern has become typical; it appears with special clarity in the years 1966 through 1972. By contrast, distributions drawn from data on earlier elections are quite different. Earlier dis-tributions are not bimodal but unimodal, with high proportions of incumbent districts clustering in the competitive region.[4] Again, the overall trend is one of declining marginality.

Figure 3-1   Frequency Distributions of Democratic Percentages of the Two-Party Vote in House Districts with Incumbents Running, 1972 and 1974

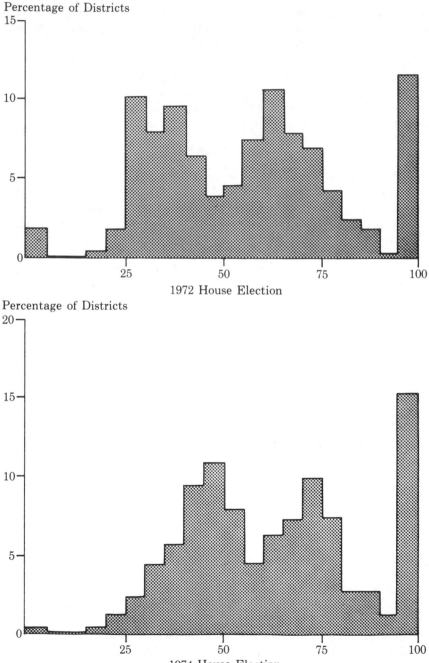

Percentage of Districts

1972 House Election

Percentage of Districts

1974 House Election

The 1974 election, graphed in the bottom of the figure, offers in one respect an interesting exception to the recent trend.[5] Although the bimodal pattern is as prominent as in 1972, the entire distribution has shifted to the right, populating the marginal range with districts that earlier were solidly Republican. What happened in 1974, of course, was that a post-Watergate national swing rendered safe Republican seats marginal. The Democratic share of the national two-party House vote rose a sizable 6 percent between 1972 and 1974, giving the Democrats, at 58.8 percent, their highest vote mark of the twentieth century. Thirty-six Republican incumbents (and four Democrats) lost their seats. The 1974 results make it clear that, the bimodal pattern notwithstanding, a large vote swing can still drive out incumbents and turn safe seats marginal. The results also suggest a subtler point: in a bimodal electoral universe the ratio of seat swing to vote swing is likely to vary with size of vote swing. To be more concrete, in a House election following one like that of 1972, the difference in seat yield between a 4 percent and a 6 percent national swing is likely to be greater for a favored party than the difference between a 1 percent and a 3 percent swing. In short, it takes a big vote swing to defeat very many incumbents when not many are marginal to begin with.

Figure 3-2 supplies data on the 1978 election. The House graph in Figure 3-2 is built according to the same rules as the two graphs in Figure 3-1. A bimodal pattern is apparent (though the 1978 distribution depicted in Figure 3-2 is generally flatter than the ones of 1972 and 1974), no single 5-percent interval (except the 95-100 percent Democratic) comes close to including 10 percent of the districts, and the number of uncontested Republican seats has risen. The flight from marginality remains evident. For contrast, Figure 3-2 also depicts a distribution of presidential vote percentages — the 1976 Carter share of the major party vote in each of the same set of districts (377 of them) used to plot the votes of the 1978 House incumbents. The contrast is clear. A close presidential election produces narrow outcomes in a sizable majority of House districts. But many fewer of those same districts return close verdicts on their incumbent representatives.

ANALYSIS OF MARGINALITY DECLINE

Why the general reduction in House marginality? An inspection of the election careers of individual members supplies a proximate answer. In particular, an examination of critical points in these career patterns shows that the electoral advantage of running as an incumbent has increased in recent years. We should emphasize at the start that it has increased *on the average*. Whatever it is that is benefiting

Figure 3-2   Frequency Distribution of Democratic Percentages of the Two-Party House Vote in 1978 and Presidential Vote in 1976, in House Districts with Incumbents Running in 1978

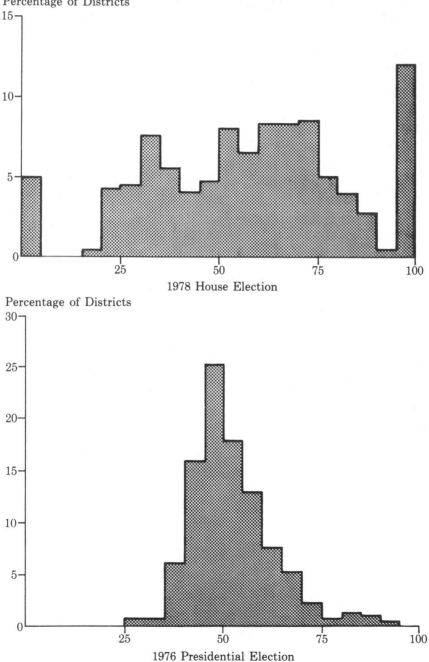

Percentage of Districts

1978 House Election

Percentage of Districts

1976 Presidential Election

incumbents, it certainly is not benefiting all of them equally. Some incumbents lose; others always win by narrow margins; others win narrowly at the start of their careers but easily thereafter; others bob in and out of the marginal zone. There is a good deal of variation around the sorts of averages we shall present, and the variation itself is a subject for analysis.[6] But here we shall deal in averages, and the averages are important.

Two career points meriting special attention are an incumbent's first and final re-election bids. Running as an incumbent for the first time, a member ought in general to do somewhat better than in his or her first successful election effort. Therefore, we should expect to observe a "sophomore surge" when these first and second elections are compared. The magnitude of this surge is one good measure of the electoral advantage of incumbency.

A second measure can be developed by seeing what happens to the nominee of the incumbent's party immediately after an incumbent voluntarily retires. In general we should not expect the incumbent's successor nominee to do as well as the incumbent did in his or her final re-election effort. If the successor does not have as much support, then we shall observe a fall-off in the party's vote immediately after its incumbent retires. The "retirement slump" constitutes a second measure of how much incumbency is worth.

House Elections: Sophomore Surge and Retirement Slump

Table 3-3 presents sophomore surge and retirement slump data for House elections from 1962 through 1978. Entries in the sophomore surge column were calculated in a fairly straightforward fashion. Consider, for example, the entry for 1962. Forty-six freshmen first elected in 1960 also contested the 1962 election. For each of these members — all with major party opposition both times — we calculated the 1960-62 vote change percentage, using for each year the representative's percent of the total House vote in his or her district. The vote change data were then adjusted to take into account the 2.2 percent pro-Republican swing in the national House vote between 1960 and 1962. For each Republican member 2.2 percent was subtracted from the change score; for each Democrat 2.2 percent was added. The 1962 entry, +2.1 percent, is the mean of the 46 adjusted change scores. A similar procedure was used for the entries in the retirement slump column. In the retirement column swing adjustments were applied to changes in a party's share of the total vote upon the retirement of its incumbent.

On balance, first-term incumbents do surge, and a party's vote does slump when its incumbent leaves Congress. These results should be noted at the outset. More interesting, however, are changes in the magnitude of incumbency advantage over time. The data in

Table 3-3 Sophomore Surge and Retirement Slump for House Members, 1962-1978

Years of Sophomore or Successor-Nominee Elections	Mean Sophomore Surge (adjusted)	N	Mean Retirement Slump (adjusted)	N
1962	+2.1%	46	− 1.4%	17
1964	+1.6	54	− 1.4	25
1966	+3.3	69	− 4.7	13
1968	+6.5	54	− 7.6	19
1970	+6.7	31	− 6.6	36
1972	+7.5	43	−11.0	27
1974	+5.8	57	− 6.7	44
1976	+6.8	87	− 6.0	41
1978	+7.2	51	− 8.9	42

SOURCE: Sophomore surge data for 1962-74 were taken from Albert D. Cover, "The Advantage of Incumbency in Congressional Elections" (Ph.D. diss., Yale University, 1976), p. 21; for 1976 from Thomas E. Mann, *Unsafe at Any Margin* (Washington, D.C.: American Enterprise Institute for Public Policy Research, 1978), p. 88. Retirement slump data for 1962-72 are from David R. Mayhew, "Congressional Elections: The Case of the Vanishing Marginals," *Polity* 6 (1974): 309; for 1974 from Cover, p. 19; for 1976 from Mann, p. 86. All data for 1978 are based on Congressional Quarterly figures. Data for both sophomore surge and retirement slump are adjusted to discount for interelection swings in the national House vote. For 1976-78 the overall swing figure used is 2.7 percent Republican. This is based on data available early after the 1978 election, on 339 House districts in which both Democrats and Republicans fielded candidates in *both* 1976 and 1978 elections.

Table 3-3 only go back to 1960 but both the surge and retirement columns indicate that the value of incumbency in House elections amounted to only one or two percent prior to the mid-1960s. This jibes well with a finding of Robert Erikson, based on somewhat different calculations, that the electoral value of House incumbency was about two percent in the years 1952-60.[7] Both of the key columns in Table 3-3 suggest that the value of running as an incumbent representative increased substantially in the mid-1960s — particularly after 1966. They differ somewhat in the precise value they ascribe to incumbency, but they both indicate a definite increase at about the same time.

The impact of this increase may be illustrated with a brief example. Between 1972 and 1974 the Republican share of the national House vote fell by 6 percent. For Republican freshmen first elected in 1972, the median vote change was −1.3 percent. These freshmen did remarkably well, almost overcoming the pro-Democratic vote shift. In contrast, for seats with Republican retirements in 1974, the median interelection vote change for the party was −15.4 percent. If for some reason the Republican party had been deprived of all its incumbents in 1974, its seat loss surely would have been much greater than it was in fact.

Senate Elections: A Different Pattern

The analysis of critical career points for incumbent senators is a bit more difficult because any given election year has relatively few sophomores or retirees, but aggregating over several elections permits us to explore changes in the value of incumbency for senators. Table 3-4 summarizes the relevant data for all usable Senate elections regardless of region. In essential respects the arrangement of this table is the same as that of Table 3-3 on House incumbency. To generate samples large enough for comparisons over time, however, Table 3-4 goes back to 1934 and aggregates data by decade into election quintuplets. Thus, the 1940-48 row in the table includes entries, under "sophomore surge," for senators who initially won their seats in regular elections in any of the years 1934-42 and who ran again a full term later in any of the years 1940-48. Under "retirement slump," the 1940-48 row includes entries for senators who ran their last races in 1934-42 and gave way to successor nominees a term later in 1940-48. In this Senate table adjustments for national trend are based on six-year interelection swings in the two-party share of the national House vote.

These Senate data are scanty but worth comment. The "sophomore surge" column shows no change over time. On the average, U.S. senators, in the 1970s as in the 1940s, have been running little better in their second elections than in their first. This makes it difficult to argue that senators, on the average, derive much of an electoral

Table 3-4 Sophomore Surge and Retirement Slump for Senators, 1940-1978

Years of Sophomore or Successor-Nominee Elections	Mean Sophomore Surge (adjusted)	N	Mean Retirement Slump (adjusted)	N
1940-48	+0.8%	33	−1.4%	26
1950-58	+1.0	51	−3.5	17
1960-68	+3.4	33	−4.3	18
1970-78	+1.9	34	−8.1	32

SOURCE: Data were taken from *Guide to U.S. Elections* (Washington, D.C.: Congressional Quarterly, 1975), pp. 485-509. Adjustments for national trends are based on six-year interelection swings in the two-party share of the House vote. Senators beginning their Senate service by appointment or by special election are excluded from the sophomore surge data.

advantage from incumbency. But values in the "retirement slump" column do change over time, reaching quite an impressive −8.1 percent in the 1970s. If Senate incumbents gain little (at least at the start) by holding office, their parties now are certainly losing when they relinquish office. Some of the recent partisan losses have been quite large: the Republicans dropped 20.8 percent in Nebraska when Carl Curtis retired in 1978, and 18.7 percent in New Jersey when Clifford Case lost out to a successor nominee in 1978; the Democrats fell 16.3 percent in Michigan when Philip Hart died in 1976, and 25.5 percent in Rhode Island when John Pastore retired in 1976.

Real changes seem to be taking place in Senate elections, but they hardly add up to a case for incumbency advantage. Senate politics is looking more like a politics of extreme personalism, with the partisan complexion of states counting for less and less in electoral outcomes. Of the 100 senators who held seats in 1979 at the start of the 96th Congress, no fewer than 67 had succeeded members of the opposite party when they took office initially.

EXPLANATIONS OF INCUMBENCY ADVANTAGE

For the House, however, the evidence is compelling that the electoral value of incumbency has increased since the early 1960s. This increase presumably helped propel many incumbents out of the dangerous marginal category. The evidence presented thus far raises an obvious question: Why are incumbents doing better now than they did only a few years ago? No definitive answer is yet possible, but we can explore some promising avenues with data collected on House elections with incumbent candidates.

Redistricting Benefits

One plausible explanation offered by Edward Tufte is that House incumbents have recently benefited more from redistricting than they had previously.[8] This suggestion gains particular credibility from the upsurge of redistricting activity that followed from *Baker* v. *Carr,* the Supreme Court's 1962 decision affirming the federal judiciary's authority to consider apportionment cases. During the 1960s most states revised district lines at least twice, and some adopted four different redistricting schemes in efforts to meet increasingly precise judicial guidelines. The very precision of these guidelines expanded opportunities for members of Congress and their allies back home to use redistricting for political gain because the guidelines effectively required states to ignore county lines in drawing district boundaries. Unfettered by this time-honored constraint, states had more freedom in their redistricting arrangements.

Preliminary evidence suggests that incumbent representatives may indeed have derived political benefit from redistricting during the 1960s. If we examine cases in which an incumbent contests both the last election before district boundaries are redrawn and also the first election after lines are changed, then we can ask whether or not incumbents generally do better after redistricting than they did before it. In making this comparison we should probably discount national interelection partisan swings to determine what effect redistricting itself has on incumbent vote margins. Of 252 incumbent representatives meeting the relevant criteria in 1962-70, 158 did better than the swing and only 94 fell behind the swing.[9] Although more elaborate controls could reduce this disparity, the preponderance of cases in which incumbents do better after redistricting than they did before suggests that redistricting might have been electorally useful for many.

On the other hand, if redistricting did benefit incumbents, then we should expect the proportion of marginal seats to be lower in sets of redistricted seats than in sets of seats left untouched. In fact, the proportion of marginal seats in the redistricted set did decline in the 1960-74 period, but a decline also occurred in districts that were not redrawn.[10] Furthermore, there is no clear relation between volume of redistricting and the values for incumbency advantage picked up for individual election years in Table 3-3. For example, there was scarcely any redistricting in either the 1968-70 or the 1972-74 interelection biennium, and none in 1974-76 or 1976-78, yet the sophomore surge and retirement slump figures yield high readings for House incumbency advantage in 1970, 1974, 1976, and 1978.

While evidence on the contribution of redistricting to the growing advantage of incumbency is weak and inconclusive, stronger evidence is available on the contribution of changes in mass electoral behavior. In particular, we can show that the decline of partisanship in the electorate has benefited incumbents in House elections.

Decline of Partisanship

In 1966 Philip Converse wrote of the "serene stability in the distribution of party loyalty" and of the "remarkable individual stability in party identification, even in this period of extravagant vote change."[11] Even then, however, this serene stability was beginning to crumble. Between 1952 and 1964 the distribution of partisan identification did indeed remain remarkably stable, but the next decade witnessed a slow erosion in the proportion of the eligible electorate identifying with either of the major parties. Between 1964 and 1974 Independents increased from 8.2 percent of the electorate to 15.1 percent. If we also consider Independent Democrats and Independent

Republicans, the most weakly affiliated partisans, then this augmented pool increased from 23.5 percent of the electorate to 37.5 percent during the same period.[12]

Noting that the growth of Independents coincided with the growth of the incumbency advantage, Robert Erikson suggested that "because the recent increase in the number of Independent voters has allowed the incumbent's visibility to tip the balance in an increasing number of voter decisions, the size of the incumbency advantage appears to have grown."[13] This logic is appealing. Evidence developed elsewhere indicates that changes in the distribution of partisanship, in fact, have benefited incumbents.[14]

The decay of partisanship has had a second, and in some ways more subtle, influence on the advantage of incumbency. Thus far we have been speaking of this decay in terms of the declining proportion of the electorate identifying with the major parties. Even for those continuing to identify with one of these parties, however, party labels may be of less significance than they once were. In particular, partisan identifiers may place less weight on party as a voting cue than they did previously. If so, incumbents may be able to take advantage of this situation. As Mayhew has suggested, "voters dissatisfied with party cues could be reaching for any other cues that are available in deciding how to vote. The incumbency cue is readily at hand."[15]

Of course, an upsurge in defections from partisan identification *may* help incumbents, but defections will not necessarily have this effect. Consider, for example, the presumably typical case of a district in which the incumbent carries the party label with which a modal share of voters identifies. A *general* increase in the defection rate will produce a net *loss* of support for the incumbent, since defections favoring the challenger will outnumber defections from the challenger's party. A decline in the importance of partisanship will help incumbents only if defections are "properly" distributed. Survey data allow us to see whether or not defections from party have on balance benefited incumbents and whether the proportions of the pro-incumbent and anti-incumbent defections have changed over time.

Using data on party identifiers from the University of Michigan's Survey Research Center, Cover examined defections from party in contested House races involving an incumbent from 1958 through 1974.[16] Defections were divided into two classes, those by respondents identifying with the challenger's party (pro-incumbent defections) and those by respondents identifying with the incumbent's party (anti-incumbent defections). Table 3-5 presents data on the proportion of all defections favoring the incumbent.

Throughout this period most defectors were voters identifying with the challenger's party. This hardly comes as a surprise, since we should generally expect incumbents to draw off more support

Table 3-5 Proportions of Voter Defections from Party Identification Favoring Incumbents: House Elections, 1958-1974

Year	Proportion of Pro-Incumbent Defections	N
1958	56.6%	83
1960	65.0	117
1962	*	—
1964	62.4	125
1966	70.7	92
1968	66.0	141
1970	83.6	73
1972	83.2	113
1974	73.8	126

* Data not available.

SOURCE: Data on percentage of defections provided by the Inter-University Consortium for Political Research. Only data from contested elections involving an incumbent are included. Percentage defections in 1958, 1960, and 1974 are based on weighted responses.

from the local minority party than challengers draw off from the incumbent's party. Although the number of usable respondents is not large, the trend toward increasingly pro-incumbent defections seems well-established. From 1970 to 1974 three-fourths or more of all defections came from the challenger's party. About 89 percent came from the challenger's party in a recent study of the 1978 elections done by Thomas E. Mann and Raymond E. Wolfinger.[17] The figures on defection capture an important shift in mass electoral behavior.

Activities of Incumbents

What lies behind the growing preponderance of pro-incumbent defections? One possibility is that incumbents are *inducing* defections through a variety of re-election-oriented activities. There is abundant evidence that incumbents have engaged more energetically in such activities since the mid-1960s. For example, the volume and cost of franked mail sent out from congressional offices increased dramatically in both the 1960s and 1970s. Members of Congress and others authorized to use the frank sent 190 million pieces of mail that cost a total of $11,224,000 in 1970. For fiscal 1979 the volume and cost had jumped to an estimated 357 million pieces and $64,944,000. On the House side, district travel allowances, first instituted during the 1964 fiscal year, have increased in recent years as have allowances for office equipment leasing, district office leasing, telecommunications, stationery, constituent communications, computer services, and other official expenses.[18] These data are obviously quite suggestive, but they do not establish that incumbents have been successful in altering mass electoral behavior.

Even if these efforts did pay off, it is not clear exactly what the route to payoff would be. One argument is that the upsurge in incumbent activities should help incumbents by boosting their recognition among constituents. If this is the path through which incumbent activity is translated into votes, then the activity has been a failure. Since 1958 all but two of the Survey Research Center postelection polls have contained some variant of the question "Do you happen to remember the name of the candidates for Congress — that is, for the House of Representatives in Washington — that ran in this district this November?" Responses to this question permit us to determine which candidates, if any, those surveyed were able to recall. The data for 1958-74 are shown in Table 3-6. Surprisingly, the share of respondents recalling *neither* incumbent nor challenger shot up over this period — from about half to over three-fifths. The proportions recalling only the incumbent's name remained stable, and the proportions recalling only the challenger's name remained negligible. Thus, incumbents have apparently come to inspire *less* rather than *more* name recall than they did in the early 1960s, and the incumbent-challenger gap in name recall has not widened.[19]

The full impact of incumbent activity may not be mediated through candidate recognition. In an analysis of survey data for 1964-70, John Ferejohn concluded that "voters were apparently using incumbency as a voting cue whether or not they could recall the names of the incumbent candidate in the interview situation."[20] This suggests that recognition does not capture the full advantage of incumbency,

Table 3-6   Postelection Recall of House Candidates

	Percentage of Respondents Recalling Names of Candidates						
	1958	*1964*	*1966*	*1968*	*1970*	*1972*	*1974*
Incumbent Only	18.1	21.7	17.7	18.3	19.8	17.8	18.7
Challenger Only	1.6	1.8	1.2	2.5	0.9	1.2	0.4
Both	26.1	30.3	21.9	31.4	14.9	17.7	15.5
Neither	54.1	46.2	59.3	47.9	64.4	63.3	65.4
Total	99.9	100.0	100.1	100.1	100.0	100.0	100.0
	N=1240	N=1117	N=1002	N=1057	N=1096	N=774	N=1778

SOURCE: Data provided by Inter-University Consortium for Political Research. Respondents have been excluded unless they were in districts with contested races involving an incumbent. The 1958 and 1974 data are weighted.

and it implies that re-election-oriented activities may have an impact through channels other than the one involving name recall.

Alan Abramowitz's analysis of Oregon survey data shows that voters can indeed formulate reasonably rich visions of House candidates and act on them without being able to pass the name recall test. Abramowitz argues for a plumbing of candidate "reputations" among voters.[21] In the case of incumbents, it may be that word of their activities reaches many voters by ripple effect, with awareness of name not traveling as far as the ripples but recoverable when needed.

Moreover, there is the possibility that electorally relevant activities of incumbents have changed in nature, inducing contemporary voters to *like* their representatives more without necessarily knowing them any better. Morris Fiorina offers an underpinning for this case with his argument that members of the House have seized an opportunity supplied by the recent growth of the federal bureaucracy.[22] The modern member is more and more an ombudsman, and the beauty of the ombudsman role is that its occupant sends out issue-neutral signals. Cutting red tape can generate pleasure and perhaps support among voters of all political persuasions.

Pro-incumbent Defections

The growing preponderance of pro-incumbent defections can be explained in two ways. First, as we have seen, the change in mass electoral behavior may be induced by the activities of incumbents. While this explanation is in many ways an appealing one, a second possibility is also plausible. It is conceivable that incumbents are the accidental beneficiaries of behavioral changes they had no part in creating or fostering — most likely a simple unraveling of party allegiance among voters and a resulting shift to the incumbency cue in voter decisions. This is a model of noninduced cue substitution — or at least one in which no shift of cues has been induced by changes in the activities of incumbent members of the House. This is the explanation favored by Walter Dean Burnham.[23] It draws its attractiveness from the abundant evidence of contemporary party erosion, even though we cannot be sure of the specific effects of that erosion.

We write this essay as a new wave of research on congressional elections is beginning to appear at conventions and in journals.[24] The 1978 and 1980 national surveys of the Center for Political Studies (University of Michigan) have included a number of new questions designed to supply evidence about relations between congressional candidates and the public — and in particular about incumbency advantage. In one set of questions, respondents are asked to remember whether congressional candidates (including incumbents) have reached them: "Have you come into contact with or learned anything about (him/her) through any of these ways?" — i.e., via meeting personally, attending a meeting, talking to staff, receiving something in the mail, reading about in a newspaper or magazine, hearing on radio, or seeing on television. Another set probes for contacts initiated by citizens: "Have you ever contacted Representative X or anyone in his/her office?"

In another improvement respondents are asked to *recognize* the names of congressional candidates rather than just *recall* them. For 1978 this turns up a 97 percent recognition rate for House incumbents and a 63 percent rate for challengers.[25] The post-1978 research has not supplied any single or simple clue to explaining incumbency advantage, though most current investigators would accept an overall model of politician-induced electoral behavior — i.e., that in general House members build up their electoral margins by doing calculated things their challengers are in no position to match.

CONSEQUENCES OF MARGINALITY DECLINE

Although it is too early to perceive the full consequences of diminishing House marginality, a few comments are worth making.

Decline of 'Swing Ratio'

First, the shift to safe incumbent seats carries with it an overall change in the sensitivity of the electoral mechanism. The 1974 election notwithstanding, an electoral system with fewer marginals is one in which partisan vote swings yield less in the way of legislative seat swings. The "swing ratio," as Tufte points out in his treatment of House elections, has been declining.[26]

Whether the fall in this ratio should be lamented is unclear. The older American tradition — like the British and the Canadian — was one of electoral exaggeration, with House seat swings magnifying partisan vote swings rather than just reflecting them. This gave great volatility to congressional politics over time, and on occasion it bolstered popular presidents by giving them lopsided House majorities to work with. The argument for high swing ratios is not that they supplied efficient reflection of public opinion at the instant, but that they provided clear political change and empowered party majorities to govern. Lower House swing ratios, reflecting or understating vote swings, bring their own mix of effects: greater stability in partisan seat holdings over time, Congresses less affected by presidential land-slides, a clearer separation-of-powers cast to the regime, and possibly a displacement of interest onto presidential elections among voters wishing abrupt political change. Membership renewal in the modern Congress becomes more a matter of continuous creation than of big bangs, with the stakes especially high in contests where retirements have supplied "open seats."

A One-and-a-Half Party System?

Mention of membership stability raises the question of whether we have a two-party system or a "one-and-a-half party system" at the congressional level. The Republicans were out of power in both houses from 1954 to 1980 — a longer drought than any party had suffered since the 1830s. Finally, in 1980, they gained control of the Senate. The chief reason for prolonged Republican frustration is clear enough: a deficiency of Republican identifiers among voters. Yet the rise in incumbency advantage in the House has created an additional burden for the minority party. Most beneficiaries of incumbency advantage are, after all, Democrats. The lowering of swing ratios reduces the probability — both actual and subjective — that a healthy electoral swing will boost the minority into power. Blighted hopes hinder efforts to recruit candidates and marshal electoral resources. The national partisan vote percentage becomes itself in small part an artifact of incumbency advantage.

The Democratic share of the House vote dropped to 50.9 percent in 1968, but it might have gone to half or under with a discounting for the fact that more Democrats than Republicans were winning incumbency points. In a highly volatile electoral system a minority party can hope to come to power once in a while; in a more stable system victory may be denied forever.

The division of House Democrats and Republicans into permanent winners and permanent losers seems to be bringing about other structural asymmetries. Voluntary retirement rates have risen higher among Republican members than among Democrats.[27] Dave Martin (R-Neb.), ranking minority member on Rules, retired in 1974 in part because "it is possible that Republicans will never again be in the majority in the House, if you are realistic about it. . . ."[28] Craig Hosmer (R-Calif.), ranking member on Joint Atomic Energy who also stepped down in 1974, lamented that "as a Republican you don't have many opportunities for promotion in the sense that a ranking member around here doesn't mean very much in relation to what a chairman means. I've been in the minority for twenty years."[29] Most House Democrats can hope to stay around Congress long enough to win at least the chairmanship of a subcommittee; no Republican can entertain such hopes.

In 1979, at the beginning of the 96th Congress, 33 House Democrats (including 27 northerners) had already served 10 or more consecutive terms; only eight Republicans had stayed that long. In the mid-1970s Republican recruitment efforts sagged in both House and Senate elections.[30] One gets the sense that in recent years the public and the media have simply given nationwide congressional elections less attention; the last publicized party square-off came in 1970, and then only on the Senate side. The Republican party's chances of winning majorities in the Senate are clearly better than in the House. Its candidates won most of the Senate seats up in 1978 and 1980. Given the personalism of Senate elections, Republicans might be able to marshal the candidates and resources needed to maintain a majority in the 1980s. House Democrats look less vulnerable.

Member Individualism Flourishes

But should we be worrying about partisan configurations at all? Probably less than we used to. Incumbency advantage accrues, after all, to individuals rather than to parties, and consequently it can be expected to foster member individualism on Capitol Hill. Members of Congress do not understand the causes of the rise in incumbency advantage any more than we do, but, in line with John Kingdon's "congratulation effect,"[31] they are likely to claim, "I did it all myself" and seek out ways to continue doing it all themselves. Hence, the electoral patterns probably inspire quests for individual assertion in congressional office.

At least on the House side, party voting has reached new lows in recent times.[32] Current institutional reforms have been decentralizing, yielding a House that looks more like the Senate. The revved-up House Democratic Caucus has been used less for making policy than for weakening committee chairmen, and the influence of the Ways and Means Committee, the chief unit for packaging general policy in the House, has declined precipitously in recent years. The effects of this decline have been evident in House handling of energy, taxation, health insurance, and welfare programs. In short, the House of the early 1980s is characterized by weak party leadership, nonhierarchical committees, a vast array of subcommittees in which members can do their own thing, and an ethic of member equality and member individualism. The Congress we shall have to cope with in the foreseeable future is one less of party management than of decentralized individualism — for better or worse a reversion to the original constitutional design.

NOTES

1. See Walter Dean Burnham, "Insulation and Responsiveness in Congressional Elections," *Political Science Quarterly* 90 (1975): 413.
2. See David R. Mayhew, "Congressional Elections: The Case of the Vanishing Marginals," *Polity* 6 (1974): 298-302.
3. Note that Table 3-1 is based on general election data. This leaves open the possibility that the decline of competition in general elections

has been counterbalanced by increased competition in primary elections contested by incumbents. This has not happened. See Albert D. Cover, "The Advantage of Incumbency in Congressional Elections" (Ph.D. diss., Yale University, 1976), pp. 34-35.

4. For example, see Mayhew, "Vanishing Marginals." For scattered distributions from earlier years, see Donald E. Stokes, "Parties and the Nationalization of Electoral Forces," in *The American Party Systems: Stages of Political Development,* ed. William Nisbet Chambers and Walter Dean Burnham (New York: Oxford University Press, 1967), p. 200; and Burnham, "Insulation and Responsiveness," p. 423.

5. On the 1974 election generally, see Burnham, "Insulation and Responsiveness," pp. 411-435.

6. For an excellent treatment of House elections at the constituency level that emphasizes district-specific causes of electoral variation, see Thomas E. Mann, *Unsafe at Any Margin: Interpreting Congressional Elections* (Washington, D.C.: American Enterprise Institute for Public Policy Research, 1978).

7. Robert Erikson, "The Advantage of Incumbency in Congressional Elections," *Polity* 3 (1971): 404.

8. Edward R. Tufte, "The Relationship Between Seats and Votes in Two-Party Systems," *American Political Science Review* 67 (1973): 540-554; Tufte, "Communication," *American Political Science Review* 68 (1974): 211-213.

9. Albert D. Cover, "One Good Term Deserves Another: The Advantage of Incumbency in Congressional Elections," *American Journal of Political Science* 21 (1977): 529-530.

10. Cover, "Advantage of Incumbency," pp. 36-44. See also John A. Ferejohn, "On the Decline of Competition in Congressional Elections," *American Political Science Review* 71 (1977): 167-169.

11. Philip E. Converse, "The Concept of a Normal Vote," in *Elections and the Political Order,* ed. Angus Campbell, Philip E. Converse, Warren E. Miller, and Donald E. Stokes (New York: John Wiley & Sons, 1966), p. 12.

12. For 1952-72 data, see Dan D. Nimmo, *Popular Images of Politics: A Taxonomy* (Englewood Cliffs, N.J.: Prentice-Hall, 1974), p. 122. The data are extended through 1974 in Cover, "Advantage of Incumbency," p. 47.

13. Robert Erikson, "A Reply to Tidmarch," *Polity* 4 (1972): 529.

14. Cover, "One Good Term Deserves Another," pp. 531-536.

15. Mayhew, "Vanishing Marginals," p. 313.

16. Cover, "One Good Term Deserves Another," pp. 534-536.

17. Thomas E. Mann and Raymond E. Wolfinger, "Candidates and Parties in Congressional Elections" (Paper delivered at the annual meeting of the American Political Science Association, Washington, D.C., August 31-September 3, 1979), Table 3. Mann and Wolfinger classify "Independent leaners" as partisans in their study.

18. Cover, "The Advantage of Incumbency," pp. 65-102. See also *Inside Congress,* 2nd ed. (Washington, D.C.: Congressional Quarterly, 1979), pp. 122-133.

19. For a fuller discussion of the recognition data, see Cover, "The Advantage of Incumbency," pp. 55-64. See also Gary C. Jacobson, "On Adding Contextual Variables to National Election Surveys: Some Examples From the 1972 and 1974 National Election Studies" (Paper delivered

at the annual meeting of the Midwest Political Science Association, Chicago, Illinois, April 1979).

20. Ferejohn, "Decline of Competition," p. 171.
21. Alan I. Abramowitz, "Name Familiarity, Reputation, and the Incumbency Effect in a Congressional Election," *Western Political Quarterly* 28 (1975): 668-684. Changes instituted in the 1978 National Election Study make this feasible. See, for example, Mann and Wolfinger, "Candidates and Parties in Congressional Elections."
22. Morris P. Fiorina, "The Case of the Vanishing Marginals: The Bureaucracy Did It," *American Political Science Review* 71 (1977): 177-181. For a fuller treatment of this theme, see Morris P. Fiorina, *Congress: Keystone of the Washington Establishment* (New Haven: Yale University Press, 1977). For some recent research bolstering parts of Fiorina's argument, see Richard Born, "Generational Replacement and the Growth of Incumbent Reelection Margins in the U.S. House," *American Political Science Review* 73 (1979): 811.
23. Walter Dean Burnham, "Communication," *American Political Science Review* 68 (1974): 210; Burnham, "Insulation and Responsiveness," pp. 414-415. See also Ferejohn, "Decline of Competition," pp. 172-175.
24. Some of the salient papers: Mann and Wolfinger, "Candidates and Parties in Congressional Elections"; Alan I. Abramowitz, "Electoral Accountability in 1978: A Comparison of Voting for U.S. Senator and Representative" (Paper delivered at the annual meeting of the American Political Science Association, Washington, D.C., August 31-September 3, 1979); Gary C. Jacobson, "Congressional Elections 1978: The Case of the Vanishing Challengers" (Paper delivered at the Conference on Congressional Elections, Rice University and the University of Houston, Houston, Texas, January 10-12, 1980).
25. Mann and Wolfinger, "Candidates and Parties in Congressional Elections," Table 5.
26. Tufte, "Seats and Votes," pp. 549-553.
27. Cover, "Advantage of Incumbency," p. 146.
28. Julius Duscha, "Departures: Fun Is Gone," *Washington Post,* September 15, 1974, p. B1.
29. Ibid.
30. See, for example, "Little Evidence of Republican Comeback," *Congressional Quarterly Weekly Report*, February 21, 1976, pp. 351-353.
31. John W. Kingdon, *Candidates for Office: Beliefs and Strategies* (New York: Random House, 1968), p. 31.
32. Julius Turner, *Party and Constituency: Pressures on Congress,* rev. ed., edited by Edward V. Schneier, Jr. (Baltimore: Johns Hopkins Press, 1970), chap. 2.

4

The Congressional Career in the 1970s

Joseph Cooper and William West

During the last decade, changes in the membership of Congress have been analyzed in greater detail than ever before. Two basic findings have characterized the results of these inquiries. First, service in Congress for the average member is no longer the temporary occupation it was in the nineteenth century when tenure was quite limited and turnover usually very high. During the course of the twentieth century, congressional service has become for most members a stable profession comparable to careers in law, medicine, or business.[1] Second, the advantages of being an incumbent have increased in recent decades. It is now far more difficult for challengers to defeat sitting members than it was in the late 1940s, 1950s, or early 1960s.[2]

Although most of the work regarding these trends has centered on the House, evidence has been gathered for both the House and Senate and applied generally to explain critical aspects of member behavior and institutional performance in the contemporary Congress.[3] It is thus ironic that within a short time after students of Congress discovered "career" and "incumbency" and began to treat them as key explanatory variables, striking anomalies have become apparent.

In the House, although the incumbency effect has remained strong, the rate of voluntary retirement has increased substantially. More and more members are opting to leave voluntarily even though seats

Table 4-1   Sources of Congressional Turnover, 1957-1979

	85th-90th Congresses (1957-1969)	*91st-95th Congresses (1969-1979)*
House		
Retirements: End of Term and Intra-Term	194.0	232.0
Average per Congress	32.2	46.4
Defeats: Primary and Election	220.0	136.0
Average per Congress	36.7	27.2
Deaths	55.0	31.0
Average per Congress	9.2	6.2
Senate		
Retirements: End of Term and Intra-Term	30.0	36.0
Average per Congress	5.0	7.2
Defeats: Primary and Election	34.0	37.0
Average per Congress	5.7	7.4
Deaths	20.0	8.0
Average per Congress	3.3	1.6

are safer than ever. As Table 4-1 illustrates, voluntary retirement in the 1970s has supplanted electoral defeat as the prime source of turnover in the House.[4] Moreover, voluntary retirement has not only increased in the 1970s, but appears to be gathering momentum. The number of voluntary retirees per Congress for the five Congresses ending in the 1970s has increased as follows: 35, 44, 47, 51, and 55.[5]

The figures in Table 4-1 also testify to an increase in the rate of voluntary retirement in the Senate, where only some 30 members are subject to election each Congess. In the Senate as well as in the House, the phenomenon appears to be accelerating. The number of voluntary retirees per Congress for the five Congresses ending in the 1970s has increased as follows: 4, 6, 8, 8, and 9.[6] However, in contrast to the House, there was also a complementary increase in the number of senators defeated in primaries or general elections.

These results are puzzling and potentially of great importance. The aim of this article is to analyze the causes and implications of the increased and increasing rate of voluntary retirement in Congress. In so doing we shall focus on the House, but also apply our conclusions to examine similarities and differences with respect to the Senate.

DETERMINANTS OF HOUSE RETIREMENTS

Why do members of the House choose to retire? Age, political vulnerability, and/or political ambition are the three factors that have generally been relied upon in the past to explain retirement patterns. More recently, however, a new factor has been suggested as a contributing cause: disaffection with House service per se.[7] Since we shall argue that disaffection is, in fact, the primary cause of retirement trends in the House today, let us begin our analysis with the more traditional explanations.

Age, Vulnerability, and Ambition

Age. The claim that age exists as a substantial or significant explanation of retirement trends in the 1970s rests both on the assumption that a larger proportion of members reached retirement age levels than in prior decades and on the assumption that the prevalence of this group accounts for the increase in voluntary retirement. Neither assumption can be sustained.

In the period from 1969 to 1979, the average age of all House members was 50.9; the average age of all voluntary retirees was 55.1; and the average number of members 65 or older was 55.5. However, from 1957 to 1969 the comparable figures were all higher: 52.3, 57.2, and 59.4. Equally important, in Congresses ending in the 1970s a larger proportion of voluntary retirees derived from the ranks of younger members than in Congresses ending in the late 1950s and 1960s. In the period from 1957 to 1969, members 65 and over accounted for 29.9 percent of the retirements and members 55 to 64 for 28.8 percent. In the period from 1969 to 1979, the comparable figures were 22.4 percent and 27.6 percent. Similarly, in the period from 1957 to 1969 members 55 or older accounted for 114 of the 194 retirements, whereas from 1969 to 1979 they accounted for only 116 of the 232 retirements.

Political Vulnerability. The rationale for according political vulnerability a major role in causing voluntary retirements is that fear of electoral difficulties or defeat motivates members to leave the House. Two specific types of linkage between vulnerability and retirement have been suggested: marginality and redistricting. Once again, however, the evidence is not convincing in either case.

Most voluntary retirees in the 1960s and 1970s came from safe districts, i.e., districts they won in the preceding election by 55 percent or more of the vote.[8] Equally important and in line with the general trend for all House members, the percentage of retirees who win their seats by less than 55 percent of the vote has declined since the late 1950s and early 1960s when about 30 percent of retirees were "marginal." In the 95th and 96th Congresses, however, only 16 of 106 retirees or 15 percent had won their seats by less than 55 percent of the vote in the preceding election.

The effects of redistricting on vulnerability are problematic. It has been used both to strengthen and weaken incumbents. What is beyond dispute, however, is that the pace of redistricting has substantially declined in the 1970s.[9] This decline has been accompanied by an increase in the rate of voluntary retirement. In short, whatever effects redistricting had in the 1960s due to reapportionment pressures imposed by the federal courts, neither it nor marginality can be relied upon to explain retirement trends in the 1970s.

Political Ambition. A final traditional explanation of voluntary retirement is political ambition. However, this factor cannot explain the behavior of most voluntary retirees. In the Congresses ending in the late 1950s and 1960s, 58 percent of those who voluntarily retired did not run for or assume other federal, state, or local offices. In the Congresses ending in the 1970s, 54 percent did not run for or assume other public office.

Moreover, even in the case of those members who did run for or gain appointment to other public positions, it should not be presumed a priori that ambition was the only or even the major motivating factor. About three-fourths of this group left to run for or assume the office of senator or governor. Yet, the average number of such retirees per Congress almost doubled in the period from 1969 to 1979 as compared with the period from 1957 to 1969 (16.8 to 9.2). Equally important, the success rate of those who ran in the 1970s was about 10 percent lower than in the late 1950s and 1960s. In short, more members were leaving to run for senator or governor, even though prospects for success were less. Both of these facts strongly suggest that in the 1970s powerful forces other than ambition were at work, even among the members whose departures are usually explained wholly or largely in terms of ambition.[10]

Disaffection

As we have seen, the traditional explanations of voluntary retirement in the House no longer suffice. While age, political vulnerability, and political ambition may have been adequate to account for such behavior in the past and still retain some causal impact, they cannot account, either singly or in combination, for the explosive increase in retirements in the 1970s. Rather, the key causal factor at present is something that is quite new in the twentieth century: growing dissatisfaction with service in the House as a career. In large part members are now retiring simply because they no longer desire to continue, because, as one member put it, "not only is the job not fun anymore, it's downright distasteful."[11]

To demonstrate the validity of this argument, it is necessary first to explain why the benefit-cost ratio of service in the House declined over the course of the last two decades and second to provide evidence of strong disaffection linked to retirement. Both can be done without difficulty.

Benefit-Cost Ratio of Service. In the late 1950s and early 1960s there was considerably less disaffection with service in the House as a career.[12] The reason for the change in the 1970s lies in a number of mutually reinforcing trends that have served to increase the costs of service while decreasing the benefits.

For a variety of reasons, the personal costs of service have greatly increased. Issues are more numerous, complex, and interrelated than they used to be. The current House spends far more time in session, in committee, and simply voting than the House under Speakers Sam Rayburn or John McCormack. Nonetheless, the combined effects of a growing workload and cumbersome organization and procedures have canceled out the benefits of added inputs of time and attention on the part of members. Though legislative pressures and demands on members have increased, the House's ability to handle its work in a coherent and deliberate fashion has declined, as has the ability of members to master even the most critical issues of a session. Moreover, the appearance of scarcity politics and single-issue voting groups has made the tasks of representing constituent interests and working with other members more difficult and frustrating. Last, but not least, the demands of the constituent workload, the need for trips back to the district, and the amount of funds required for re-election campaigns have grown substantially. In short, serious sources of strain proceed both from the political and the technical or organizational dimensions of legislative life in the contemporary House.[13]

As a result, the job of a member of Congress is far more onerous and unpleasant than a few decades ago. Members now lead very hectic and frenetic lives. The combination of their Washington and district duties results in long office hours and frequent travel. They have little time left to spend with their families. When in Washington, members are confronted by the need to vote on hosts of issues they know little about, frustrated by scheduling conflicts in committee meetings and overlaps in jurisdictions, and debilitated by the need to race continually back and forth from office to committee to floor. Practicing the basic politician's art of compromise is far more difficult. Considerable internal conflicts arise between members' desire to spend their time as legislators working on substantive policy questions that interest them and their perceived need to satisfy constituent requests, maintain a personal presence in their districts, and electioneer. Indeed,

Table 4-2   Voluntary Retiree Characteristics, 1957-1979

| | Retirees 85th-90th Congresses, 1957-69 (N=194) | | | Retirees 91st-95th Congresses, 1969-79 (N=232) | | |
	Number	Percent of All Retirees	Average per Congress	Number	Percent of All Retirees	Average per Congress
Under 65 With More Than 3 Terms	86	44.3	14.3	114	49.1	22.8
Under 65 With Less Than 3 Terms	50	25.8	8.3	66	28.4	13.2
Republicans	98	50.5	16.3	106	45.7	21.2
Committee, Subcommittee, and Party Leaders*	98	50.5	16.3	140	60.3	28

* Includes Chairmen, Ranking Minority Members, Speaker, Majority and Minority Leaders, and Chief Whips.

many find voting on hundreds of minor bills, attending banquets, raising campaign funds, and other aspects of their jobs highly irksome.[14]

It is true, of course, that members now enjoy greater aids in terms of staff and allowances and that most districts are "safe." However, these benefits are not free. They come at a price. The price of staff and allowances is a heavier workload; these resources permit — indeed generate — extra work, especially on the constituent side.[15] Similarly, the price of re-election "safety" is constant attention and vigilance.[16] It is also true that the frustrations listed above are usually not as intense in the first few terms, when the excitement of being in Congress is fresh, as in subsequent terms. Nonetheless, as data presented in Table 4-2 indicates, frustration builds more quickly now than in the past.

Increases in the costs of service have been accompanied by decreases in the rewards or benefits. Congressional salaries, although at an all-time high, have not kept pace with cost of living increases during the late 1960s and 1970s. At the same time, opportunities to earn outside income have been limited and disclosure requirements tightened. Conversely, opportunities for retired members to earn more money working as lobbyists, in law firms, and in private business appear to have expanded.[17] Moreover, the prestige of Congress as an institution has fallen as have the rewards that derive from feelings of camaraderie and close personal friendship among members. Committee and subcommittee chairmanships do not carry with them the same amounts of prestige and power as in the years before the caucus reforms of the early 1970s. Finally, the satisfactions members receive from realizing policy goals have declined as the difficulties of building majorities behind coherent and meaningful programs have increased. More and more members today doubt that they can have an impact on the course of our nation, that they can play a vital and significant role in shaping national policy. Two of the most positive critical motivations, identified by Richard Fenno — power and policy — have thus been undermined and several subsidiary ones negatively affected as well.[18]

Expressions of Dissatisfaction. The consequence of increasing costs and decreasing rewards has been greater disaffection with service in the House as a career. Such disaffection is clearly visible in current assessments by individual members of their jobs and of the House as an institution.

On the negative character of change in the broad personal and political climate of the House, note the words of two highly respected members, Minority Leader John J. Rhodes (R-Ariz.) and David R. Obey (D-Wis.):

> ... Congress has changed. Of this there can be no doubt. The atmosphere in and around Congress today is far more acrid than

at any time during my career. The members are louder, more uptight, hostile, and devious. The average Congressman has always been partisan, but never so partisan as he is today. Today's members — particularly many of the newer members — have failed to master the art of disagreeing without being disagreeable.

Yes, government is getting bigger, but what's eating this place alive is the growth of one-issue groups — pro and anti-abortion, pro and anti-B-1 bomber, pro and anti-nuclear power. Neither side wants to listen to the other. Consensus can't be achieved. You take that kind of pressure, add the fact that one-half of the people in the Congress were elected in the last five years, plus the fact that the party system is collapsing, and you see the fragmentation and frustration. . . . Moses couldn't lead the country today."[19]

For more specific comments on the increasing costs of service in the House, note these comments by recent retirees:

What it takes to get the job done is 80 hours a week. That's not compatible with how much time I'd like to spend with my family. I just wanted to get to know my kids before it was too late.

. . . at least half the time you're at work, your schedule demands that you literally be two places at the same time. A few years around here can turn you into a marathon runner — and that's if you're lucky."

Because of the proliferation of problems for which Congress is expected to find solutions, you can't concentrate on anything very long. You wind up with an attention span microseconds long. Some of us don't like that.

Congress is still workable, still viable. . . . But the job is more demanding, more time-consuming . . . you'll find greater turnover in the future . . . political careers will be shorter. The life is just too intense.

You simply burn yourself out. You get to a point where something has to give. Either your health suffers or your constituents suffer.

Being expected to put in a full day's work at the office and a full night's appearance on the banquet circuit can get to be and has come to be a bore. . . . People bug me more than they used to. They are asking their government to do more for them and are willing to do less and less for themselves. . . . So much of the work is nit-picking trivia.[20]

Complaints by members of the House are not limited to the costs of House service. The following statements by recent retirees testify to members' strong dissatisfaction with the current rewards of House service:

I just don't want to be a Congressman anymore. I want to practice law while I'm still young enough to pursue another career. I'm going to triple my income.

Congress is a disappointment. I don't see movement or progress. When I was mayor of Syracuse, I could watch downtown being rebuilt. The legislative process here is cumbersome; the system isn't designed to take on major reforms. I ran because I was unhappy with the political scene. I'm still unhappy and I don't believe in doing something I don't like.

Chairmanships are not the satisfying commands they once were. . . . The Democratic caucus has brought about a sharp change in the operation of the House — for good or for bad.

You want to have pride in what you're doing, but it is hard — very hard — when you see Congress continually cast in a bad light. Lately, it is assumed that we're both undisciplined and immoral. That isn't true, but it is increasingly the perception.

I've fought all I can fight and sometimes I feel I can't make a dent.[21]

Comments such as these regarding the high costs and inadequate rewards of House service are now legion, and many more could be cited. But the case for disaffection as the primary factor in recent retirement trends can also be supported by statistical evidence. Table 4-2 indicates that disaffection among House members in Congresses ending in the 1970s was not an isolated or segmented phenomenon, but rather a highly pervasive one. Three points are worth noting.

First, voluntary retirement has increased among members who have served six years or more and among members who have attained leadership positions. Thus, disaffection has grown in the ranks of those members who ought to be the most resistant to it: among members who have made substantial personal commitments to and investments in House careers and who have attained important institutional rewards for their service.

Second, voluntary retirement has also increased among members who have served less than six years. This fact provides additional evidence of the pervasive character of disaffection by indicating that it has also had an impact on those who are still deciding on whether to invest heavily in a House career.

Third, voluntary retirement has increased among Democrats as well as Republicans. Given the frustrations involved in long and continued minority status, it might be expected that Republicans would be highly disaffected. And they are. In the past several decades Republicans have constantly provided a higher percentage of retirees than their numbers would warrant. Nonetheless, in the 1970s Democratic retirees have outpaced Republican retirees both in number and in rate of increase relative to the late 1950s and 1960s.

SIGNIFICANCE OF HOUSE RETIREMENT TRENDS

Disaffection with congressional service produced by increasing costs and declining rewards accounts for the increased and increasing rate of voluntary retirement in the House. The major role that disaffection now plays in motivating voluntary retirement is quite new in the twentieth century. In this section we shall consider the significance of House retirement trends and their implications for the future.

It is important to note that the impact and implications of recent retirement trends in the House pertain to the organizational or institutional context of decisionmaking in that body — not to immediate policy outcomes. In his study of departees from the House between 1966 and 1974, Stephen Frantzich found that substantial amounts of change in liberalism scores occurred *solely* in the case of defeated members who were replaced by opposing partisans. Only marginal amounts of change took place in policy orientations in the case of members who replaced voluntary retirees.[22]

This is not surprising. The existence of a strong tie between policy change and switched seats has been demonstrated repeatedly in the existing literature. In the great majority of cases, however, voluntary retirees are replaced by fellow partisans (73 percent of the time in the 92nd-95th Congresses). Significant changes in policy voting therefore do not occur. Nor are the underlying causes or determinants of such stability difficult to understand. The fact that few party switches occur in the case of retirees means that the controlling electoral forces here are similar to those that support incumbency. That is to say that local and idiosyncratic constituency factors, rather than parties as overarching and competitive policy coalitions, dominate the scene. Results with respect to voluntary retirement as with respect to incumbency thus testify to party weakness and may well be expected not to produce any major policy changes in voting.[23]

Organizational Trends

Although voluntary retirement has not had a direct and substantial policy impact, it is nonetheless an important phenomenon that must be understood in its historical context. Norms, structures, and leadership styles in the House differ over time in response to changing environmental constraints and internal pressures.[24]

From the late 1930s to the late 1960s, a very distinctive type of House existed. It took shape over several decades in response to the breakdown of the highly centralized and party-dominated House of Speakers Thomas Reed (1889-91, 1895-99) and Joseph Cannon (1903-11). This House, which for convenience may be called the Rayburn House, was distinguished by the high degree of allegiance commanded by a constellation of norms quite familiar to the present generation of political scientists: seniority and apprenticeship, reciprocity, specialization, civility, accommodation, tempered partisanship, and institutional patriotism. It was also distinguished by the high degree of power wielded by committees and committee chairmen and by the dormant status of majority party units, such as the party caucuses and steering or policy committees. The prevailing leadership style was accordingly highly personal, informal, permissive, and consensus-oriented. Epitomized by Speaker Sam Rayburn (1940-47, 1949-53, 1955-61), it was a style that differed radically from that of Speaker Cannon in the early 1900s or even Speaker John Garner in the early 1930s.[25]

By virtue of historical accident, this type of House was at full strength at the time of the behavioral revolution in political science. Consequently, its norms, structures, and leadership style were treated for many years as if they were permanent or inherent features of congressional politics. Indeed, this was largely true even when students began to view the House developmentally.[26]

Events since 1969, however, have shattered the illusion of an historic or even archetypal House. Rules and practice in the House have altered substantially due to a series of Democratic Caucus reforms and to more basic underlying forces of which these caucus reforms were only an expression.[27] What has become clear with the passage of time is that a new and very different type of House has been emerging in the 1970s. In terms of norms — adherence to seniority, respect for apprenticeship, deference to committees, willingness to compromise, and the "to get along, go along" Rayburnian ethic — all have greatly declined in strength. So too in all probability have tempered partisanship, civility, and institutional patriotism. In terms of structure, both the Speaker and subcommittees have gained power at the expense of committees, and majority party units have been revived and become quite active. In terms of leadership style, there is less tolerance for partisan defection on crucial votes and less willingness to cooperate or exchange favors with Republican leaders, although the basic mode of operation remains highly personal and informal.

Nonetheless, the net result of these changes has been greater fragmentation. The increase in partisan spirit, to the degree that it has occurred, has been confined in impact to personal relations and the distribution of rewards. It has had little impact on party unity or coherence, but rather has served to increase levels of strife or dissension. The increased powers of the Speaker have not compensated for the proliferation of subcommittees, the declining ability of party to provide a nexus for building majorities on critical issues, or the emergence of a host of ad hoc caucuses, such as the Black Caucus, the Rural Caucus, and the Steel Caucus.

As for the revival of majority party units, the current Democratic Caucus and Democratic Policy Committee bear only superficial resemblance to their predecessors in eras when party allegiance and coherence were strong. Although both met regularly in the 1970s for the first time since the 1930s, they serve primarily as arenas for intraparty conflict and maneuvering — not as instruments for party unity or discipline. The leadership therefore approaches the policy committee and especially the caucus with caution, not confidence. On the whole, it is individual members and particular blocs of members that have gained increased independence, power, and flexibility at the expense of institutional capacity for integration. The hallmarks of the modern House are heightened individualism, conflict, and fractionalization. Even the revival of the Democratic Caucus reflects this general trend.[28]

Organizational Impacts

Recent trends in voluntary retirement exist as an integral aspect of the emergence of this new type of House. On the one hand, voluntary retirement has contributed significantly to the alterations in norms and structures that have taken place. On the other hand, voluntary retirement testifies to changes in the incentive system that are of great and general significance.

It is commonly recognized that junior members have increased in number in the past decade and that they have played an important role in altering House procedures and practices, especially in the mid- and late 1970s.[29] Table 4-3 shows that the number of junior members has indeed increased. It may be noted that the proportion of members who served less than four full consecutive terms during the 96th Congress was 52.4 percent; that the trend toward increases

Table 4-3   Tenure Distribution of House Members, 1957-1981

Congress	*Full Consecutive Terms*			
	1-3 N (%)	*4-6* N (%)	*7-9* N (%)	*10+* N (%)
85th (1957-59)	172 (39.7)	135 (31.2)	68 (15.7)	58 (13.4)
86th (1959-61)	182 (41.8)	137 (31.5)	63 (14.5)	53 (12.2)
87th (1961-63)	166 (38.2)	132 (30.3)	72 (16.6)	65 (14.9)
88th (1963-65)	190 (43.8)	105 (24.2)	74 (17.1)	65 (15.0)
89th (1965-67)	203 (46.7)	96 (22.1)	75 (17.2)	61 (14.0)
90th (1967-69)	192 (44.1)	104 (23.9)	70 (16.1)	69 (15.9)
91st (1969-71)	179 (41.1)	123 (28.3)	62 (14.3)	71 (16.3)
92nd (1971-73)	163 (37.8)	121 (28.0)	66 (15.3)	82 (19.0)
93rd (1973-75)	166 (38.4)	130 (30.1)	62 (14.4)	74 (17.1)
94th (1975-77)	205 (47.1)	98 (22.5)	74 (17.0)	58 (13.3)
95th (1977-79)	221 (50.8)	87 (20.0)	68 (15.6)	59 (13.6)
96th (1979-81)	227 (52.4)	89 (20.6)	68 (15.7)	49 (11.3)

in the proportion of House "careerists" (members with 10 or more full consecutive terms) has been reversed; and that members on the brink of making a permanent commitment to a House career (members with four but less than seven full consecutive terms) are opting to leave far more often than in the past. What has been overlooked, however, is the key role increasing rates of voluntary retirement have played in expanding the ranks of junior members.

Part of the impact voluntary retirement has had lies simply in numbers. As pointed out earlier in this article, voluntary retirement, rather than election or primary defeats, has been the single greatest source of turnover in the 1970s. Nonetheless, the sheer number of departees who were voluntary retirees is less important as a cause of the increased proportion of junior members than another facet of voluntary retirement: wide dispersion across tenure classes or categories.

Turnover data for the past several decades contain a startling fact: the number of departures from the House per Congress has been relatively stable.[30] Indeed, the total amount of turnover in the 85th through 87th Congresses (1957-1963) was virtually the same as in the 93rd through 95th Congresses (1973-1979). The respective totals are 56.1 percent and 59.1 percent. Yet, as Table 4-3 indicates, the proportion of members in various tenure ranks remained quite stable and relatively balanced in the late 1950s and early 1960s, whereas it has changed markedly and become far less balanced in the 1970s.

What is critical, then, is not simply the amount of turnover, but its dispersion. Otherwise, persons of only junior rank can turn over without altering the relative proportions of the various ranks.

Table 4-4 Tenure of Defeated House Members as Compared with Voluntary Retirees, 1957-1963 and 1973-1979

Selected Congresses	*Full Consecutive Terms*			
	1-3 *N (%)*	*4-6* *N (%)*	*7-9* *N (%)*	*10+* *N (%)*
Members Defeated*				
85th-87th (1957-63)	59 (56.2)	26 (24.8)	13 (12.4)	7 (6.7)
93rd-95th (1973-79)	46 (52.3)	23 (26.1)	9 (10.2)	10 (11.4)
Total Number	105	49	22	17
Members Voluntarily Retired				
85th-87th (1957-63)	28 (26.9)	36 (34.6)	18 (17.3)	22 (21.2)
93rd-95th (1973-79)	43 (28.1)	37 (24.2)	32 (20.9)	41 (26.8)
Total Number	71	73	50	63

*In elections or primaries.

It is here that voluntary retirement assumes its greatest significance. Turnover caused by electoral defeat tends to be confined to junior ranks; in contrast, turnover caused by voluntary retirement tends to be widely dispersed across tenure ranks. This is clearly shown in Table 4-4, which provides evidence of the differential impacts of electoral defeat and voluntary retirement across tenure ranks for the late 1950s, early 1960s, and 1970s. In sum, the shift from electoral defeat to voluntary retirement as the predominant source of turnover did far more than simply maintain the overall level. It altered the range and impact of turnover and in so doing negatively affected tenure trends that had prevailed throughout the twentieth century.[31]

The impact of voluntary retirement, however, is not limited to the role it has played in increasing the number and proportion of junior members. What the increased rate of voluntary retirement bears testimony to, given the fact that it has been fueled largely by disaffection, is a significant change in the incentive system of the House. An organization dominated by such norms as seniority, reciprocity, and civility is an organization in which members expect and desire long and stable careers. When disaffection for continued service grows, so does acceptance of the limitations sanctioned by these norms. This is true both because senior members who adhere to these norms become disenchanted and leave and because members of only moderate tenure and new members begin to resist them more strenuously. The incentives provided are no longer able to motivate the high degrees of tolerance, patience, cooperation, and self-denial these norms require to be fully operative and controlling. To be sure, they do not disappear, but they do erode and become less influential determinants of behavior.

In short, as the benefit-cost ratio of service in the House altered, there was an inevitable impact on norms and structure. Thus, it was not simply the desire of non-senior members for more power, for a greater piece of the action, that made them a force for change in the Democratic Caucus, but also the weakening of the rewards or satisfactions of membership that in past years had buttressed existing norms and structures. Other factors also contributed to the reforms of the 1970s, such as the growing numerical dominance of northerners within the Democratic party and the policy dissatisfactions associated with southern control of chairmanships. But the passage of time would eventually ameliorate this aspect of the problem.[32] Full explanation requires attention to a factor that has largely escaped notice — the impact of a declining benefit-cost ratio with regard to service in the House, especially in the case of members with only moderate or limited amounts of seniority.

Organizational Implications

The new House that is emerging is more junior, more fragmented, more factious, and more individualistic than its predecessor. To be sure, changes in the incentive system are not solely responsible. The general decline of party that has taken place over the past several decades has also played a critical role. Nonetheless, the reduction in the net level of member job satisfaction has had an important impact both directly and indirectly through growing rates of voluntary retirement.

What we appear to be returning to is a House that in a number of key respects resembles Houses in the nineteenth century, even though more elaborate or sophisticated in terms of resources, structures, and procedures. These Houses also had problems with the net level of member job satisfaction. These Houses also were highly junior, factious, fragmented, and individualistic.[33] Indeed, if the trend toward voluntary retirement intensifies and/or the rate of electoral defeats increases, the amount of turnover could again approach nineteenth-century levels.

Whether this will happen is, of course, not clear, though some scholars argue persuasively that the present incumbency advantage may disappear in the future.[34] What does seem clear is that as long as the rate of voluntary retirement does not diminish and nothing occurs to resuscitate party as an electoral and legislative force, the type of House that has emerged in the 1970s will become further stabilized and entrenched in the 1980s. As this occurs, it is also quite possible that a new type of member will begin to be recruited for service, a type of member more attuned to the benefit-cost ratio that now prevails.[35] Future members of Congress will probably be even more self-oriented and independent than those now in office. Current tendencies toward fragmentation, factiousness, and exploitation of position will therefore be intensified.

Although the present generation of political scientists has made much of the increased strength of incumbency and its policy implications, the dynamic aspects of this development have been largely ignored. The irony of a strengthened incumbency effect combined with an increased rate of retirement was noted at the start of this article. The key to understanding this anomaly lies in understanding underlying causes and effects. Many of the factors that have worked to the advantage of incumbents (party weakness, bureaucratic power, and constituent service) have also worked to increase the costs and decrease the benefits of House service. A concomitant feature of a heightened advantage for incumbents has thus been an erosion of the incentives that supported the traditional institutional order. For this and other reasons, a new type of House has emerged and so too, perhaps, will a new type of member. Yet, the ability of this type of House to mobilize its norms, structures, and incentives to conquer the problems of fragmentation and provide the policy accomplishments and rewards on which the maintenance of its institutional role so vitally depends appears highly conjectural. What is more likely is growing disaffection both within and without the House, leading ultimately to greater institutional debility or weakness.

SENATE COMPARISONS

Senate data on retirements and defeats are more difficult to interpret than House data in part because of the smaller number of cases and in part because the evidence is more mixed. Nonetheless, the Senate presents an informative contrast with the House and raises some important questions that are difficult to answer on the basis of existing evidence.

Incumbency Trends

Table 4-1 indicates a marked difference between the House and Senate with respect to the role and significance of primary and election defeats as a source of member turnover. The average number of incumbents defeated in the Senate per Congress has increased from 5.7 in the period from 1957 to 1969 to 7.4 in the period from 1969 to 1979, whereas in the House the number has declined from 36.7 to 27.2. Moreover, to place these figures in proper perspective it should be remembered that only about one-third of the Senate is subject to re-election every two years. Thus, in the 1970s incumbent defeat resulted on average in the turnover of 22 percent of the senators whose terms expired each Congress, though the comparable percentage for the late 1950s and 1960s is only 17 percent. In the House, however, the average impact of incumbent defeat on member turnover per Congress has declined from 8 percent to 6 percent for the same time periods.

Table 4-5 presents data on incumbency advantage in the House and Senate for the 85th-95th Congresses (1957-1979). It confirms that in this period the incumbency effect has generally been more of a House than a Senate phenomenon. More importantly, it provides further evidence of a difference in trend which thus far has been overlooked. Whereas the advantage of incumbents in elections does appear to have increased for House members in the late 1960s and 1970s, the reverse appears to be true for Senate members. This is clearly indicated by the trends regarding the percentages of House and Senate incumbents who seek and win re-election. It is also strongly suggested by the trends regarding the percentages of such members who win by 60 percent or more of the vote.

Table 4-5 Incumbency Advantage in Congress: 1958-1978 Elections (in Percentages)

	Successful House Incumbents	Successful Senate Incumbents	Senate-House Difference	House Incumbents Winning by More Than 60%	Senate Incumbents Winning by More Than 60%	Senate-House Difference
1958	89.6	64.5	−25.1	63.1	66.7	+ 3.6
1960	92.1	96.6	+ 4.5	58.9	41.3	−17.6
1962	93.4	82.9	−10.5	63.6	26.4	−37.2
1964	87.5	84.8	− 2.7	58.5	46.8	−11.7
1966	87.7	87.5	− .2	67.7	41.3	−26.4
1968	98.0	71.4	−26.6	72.2	37.5	−34.7
1970	95.2	76.7	−18.5	77.3	31.0	−46.4
1972	93.4	74.1	−19.3	77.8	52.0	−25.8
1974	87.7	85.2	− 2.5	66.4	40.0	−26.4
1976	95.8	64.0	−31.8	69.2	40.0	−29.2
1978	93.7	60.0	−33.7	76.6	31.8	−44.8

SOURCE: *Congressional Quarterly Weekly Report,* March 25, 1978, p. 755 and *Congressional Quarterly Weekly Report,* July 7, 1979, p. 1351. Both primary and election defeats are included in calculations of the percentage of incumbents who win re-election.

Since the mid-1970s, students of Congress have been wrestling with the causes of the increased incumbency effect in the House.[36] The decline of this effect in the Senate at the same time that it increased in the House raises yet another puzzling question about incumbency. Recent studies of the 1978 congressional elections, based on data collected by the Center for Political Studies at the University of Michigan, have shown in great detail that Senate incumbents have far less electoral advantage than House incumbents. The greater visibility of Senate challengers and the greater ability of House incumbents to control information about their activities are two of several factors cited to explain this finding.[37] These conclusions are both plausible and convincing, but they do not explain why the incumbency effect in the Senate has declined over time both in absolute terms and relative to House trends.

Retirement Trends

The data on Senate retirements in Table 4-1 suggests a pattern of increase similar to that in the House. For the periods from 1957 to 1969 and from 1969 to 1979, the average number of retirees per Congress increased from 32.2 to 46.4 in the House and from 5 to 7.2 in the Senate. Thus, voluntary retirement in the House has resulted on average in a member turnover of 11 percent per Congress during the 1970s in contrast to 7 percent in the late 1950s and 1960s. In the Senate during the 1970s, it has resulted on average in a turnover of 22 percent of those whose terms expired each Congress in contrast to 15 percent in the late 1950s and 1960s. Moreover, as suggested earlier, the rate of voluntary retirement seems to be increasing in both bodies. In the last three Congresses the Senate average has increased to 8.3 and the House average to 51.

Nonetheless, the determinants of retirement trends in the modern Senate appear quite different. In contrast to the House, age, marginality, and ambition can be seen to account for the preponderant number of Senate retirees in the 1970s. Of the 36 senators who retired during the past decade, two-thirds were 65 or older and most of these were 70 or older. Of the 12 Senate retirees under 65, only 2 did not face serious electoral difficulties, accept higher appointments, or have severe health problems.[38]

That disaffection with congressional service remains far lower in the Senate than in the House is not surprising. Due to its smaller size, greater informality, and traditions, individuals in the Senate have always had greater power in the body and more ability to influence policy results than individuals in the House. This continues to be the case. Similarly, the prestige attached to membership in the Senate has been and remains far higher than in the House. In addition, senators have the decided luxury of facing the electorate only every six years.

Even so, the potential for increasing disaffection among senators as well as House members should not be discounted. Time pressures, constituent service burdens, campaign costs, and policy frustrations have increased in the modern Senate as well as in the modern House.[39] Moreover, some evidence suggests that dissatisfaction with Senate service is already on the increase. Two of the nine senators who retired in 1978 at the end of the 95th Congress were definitely motivated to some substantial degree by the frustrations of a Senate career, and they expressed their unhappiness in words quite similar to those frequently used by recent House retirees. Note the following comments of Senators James Abourezk (D-S.D.) and James Pearson (R-Kan.):

> My family is part of it, of course, but I can't take any more of this stuff. I resent that I don't have time to think, maybe to write, to take photographs, to play my guitar. I need to make more money and retire some debts. . . . And each time you run, you have to peel off a principle here, a principle there. I'm not disillusioned, just realistic.

> Several factors are pushing in on us today. We have an enormous increase in the amount of business to be done and a great increase

in time pressure. And the parochial demands from back home are greater. People today, more than ever before, expect you to come home to your state just about every weekend. . . . [I]f this government ever falls, it won't be from any external pressure. It will be because those people assigned to make judgments never had any time to read or contemplate or think.[40]

Institutional Impacts

The period from 1957 to 1979 has witnessed important changes in the institutional character of the Senate as well as the House. The oligarchic Senate of the late 1940s, 1950s, and early 1960s, which was dominated by an inner club or establishment, has disappeared. Seniority and apprenticeship norms have grown much weaker as have the norms that favored free and unlimited debate. Committee and subcommittee chairmanships have increased and become more widely distributed. Policy divisions among Democratic senators have become more complex and intense. Leadership style has altered substantially in the transitions from Lyndon Johnson to Mike Mansfield to Robert Byrd. The Senate thus has also become a more fragmented and individualistic body. On the whole, however, change has been more gradual and incremental than in the House.[41]

What role has voluntary retirement played in causing these changes? The answer is a far more limited one than in the House. To be sure, in the House as well as the Senate the changing balance of power between Northern and Southern Democrats has been a major catalyst of change.[42] Nonetheless, change in the House has been more concentrated in the 1970s and significantly influenced both by disaffection per se and by increases in the proportion of junior members caused by retirements based on disaffection. These factors have been much less important in the Senate.

On the one hand, dissatisfaction with service in the Senate as a career has not been a matter of any substantial importance in the 1960s or 1970s. Traditional incentives for continued service thus have remained strong, and changes in traditional norms have been more limited than in the House.[43] On the other hand, recent retirement trends, which appear to be based largely on aging, have not resulted in any secular increase in the proportion of junior members. For example, the proportion of members with less than six years service was about 42 percent in the early 1960s, declined to about 30 percent in the late 1960s, and then rose again to about 45 percent in the late 1970s.

This, however, is not to say that retirement has had no impact. It played a role in the displacement of senior Southern Democrats in the 1960s and 1970s and in increasing the proportion of junior members in the mid- and late 1970s. This increase, in turn, was a factor in the limits imposed on chairmanships and assignments in 1977.[44] Nevertheless, even in these instances it was complemented or reinforced to a significant extent by other sources of turnover: by incumbent defeat in the latter instance and by incumbent defeat and death in the former.

In conclusion, the causes of voluntary retirement are more important than its proportions in any single decade. Recent trends in the Senate should not be equated with those in the House. Indeed, since the average age of senators declined to 52.7 in 1979, as compared with 56.6 in 1969 and 57.1 in 1959, it is quite possible that the trend toward increased retirement will reverse in the 1980s unless levels of disaffection begin to approach those in the House. Some indicators suggest that such a development may be under way. Whether these fragments of evidence are illusory or predictive, however, remains a question only the future can resolve.

NOTES

1. See T. Richard Witmer, "The Aging of the House," *Political Science Quarterly* 79 (1964): 526-542 and Nelson W. Polsby, "Institutionalization in the U.S. House of Representatives," *American Political Science Review* 62 (1968): 144-168.
2. See David R. Mayhew, "Congressional Elections: The Case of the Vanishing Marginals," *Polity* 6 (1974): 295-317 and Albert D. Cover, "One Good Term Deserves Another," *American Journal of Political Science* 21 (1977): 523-541.
3. See Morris P. Fiorina, *Congress: Keystone of the Washington Establishment* (New Haven: Yale University Press, 1977); H. Douglas Price, "Congress and the Evolution of Legislative Professionalism," in *Congress in Change: Evolution and Reform,* ed. Norman J. Ornstein (New York: Praeger Publishers, 1975); and Albert D. Cover and David R. Mayhew, "Congressional Dynamics and the Decline of Competitive Congressional Elections," in this volume.
4. Unless specifically noted, all data reported in this article have been compiled from the annual *Congressional Quarterly Almanacs* for the period 1957 to 1979 and *Congressional Directories* for the 85th-96th Congresses (1957-1981).
5. The number of voluntary end of term and intra-term retirees in the House per Congress for Congresses ending in the late 1950s and 1960s, i.e., the period from 1957 to 1969, are as follows: 36, 28, 40, 37, 26, 27.
6. The number of voluntary intra-term and end of term retirees in the Senate per Congress for Congresses ending in the late 1950s and 1960s, i.e., the period from 1957 to 1969, are as follows: 7, 5, 5, 4, 5, 6.
7. See Stephen Frantzich, "Opting Out: Retirement from the House of Representatives," *American Politics Quarterly* 6 (July 1978): 251-274.
8. Ibid. See also Stephen Frantzich, "Derecruitment: The Other Side of the Congressional Career Equation," *Western Political Quarterly* 31 (1978): 105-126.

9. For conflicting evaluations of the political impacts of redistricting as well as evidence of its declining role in the 1970s, see *Electing Congress* (Washington, D.C.: Congressional Quarterly, 1978), p. 35; and Morris P. Fiorina, David W. Rohde, and Peter Wissel, "Historical Change in House Turnover," in *Congress in Change;* and John Ferejohn, "On the Decline of Competition in Congressional Elections," *American Political Science Review* 71 (1977): 166-177.

10. The impact of ambition in motivating those members who left to run for or assume public positions other than senator or governor also cannot simply be assumed on an a priori basis. Some retired for offices that are clearly more desirable than a House seat, e.g., a cabinet post. But others did so for offices whose superior desirability is problematic, e.g., state offices and judgeships.

11. The member quoted is Rep. David R. Obey (D-Wis.). See *Parade,* November 5, 1978, p. 11. For examples of similar comments by other members, see *National Journal,* March 11, 1978, pp. 391-393.

12. See Charles Clapp, *The Congressman: His Work as He Sees It* (Washington, D.C.: Brookings Institution, 1963), p. 437.

13. On the growth of the workload, time pressures on members, information needs, committee conflicts, etc., see the *Final Report of the Commission on Administrative Review,* vol. 1, H. Doc. 95-272, pp. 11-43 and 613-694. On the growth of campaign costs and new forms of lobbying, see *National Journal,* April 30, 1977, p. 686; April 8, 1978, pp. 557-561; and August 5, 1978, p. 1257.

14. See comments of members on various facets of service they dislike in *Parade,* November 5, 1978, pp. 11-5; *U.S. News and World Report,* May 1 and June 5, 1978, pp. 37-38 and 23-24; and *National Journal,* June 24, 1978, p. 1023 and March 11, 1978, pp. 391-393. For data on conflicts in member role orientations, see Wave I Member Survey of Commission on Administrative Review, Tables 5, 6, 7a, 7b and 8a in the *Final Report,* vol. 2, H. Doc. 95-272, pp. 874-885.

15. For information on member allowances, see *National Journal,* February 4, 1978, pp. 180-183. See also Public Survey of the Commission on Administrative Review, Tables 15a and 17 in the *Final Report,* vol. 2, H. Doc. 95-272, pp. 830 and 835. The data in these tables are very interesting. They indicate that only a small percentage of constituents request help from members and that the great majority of contacts are either initiated by members or mediated by the press. In the latter regard it should be remembered that most member offices now include a press specialist.

16. See Robert Erikson, "Is There Such a Thing as a Safe Seat?" *Polity* 8 (1976): 623-632 and Thomas Mann, *Unsafe At Any Margin* (Washington, D.C.: American Enterprise Institute, 1978).

17. For information on salary and alternative job opportunities, see the report of a recent federal salary commission reprinted in *Financial Ethics, Hearings Before the Commission on Administrative Review,* 95th Cong., 1st sess. (1977), pp. 311-472. For information on outside income limitations and disclosure, see *1977 Congressional Quarterly Almanac,* pp. 763-771.

18. Richard F. Fenno, Jr., *Home Style: House Members in Their Districts* (Boston: Little, Brown & Co., 1978), p. 137. Improving pension benefits has played a role in inducing retirement. Nonetheless, this factor serves primarily to reinforce the impact of disaffection and is subsidiary to it. The percentage of voluntary retirees per Congress eligible for full benefits has declined as the number of retirees has increased. For example,

the average for 1957 to 1976 is 44.3 percent, as opposed to 38.8 percent for 1971 to 1979.

19. The Rhodes quote is from John Rhodes, *The Futile System* (McLean, Virginia: EPM Publications, 1976), p. 7. The Obey quote is from *Parade,* November 5, 1978, p. 15.

20. The speakers and sources of the quotes are in order of their appearance in the text as follows: Rep. Gary Myers (R-Pa.), *Parade,* November 5, 1978, p. 11; unidentified House retiree, *U.S. News and World Report,* May 1, 1978, p. 37; Rep. Thomas Rees (D-Calif.), *U.S. News and World Report,* May 1, 1978, p. 37; Rep. Paul Rogers (D-Fla.), *Parade,* November 5, 1978, p. 11; Rep. David Henderson (D-N.C.), *Washington Post,* April 16, 1976, p. A5; and Rep. Otis Pike (D-N.Y.), *Parade,* November 5, 1978, p. 15.

21. The speakers and sources of the quotes are in order of their appearance in the text as follows: Rep. Charles Wiggins (R-Calif.), *Parade,* November 5, 1978, p. 12; Rep. William Walsh (R-N.Y.), *Parade,* November 5, 1978, p. 12; Rep. George Mahon (D-Texas), *Houston Post,* March 3, 1978 (AP story); Rep. John Moss (D-Calif.), *Parade,* November 5, 978, p. 12; and Rep. Leonor Sullivan (D-Mo.), *Houston Chronicle,* April 11, 1976, p. 25 (UP story).

22. Frantzich, "Opting Out," pp. 251-274; Frantzich, "Derecruitment," p. 105-126.

23. On the relation between switched seats and policy change and the importance of party strength as a factor in policy change, see Patricia Hurley, David Brady, and Joseph Cooper, "Measuring Legislative Potential for Policy Change," *Legislative Studies Quarterly* 2 (1977):385-399 and David Brady, Joseph Cooper, and Patricia Hurley, "The Decline of Party in the House of Representatives," *Legislative Studies Quarterly* 4 (1979): 381-409.

24. See Joseph Cooper and David Brady, "Organization Theory and Congressional Structure" (Paper delivered at the annual meeting of the American Political Science Association, New Orleans, Louisiana, September 4-8, 1973) and Lawrence C. Dodd, "Congress and the Quest for Power," in *Congress Reconsidered,* 1st ed., edited by Lawrence C. Dodd and Bruce I. Oppenheimer (New York: Praeger Publishers, 1977), pp. 269-307.

25. On the emergence and character of the Rayburn House, see Joseph Cooper, *The Origins of the Standing Committees and the Development of the Modern House* (Houston: Rice University, 1970), pp. 116-130. See also Richard Bolling, *Power in the House* (New York: E. P. Dutton, 1968); Richard F. Fenno, Jr., "The Internal Distribution of Influence: The House," in *The Congress and America's Future,* ed. David Truman (Englewood Cliffs N.J.: Prentice Hall, 1965); and Clapp, *The Congressman.*

26. See Polsby, "Institutionalization in the House."

27. For a survey of House reforms during the 1970s, see Lawrence C. Dodd and Bruce I. Oppenheimer, "The House in Transition," in this volume.

28. The best sources of evidence on the character of the House that have emerged in the 1970s are from Congressional Quarterly and the *National Journal.* In the former case see *Inside Congress,* 2nd ed. (October 1979). In the latter case see the following pages: pp. 1731-1737 (1976); pp. 940-946, 1028-1038, 1080-1081, 1756-1762, 1994-1995 (1977); pp. 4-9, 630-632, 677-679, 712-714, 844-845, 1203-1205, 1384-1388 (1978); and pp. 150 and 1326-1331 (1979). See also Richard F. Fenno, Jr., "If, as Ralph Nader Says, Congress is 'the Broken Branch,' How Come We Love Our

Congressmen So Much?" and Herbert Asher, "The Changing Status of the Freshman Representative," in *Congress in Change*. Although much has been made of Fenno's point regarding the tendency of members to run against Congress, the implications of his insight with respect to changing House norms have been ignored. Yet, such behavior strongly suggests a decline in institutional patriotism, and thus it is probably no accident that this phenomenon was first identified in the literature in the early 1970s.

29. See *National Journal*, pp. 1881-1890 (1974); pp. 129-134 (1975); pp. 189-196 and 370-374 (1976); pp. 1080-1081 and 1994-1995 (1977); pp. 1203-1205 (1978); and p. 150 (1979).

30. Figures for turnover vary slightly depending on whether entrances or departures are counted. Measured in terms of departures (including death, retirement, and defeat), the percentages per Congress from 1957 to 1979 varied — with one exception (10 percent in 1968) — from 15 percent to 23 percent. Moreover, in 6 of the 11 Congresses involved, the rate varied only from 16 percent to 19 percent.

31. See Witmer, "The Aging of the House" and Polsby, "Institutionalization in the House."

32. See Norman J. Ornstein and David W. Rohde, "Seniority and Future Power in Congress," in *Congress in Change*.

33. For two classic studies of the House in the nineteenth century, see James S. Young, *The Washington Community: 1800-1828* (New York: Columbia University Press, 1966) and Woodrow Wilson, *Congressional Government* (Cleveland: Meridian Books, 1965). In addition, see Polsby, "Institutionalization in the House"; Price, "Congress and the Evolution of Legislative Professionalism"; and Bolling, *Power in the House.*

34. Mann, *Unsafe At Any Margin*, pp. 106-107.

35. See James Payne, "The Personal Electoral Advantage of House Incumbents, 1936-1974," unpublished paper, 1979; and *Electing Congress*, pp. 38-40.

36. For a review of varying explanations see Mann, *Unsafe At Any Margin*, pp. 11-18.

37. See Alan Abramowitz, "Party and Individual Accountability in the 1978 Congressional Election" and Thomas Mann and Raymond Wolfinger, "Candidates and Parties in Congressional Elections" (Papers delivered at the Rice-Houston Conference on Congressional Elections, 1980). See also Barbara Hinckley, "House Reelections and Senate Defeats" (Paper delivered at the annual meeting of the American Political Science Association, Washington, D.C., August 31-September 3, 1979).

38. These two are Harold Hughes of Iowa in 1972 and James Pearson of Kansas in 1978. However, two others were motivated to some substantial degree by disaffection with a Senate career: Eugene McCarthy of Minnesota in 1970 and James Abourezk of South Dakota in 1978.

39. See the *Final Report of the Commission on the Operation of the Senate*, S. Doc. 94-278.

40. The Abourezk quote is from *Parade*, November 5, 1978, p. 11 and the Pearson quote is from *U.S. News and World Report*, June 5, 1978, p. 24.

41. For material on the institutional character of the Senate from 1957 to 1979, see William S. White, *The Citadel* (New York: Harper & Brothers, 1956); Randall Ripley, *Power in the Senate* (New York, St. Martin's Press, 1969); Nelson W. Polsby, *Congress and the Presidency* (Englewood Cliffs, N.J.: Prentice Hall, 1976); and Norman J. Ornstein, Robert L. Peabody, and David W. Rohde, "The Contemporary Senate: Into the

1980s," in this volume. For information on the decline of southern power in the Senate in the 1960s and 1970s, see Ripley, *Power in the Senate,* pp. 53-77 and William Keefe, *Congress and the American People* (Englewood Cliffs, N.J.: Prentice Hall, 1980), p. 76. For information on the increase in fragmentation and individualism in the Senate, see Lawrence C. Dodd and Richard Schott, *Congress and the Administrative State* (New York: John Wiley & Sons, 1979), pp. 118-124.

42. See Joseph Cooper, "Strengthening the Congress: An Organizational Analysis," *Harvard Journal on Legislation* 12 (April 1975): 359-360.

43. See Ornstein, Peabody, and Rohde, "The Contemporary Senate," in this volume.

44. However, the pressures of the workload and the impossible number of committee and subcommittee assignments per senator (an average of 18) were probably more important motivating factors. See Judith Parris, "The Senate Reorganizes Its Committees, 1977," *Political Science Quarterly* 95 (Summer 1979): 319-339 and *National Journal,* January 15, 1977, pp. 106-111.

5

Two Avenues of Change: House and Senate Committee Reorganization

Roger H. Davidson

How do institutions change? This question intrigues social scientists and historians, and answering it is not just an academic exercise. All institutions must change in order to survive and fulfill their social functions. Whether these changes respond sufficiently to the challenges of the times or whether they are irrelevant spells the difference between life and death for an institution.

The American Congress is no exception. Despite its unflattering media image — as a fusty place inhabited by obdurate and senile politicians — Congress has undergone profound changes throughout its history. Indeed, in the last two decades Congress has become arguably the most radically altered of all our major governmental institutions. The changes have touched virtually every nook and cranny on Capitol Hill — its membership, structures, procedures, folkways, and staffs.

Like all organizations, Congress strives to preserve itself and, if possible, expand its span of influence.[1] For many organizations, like the proverbial Mom and Pop grocery store, survival is a day-

---

The views expressed in this chapter are the author's and do not necessarily reflect those of the Congressional Research Service.

to-day challenge in which keeping the doors open for business is often a struggle. For Congress the imperative is more subtle but no less real: Can it preserve and even enhance its independence and its sphere of influence? In our constitutional framework of blended powers, which the late Edward S. Corwin called an "invitation to struggle," Congress competes with many other institutions — including the White House, executive agencies, the courts, and even private bodies.

FORCES FOR CHANGE

If an institution is to survive — whether a family business or the U.S. Congress — it must adjust to *external demands* and cope with *internal stresses.* These outside and inside pressures for innovation, operating alone or in tandem, can force an organization to reassess its traditional ways of doing things. Congress faces problems of both sorts.

External Demands

Our age is called antiparliamentary, a label that reflects staggering and ever-shifting challenges emanating from the external environment. Most analysts agree that Congress's "crisis of adaptation" is serious and of long standing.[2] The crisis is typified by executive ascendency, as Congress relies increasingly on the president and the bureaucratic apparatus for its legislative agenda and delegates ever larger chunks of discretionary authority to bureaucrats. The crisis is felt acutely on Capitol Hill. It often stretches legislative structures and procedures beyond their limits, and it drains legislators' morale and institutional loyalty.

Many elements of Congress's external environment contribute to this crisis. Demands upon the House and Senate are enormous and show no signs of abating; by most objective measures (committee meetings, votes, constituency mail, hours in session), the workload has just about doubled in the past 20 years.[3] Moreover, today's complex problems transcend traditional agencies and jurisdictions. President Carter's 1977 energy package embraced more than 110 separate bills that were referred to half a dozen committees in each house. Because we live in an era of limits, both in resources and in public tolerances, relative resources for resolving political demands in attractive ways have dwindled. Congress's external environment is also characterized by conflicts between the executive and legislative branches. Conflicts with the White House, at a high point during the Nixon years, remain salient in such fields as budgeting, economic policy, social programs, and foreign affairs. Finally, public support for Congress as an institution is notoriously low. In one Harris poll two-thirds of the respondents gave Congress a negative rating, while only 22 percent gave it positive marks.[4] In view of these external pressures, it is no wonder that voluntary retirements from Congress have accelerated and that many retirees express weariness and relief at getting out.

Internal Pressures

Another set of pressures for change emanates from forces within Congress — primarily the goals and careers of individual members. Legislators harbor a variety of personal goals.[5] Most legislators want to gain re-election, and some have no other interests. But even political men and women do not live by re-election alone; they want a chance to contribute, to shape public policy, to see their ideas come to fruition, to gain respect for their work. Hence, legislators make a variety of claims upon the institution, shaping its structures and procedures to serve their own needs as well as the demands of the outside environment.

Internal stresses and strains are no novelty in Congress, whose members are quasi-independent political entrepreneurs of relatively equal formal power who represent diverse constituencies and viewpoints. Sometimes the effects of external demands ricochet and create interpersonal stresses — as when a ballooning workload (external demand) produces personal or committee scrambles for jurisdiction (internal stress). Other tensions flow from shifts in personnel, factional balances, and members' attitudes or norms. Such conflicts surface in recurrent bickering over perquisites, committee jurisdictions, rules, scheduling, seniority, and aspects of budgetary decisionmaking.

Types of Innovation

These external demands and internal stresses must be held in check if any institution is to survive. In the case of Congress, this means it must respond to demands made upon it by others (presidents, administrators, lobbyists, the press, and general and specialized publics) or at least shape or modify those demands into more manageable dimensions. At the same time it must provide its own participants (primarily members and their staffs) with outlets for realizing their own goals.

Outside and inside pressures for change produce two distinctive types of innovation: *adaptation* and *consolidation*. Adaptation refers to shifts in practices or work habits designed to adapt to external pressures. Consolidation refers to adjustments in procedures or power relationships designed to help members realize individual goals or relieve internal tensions. These two types of innovation flow from divergent sources and exert independent effects upon the institution. What is more, adaptation and consolidation may pull in opposing directions, forcing the institution to make difficult and costly choices. An organization may adapt well to outside demands, but at painful human costs to its participants; or it may handle its internal affairs effectively, only to fall more and more out of touch with its larger environment.

FISSURES IN THE COMMITTEE SYSTEM

Pressures for change frequently converge upon congressional committees and subcommittees. These work groups are the nerve ends of Congress — gatherers of information, sifters of alternatives, refiners of legislation. As Woodrow Wilson wrote in 1885, "It is not far from the truth to say that Congress in session is Congress on public exhibition, whilst Congress in its committee-rooms is Congress at work."[6] Typically, it is in the committees and subcommittees that members' reputations are made and careers nurtured.

External pressures on the committees usually emanate from the number and type of problems presented to Congress for resolution. As the number and scope of public issues has grown, so has the trend toward work group proliferation on Capitol Hill through committees and, more recently, subcommittees. By the same token, committee jurisdictions shift as novel topics appear and old topics fade from view. The creation (and sometimes abolition) of major committees corresponds with historical events or shifting public problems — in the House, for example, Commerce and Manufactures (1795), Public Lands (1805), Freedmen's Affairs (1866), Roads (1913), Science and Astronautics (1958), and Ethics (1967), to name a few.[7]

Internal or consolidative pressures upon the committee system in the past generation took the form of factional conflict over committee and subcommittee chairmanships and memberships. The resulting war over the seniority system was essentially an ideological and generational dispute within the Democratic ranks caused by a temporary mismatch between the party's senior leadership (conservative, southern) and its rank and file (increasingly northern and liberal). By the late 1960s this internal contradiction was resolved in favor of youth and liberalism. In the House skirmishes were spasmodic and occasionally bloody, punctuated by a series of intracommittee revolts against recalcitrant chairmen, dispersion of power into the subcommittees (1971 and 1973), and finally overthrow of several unpopular committee chairmen (1975).[8] In the Senate the transformation was noticeably more rapid and smooth because burgeoning subcommittees and staffs gave nearly every senator a chance to participate.

The dispersion of the committee system, effected in the 1960s and 1970s to equalize participation, has yielded a new generation of problems, consolidative as well as adaptive. Studies in 1976 showed that the average House member had 6 committee and subcommittee assignments, the average senator almost 18.[9] With so many assignments, members are harder pressed than ever to manage their crowded schedules. Scheduling problems are endemic, with committee quorums difficult to achieve and members' attention less focused than it once was. During midweek peak days (Tuesday through Thursday mornings), it is commonplace for members to face scheduling conflicts of two, three, or more of their committees.

Even more vexing was the unwieldy nature of committee jurisdictions. Aside from sporadic attempts to consolidate proliferating committees, the first broad-scale effort to bring order to jurisdictions was the Legislative Reorganization Act of 1946. "Modernization of the standing committee system," wrote the staff expert who drafted the law, "was the first objective of the Act and the keystone in the arch of congressional reform."[10] The act codified jurisdictional precedents and embodied them in House and Senate rules. It also trimmed the number of committees from 48 to 19 in the House and from 33 to 15 in the Senate.

In a fast-changing world, time quickly outran the 1946 reforms. Although the number of committees was curtailed, subcommittees sprouted in their place; by the 93rd Congress there were 57 standing and special committees (House, Senate, joint) and 288 standing and special subcommittees — a total of 345 work units for 535 legislators. When new issues arose, new panels were created or, more frequently, several committees maneuvered for their "piece of the action." Workloads varied widely. In a "Dear Colleague" letter dated December 29, 1972, proposing a concerted study of the committee system, then-Representative John C. Culver (D-Iowa) summarized the situation:

> Some of our committees are already catch-basins for miscellaneous or tenuously related subjects; others have acquired an unmanageable breadth of subject matter. . .; still other standing committees have jurisdictions too archaic or too narrowly conceived when viewed against modern public policy issues. And there are other policies . . . such as urban affairs, health services, the environment, economic conversion, energy, national population distribution and growth which fit at best uncomfortably and sometimes not at all into the committee structure within which we now operate.

By the early 1970s the committee system was in serious disarray. Some of the problems were external (adaptive): committee jurisdictions and emerging public issues were mismatched, and the dispersed committee system often failed to aggregate related pieces of a policy.

Yet internal (consolidative) consequences occurred as well, such as jurisdictional rivalries and scheduling conflicts. Legislators themselves professed to be profoundly dissatisfied with the committee structure. In a 1973 survey of 101 House and Senate members, a foreign policy study commission discovered that 81 percent were dissatisfied with "committee jurisdictions and the way they are defined in Congress."[11] Only one percent of the legislators were "very satisfied" with the jurisdictional situation, while 13 percent were "very dissatisfied."

The two houses endeavored to tidy up their deteriorating committee systems. The House established a Select Committee on Committees (the Bolling Committee) in 1973. Its wide-ranging report, presented in March 1974, triggered intense opposition from committee leaders who opposed curbs on their jurisdictions, not to mention those alliances known as "iron triangles" (composed of committee members and staffs, lobby groups, and executive agencies), that feared that structural shifts would unwire their mutually beneficial alliances. A weaker substitute plan, drafted hastily by a Democratic Caucus group, was adopted in October 1974 and took effect in the 94th Congress.

In the Senate, pressure for a similar study was mounting, and in March 1976 the Temporary Select Committee to Study the Senate Committee System (the Stevenson Committee) was created. Within six months a committee reorganization plan was produced, and a modified version was adopted in 1977 at the opening of the 95th Congress.

Committee organization is the province of both houses of Congress under the constitutional mandate in Article I, section 5, that "each house may determine the rules of its proceedings." Yet modifying the committee system presents an acute political challenge that threatens to upset the institution's internal balance, affecting not only legislators' and staff members' careers but also their mutually supportive relationships with potent outside clientele groups. Although the present committee structure may fit imperfectly with categories of public problems, it is buttressed by the so-called "iron triangles."

The House and Senate efforts at realigning their committees, though addressed to the same problem, had different origins, followed different courses, and enjoyed different results. The story of these efforts at committee reorganization reveals much about the contemporary House and Senate and their processes of change.

THE BOLLING COMMITTEE (1973-1974)

Origins of the Committee

Late in 1972 Speaker Carl Albert, Minority Leader Gerald Ford, and senior Rules Democrat Richard Bolling from Missouri agreed the time was ripe to re-evaluate the committee system in the House.[12] Although as leaders they were held publicly accountable for congressional performance, they lacked the tools to coordinate or schedule the legislative program. Especially troublesome was the Arkansas Democrat Wilbur Mills's Ways and Means Committee, which followed its own deliberate timetable in handling its vast jurisdiction. Although John Culver (D-Iowa) and a number of other legislators were calling for committee reform, initiative for the inquiry belonged to the leadership.

As drafted by Bolling and approved by Albert and Ford, the strategy called for a small bipartisan committee — seats, staff, and funds divided equally between Democrats and Republicans — to study the problem and present its recommendations to the House before the close of the 93rd Congress. The House resolution (H. Res. 132) establishing the committee was adopted 282-91 — a comfortable margin, but far from unanimous. Many members had their own ideas about how the study should proceed.

Bolling and Dave Martin (R-Neb.), the Rules Committee ranking Republican and cosponsor of the resolution, served as chairman and vice-chairman respectively of the Select Committee on Committees. The other eight members (4 Democrats, 4 Republicans) named by the Speaker were geographically and ideologically balanced.[13] However, there was a bias that was not immediately apparent: virtually all the members were considered electorally "safe." This meant they had time to study the House and freedom to reach their own conclusions. And while four subcommittee chairmen and two ranking minority members sat on the committee, they were, with one or two exceptions, reform-minded members. (All the Democrats were associates of Bolling, a strong-willed, reform-minded student of the House who was once a protégé of the legendary Speaker Sam Rayburn.) Hence, they acted as independent "trustees" rather than instructed delegates from constituencies in or out of the House. Although this progressive outlook helped the members of the Bolling Committee take a fresh look at the committee system, it set them apart from many of their colleagues.

Evolution of the Blueprint

To gather information on the House "reform market," the committee employed several techniques with varying success. An effort by committee members to interview their colleagues for ideas soon lagged as the session proceeded and schedules became crowded. Committee staff members interviewed more than 150 staff personnel from other committees. Staff and consultant studies were undertaken on specific topics. Thirty-seven days of hearings were held, and testimony from House members was heard. Sixty-eight members (including 13 chairmen) appeared or submitted statements, while 39 experts and 16 public witnesses presented views on a variety of topics. The 1,765 pages of record add up to a detailed portrait of the House of Representatives as seen by members, lobbyists, scholars, and other observers.[14]

During the fall of 1973, a preliminary committee plan was drafted in several stages. First, an intensive working session was held one weekend at Bolling's country home. Then, Paul Sarbanes (D-Md.) and William Steiger (R-Wis.) were delegated to work with the staff on a draft report for discussion purposes. The full committee refined this draft, releasing it as a trial balloon just before the Christmas recess.

Reactions to the trial balloon were not long in coming. As Bolling remarked wryly, "It took awhile to get everyone's attention, but I think now we've got it." The draft report was then worked over in a series of remarkably candid open markup sessions. Adjustments were made to incorporate new information, correct errors, and placate anticipated opposition. The committee's final report, presented unanimously on March 21, 1974, contained a wide range of recommendations for committee jurisdictions, member assignments, staffing, information resources, and rules and procedures. A resolution embodying many of the proposals (H. Res. 93-988) was introduced at the same time.

The Bolling Plan

The Bolling plan (as it came to be known) was a compromise. A majority within the committee favored a "single-track" approach, with each legislator assigned to a single committee whose jurisdiction would be broad and relatively equal to that of other committees. A minority favored multiple assignments, perhaps even with increased numbers of narrowly based committees. Practical and political objections to the single-track approach forced a compromise calling for 15 exclusive and 7 nonexclusive committees:

Exclusive Committees

Agriculture and Forestry; Appropriations; Armed Services; Banking, Currency and Housing; Commerce and Health; Education; Energy and Environment; Foreign Affairs; Government Operations; Judiciary; Labor; Public Works and Transportation; Rules; Science and Technology; Ways and Means.

Nonexclusive Committees

Budget; House Administration; Standards of Official Conduct; Merchant Marine and Fisheries; Small Business; District of Columbia; Veterans Affairs.

The plan embraced scores of jurisdictional shifts. Two standing committees (Internal Security; Post Office and Civil Service) would have been eliminated; 14 others were affected significantly.

Four principles underlay the reorganization plan: subject matter coherence, balance of interests, equality of workload, and political salability. The first two goals were primarily adaptive in character, focusing upon the organization of demands and tasks imposed by the external environment. The remaining goals were primarily matters of internal equity. The resulting package was a patchwork of compromises rather than a consistent model of how the House should operate. As it turned out, even these compromises proved insufficient.

Rather than pursuing the illusory goal of total subject matter coherence, the Bolling plan focused on a few pressing issue areas: energy, the environment, transportation, health, and international economic affairs. Energy and environmental concerns would be consolidated; transportation would become the vortex of an expanded Public Works Committee; the Commerce Committee would gain a new health domain, including nontax aspects of Medicare (from Ways and Means); and international economics would become the province of the Foreign Affairs Committee. In other areas the Select Committee on Committees contented itself with correcting the most glaring anachronisms that had crept into jurisdictional alignments.

According to the so-called "balanced committee concept," broad-based panels would attract a wider cross section of members and produce more equitable policy. Biased membership is a problem in many committees, especially those with traditional "pork" or "interest" focuses. For example, farm-belt legislators are drawn to Agriculture, westerners to Interior, and those from port cities to Merchant Marine.[15]

The reorganization plan tackled this problem unevenly. An early suggestion for attaching resource policies to Agriculture drew such angry cries from environmentalists that the committee retreated, suggesting instead additions primarily in public lands and forestry. A proposal to abolish Merchant Marine and Fisheries and transfer its functions to more broad-based panels was also withdrawn because of vocal objections from maritime interests. The committee's plan did, however, include an innovative marriage of energy and environmental matters into a single committee, as well as linkage of transportation to traditional public works affairs (including highways).

Unequal committee workloads hamper efficiency, and the Bolling plan sought to trim the most glaring disparities. Research showed that several committees — most notably, Ways and Means, Commerce, and Education and Labor — were seriously overburdened by far-ranging duties and a heavy flow of bills. Other committees, including Agriculture, Foreign Affairs, Internal Security, Merchant Marine, Post

Office and Civil Service, Public Works, and Science and Astronautics, were underutilized. Adjustments were proposed to alleviate these inequities such as phasing out the Internal Security and Post Office panels.

In the markup sessions Bolling and his colleagues made numerous concessions to placate those threatened with losses. So many compromises were made, in fact, that much of the plan's original symmetry was lost. Yet for members and staff affected by the plan, the Bolling group offered little aside from a recommendation that party caucuses take account of members' jurisdictional losses in making new committee assignments. This was considered a caucus matter and outside the select committee's jurisdiction. Nor did Bolling's committee attempt to negotiate further once the reform package was reported. Bolling held that as chairman he was obliged to support the committee's product; neither Speaker Albert nor other leaders stepped in to mediate. Thus the plan appeared as an adaptive change that held little attraction for individual members aside from the overall efficiency it promised to bring to the House.

Ambushing the Plan

The reorganization plan touched the hypersensitive nerve ends of a decentralized House: that is, legislators' and staff members' individual careers and their relationships with outside clienteles. While Bolling and his colleagues had few illusions about the sources of their opposition, they severely underestimated its intensity. As Majority Leader Thomas P. O'Neill Jr. (D-Mass.) put it then, "The name of the game is power, and the boys don't want to give it up."

The plan aroused bitter, personal opposition. While members were not well-informed about the plan as a whole, they quickly fixed on those provisions that affected them directly. Those who would lose power were more vocal than those who stood to gain; assets that were in jeopardy seemed more tangible than expected benefits. Thus H. Res. 988 split the majority Democrats, lost the support of most House leaders, and won few vocal supporters. All too often, Bolling and his colleagues were preoccupied with defending their plan against criticisms rather than urging its merits.

The reorganization plan fell victim to a reverse-lobbying process in which committee members and staffs, fighting to preserve their positions, mobilized support from outside groups that had previously benefited from committee decisions. Many congressional panels are key links in alliances known as subgovernments or "iron triangles," as we have already mentioned. Outside groups, especially in organized labor, rallied to protect the alliances they had established on the Hill. Jurisdictional realignment threatened some of these mutually beneficial networks. As one journalist explained, "Carefully nurtured contacts with key congressmen and their aides, as well as years of selective campaign contributions, will all come loose when a new, unfamiliar committee takes jurisdiction."[16]

Opposition to the Bolling Committee's efforts solidified in the Democratic Caucus, which decided by a 16-vote margin to refer the plan to the "Committee on Organization, Study and Review," then called the Hansen Committee after its chairwoman, Julia Butler Hansen (D-Wash.). This was the same caucus committee that in 1971 and 1972 had drafted subcommittee decentralization rules. Many of the beneficiaries of the "subcommittee bill of rights," which broadened participation among younger, more liberal Democrats, found themselves in an awkward, antireform posture as they lobbied to bury the Bolling plan.

Because of the vocal opposition of the Hansen group, reorganization of the committee system might have been shelved altogether had it not been for a drumbeat of criticism kept up by reform-minded Republicans, proreform groups such as Common Cause and Americans for Democratic Action, and a host of newspaper editorial writers. Several members, including Mrs. Hansen, insisted that the group produce a counterproposal. In the wake of the Watergate revelations, with public approval of Congress at an all-time low, it would have been politically unthinkable for the majority Democrats to scuttle reform altogether. Thus a Hansen Committee plan was unveiled on July 17, 1974.

The Hansen substitute was a hastily assembled pastiche of provisions acceptable to the group's various members. In most respects the Hansen plan was simply the Bolling plan with its controversial features excised. Jurisdictional shifts were minimized to make reorganization palatable to Democrats whose committees would have been adversely affected by H. Res. 988. Education and Labor was kept intact, Post Office and Civil Service was retained, and Merchant Marine and Fisheries strengthened rather than emasculated — moves aimed at appeasing key labor unions. Ways and Means lost little of its vast authority, although internal dispersion of power through subcommittees was mandated. Committees that Bolling sought to strengthen — mainly Foreign Affairs, Public Works, Science and Astronautics, and Government Operations — gained fewer new duties than under the earlier scheme.

As the 93rd Congress edged toward adjournment, public attention was riveted on the Nixon impeachment hearings and subsequent resignation. Meanwhile, foes of the House reorganization staged prolonged battles in the caucus (July) and the Rules Committee (September). Despite this opposition, the Bolling and Hansen resolutions reached the House floor September 30, 1974. Six days of sometimes tedious, sometimes raucous debate ensued. On the key vote on October 8th the Hansen substitute with some further modifications was adopted over the Bolling plan, 203-165.

Unfinished Agenda

The final reorganization was a pale shadow of what the Bolling Committee had recommended, but some noticeable gains were made. All major categories of transportation except railroads — a special interest of Commerce Chairman Harley O. Staggers (D-W.Va.) — were gathered into Public Works and Transportation. An invigorated Science and Technology Committee assumed overall responsibility for government research and development programs. Foreign Affairs began to operate under broadly worded new language. And most health responsibilities became concentrated in Commerce, although Ways and Means retained most of its leverage on medical financing through payroll taxes. Energy and environmental issues remained as scattered and uncoordinated as ever.

More notable gains occurred in nonjurisdictional matters. Following the Bolling group's recommendation, the House adopted a provision broadening the Speaker's power of referring bills to committees. The Speaker may now refer a bill jointly, in parts, or sequentially, to two or more panels. Joint, split, and sequential referrals have been employed for thousands of bills. The House also adopted a provision enabling the Speaker to create ad hoc committees to process bills falling between two or more standing committees.

Despite these palliatives, the House committee system remains in need of major repair. Scheduling problems are as numerous as ever, especially during prime mid-week hours. Jurisdictional conflicts among committees have escalated, hampering policymaking in dozens of areas. Ad hoc committees are convenient for a few pressing issues, but they add another layer to the committee system and cannot be employed every time two or more committees lay claims upon a bill.

House members profess to want committee reorganization but have been reluctant to pay the price to remedy the defects. In interviews with 153 members of the House in 1977, committee structure was the most frequently mentioned "obstacle" preventing the House from doing its job.[17] "Scheduling" and "institutional inertia" were next in line. By far the most frequently mentioned suggestion for improving Congress was reforming the committee structure: 41 percent of the representatives interviewed mentioned it. Yet later that same year the House summarily rejected the report of its Commission on Administrative Review (the Obey Commission), which included a call for a new committee investigation.

Needless to say, the 1974 innovations were inadequate to cure the House committees' ills. Complaints by members themselves about the unwieldiness and inefficiency of the committee structure persisted. In January 1979 both the Democratic Caucus and the Republican Conference voted in favor of a new Select Committee on Committees. Approved two months later, the 15-person panel was directed to study committee structures, jurisdictions, rules and procedures, media coverage of meetings, staffing, and facilities. The new select committee was to report its findings by February 1, 1980. The resolution creating the panel (H. Res. 118) was approved by the narrow margin of 208-200, and its funding by a 212-180 vote — hardly a resounding sendoff!

"Without strong leadership backing," Lee Hamilton (D-Ind.) predicted, "there won't be major changes."[18] In fact, Democratic leaders were unenthusiastic about this new inquiry. None of the top leaders — Speaker O'Neill, Majority Leader James Wright (D-Texas), and Chief Whip John Brademas (D-Ind.) — had supported the 1974 Bolling plan, and their coolness toward committee realignment had not abated. Wright was quoted as remarking that committee restructuring was "taking things from one box and putting them in another. I never thought it made much difference."[19]

Despite their ambivalence, leaders had a stake in the committee inquiry. For one thing, it provided a post for Jerry Patterson (D-Calif.), an amiable, low-key third-termer who was named to chair the inquiry. Earlier Patterson had been the choice of California Democrats for a Rules Committee vacancy, but at the urging of Rules Chairman Bolling another Californian (Anthony Beilenson) got the nod. More importantly, the leadership could benefit from committee realignment, particularly in the area of energy policy that involved some 83 House committees and subcommittees. Previous leadership efforts to coordinate the scattered energy jurisdiction had not resolved the basic jurisdictional confusion. Especially controversial was John Dingell's Commerce Subcommittee on Energy and Power, a panel more powerful than many committees and criticized as a bottleneck on such issues as synthetic fuels and the Energy Department authorization.

Rather than risking a full-scale committee realignment plan, the Patterson group decided to concentrate on consolidating energy jurisdiction. At least four influential House Democrats were jockeying for position: Interior Chairman Morris K. Udall (D-Ariz.), Science and Technology Chairman Don Fuqua (D-Fla.), Energy and Power Subcommittee Chairman Dingell, and Thomas Ashley (D-Ohio), an ally of the Speaker who had chaired the ad hoc energy panel in the 95th Congress. Testifying before the Patterson panel, Ashley made a forceful case for a new, separate energy committee. Ashley's proposal apparently had the backing of Speaker O'Neill.

The modest plan for a new energy panel stirred up fierce opposition among those who stood to forfeit jurisdiction. A parade of committee leaders appeared before the Rules Committee to denounce the plan; and the affected leaders rushed to embrace a conciliatory proposal authored by Jonathan Bingham (D-N.Y.) and designed to apportion the jurisdiction among those committees already exercising authority. The Bingham substitute, cemented by an elaborate series of agreements signed by all the relevant chairmen, was eventually adopted by the House, 274-134.

On the eve of the floor debate, Speaker O'Neill told reporters that "the cardinals of the House" had rallied behind the Bingham scheme to give Commerce more jurisdiction and leave everything else alone. O'Neill actually claimed to favor a GOP plan, endorsed by Patterson at the last minute, but because that plan was procedurally to be offered as a Republican motion to recommit with instructions, O'Neill felt he could not support it.[20] In essence, the Speaker walked away from the issue, leaving his colleagues free to vote as they wished.

Without leadership support — O'Neill was conspicuously absent from the floor debate — Ashley declined to speak out for a separate committee, even though he was the presumed beneficiary. The predicament was not lost on House observers. The bitterest criticism came from Toby Moffett (D-Conn.), who declared that "maybe nothing is the answer today until we get the leadership and everyone else who is interested in a regular energy committee to come forward, to get behind somebody to put an energy committee together and to offer it as an alternative."[21]

THE STEVENSON COMMITTEE (1976-1977)

In the Senate, committee realignment was initiated by agitation from junior members — not, as in the House, by the leadership. Complaints about the Senate committee system, sporadic during the 1960s, mounted in the 1970s. Prominent among the critics were junior senators Fred Harris (D-Okla.), Adlai Stevenson III (D-Ill.), Charles Mathias (R-Md.), and Bill Brock (R-Tenn.). Undeterred by the mixed results of the 1974 House reorganization effort, Stevenson and Brock in March 1975 introduced S. Res. 109, which called for the establishment of a temporary select committee to investigate a variety of committee-related problems. The resolution stated that changes were needed to promote:

> optimum utilization of Senators' time, optimum effectiveness of committees in the creation and oversight of Federal programs, clear and consistent procedures for the referral of legislation falling within the jurisdiction of two or more committees, and workable methods for the regular review and revision of committee jurisdictions.

Although the Stevenson-Brock resolution gained no less than 55 cosponsors — a majority of the Senate — it languished for nearly a year in the Rules and Administration Committee before gaining new life in February 1976 when the Subcommittee on the Standing Rules of the Senate, chaired by Robert C. Byrd (D-W.Va.), held hearings on it. With the proposed committee's budget trimmed and its timetable compressed from two years to eleven months, S. Res. 109 was reported by the Rules Committee on March 30 and adopted by a voice vote the next day. The crucial decision to proceed with the inquiry was made by Byrd, the Majority Whip and a master mechanic of the Senate's procedures. The retirement of Majority Leader Mike Mansfield (D-Mont.) had just been announced. Byrd presumably sought to bolster his chances to succeed Mansfield by demonstrating sympathy for reform and responsiveness to younger members' desires. Although the impetus for the Senate's inquiry into its committee system came from the back benches, the decision to proceed, and the tacit sponsorship implied by that decision, came from the leadership — more precisely from Robert Byrd.

The Temporary Select Committee to Study the Senate Committee System, chaired by Stevenson and cochaired by Brock, manifested certain of the biases of its House counterpart. Its 12 members, equally divided between the parties, were somewhat more junior than the Senate average, and the only committee chairmen in the group were from minor panels.[22] Like the Bolling Committee, a disproportionate number of the members of the Stevenson Committee came from the ranks of those anxious to take a fresh look at committee structure and willing to see substantial alterations. As the House experience proved, this can be a mixed blessing. Although it makes for a more dedicated, cohesive investigating unit, it also sets them somewhat apart from their colleagues.

Drafting the Blueprints

The Stevenson Committee's information-gathering process differed from the House pattern in two respects.[23] First, it was accomplished far more quickly. The abbreviated schedule was a matter of necessity. By the time the committee began its work, the second session of the 94th Congress was well under way with adjournment less than six months off. It was decided that recommendations on committee assignments and jurisdictions should be prepared by adjournment, so that the Senate could consider them early in 1977 at the outset of the 95th Congress. Less pressing matters, such as committee staffing, facilities, procedures, and jurisdictional review, would be dealt with later. This timetable made lengthy hearings and panel discussions such as those that had marked the House inquiry impossible. Indeed, the work done by Bolling and his colleagues benefited the Senate reformers by identifying salient issues and showing which approaches were fruitful and which were not. In short, a duplicate effort in the Senate was simply not required.

A second hallmark of the Senate investigation was that it was accomplished almost entirely by staff, rather than cooperatively by staff and members. This reflects a basic difference in the traditional operation of the two bodies — a difference that has faded markedly in recent years. In accord with traditional House norms, Bolling and a majority of his colleagues insisted on gaining personal mastery of the subject matter. They used staff aides to collect data but not to formulate solutions or make decisions. In contrast, senators rely upon staff aides not only for background research but also for many decisions, reserving for themselves the most basic strategic and political considerations.

Stevenson and Brock were briefed frequently on the staff's activities and soon gained familiarity with the subject. Other members' knowledge was more generalized, excepting the information they possessed from their other committee assignments. In the markup sessions the divergent staff role was manifested in a subtle but significant way: during the House deliberations staff members remained discreetly behind the legislators, who sat at the table, but Senate staff members sat with the senators or at the witness table.

The bulk of the staff's research was completed during the bicentennial summer of 1976. Lengthy, structured interviews were conducted with designated majority and minority staff aides from all of the Senate committees and many of the subcommittees. Massive data-collection projects concerning committee assignments, jurisdictions, workloads, and staffing were commissioned from the Library of Congress's Congressional Research Service. The result was a factual compendium entitled *The Senate Committee System,* detailing the history and problems of the Senate's committee system.[24] The staff report documented the widely held assumption that senators were acutely overextended by their committee assignments. The average senator, it was discovered, served on no less than 20 committees, subcommittees, joint bodies, boards, and commissions.

Also documented were jurisdictional overlaps. For example, 17 committees and at least 40 subcommittees held some jurisdiction over the energy problem. Nor was the situation much different in other pressing fields — economic growth, the environment, education, science and technology, transportation, and welfare, to name a few. In summarizing the case against the existing committee setup, the staff asserted:

> Jurisdictional overlaps, however desirable when maintained at moderate levels, have gotten out of hand. ... The Senate rarely, if ever, takes a comprehensive look at such problems as transportation or energy. Rather, what passes for policy in these matters is a series of disparate and sometimes contradictory enactments, frequently proceeding in wholly different directions. Mechanisms for intercommittee cooperation, while highly developed in the Senate (in contrast to the other body), are cumbersome and time consuming. It is questionable, moreover, whether these procedures actually achieve integrated policymaking, or whether they merely serve to protect the interest of the committees involved.[25]

Armed with these findings, the committee "went public" with their first hearings. As in the House, it proved difficult to capture the attention of other legislators who, not without reason, doubted that anything would come of the reform effort. Only 13 senators appeared to testify. The witnesses, mostly Republicans and junior Democrats, proposed a bewildering variety of innovations. Most asked for fewer committees and subcommittees, limits on assignments, and jurisdictional realignment. All complained about crowded schedules, and all supported the overall goal of committee reorganization.

Like their House counterparts, the Senate reformers discovered they needed a trial balloon to grab the attention of their colleagues. In August 1976 they set loose a second staff report that unveiled three specific starting points for reorganizing Senate committees:[26]

(I) *Minimal-change Plan.* The existing committees would be modified incrementally with somewhat modernized jurisdictions, smaller committees, assignment and chairmanship limits, a new scheduling service, and stronger party leadership. This approach was essentially a tidying up of the existing committee system.

(II) *Twelve-Committee Plan.* Twelve committees with broad, functionally based jurisdictions formed the core of this plan, which was designed to "rationalize the jurisdictions of committees and minimize overlap among them by organizing the committee system according to major functional categories." Limits would be placed upon committee assignments (two per senator), chairmanships (one full committee chairmanship per senator, two subcommittee chairmanships), and the number of subcommittees (120). The leadership would have increased referral powers.

(III) *Five-Committee Plan.* Five "functional-management" committees of 20 members each (Governmental Resources; Human Resources; Financial Resources; Defense and Foreign Policy; Natural

Resources) would manage their respective agendas, whereas detailed legislative work would be handled by 60 subcommittees. Each senator would be assigned to one committee and three subcommittees; assignments and chairmanships would be rotated periodically.

These three starting points, especially the most radical five-committee plan, had the anticipated effect of throwing serious attention on the Stevenson Committee's work. On September 8, Majority Leader Mansfield presented a floor statement on the alternative plans, and the *National Journal* ran a story stressing the five-committee option.[27]

When the select committee held further hearings in mid-September, 24 senators appeared or wrote letters to Stevenson and Brock. Such Senate heavyweights as John Stennis (D-Miss.) and Frank Church (D-Idaho) were on hand to combat a suggested merger of their Armed Services and Foreign Relations Committees (part of starting points II and III). Senators Frank Moss (D-Utah) and Barry Goldwater (R-Ariz.), chairman and ranking minority member of the Aeronautical and Space Sciences Committee, proposed a new science panel in an attempt to preserve their positions. Environmental lobbyists also got in the act. They protested linking energy and environmental issues (starting points II and III). House committee reformer Richard Bolling wrote to object to the projected elimination (starting points II and III) of the Joint Economic Committee on which he served as vice chairman.[28]

Stevenson, Brock, and their colleagues adopted the 12-committee plan, starting point II. The Senate was not ready to accept the five-committee managerial scheme. On the other hand, the committee's members were not content merely to tinker with existing arrangements. They believed they should begin with a bold blueprint, knowing that accommodations would have to be made. As Stevenson later remarked, the committee asked for 140 percent of what they wanted in order to get 75 percent. It then took Stevenson's group seven days of open markup sessions to refine starting point II into a workable plan, introduced at the close of the 94th Congress as S. Res. 586.

The Stevenson Plan

Although tailored to the realities of Senate power, the Stevenson plan was surprisingly bold and symmetrical. It was, in other words, a blend of adaptive and consolidative elements. According to the proposal, the number of committees would be slashed from 31 to 15:

> Agriculture and Small Business; Appropriations; Armed Services; Banking, Housing and Urban Affairs; Budget; Commerce, Science and Transportation; Energy and Natural Resources; Environment

and Public Works; Finance; Foreign Relations; Governmental Affairs; Human Resources; Judiciary; Rules, Administration, and Standards; and Select Intelligence.

Four standing committees — District of Columbia, Post Office and Civil Service, Aeronautical and Space Sciences, and Veterans Affairs — would be abolished under the reorganization. Except for the Intelligence panel, all select, special, and joint committees were to be eliminated.

In addition, scores of major jurisdictional shifts were scheduled. Energy matters would be consolidated from several committees into one (the old Interior panel). International economics would go to Banking, environmental affairs to the old Public Works panel. Human Resources (Labor and Public Welfare) would gain veterans' affairs, aging, and macroeconomic planning. Governmental Affairs would assume major legislative jurisdiction over civil service, Postal Service, District of Columbia, and insular affairs. And the Commerce panel would become a holding company for science, transportation, and communications.

Other adaptive problems were addressed by nonjurisdictional innovations. The concept of "comprehensive policy oversight" was developed to give committees oversight duties over broad-gauged issues, even for specific portions of a policy within another panel's jurisdiction. Computerized scheduling of committee meetings would be introduced. Majority and Minority Leaders were authorized to give continuing review to the committee system.

Starting from a rigorous blueprint, Stevenson and his colleagues had made numerous adjustments to placate key senators. It is said that the Senate no longer has an "inner club" — a privileged group of powerful senior members dominating the institution. Yet certain senators are decidedly more equal than others, and Stevenson's group was counselled to avoid alienating such senior chairmen as John Stennis (D-Miss.), Jennings Randolph (D-W. Va.), Warren Magnuson (D-Wash.), Henry Jackson (D-Wash.), Russell Long (D-La.), and Abraham Ribicoff (D-Conn.). It was no accident that Magnuson's Commerce Committee and Jackson's Interior panel were big "winners" in the Stevenson plan, or that Long's vast Finance jurisdiction (five of whose members sat on the select committee) went virtually untouched. The notion of a combined energy-environment panel was scuttled, not to placate environmentalists (as in the House), but to preserve the separate domains of Jackson (energy) and Randolph (environment). The most painful decision reached by the Stevenson group was to eliminate the space committee. This decision particularly angered two members of the panel — Frank Moss, who was waging a losing re-election battle, and Barry Goldwater.

Even more important consolidative features of the plan were those aimed at spreading out committee assignments and leadership posts. Senators would be limited to eight assignments — three committees (two major panels and a "third" one) and five subcommittees (two within each major panel and one on the "third"). No senator could hold more than one committee chairmanship and one subcommittee chairmanship per committee. These rules were intended to end the hoarding by certain senior senators of choice leadership posts and to give junior senators better assignments.

Negotiating the Final Plan

The fall elections gave further impetus to reorganization. Eighteen new senators entered the Senate in January 1977 — the largest freshman class in a generation. Nearly half the Senate had arrived after 1970, when Stevenson had first been elected. Although Cochairman of the Stevenson Committee Bill Brock was an electoral casualty, also defeated were three senators whose committees were slated for elimination: Frank Moss (D-Utah) of Aeronautics and Space, Gale McGee (D-Wyo.) of Post Office, and Vance Hartke (D-Ind.) of Veterans' Affairs.

Stevenson and Robert Packwood (R-Ore.), Brock's successor as cochairman, arranged with Senate leaders for the reorganization package to receive a speedy hearing in the Rules and Administration Committee, followed by debate in the full Senate.[29] In the meantime, no new committee assignments would be made. (Under pressure from new senators, however, "temporary" assignments were awarded.) Cloture and other rules changes, subject to filibuster, would be delayed until after reorganization had been accomplished. These conditions were adopted by unanimous consent — a typical Senate scheduling technique — when Stevenson introduced the package in the new Congress as S. Res. 4.

Final bargaining over committee reorganization took place in the Rules and Administration Committee during five days of hearings and six days of open markup sessions. Parading before the committee were veterans, public employees, native Americans, small businessmen, the elderly, and other lobbyists who feared the reorganization would hurt their groups. Thirty-nine senators affected by the committee shuffle appeared to plead their cases. Stevenson and Packwood were on hand to present the plan, outline its advantages, and defend it against destructive amendments. Key Rules and Administration negotiators included Chairman Howard Cannon (D-Nev.), Dick Clark (D-Iowa), and of course Majority Leader Byrd — a continuing presence even though not always physically present.

The Rules and Administration panel made scores of accommodations, large and small, to senators, staff members, and lobby groups.

New life was given to five panels slated for elimination under Stevenson's plan: Veterans' Affairs, Standards and Conduct (renamed Ethics), Select Small Business, Joint Economic, and Joint Internal Revenue Taxation. The committee also rejected several proposed jurisdictional shifts. On one occasion Senator Magnuson and four of his Commerce Committee colleagues showed up unannounced at the markup to protest a decision to shift environmental aspects of oceans to the Environment and Public Works Committee. These five senators remained at the witness table, filibuster-like, until Rules and Administration voted to give oceans back to Commerce!

The panel relaxed the assignment limits, raising the committee and subcommittee maximum to 11 from the 8 set by the Stevenson group. Certain assignments were exempt from limitations. Rules and Administration also voted more committee staff for the minority GOP. Finally, the committee adopted a sense-of-the-Senate provision, sponsored by Dick Clark, which stated that all members should have one subcommittee assignment within a committee before any others were allowed a second assignment. This gave junior members a better chance for choice subcommittee slots that could otherwise have been hoarded by senior members.

These features broadened the plan's appeal. The Rules and Administration Committee reported it unanimously, and from January 31 to February 4, 1977, it was debated on the Senate floor. Floor debate focused upon the abolition or retention of the Post Office and Civil Service, Special Aging, and Select Nutrition Committees. Aging was reinstated, though its membership was cut down. It was voted to phase out Nutrition gradually, retaining it through 1977 with fewer members. A motion to retain Post Office was tabled — a major victory for reformers. Broadening still further the plan's utility for junior members, the Senate adopted a Clark amendment prohibiting full committee chairmen from heading more than two subcommittees on major panels, plus one other chairmanship on a nonmajor panel. Not surprisingly, every full committee chairman who was present voted to table this amendment.

After five days of debate all controversies were resolved. The Senate passed S. Res. 4 by a vote of 89 to 1. Only Quentin Burdick (D-N.D.), in line to chair the Post Office panel, dissented. In its traditional style the Senate had composed its differences and produced a consensus product.

Results of Reorganization

The Senate committee reorganization was incremental, but by no means insignificant. The number of Senate committees (standing, special, joint) was reduced nearly a quarter, from 31 to 24. Sub-committees were cut by one third, from 174 to 117. Average assignments dropped from 18 committee and subcommittee assignments in the 94th Congress to 11 in the 95th.

The Stevenson Committee's reorganization plan has also reduced jurisdictional overlap and competition. Scheduling conflicts for committee meetings and hearings have declined markedly. Workloads have been equalized to the extent that assignments are trimmed and jurisdictions consolidated. Junior senators gained some notable committee and subcommittee posts. In these ways, S. Res. 4 has made the Senate a more viable work environment for the bulk of its members. Realignments have enhanced the coherence of the committees' jurisdictions. Notable gains are seen in the fields of energy, science and technology, human resources, and governmental affairs. Less successful were efforts to consolidate environmental matters, transportation, or international economics. Moreover, the Finance Committee still holds a tight grip on a vast array of substantive issues linked only by their proximity to tax codes.

Gains in nonjurisdictional items have been less extensive than those in the House. Presumably at Byrd's suggestion, leadership authority to propose ad hoc authorizing committees was omitted from the plan, though language was retained mandating review of the committee system by the Rules and Administration Committee in consultation with the joint leadership. The concept of "comprehensive policy oversight," although not immediately exploited, is a potential tool for oversight and policy review that transcends narrow jurisdictional boundaries.

When Adlai Stevenson declared that the Senate had approved "the most extensive reorganization since the committee system was created in the early nineteenth century," he did not exaggerate.[30] Although numerous compromises marred the original plan's logic, these adjustments bolstered the reform's consolidative features and facilitated acceptance by the Senate. By containing conflict, moreover, these compromises helped insure that the new system would be implemented with a minimum of evasion or backsliding.

CONCLUSION: THE PROCESS OF INNOVATION

It is no accident that in the 1970s Congress adjusted its committee structures. External pressures — manifested in escalating public demands and complex, interwoven, and fast-moving problems — challenged both houses to adapt their mechanisms for processing legislation. Internal stresses, reflected in jurisdictional competition and scheduling conflicts, stretched the 1946-vintage committee structure toward its breaking point.

The two chambers responded in parallel fashion. Both created select committees to investigate the committee structure and make recommendations. The proposed reorganizations followed a similar design: consolidate and rationalize jurisdictions; reduce the number of committees, subcommittees, and member assignments; systematize scheduling; and strengthen the leadership's coordinating powers. Members and staffs in the House and Senate resisted giving up assignments or jurisdictions, and outside groups resisted change in both bodies because of real or imagined threats to their access.

Despite opposition, reforms were actually adopted, which testifies to the magnitude of adaptive and consolidative pressures for change. In final form the changes bore the imprint of each chamber. The House made minimal alterations in committee jurisdictions and none at all in controlling assignments — matters that many viewed as too partisan for the Bolling Committee's approach. The Senate, on the other hand, had no conceptual difficulty with such matters, even though given changes were often stoutly resisted.

At the same time, the House moved in one direction deliberately avoided by the Senate. This was strengthening its leadership by investing the Speaker with wider referral powers. Despite the independence of modern legislators, the House enjoys a stronger tradition of leadership than does the Senate. That is why such students of the House as Rayburn, O'Neill, and Bolling advocated careful but systematic strengthening of leadership powers, especially those of the Speaker. Equally conspicuous is the Senate's tradition of unobtrusive, personalized leadership. Byrd acknowledged this tradition by seeing to it that his referral powers were not augmented.

Although the Bolling plan was rejected and the Stevenson plan adopted, it would be an overstatement to say that the House effort "failed" whereas the Senate effort "succeeded." The differences in outcome were more subtle: large portions of the Bolling plan were included in the Hansen substitute, and by the time the Stevenson plan reached the Senate floor, amendments had watered it down. Nevertheless, it is not inaccurate to conclude that the Senate innovations were both more extensive and less controversial than those in the House. Why was this so?

Timing is a key factor in the origin and acceptance of innovations. The decade of the 1970s witnessed a remarkable (for modern times) turnover in membership of the two houses. This process was further advanced in 1977, when the Senate voted its reorganization, than when the House chose the Hansen substitute over the Bolling plan in 1974. By the time the Senate acted on S. Res. 4, a majority of its members had arrived after 1970; the House of three years earlier contained relatively fewer members of similar juniority. Had the House voted on reorganization when the Senate did, 55 percent of those voting would have arrived in 1971 or later — including the 92 members of the Watergate class and the 69 members of the class of 1976.

Junior members, who have less power to lose and less attachment to traditional procedures, comprise a powerful clientele for innovation. Significantly, the House inquiry was initiated by the leadership with what can only be described as an indifferent response from the bulk of House members. By contrast, the Senate inquiry was urged by backbenchers, with 55 senators cosponsoring the Stevenson-Brock resolution. For their own reasons the leaders eventually bowed to the pressure and agreed to the inquiry.

Once reorganization plans were drafted, the leaders' behavior in the two houses virtually reversed itself. While Speaker Albert made a series of phone calls to drum up support for the Bolling plan, neither he nor anyone else stepped forward to sponsor the delicate negotiations that would have transformed adaptive innovations into ones acceptable to a majority of members. Majority Leader Byrd and other Senate leaders, however, actively negotiated compromises between the Stevenson group and affected interests.

As a result, the Bolling plan was not as attractive to members as the Stevenson plan. It represented adaptive change that promised to make the House more effective while holding few tangible benefits for individual members. As Representative Joe Waggonner (D-La.) remarked, "It was too drastic, it went too far too quick." Senators, more harassed by multiple assignments and unworkable schedules, were ready to accept jurisdictional and assignment consolidations as a personal convenience, rather than as a threat to their influence. In short, adaptive and consolidative features were better balanced in the Senate plan than in the House version.

The Senate's readiness to acknowledge the adaptive features of committee realignment is not unrelated to a subtle but significant difference in the role of committees in the two houses. Decisionmaking is less committee-dominated in the Senate than it is in the House.[31] Senators do not specialize as intensely, or as exclusively, in committee work as do their House counterparts. Because Senate committees are more permeable to outside influences, noncommittee senators can intrude more readily in the committee's subject matter. Failing this, the Senate's more open floor procedures permit negotiations during debates on committee bills.

In the House, committee membership and rank count for more. Legislators outside a given committee encounter obstacles in influencing the measures within that committee. The House's larger size and tighter procedures preclude individual members from exerting the kind of influence that a single senator can exert in floor debate. House committees' grip on the legislative process is loosening, just as it did earlier in the Senate, because of deteriorating specialization norms and relaxed rules of floor participation. For the time being, however, House committees are regarded by members, not to mention staff and outside interests, as less mutable than Senate committees.

The story of House and Senate committee reorganization illustrates many facets of institutional innovation: its origins, its politics, its results, and its relation to institutional and environmental settings. One key issue, however, cannot be answered at such close range: the issue of institutional survival. What degree of innovation is needed to enable an institution to solve its adaptive and consolidative problems? Specifically, are the committee innovations of the 1970s adequate to preserve Congress's influence and autonomy in processing today's complex legislation? Only time can answer these questions.

NOTES

1. In this discussion a simplified theory of organizational change is applied to the U.S. Congress. See, for example, Joseph Cooper, "Strengthening Congress: An Organizational Analysis," *Harvard Journal on Legislation* 12 (April 1975): 307-368; Roger H. Davidson and Walter J. Oleszek, "Adaptation and Consolidation: Structural Innovation in the U.S. House of Representatives," *Legislative Studies Quarterly* 1 (February 1976): 37-65.
2. Joseph Cooper and David W. Brady, "Organization Theory and Congressional Structure" (Paper delivered at the annual meeting of the American Political Science Association, New Orleans, Louisiana, September 4-8, 1973).
3. U.S., Congress, House, Commission on Administrative Review, *Administrative Reorganization and Legislative Management,* 95th Cong., 1st sess., September 1977, H. Doc. 232, Part II, pp. 20-26; U.S., Congress, Senate, Commission on the Operation of the Senate, *Toward a Modern Senate,* 94th Cong., 2nd sess., December 1976, S. Doc. 94-278, pp. 4-5.
4. House Commission on Administrative Review, *Final Report,* 95th Cong., 1st sess., December 1977, H. Doc. 272, Part II, pp. 816-821.
5. Richard F. Fenno, Jr., *Congressmen in Committees,* (Boston: Little, Brown, & Co., 1973), chap. 1.
6. Woodrow Wilson, *Congressional Government* (New York: Mentor Books Edition, 1954), p. 79.
7. U.S., Congress, House, Select Committee on Committees, *Committee Reform Amendments of 1974,* 93rd Cong., 2nd sess., March 1973, H. Rept. 916, p. 13.
8. An historical overview is presented in Roger H. Davidson and Walter J. Oleszek, *Congress Against Itself* (Bloomington: Indiana University Press, 1977), pp. 32-50.

9. House Commission on Administrative Review, *Administrative Reorganization and Legislative Management,* Part II, p. 26; U.S., Congress, Senate, Temporary Select Committee to Study the Senate Committee System, *The Senate Committee System,* 94th Cong., 2nd sess., July 1976, p. 6.
10. George B. Galloway, *The Legislative Process in Congress* (New York: Thomas Y. Crowell Co., 1953), p. 591.
11. Commission on the Organization of the Government for the Conduct of Foreign Policy, *Report* (Washington, D.C.: U.S. Government Printing Office, 1975), Appendix Volume V (Appendix M). The question asked was: "Are you very satisfied, satisfied, dissatisfied, or very dissatisfied with the way committee jurisdictions are defined in Congress?"
12. The full story of the Bolling Committee is found in Davidson and Oleszek, *Congress Against Itself.*
13. The Democratic members of the House Select Committee on Committees (the Bolling Committee) were Richard Bolling (Mo.), Robert Stephens (Ga.), Lloyd Meeds (Wash.), John Culver (Iowa), and Paul Sarbanes (Md.); the Republican members were Dave Martin (Neb.), Peter Frelinghuysen (N.J.), Charles Wiggins (Calif.), William Steiger (Wis.), and C.W. Bill Young (Fla.).
14. House Select Committee on Committees, *Committee Reorganization in the House,* 94th Cong., 1st sess., 1974, H. Doc. 187, 3 vols.
15. For a more detailed exposition of this argument, see Roger H. Davidson, "Breaking Up Those 'Cozy Triangles': An Impossible Dream?" in *Legislative Reform and Public Policy,* ed. Susan Welch and John G. Peters (New York: Praeger Publishers, 1977), pp. 30-53.
16. *Washington Post,* April 29, 1974, p. A-2.
17. House Commission on Administrative Review, *Final Report,* Part II, pp. 868-869, 871-873.
18. "Tinkering with House Rules," *National Journal,* August 25, 1979, p. 1417.
19. Quoted by Richard L. Lyons in "On Capitol Hill," *Washington Post,* April 25, 1979, p. A3.
20. Richard L. Lyons, "On Capitol Hill," *Washington Post,* March 25, 1980, p. A-7.
21. U.S., Congress, House, *Congressional Record,* 96th Cong., 1st sess., March 25, 1980, 126: H2152.
22. The Democratic members of the Temporary Select Committee to Study the Senate Committee System (the Stevenson Committee) were Adlai Stevenson (Ill.), Lee Metcalf (Mont.), Gaylord Nelson (Wis.), Lloyd Bentsen (Texas), Lawton Chiles (Fla.), and Frank Moss (Utah); the Republican members were Bill Brock (Tenn.), Clifford Hansen (Wyo.), Barry Goldwater (Ariz.), Robert Packwood (Ore.), Peter Domenici (N.M.), and Jesse Helms (N.C.).
23. This account of the Stevenson Committee's activities is drawn from the public record, from my own experiences as Special Research Consultant to the committee, and from a useful summary account written by a committee staff colleague, Judith H. Parris. See her article entitled "The Senate Reorganizes Its Committees, 1977," *Political Science Quarterly* 95 (Summer 1979): 319.
24. U.S., Congress, Senate, Temporary Select Committee to Study the Senate Committee System, *The Senate Committee System,* 94th Cong., 2nd sess., July 1976.

25. Ibid., pp. 104-105.
26. Senate Temporary Select Committee to Study the Senate Committee System, *Senate Committee System Hearings,* 94th Cong. 2nd sess., September 1976, Part II, pp. 179-222.
27. U.S., Congress, Senate, *Congressional Record,* 94th Cong., 1st sess., September 8, 1976, 122: S15366; *National Journal,* August 21, 1976, p. 1189.
28. *Senate Committee System Hearings,* Part II, pp. 161-162.
29. That is, Rules Chairman Howard Cannon (D-Nev.) and members Robert C. Byrd (D-W.Va.), Howard Baker (R-Tenn.), and Robert Griffin (R-Mich.) — the last three of them candidates for the floor leadership post in their respective parties.
30. U.S., Congress, Senate, *Congressional Record,* 95th Cong., 1st sess., February 4, 1977, 123: S2315.
31. On this point, see Fenno, *Congressmen in Committees,* p. 146.

II

Congressional Processes
and
Institutions

6

House Party Leadership in the 1970s

Robert L. Peabody

On August 25, 1980, Speaker Thomas P. O'Neill, Jr. (D-Mass.) sent this sharply worded rebuke to 44 of his Democratic colleagues in the House of Representatives:

> I was extremely disappointed to note that you voted against a motion to uphold the ruling of the Chair last week.
>
> It is elementary to our procedural control of the House that the chair be supported by members of our party. That is basic to a parliamentary body. In other countries if such a vote were lost, the government would fall.
>
> You should know that from 1937 to 1968, there were no recorded votes on the Chair's rulings. From 1968 until 1979, there were four votes. Now we have seen three roll call votes in seven weeks!
>
> Members of the Steering and Policy Committee and the Whip's Organization have discussed these developments, some of them calling for disciplinary measures and meetings. I believe, however, that our best course is to call the above facts to the Members' attention.
>
> I fully understand the pressures that are brought to bear by single-issue groups on such occasions, but I believe members have to be ready to support the orderly process when a member seeks to confuse procedure with issue.
>
> I trust you will take all these facts into consideration in the future. We must work together to enact a legislative program.[1]

The vote that led to O'Neill's criticism took place on August 19, 1980, when Representative John Ashbrook (R-Ohio) offered an amendment to block an Internal Revenue Service regulation that could cause the loss of tax-exempt status by private or religious schools. The House parliamentarian had ruled the amendment out of order, and Ashbrook had appealed the ruling of the chair.[2] The House voted to support the chair's ruling, 214-182, but Speaker O'Neill and other Democrats were displeased because 44 Democrats had sided with a majority of Republicans on the losing side. Twenty-nine of these dissident votes were cast by Southern Democrats, who traditionally have made up the more conservative wing of the party.

Speaker O'Neill was not in the chair at the time of the ruling. Under House rules he had appointed one of his senior Democratic colleagues to preside over the debate. But as the increasingly partisan and rancorous second session of the 96th Congress (1979-80) progressed, O'Neill became more and more dissatisfied by what he perceived as a breach of party discipline. In the closing days of the session, his appeal for tighter party discipline, at least on procedural questions, appeared to be having an impact. On several key votes Democrats supported their leadership nearly unanimously.[3]

These efforts by the Speaker to shore up party discipline provide a partial glimpse of the operations of the complex party organizations — Democratic and Republican — that governed the House of Representatives in the 1970s. Before continuing that exploration, several points made in O'Neill's letter need brief elaboration here.

First, although the Speaker is normally the most powerful legislative leader in the House, he is not omnipresent nor all powerful. It is no longer the case, if it ever was, that "the Speaker has but one Superior and no peers."[4] He must appeal to other members for their support primarily by means of persuasion.

Second, the parties in the House are by no means monolithic. Although they act with one voice in the selection of the Speaker at the beginning of each two-year Congress, members are relatively free to follow the dictates of their consciences and to pursue the interests of their districts. Ultimately, a majority of each district's voters will decide every two years whether or not their representative should be returned to Washington.

Third, despite a rather steady erosion of party discipline over the years, identification with party remains a strong voting cue. Members continue to see themselves primarily as either "Democrats" or "Republicans." They continue to select their leaders, like Speaker O'Neill, in party caucuses or conferences. Throughout the 1970s and indeed extending back to 1930, the Democrats have organized the House with only two exceptions: the 80th (1947-48) and 83rd (1953-54) Congresses. Much of the partisan rhetoric and assertiveness characteristic of the 96th Congress can be traced to the renewed hope and sense of momentum the Republicans have felt as they endeavored to become the majority party in the House in the 1980s.

Finally, Speaker O'Neill's letter makes note of the rise of special or "single-issue" interest groups (for example, "pro-life or anti-abortion" groups), which Representative Ashbrook's amendment was designed to assist. In any given election year members on both sides of the aisle, Democrats and Republicans, become more sensitive to the special advocacies, often accompanied by campaign funding, that such groups can readily muster.

All of these themes will be amplified further in the pages to follow. This essay has four principal objectives: (1) to describe briefly the historical evolution of the most important leadership positions and the growth of parties in the House; (2) to examine the contemporary patterns of leadership recruitment and performance among Democrats and Republicans; (3) to comment on modifications in party organization and personnel over the past several Congresses; and (4) to speculate about developments in party leadership among the Democrats and Republicans in future Congresses.

THE INFLUENCE OF HISTORICAL TRADITIONS

The organizational complexity of the House of Representatives, in general, and its patterns of party leadership, more specifically, reflect many interacting forces. Among the most important are the continuing influence of historical traditions on the operations of this nearly 200-year-old institution; the development and maintenance of a controlling, if necessarily decentralized, two-party system; and the ways in which the characteristic functions of the House as a representative and lawmaking body set limits on party leadership.

The operations of the contemporary House are nested in preceding Congresses stretching back to the first U.S. Congress (1789-90) and before then to the shortcomings of the Congresses of the Confederation, to the experiences of the American colonial legislatures, and to the long-range influences of prior centuries of British parliamentary traditions. The continuing impact of these meaningful historical traditions is reflected in the major leadership position in the House: the Speakership. Its origins can be traced back to fourteenth-century English parliamentary practices. Sir Thomas Hungerford, in 1377, was the first individual to be assigned the title of Speaker in the British House of Commons. In the British experience the Speaker's role is limited to that of an impartial presiding officer. The American Speakership, however, has had a strong partisan leadership component from the beginning.[5]

The Speakership is the only House office specifically mandated by the Constitution. Article I, section 2, specifies that "the House of Representatives shall chuse their Speaker and other Officers." All other party positions, such as the floor leaders and whips, grew out of increasing demands for leadership as the House increased in size and complexity. Among the rules adopted by the first House, which convened in New York in April 1789, was one that defined the limited powers of the Speaker. The first rule of each successive compilation of the Rules of the House of Representatives has continued to set forth the "duties of the Speaker," although these duties have undergone considerable expansion over time. Moreover, every Speaker since the first, Frederick Muhlenberg of Pennsylvania, has been guided by precedents evolved from rulings of the chair (such as the one discussed earlier) and have also helped to establish and support new ones. Gradually, these precedents form a body of rulings that guide and constrain House debate.

Neither the colonial experiences, nor the formal language of the Constitution, nor the initial rules of the House of Representatives anticipated much of an active role for political parties in the legislative process. But the American Revolution experience of pro- and anti-British sentiment, differing East Coast and frontier perspectives, and northern and southern alignments gradually crystallized into Federalist versus anti-Federalist divisions in the country. These, in turn, led to the formation of political parties in the House. Initially, the various factions coalesced around New York's Alexander Hamilton, the first Secretary of the Treasury, and his principal opponents within the Cabinet and the House, Virginians Thomas Jefferson and James Madison.

The development of political parties in the House was further enhanced by the need to elect a Speaker at the beginning of each new Congress. By the early 1800s, members were taking sides for or against candidates for Speaker. As the Speaker's powers became more prominent, he would move to solidify his position by appointing loyal lieutenants as chairmen of the key legislative committees. Within the first several decades of the House, the standing committee system also emerged. Party-identified chairmen began to expand their roles in committee deliberations and as floor managers of legislation.

Perhaps the high-water marks of partisan control in the House were reached under two strong Republican Speakers, Thomas B. Reed of Maine (1889-91, 1895-99) and Joseph G. Cannon of Illinois (1903-11), who had a deep appreciation of the rules of the House and did not hesitate to discipline recalcitrant members. From 1911 to 1915, House Democrats revitalized the party caucus as a means of shaping legislation under the leadership of Majority Leader Oscar Underwood of Alabama and Speaker Champ Clark of Missouri.

Party allegiance to leaders appears to have reached a high point in the late nineteenth and early twentieth centuries. Despite a rather steady erosion since then, political party affiliation remains the single most reliable factor in predicting voting patterns in the House. That is to say, if one was restricted to a single piece of information about a given member's propensity to vote "yes" or "no" on a legislative issue, party identification — Democrat or Republican — would tell one the most about his or her voting patterns. But in the contemporary House, party remains a "weak" signal. Aside from the opening roll call vote on the Speakership, few roll call votes in the House will find all Democrats united on one side, all Republicans in agreement on the other. A wide range of cross-cutting influences frequently enter into voting: a member's personality, ethnicity, and ideology; district forces; presidential and interest group pressures; and the advice of party leadership and fellow colleagues.[6]

From a national perspective, a representative can be seen as part of a greatly decentralized, but nevertheless reasonably cohesive, community: the House of Representatives. But from another perspective, each representative controls one of 435 separate fiefdoms, only loosely coordinated and tied together by personal, committee, regional, and party ties. Given the centripetal pressures from the constituency and the weakened effect of party, if the House is to accomplish its tasks with some degree of effectiveness, it must become more and more dependent on the caliber of its contemporary leaders and the organizational machinery they have available to them.

HOUSE PARTY LEADERS

As we have seen, the Speakership is the only constitutionally designated position in the House of Representatives. All the other major leadership positions — floor leaders, whips, and the chairmen of various party organizations such as the caucus or conference — have evolved rather slowly and informally. Indeed, both parties did not have active, elected floor leaders until the turn of the nineteenth century.[7] As the legislative workload grew more complex, party whips and chairmen of policy or steering committees came into being. Major party leadership positions, together with the individuals who held these positions in the Houses of the mid-1970s, are evaluated below.

The Speaker

As Figure 6-1 indicates, the incumbent of this constitutional office sits at the apex of the formal hierarchy of the House. He ranks second in the line of presidential succession just behind the vice-president. The Speaker has a number of important responsibilities. He is (1) presiding officer of the House; (2) leader of his party; (3) chief administrative officer of the House; (4) chief ceremonial

Figure 6-1 Organization of the House of Representatives, 96th Congress (1979-1980)

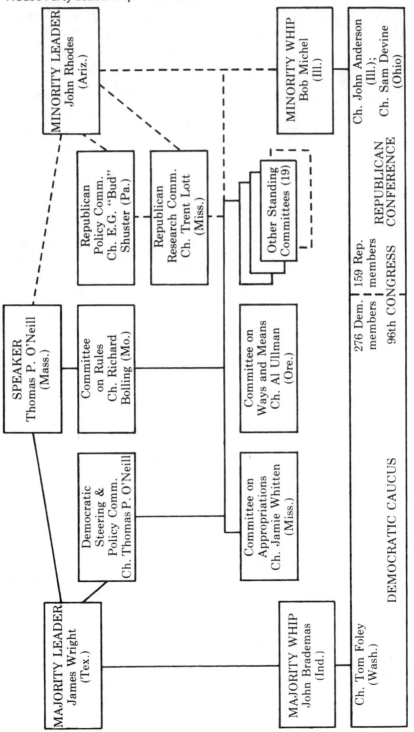

officer, as well as; (5) a member of the House with the same obligations as the other 434 members.

As chief presiding officer of the House, the Speaker opens each daily session, rules on parliamentary questions, decides which members will be recognized to speak or offer amendments, determines voice and division (standing) votes, and refers bills to committees (with the advice of the parliamentarian). One of the Speaker's most important responsibilities is appointing the chairman of the Committee of the Whole, the parliamentary mechanism through which the House considers most legislation. In all of these activities, the Speaker is expected to carry out his responsibilities in a fair and impartial manner, looking after the rights of minority, as well as majority, members.

The Speaker is also leader of the majority party, and it is his responsibility to try to implement his party's legislative program. If the president is of the same party as his own, then the objective becomes to adopt the administration's program. Skilled legislative leaders like Presidents Kennedy and Johnson will make every effort to consult closely with the Speaker and other party and committee leaders of the House and Senate *before* major legislation reaches the priority-setting and implementation stages. Generally, the top party leaders will breakfast with a president of their own party each Tuesday morning to go over the legislative schedule for that and upcoming weeks.

One of the most powerful tools of a Speaker for accomplishing his legislative leadership is his control of his party's policy committee. Under Speakers Carl Albert (D-Okla., 1971-76) and O'Neill (1977-), Democrats have revitalized their Democratic Steering and Policy Committee. Of the 24 members on the committee, 12 are selected by region, and 12 are made up of House leaders or members appointed by the Speaker. Under O'Neill's direction, the committee has met several times a month during the legislative session to discuss forthcoming legislation and initiatives to recommend a Democratic position to be adopted by all Democratic members meeting in caucus.

The other main responsibility of the Steering and Policy Committee is to make committee assignments. At the beginning of each new Congress, the committee will receive requests for preferred committees from each entering Democratic freshman. More senior members who wish to transfer from one committee to another will also submit their requests. In the process of overseeing committee assignments, a Speaker has one of his best opportunities to reward the party faithful and to build credit toward future needs.

The Speaker also assigns members to conference committees, usually following the advice of his committee, and appoints the members of special and select committees and commissions. Since 1974, the Speaker has had the power to nominate members of the House

Committee on Rules, subject to Democratic Caucus approval. A Speaker's administrative and ceremonial responsibilities — looking after the Capitol building and grounds, greeting foreign dignitaries — may not be as major as presiding over the House or leading his party, but they can be very time-consuming. A senior member with office space in the Capitol dies. Who is to inherit his space? The Speaker must decide usually, but not always, according to the dictates of seniority. In any given session of Congress, two dozen or more heads of state will come to Washington and many will wish to address a joint session of Congress. It is up to the Speaker and his staff to decide how the request will be met and to make the necessary arrangements.

Although several Senate Majority Leaders have suffered electoral defeat in past decades, no incumbent Speaker has been defeated at the polls in the twentieth century. In part, this is because the office is highly respected and reflects well upon the people back home. But it is also because Speakers are members of the House, and they and their staffs work hard at representing their home district as well as serving as a national leader.

"Tip" O'Neill has represented the eighth district of Massachusetts (Cambridge and parts of Boston) since 1953. A former Speaker of the Massachusetts House of Representatives, he won his seat when John F. Kennedy left to become a senator. A large, heavyset Irishman with a genial temperament and a facility for telling stories with a message, O'Neill was quickly assimilated into Democratic leadership circles. John McCormack of Massachusetts, then Majority Leader and later Speaker (1962-71), became his mentor. O'Neill was placed on the Committee on Rules just one term after he came to the House.

In 1971, after Majority Leader Carl Albert advanced to the Speakership and Majority Whip Hale Boggs of Louisiana was elected Majority Leader, they appointed O'Neill as whip. Two years later when Boggs was killed in an Alaskan airplane crash, O'Neill moved up to Majority Leader.

By 1980, O'Neill was serving his fourth year as Speaker. Some observers have judged him to be the strongest, most persuasive Speaker since Sam Rayburn (D-Tex., 1940-47, 1949-53, 1955-61). A committed national Democrat, O'Neill nevertheless continues to look after his people back home. "All politics," he has observed, "is local politics."

Floor Leaders

The primary responsibility of floor leaders — majority and minority — is to marshall their party's forces to develop winning coalitions on key amendments and on final passage. If the president is of the same party, it is generally the "administration's program" that the floor leader attempts to implement. If the president is of the opposite party, then floor leaders try to defeat the president's program and develop alternative legislative proposals.

Working closely with the Speaker, a Majority Leader's responsibility is to prepare the weekly schedule of legislation coming to the floor. In a typical week the schedule may go through more than 10 revisions as decisions are made as to timing and the amount of support a given bill may have. Above all, a Majority Leader waits, watches, and builds support for the time when there will be a vacancy in the Speakership. By tradition, he is the leading candidate to succeed the Speaker.

The Minority Leader plays a similar role to the Majority Leader. At the beginning of each new Congress, he is nominated by his party for the Speakership, a contest he will inevitably lose on a strict party-line vote. Thereafter, he works as closely as possible with his Senate counterpart, either to assist the legislative programs of a president of his own party or to modify or thwart the bills of a president of the opposite party. Republican congressional leaders generally cooperated with Presidents Nixon (1969-74) and Ford (1974-76), but usually opposed President Carter's legislative objectives in the 95th (1977-78) and 96th (1979-80) Congresses.

All floor leaders — Democratic or Republican, majority or minority — are involved almost continuously in five broad areas of policymaking: (1) monitoring internal party organization, especially maintaining relationships with committee and other party leaders; (2) formulating and implementing legislative agendas; (3) keeping in touch with other House members, especially from their own state delegations and regions; (4) overseeing the activities of key staff; and (5) engaging in a wide range of external relationships, especially with White House and executive branch officials, interest group representatives, and media personnel.

Over the past several Congresses, James Wright (D-Tex.) has served as Majority Leader and John Rhodes (R-Ariz.) as Minority Leader. Wright was first elected to the House in 1954, ran unsuccessfully for the Senate in 1961, and was about to become chairman of the House Public Works Committee when he decided to run for Majority Leader in 1976. Rhodes entered the House in 1953 and, once appointed, rose steadily through the ranks of minority members on the Appropriations Committee. He became chairman of the House Republican Policy Committee in 1965. When Minority Leader Gerald Ford was selected by President Richard Nixon as his vice president, Rhodes advanced to Minority Leader with only token opposition.

Party Whips

The whip is generally viewed as the third-ranking leader in the House majority party and the second-ranking official in the minority party. By tradition, the leaders of the Democratic party appoint their whips. They are usually the Speaker's choice, but floor leaders may from time to time have a strong input in the selection. The choice of a whip can determine future party selection for a decade or more, since the whip often, but not always, is elevated to Majority Leader. Republicans, in contrast, elect their whip, usually at their biennial party conferences.

The tasks of whips, regardless of party, are essentially twofold: (1) to maintain a nearly constant communication with their party colleagues — on the floor, in the corridors, by telephone, and through whip notices and advisories; and (2) to help their leaders obtain the most up-to-date and sensitive information concerning how their colleagues feel about forthcoming legislation, especially key floor amendments. Often on major legislation the party whip organizations will poll their members, that is, sound them out on how they regard the forthcoming votes — are they in favor, opposed, or undecided. Both party whip systems are elaborately organized by regional and state (or assistant) whips in order to facilitate these processes. Whips circulate on the floor, confiding in their colleagues, arguing the merits of the legislation.

As the pace of legislation increases, a number of polls may be going simultaneously. Frequently, the regular House polls are supplemented by same-party White House assessments and information obtained from friendly or involved interest groups.

John Brademas (D-Ind.) was appointed deputy whip by Speaker Albert and Majority Leader O'Neill in 1973. A former Rhodes scholar and a liberal, Brademas entered the House 15 years earlier and had become an expert on education policy as a member and later subcommittee chairman of the House Education and Labor Committee. In 1977, when O'Neill was elected Speaker, he selected a fellow liberal, Brademas, as his whip.

Bob Michel (R-Ill.) was first elected to the House in 1956 and was appointed almost immediately to the Appropriations Committee. Highly respected by his colleagues, Michel won the Republican whip's position in 1974. A vacancy had been created when Les Arends, also from Illinois, retired after 30 years service as whip.

Other Party Offices

Democrats and Republicans have also created other party offices of which the most important are the chairmen of their respective party caucuses and policy committees. In past Congresses, meetings of all incoming party members were generally confined to an opening-day session designed to select nominees for the Speakership. But from the mid-1960s on, both parties began to hold meetings almost every month in order to discuss party and committee reforms and other legislative matters. As a consequence, the chairmen of both the Democratic Caucus and the Republican Conference began to emerge as important party leaders who no longer served as mere party functionaries.

Both parties have also reactivated "policy committees" in recent decades for the purpose of discussing and taking party positions on major legislation. Republicans have made consistent use of this party mechanism for about two decades; Democrats, only since about 1974. As long as the Democrats continue in the majority, their Speaker will preside over their Steering and Policy Committee. As already noted, in addition to evaluating party positions, this group makes committee assignments. Republicans assign committee positions through a separate committee, called a "Committee on Committees," mainly controlled by the heads of large state delegations through a weighted voting system (one vote for each Republican member in their delegation).[8]

REFORMS IN THE 1960s AND 1970s

Both parties in the House of Representatives undertook a wholesale series of organizational reforms in the 1960s and 1970s. Major Democratic reform efforts can be dated from the creation of the Democratic Study Group (DSG) in the late 1950s as well as from Speaker Sam Rayburn's decision to win back control of the House Rules Committee through enlargement of its membership in Janury 1961. Increasingly, junior members, railing against the seniority system and other hallowed House norms, have been able to help organize and vote through committee and caucus reforms, especially in the 1970s.[9]

One of the most critical developments for party leadership and reform activities in both parties has been the reactivation of party caucuses or conferences. For Republicans, their renewed emphasis dates from the election of Gerald Ford to the chairmanship of the Republican Conference in 1963. Although Ford's reform contribution was modest, he used the position as a springboard for the ousting of Minority Leader Charles Halleck of Indiana two years later. As chairman, Ford was able to call and organize a mid-December Republican conference in Washington in 1964. Following upon substantial election losses in the House, dissident Republicans hostile to Minority Leader Halleck capitalized upon this change-oriented climate to replace him with Ford. A number of decentralizing modifications in House GOP party and committee structure followed.[10]

Under reform procedures adopted in the 93rd Congress, both parties are directed to return to Washington about a month before a new Congress convenes. These early caucuses have had several, sometimes cross-cutting consequences. An entrenched leadership can use the time to indoctrinate an incoming freshman class, which was primarily the goal for the House Democratic party after the 1978 elections. But such caucuses also provide party reformers — leaders or nonleaders — additional time and an appropriate climate within which to bring about change.

The three pre-Congress Democratic Caucuses of 1974, 1976, and 1978, each held in December, were characterized by quite different reform climates and results. In each case the number or mood of the incoming freshman class largely set the tone and substantially influenced the outcomes.

The 75-member Democratic class of 1974 constituted the largest incoming one-party class since the 1930s. More than 50 had succeeded in capturing seats traditionally held by Republicans, in large part a response to Watergate issues. Spurred on by these reform-oriented freshmen, the Democratic leadership sponsored a series of major changes. Most important were the ousting of three senior southern chairmen — Wright Patman and William Poage of Texas, and F. Edward Hebert of Louisiana — and the shift of committee assignment powers away from the Democratic members of the House Ways and Means Committee and into the hands of the leadership-dominated Steering and Policy Committee.

The December 1976 Democratic Caucus found most membership energies directed away from committee and caucus reform into an intensive four-way contest for the House majority leadership.

The net effect of the House Democratic party reforms of the 1970s is still being evaluated, but several preliminary conclusions can be advanced. Although committee chairmen lost some ground to the leadership, overall, individual members gained the greatest autonomy. In the pendulum shifts characteristic of House reforms, the contemporary moods appear to call for further changes designed to strengthen the party leadership.

Leadership Turnover in the 94th and 95th Congresses

Each Congress has its unique characteristics, its perennial as well as changing issues, its distinctive place in history. But every Congress also shares many political and organizational aspects in common with its predecessors. Thus any given Congress is most likely to approximate the Congress immediately before it, and its characteristics and accomplishments, in turn, will bear heavily on the Congress to follow.

One major reason for these approximations is overlapping personnel. In recent elections more than 300 — sometimes close to 400 — House members have sought re-election. So powerful are the advantages of incumbency that proportionately more than 90 percent of all these members who run will find themselves re-elected to the next Congress.[11] Except for those rare Congresses with relatively high turnover — a fifth or more of their members — stability in personnel and practices is almost guaranteed. Moreover, as already noted, leadership continuity rather than change is traditional with the House of Representatives. Leaders typically reach high office after two decades or more of service in the House. Innovative leadership is the exception rather than the rule.

Nevertheless, the circumstances and pace at which the House operates can change substantially through structural developments as well as leadership turnover. Although the 95th Congress (1977-78) had much in common with the 94th (1975-76), there were critical differences. For the first time in eight years, Democrats controlled the executive branch as well as the House and Senate. President Jimmy Carter and a new House Democratic leadership were confronted with a broad range of issues, chief among them ethics, governmental reorganization, energy programs, and tax reductions. Still, the party ratios in the 95th — 62 Democrats to 38 Republicans in the Senate, 292 Democrats to 143 Republicans in the House of Representatives — closely approximated those of the previous Congress. A trend toward younger representatives and senators serving in Congress continued. Members with law backgrounds remained especially important in the Senate, but other professions continued to increase their numbers in the House.[12]

Another major difference between the two Congresses was a wholesale change in the House Democratic leadership. Albert retired after three terms as Speaker. O'Neill, Majority Leader in the previous two Congresses, succeeded him as the 47th Speaker of the House. With 24 years experience in the House, including 20 years of service on the Committee on Rules, O'Neill was widely regarded by his colleagues as an effective and popular leader. At a pre-95th Congress caucus, O'Neill was unanimously selected as his party's nominee.

A four-way contest for Majority Leader preoccupied House Democrats through the summer and fall of 1976.[13] The four candidates, all with extensive leadership and legislative experience, were John McFall of California, the Democratic whip; Phillip Burton of California, chairman of the Democratic Caucus; Jim Wright of Texas, one of three regional whips; and Richard Bolling of Missouri, the second-ranking member on the Committee on Rules and a long-time advisor to Speakers on parliamentary procedures.

On December 6, 1976, it took most of the afternoon and three ballots to choose a Majority Leader. Jim Wright of Texas, the least liberal candidate, finally edged Phil Burton, the most liberal candidate, by one vote, 148 to 147. Although there were more liberals than conservatives among House Democrats, Wright's lower-keyed, less abrasive personality may have carried the day. The Bolling supporters, most of them moderate to liberal, would in most circumstances have been expected to pick a fellow liberal. Yet they split about three to two in favor of Wright. Still, for the lack of one vote, Burton, not Wright, would have become Majority Leader and the heir apparent to the Speakership. Burton and his followers would bide their time.

Later in the week, O'Neill picked John Brademas of Indiana as majority whip; Dan Rostenkowski of Illinois became deputy whip. Rostenkowski, who had campaigned extensively for the new Majority Leader, had been Wright's first choice for whip, but O'Neill's preference for Brademas carried the greater weight. Thomas S. Foley of Washington, the newly elected chairman of the caucus, rounded out the Democratic leadership.

The top Republican House leaders during the 94th and 95th Congresses, in contrast, remained substantially unchanged: Minority Leader John Rhodes of Arizona, Minority Whip Robert Michel of Illinois, Chairman of the Republican Conference John Anderson of Illinois.

By the summer of 1977, the new House Democratic leadership could rightly claim substantial credit for the passage of important legislation. Some bills emanated from the new administration, but most had their roots in the committee actions and floor deliberations of previous Congresses. After an uneasy start, a positive working relationship developed between President Carter, Speaker O'Neill, and Majority Leader Wright. The combination of already prepared legislation and skilled House and Senate leadership was instrumental in a relatively successful first session performance.

In the crucible of the election year of 1978, more conflict and less cooperation characterized the relationships between the House leaders and rank-and-file members. Moreover, there was less cooperation between the Senate and the House and between Congress and the executive branch. Representatives of the classes of '74 and '76 in particular played more important and independent roles than their counterparts in previous Congresses. Nevertheless, in the closing hours of the 95th Congress, President Carter with the help of the Democratic leadership in both houses was able to secure the final passage of energy and tax legislation. Although Congress did not grant him what he had initially asked for, it was still legislation he could sign.

By the spring of 1978, the likelihood of a liberal challenge led by Phil Burton against Majority Leader Wright had largely abated.

If Wright was viewed as more conservative than O'Neill, his own votes had moved him closer to the moderately liberal, centrist positions within the party. In the crucial debate over the administration's energy package, Wright had, in the main, defended the program despite intense cross-pressures from home to side with Texas's oil and gas industries. In retrospect, a strong minority of House Democrats might have favored a more liberal Majority Leader such as Burton, but Wright's conduct as a loyal number two man, coupled with O'Neill's probable open support in a contest, had neutralized any opposition.

Burton's remaining hope for an early challenge depended upon favorable Democratic outcomes in the fall 1978 elections. The great majority of his supporters among incumbent Democrats would have to hold their own. Moreover, they would have to be joined by a large, fresh crop of liberal, reform-oriented members. Instead, Republicans made a net gain of 12 seats in the House, reducing the Democratic majority in the new Congress to 276-159. Fourteen Democratic incumbents, compared to five Republicans, lost their seats in 1978. The heaviest Democratic losses — seven in all — were from the reform-oriented class of '74. Members of this class had been a strong element in Burton's support in the House. Moreover, in Texas, where six Democratic incumbents retired, only one of these seats was lost to a Republican. By election night it was apparent that Wright could more than hold his own among the 42 incoming freshmen Democrats.

96th Congress Contests

No contests developed for House Democratic leadership positions at the beginning of the 96th Congress (1979-80). Thus, when the 276 Democratic incumbents and freshmen-elect members caucused on the House floor in mid-December 1978, Speaker O'Neill, Majority Leader Wright, and Caucus Chairman Foley were renominated and elected by acclamation. Once again, O'Neill appointed Brademas and Rostenkowski as his principal whips. Whatever opposition there may have been to O'Neill and Wright bided its time. Quite simply, Burton or other possible liberal challengers did not have the members to mount a successful revolt.

The top Republican leadership of Rhodes and Michel also was routinely re-elected a month before the 96th Congress reconvened. However, John Anderson, the moderate chairman of the Republican Conference, received a challenge from conservative Tom Kindness of Ohio. With leadership support, Anderson won by a vote of 87 to 55. Later, when Anderson resigned his leadership position to launch an apparent dark horse candidacy for the presidency, his place was taken by conservative Sam Devine of Ohio. Devine edged by three votes a freshman-supported challenge by Henry J. Hyde of Illinois. In the months that followed, Rhodes's leadership came under increasing criticism, especially from newly elected conservative members. Led by Newt Gingrich of Georgia, Ed Bethune of Arkansas, and others, they argued that the Republican leadership had developed a "minority mentality." What was clearly called for was a more assertive, less compromising type of leadership.

Indeed, the election of a series of large, relatively youthful, and independent freshman classes continues to make life interesting for party and committee leaders on both sides of the aisle. In contests for subcommittee chairmanships at the opening of the 96th Congress, several junior Democrats like Toby Moffett of Connecticut and Henry Waxman of California upset more senior candidates. The 42 Democrats and 35 Republican freshmen who arrived in Washington following the 1978 midterm elections, however, were less committed to procedural change than previous classes. Regardless of party, they were almost unanimously in favor of reduced government spending, lower taxes, and the achievement of a balanced budget.

The ratio of entering Republicans compared to Democrats in the 96th Congress was the most favorable for the minority party in six years, and Republicans had high hopes of doing even better in 1980. In 1974, in contrast, all but 17 of the 92 incoming House freshmen were Democrats, an election benefit largely attributed to Watergate reactions. Republicans had an overall House election standoff in 1976, but still managed to elect 20 of the 67 incoming members.

A combination of record retirements among more senior members and the continuing re-election of most of the recent classes of freshmen made the 96th Congress one of the youngest and least senior Congresses in modern times. At the opening of the 96th Congress, 212 House members (almost half) had served for four years or less. Although most members of the House continue to be between 40 and 60 years of age, 86 members in the 96th Congress were under 40; only 14 were over 70 years of age.

FUTURE DEVELOPMENTS IN PARTY LEADERSHIP

What lies ahead? Intense competition for major leadership positions in both parties can be expected. The "who" and the "when" is more difficult to predict, especially within the House Democratic party. As long as O'Neill remains Speaker, the Democratic leadership is likely to remain stable. However, at the end of the 96th Congress, O'Neill was almost 68 years old. From time to time, rumors of a possible ailment or of O'Neill's prospective retirement make the rounds of the Democratic cloakroom. Obviously, the Speaker's continued good health and his election plans are uppermost in the minds of those limited number of House members who have realistic ambitions to advance in the Democratic party leadership.

What would happen if a vacancy occurred in the Speakership? Historical patterns of leadership succession suggest that the most probable scenario would be the advancement of the Democratic Majority Leader up the ladder, probably without a contest. With several Congresses as his party's floor leader already behind him, Jim Wright of Texas has become the strong favorite to be elected to the Speakership. But first he must survive the strongest Republican challenge to his Fort Worth seat in years. Ironically, aggregate House Democratic election defeats in either 1980 or 1982, or both, would probably serve to enhance Wright's chances. Traditionally, in the Democratic party the marginal seats have been held in the main by liberals. Thus severe election losses almost inevitably result in a more conservative House Democratic party. If Wright receives a challenge in a future contest for the leadership, it is most likely to come from a candidate to his left. Phil Burton of California and Tom Foley of Washington, the past and current chairmen of the Democratic Caucus, remain the most frequently suggested possible challengers to Wright. Another respected House leader, Dan Rostenkowski of Chicago, is less likely to challenge, given his active involvement on Wright's behalf in the December 1976 contest for Majority Leader. He is also next in line to inherit the chairmanship of the Ways and Means Committee.

Any of these individuals and perhaps younger House members as well may calculate that Wright is not vulnerable and decide instead to run for his vacated position of floor leadership. Whenever that opportunity opens up, the competition is likely to be spirited. In November 1980 John Brademas lost his seat to a 27-year-old Republican and thus opened up the position of majority whip (an appointive position). Dan Rostenkowski, the chief deputy whip, became the leading contender to succeed Brademas. If nominated by Speaker O'Neill, his acceptance would be complicated by caucus rules that would prevent him from being whip as well as inheriting the chairmanship of the Ways and Means Committee. The former chairman, Al Ullman (D-Ore.), was another major casualty of the 1980 election, along with Brademas and more than 30 other House Democratic incumbents. Although Democrats lost control of the Senate, they would organize the 97th House but with a reduced ratio of 243-192. In their pre-97th Congress conference, House Democrats will select a new Democratic Caucus chairman. Foley has served for four years and by caucus rules must retire. Gillis Long of Louisiana and Charlie Rose of North Carolina are the principal candidates.

House Republicans are heavily involved in a series of major leadership battles in 1980 that will also be decided at a pre-97th conference in early December. These events were precipitated by Minority Leader

Rhodes's announcement on December 12, 1979, that, except under unusual circumstances, he would not be a candidate for that position in the 97th Congress. "Nobody should be minority leader for more than seven years," Rhodes contended.[14] However, he reserved the right to run for the Republican nomination for Speaker in the less than likely event that Republicans gained enough seats in the 1980 elections to gain control of the House. A net change of 59 seats would be required. And he also reserved the right to re-enter the contest for Minority Leader should the campaign to succeed him turn into a bitter battle with harmful consequences for the GOP.

Two conservative Republicans — Michel, the incumbent whip, and Guy Vander Jagt of Michigan, the chairman of the National Republican Congressional Committee — became the front-running contenders to succeed Rhodes. The outcome might ride on the number of incoming, GOP freshmen, with Vander Jagt's chances presumably being enhanced by higher numbers.

Party leadership selection in the 97th (1981-82) and future Congresses will be worth watching for several reasons. First, contests, whenever they occur, are fascinating for their parallels and contrasts in the personalities and the backgrounds of the candidates — a Ford vs. a Halleck, a Wright vs. a Burton — in the ideological beliefs of their supporters — liberal, moderate, and conservative — and in the regional patterns of allegiance that develop. How, for example, will the rest of the House Democrats regard the candidacies of Long and Rose in 1980, both moderate southerners?

Second, the outcomes of leadership choices have important consequences for other members in terms of leadership positions, internal influence, and committee control. For example, the compromise choice of O'Neill as whip by Speaker Albert and Majority Leader Boggs was the first and most crucial step on his path to the Speakership. What choices will the winners of 1980 leadership contests in either party make that might influence the choice of a future Speaker?

Finally, those House and Senate leaders who are selected will play a major role interacting with the president and the executive branch. Most important, they will play decisive roles in controlling the substance, and especially the timing, of legislative policy in the years ahead.

POSTSCRIPT: On December 8, 1980, the Republican Conference elected Robert Michel as its Minority Leader. He defeated Guy Vander Jagt by a vote of 103-87. That same day Speaker Thomas P. O'Neill, Jr. and Majority Leader James Wright announced their selections for party whip: Thomas S. Foley and Bill Alexander. Former chief deputy whip Dan Rostenkowski opted to become chairman of the House Ways and Means Committee. By a 146-53 vote, Gillis Long was elected Democratic Caucus chairman.

NOTES

1. U.S., Congress, House, *Congressional Record* (daily edition), 96th Cong., 2nd sess., August 28, 1980, p. H8120. Speaker O'Neill's letter was inserted in the *Record* by Republican Representative Bob Bauman of Maryland. Republicans had taken the floor to criticize the Democratic leadership for resorting to a postelection or "lame duck" session beginning November 12, 1980.

2. Ironically, one day later, Ashbrook's amendment to H.R. 7583, the Treasury and Postal Services Act, was adopted by a vote of 300 to 107.

3. See, for example, the October 1, 1980, votes on the 1981 budget resolution and adjournment resolution. *Congressional Quarterly Weekly Report,* October 4, 1980, pp. 2910-2911, 2958-2959.

4. Quoted in *Congressional Quarterly Weekly Report*, November 17, 1961, pp. 1847-1854. Speaker Thomas B. Reed made this observation while presiding over the House of Representatives. He and his Republican successor, Joseph G. Cannon, were referred to as "czars" because of their effective use of concentrated powers.

5. M. P. Follett, *The Speaker of the House of Representatives* (New York: Longmans, Green, 1896), p. 3.

6. John W. Kingdon, *Congressmen's Voting Decisions* (New York: Harper & Row, 1973); Donald R. Matthews and James Stimson, *Yeas and Nays: Normal Decision-Making in the U.S. House of Representatives* (New York: John Wiley & Sons, 1975).

7. Randall B. Ripley, *Party Leaders in the House of Representatives* (Washington, D.C.: Brookings Institution, 1967).

8. Robert L. Peabody, *Leadership in Congress* (Boston: Little, Brown & Co., 1976), pp. 28-39.

9. For a more extensive analysis see relevant articles collected in *Changing Congress: The Committee System,* ed. Norman J. Ornstein (Philadelphia: The Annals of the American Society of Political and Social Science, 1974); *Congress in Change,* ed. Ornstein (New York: Praeger, Publishers, 1975); and *Congress Reconsidered,* 1st ed., edited by Lawrence C. Dodd and Bruce I. Oppenheimer (New York: Praeger, 1977), chap. 2.

10. Robert L. Peabody, "Political Parties: House Republican Leadership," in *American Political Institutions and Public Policy,* ed. Allan P. Sindler (Boston: Little, Brown & Co., 1969), pp. 180-229.

11. See Milton C. Cummings, Jr., *Congressmen and the Electorate* (New York: Free Press, 1966); Thomas E. Mann, *Unsafe at Any Margin: Interpreting Congressional Elections* (Washington, D.C.: American Enterprise Institute, 1978); and Albert D. Cover and David R. Mayhew, "Congressional Dynamics and the Decline of Competitive Congressional Elections," in this volume.

12. At the beginning of each Congress, Congressional Quarterly publishes profiles on the incoming representatives and senators as well as characteristics of the overall membership. For examples of each, see *Congressional Quarterly Weekly Reports,* December 30, 1978, pp. 3499-3535 and January 1, 1977, pp. 19-30.

13. This brief overview is abstracted from Bruce I. Oppenheimer and Robert L. Peabody, "The Majority Leadership Contest, 1966" (Paper delivered at the annual meeting of the American Political Science Association, Washington, D.C., September 1-4, 1977).

14. Martin Tolchin, "Rhodes to Quit House G.O.P. Post," *New York Times,* December 13, 1979; Alan Ehrenhalt, "Rhodes to Yield Minority Leader Post in House," *Washington Star,* December 12, 1979.

7

Congressional Committees in the Policy Process

David E. Price

INTRODUCTION

The early years of the Carter presidency did not produce the sort of cooperation between Congress and the executive that some expected to result from Democratic recapture of the White House. Enough instances of successful collaboration could be cited — airline deregulation, civil service reform, and the formation of a Department of Education — to make generalizations perilous. But in areas ranging from energy to welfare to public works, Congress and the president developed contrasting approaches to legislation and frequently came into conflict. Most of the president's major proposals either were not acted on by the 95th Congress (1977-78) or emerged with substantial alterations. As of early 1980, the 96th Congress had turned in a similar performance.

The explanations given for the relatively high level of presidential-congressional conflict have varied considerably. We hear, on the one hand, that Congress is more assertive nowadays, better equipped and more inclined to make policy on its own terms and in its own

The author is indebted to Steve Haeberle for research assistance and to David Garrow, Michael Malbin, Harris Miller, Norman Ornstein, Jim Ricciuti, Ronald Rogowski, and the editors of the present volume for helpful comments and suggestions.

way. On the other hand, Congress is often portrayed as an "obstacle course," immobilized by conflict, susceptible to obstruction by determined minorities, unable to respond to presidential proposals yet incapable of developing its own coherent alternatives.

These accounts are not as contradictory as they at first appear. Congress tends to balk at what the president requests in some areas and to push him farther than he wants to go in others. Nor are these variations random ones: Congress has recently mangled the initiatives of Republican and Democratic presidents alike on numerous matters of national scope that have involved painful conflicts of value and interest (e.g., energy, urban assistance, welfare, tax reform). But on less conflictful issues pushed by groups and constituencies that are firmly based in a bloc of congressional districts, it is the Congress that has often resisted presidential constraints. For example, Congress took the lead during the 95th Congress in designing a generous program of agricultural price supports and in expanding the president's preferred list of water projects.

Although Congress is inclined to handle different types of issues in different ways, the picture of congressional organization and responsiveness that emerges from a range of cases is fairly consistent. First, the policymaking process in Congress is decentralized and fragmented. As Bruce Oppenheimer has pointed out in Chapter 12, conflict among committees in both houses slowed passage of the Ford and Carter energy bills. The legislation no doubt would have passed with great difficulty in any case, but congressional fragmentation complicated the process considerably and provided checkpoints for those who were determined to oppose one provision or another.[1] No less fragmentation is usually visible on farm and public works bills, although here the element of competition between committees is missing. Congress parcels out decisionmaking authority and, as Woodrow Wilson wrote in 1885, usually meets "to sanction the conclusions of its committees as rapidly as possible."[2]

These episodes reveal, secondly, what might be termed congressional "particularism." Protagonists in the energy debate frequently spoke for energy-producing areas favoring deregulation or for high-consuming states seeking continued price controls. Opposition to President Carter's welfare reform package came from Agriculture Committee spokesmen who saw replacing food stamps with cash payments as detrimental to farm interests, while many of those working to salvage the bill were mainly concerned with giving hard-pressed state and local governments financial relief. Safeguarding district water projects or agricultural commodity programs was often a higher priority of legislators than identifying with the broader fiscal-management and consumer viewpoints that the president adopted. This is not to say that members of Congress are incapable of taking broad-gauged policy

initiatives. Indeed, as we shall see below, they are increasingly motivated to gain stature in nationally visible policy areas. Nevertheless,
a general tendency exists in Congress to give priority to constituency-
based interests, to aggregate the demands of groups and constituencies
in such a way as to minimize tradeoffs and conflict among them,
and thus to reject or modify presidential proposals that are aimed
at redistributive or other "universalistic" objectives. Congress, in Theodore Lowi's phrase, displays a penchant for "distributive" politics.[3]

Congressional fragmentation and particularism are institutionalized in the committee system. This leads us to a third generalization:
congressional policymaking is committee-centered. It is this realization
that furnishes the point of departure for the present essay. My purpose
is to give a general account of the legislative process, keeping, as
one must, the committee system in central focus. What capacities,
disabilities, and biases does Congress display by virtue of the central
place of committees in its life? How have committees come to occupy
the place they do in our national legislature, and is their continuing
pre-eminence assured? How do committees differ in their legislative
roles, and what does one need to know about a committee to understand
its role? Exploring such questions should take us beyond the contrasting
stereotypes of Congress as the "broken branch" or as the last best
hope of American government, and help us understand the kind
of public policy we get from Congress and what kind of performance
it is reasonable to expect.

CONGRESSIONAL STRENGTHS AND WEAKNESSES

As we have seen, Congress acts more readily and easily on distributive issues that are responsive to discrete constituencies than
it does on broader and more conflictful problems. And the same
organizational characteristics that often encourage both dependence
on and defiance of the executive on policies of national scope may
in fact facilitate congressional leadership on matters like agricultural
price supports, public works, and transportation subsidies. Congress's
parceling out of decisionmaking authority invites vetos by determined
minorities in areas such as energy, but on matters like tobacco or
cotton supports it gives the partisans who have worked their way
onto the relevant subcommittees a chance to write their preferences
into law and — given the norms of reciprocity and mutual deference
that have developed among members working in low-conflict, distributive policy areas — to have their decisions ratified by their
peers. This is not to say that Congress or the president makes "better"
policy of one type or the other. That is a separate question, impossible
to answer in general terms. Certainly, one cannot simply assume
that "more is better"; the constraint exercised by the president on

Congress's legislative activism in the area of public works, for example, might be quite efficacious. Thwarting initiatives may on occasion be as important as taking them. The point for now is simply that Congress is willing and able to assume policy leadership on certain *types of issues* more than others. These capacities and inclinations are related as both cause and effect to the legislature's organizational fragmentation and particularism as institutionalized in the committee system.

Similarly, one's estimate of Congress's strengths and weaknesses might depend on the *stage of the policymaking process* one is talking about. Too many accounts of presidential-congressional conflict talk as though policymaking is an undifferentiated process: it is not. Issues occasionally arise overnight in response to a catastrophe or crisis, but more often they are deliberately articulated and publicized by leaders in or out of government. Once a matter is identified as an issue, specific remedies must be formulated, further information gathered, and the range of relevant interests sought out and accommodated. Finally, sufficient political force must be mobilized to hammer out a definitive legislative compromise and secure its enactment. Publicizing, formulating, gathering information, aggregating interests, mobilizing, refining and modifying — all are important and complementary aspects of the development and enactment of new policies.[4] (We leave aside the subsequent processes of funding, implementation, and oversight for the moment.) Only rarely does any single actor in the process possess sufficient skills and resources to perform all of these functions with equal success or in isolation. Legislative case histories typically reveal a division of labor — within Congress, and between Congress and the executive — in which elements of both cooperation and conflict are present and by virtue of which responsibility for the policy product is shared.

Recognition of the multifaceted and cooperative character of policymaking undermines simplistic generalizations about congressional or executive domination of the process in general. But just as Congress displays a penchant for certain types of policy, so does it have an easier time with some stages of policymaking than it does with others. One's estimate of Congress's capacities is likely to be more favorable, in short, if one is looking at the early stages of policy formation — the generating of issues, the gathering of information, the floating of new ideas, the development of the policy agenda. One interested in the capacity to forge difficult compromises and push them through to enactment is apt to be less impressed.

Again, it is important to avoid oversimplification. Obviously, the president has a tremendous capacity, at least for the top few items on his agenda, to publicize an issue and to influence the terms of subsequent debate. And we have seen how mobilization is no problem for Congress in many of the distributive, low-conflict areas in which it specializes. But if one were to look only at the early stages of policymaking, the case for congressional preoccupation with distributive policy would seem far less strong. In fact, members are often quite anxious to publicize problems and abuses and to float legislative remedies in controversial areas of broad national scope. Most of the items in President Johnson's aid-to-education, Medicare, antipoverty, and other Great Society proposals had been kicking around Congress in one form or another for years. The same is true of most of the major legislative proposals of the Carter administration. The problem is that all too often Congress's "germination" function amounts to no more than that. On high-conflict issues Congress often needs a major push from the executive or a swelling of popular opinion if its scattered initiatives are to come to fruition.

Congress's penchant for publicizing and issue-generating, like its proclivity for distributive politics, is closely tied to its organizational characteristics. And again, what spells weakness at one point may provide strength at another. In fact, Congress's decentralized, committee-centered decision structure is ideally suited to the early stages of legislative initiative. Committee and subcommittee members, as they establish their claim to a piece of policy turf and seek the approval of interested groups and constituencies, have every reason to cajole the executive, to seek out the views of concerned parties in hearings, and to establish a position of policy leadership.

A case in point is airline deregulation, which came to legislative fruition in 1978. The issue first hit the headlines in 1974 when Edward Kennedy (D-Mass.) used his Judiciary Subcommittee on Administrative Practice and Procedure to attack the Civil Aeronautics Board's approval of fare increases and its other anticompetitive regulatory practices. Howard Cannon (D-Nev.), chairman of the Commerce Subcommittee on Aviation that had jurisdiction over the CAB, had earlier reported a bill dealing with the narrower question of CAB restriction of charter airlines. While Kennedy's intrusion annoyed Cannon, it also stimulated him to increase his efforts and strengthen his own proposals in the area of airline deregulation, a matter both senators felt to be increasing in its potential salience and appeal to the public. The fact that each had the resources of a subcommittee at his disposal and that jurisdictional overlaps created competition between them clearly made for heightened congressional activity at the publicizing, information-gathering, and formulation stages.

Congressional fragmentation threatened to have a contrary effect at later stages, however. The chairman of the full Commerce Committee, closely tied to the scheduled airlines (who opposed deregulation), was skeptical of Cannon's initial efforts — to say nothing of Kennedy's. The limited jurisdiction of the Judiciary Subcommittee over the CAB prevented Kennedy from taking his efforts beyond the hearing stage. And Cannon's counterparts in the House were not sympathetic. As it turned out, the impact of anticompetitive regulation on the economy caught on as a consumer issue, and Presidents Ford and Carter took up the deregulation cause. The seeds sown by Kennedy and Cannon thus bore fruit in the 95th Congress. But the case shows how congressional decentralization could heighten their visibility and leverage at one legislative stage even as it complicated their prospects for success at another.

COMMITTEES AS A REFLECTION OF CONGRESSIONAL INDIVIDUALISM

The congressional committee system, then, both derives from and reinforces the fragmentation of power in Congress and the particularistic policy orientations of its members. The system is well-suited to the publicizing of issues and the development of the policy agenda, and it facilitates congressional leadership in distributive, constituency-related policy areas. By the same token, however, Congress is often difficult to mobilize, particularly on high-conflict issues of broad scope.

How has a system with these legislative strengths and weaknesses evolved? A comparison with the most familiar alternative model — the parliamentary system as it is found in Britain and most Commonwealth countries — points up important elements of constitutional structure and political history. The separation of powers at the federal level has removed the president and cabinet heads from any decisive control of the legislative process. And strong and cohesive parties have not emerged to bridge the gap. Party divisions in the United States, by virtue of the country's ideological inheritance and social structure, coincide neither with basic divisions in society nor with distinctive philosophical outlooks. Organizationally and ideologically diffuse, American parties have displayed only a limited capacity to bind together the branches of the federal government — and disparate elements within the legislature — in the pursuit of well-defined policy goals.

There have been historical variations in the allegiance party has commanded both in the electorate and among officeholders. Relatively strong party and/or executive leadership has characterized a number of state legislatures and, at certain periods, the U.S. Congress itself. But the general pattern is clear: while their parliamentary counterparts have seen adherence to party discipline as the most promising pathway both to electoral security and to power and preferment within the government, members of Congress have seen it as one alternative among many and by no means always the most promising one. The looseness of the party tie in the electorate and within government, and the vagueness of the parties' ideological and programmatic appeals, have made it possible for members to respond to a broad range of cues and to develop alternative bases of electoral support and political leverage.

Thus to an appreciable extent, members of Congress, as politicians seeking election and re-election in the American setting, are "on their own."[5] They are generally nominated not by party caucuses or conventions but in direct primaries. Most of their local partisan supporters, even when cohesively organized, will be only casually concerned with the party's national platform and will offer few inducements toward teamsmanship in Washington. Most members must raise their own funds and build their own organizations at both the primary and general election stages. Less than half of the variation from election to election in most congressional districts is attributable to national partisan swings, and voter defections from party identification are becoming more and more common up and down the ballot. Understandably, members are inclined to see the services they render to their districts and their visibility there as more crucial to their electoral fortunes than whatever advantages they might gain from high presidential and partisan support scores in Washington. Certainly it should come as no surprise that when party cues and district interests clash, members of the American Congress, in contrast to their parliamentary counterparts, frequently defect from their party.

The maintenance of electoral strength involves more than "voting the district" on critical issues, however. David Mayhew has developed a typology of the kinds of activities legislators in the American setting find it electorally useful to engage in. They *advertise*, building name familiarity and a favorable image through newsletters, newspaper and radio reports to the district, and huge volumes of mail. They *claim credit*, performing thousands of favors for constituents, facilitating their dealings with government agencies, and publicizing the member's role in securing projects and allocations of funds for the district. And they *take positions*, making speeches, introducing bills, publicizing their roll call votes, assuming postures designed for maximum electoral appeal.[6] This list of congressional activities is not exhaustive; few members can be viewed purely and simply as seekers after re-election. But the collective portrayal in many respects rings true. The fact that elections are focused on single-member districts often remote from national electoral trends, and that party organizations are highly decentralized and generally in decline, places American legislators "on their own" electorally and makes advertising, credit-claiming, and position-taking a rational adaptive strategy.

It is important to recognize how congressional policymaking — characterized as it is by fragmented power, particularism, and the domination of committees — fits into this broader picture. Often electorally minded members will see little reason to defer to presidential or party leadership, but will have strong incentives to secure needed benefits for their districts, to exert leverage on critical federal agencies, and to take visible policy stands. The committee system is admirably equipped to help in this regard. Committees like Agriculture, Interior, Public Works, and Merchant Marine enable members to have a hand in the formulation of legislation crucial to their districts and to claim credit for it. Membership on Appropriations, Public Works, Armed Services, Commerce, and other committees gives members an inside track with relevant federal agencies as they plan their activities, administer projects, and allocate funds. Although most committees offer a forum for position-taking and the staff resources to underwrite policy advocacy, some, like the Foreign Relations and Government Operations Committees in both houses, have become particularly noteworthy as arenas for the exposure of alleged abuses and the publicizing of policy stances.

Members seek not only electoral security but also power and prestige within the governmental establishment. This desire gives party and executive leaders some leverage with members, but here, too, the committee system has a great deal to offer. Legendary Senate power broker Robert Kerr, as chairman of the Public Works Subcommittee on Rivers and Harbors and a key member of the Finance Committee, needed and wanted no additional institutional base, least of all the party leadership; he could bargain for virtually anything he wanted with his fellow members and the Kennedy administration. More recently, the policy role assumed by House members of modest seniority like Bob Eckhardt (D-Tex.) in consumer affairs, Lee Hamilton (D-Ind.) in Mideast policy, and Charlie Rose (D-N.C.) in agriculture would scarcely have been conceivable without the prior parceling out of power and authority through the committee-subcommittee system.[7] Committees give members expertise, a voice in policy formation, and bargaining leverage with their peers and the executive that only a few leaders would enjoy in a more hierarchical system.

Recent years have seen a heightening of the electoral and power stakes that members have perceived in the committee system and some altering of that system in the process. Government has grown, policies and programs have proliferated, and the ties that bind citizens and localities to federal agencies have become more numerous and more complicated. It has thus become increasingly important for the legislator who would be "effective" to be in a position to influence policy formulation and to intervene effectively on behalf of persons, groups, and governments with a stake in various programs. At the same time, party identifications have faded in the electorate, party organizations have eroded, districts have grown in size and heterogeneity, and television has become a dominant campaign medium. Highly visible position-taking, credit-claiming, and policy leadership have become far more important electoral techniques than they were in the days of friends-and-neighbors and clubhouse politics.

All of this has made members more anxious to gain the visibility and resources that come with committee and subcommittee leadership and at an earlier point in their careers. New members have been increasingly unwilling to defer to their party and committee elders or to adhere to the norms of apprenticeship that formerly kept junior members "in their place." On virtually every House and Senate committee there have been strong pressures over the past three decades to create more subcommittees, to give them more authority, and to spread the leadership around. For a number of years virtually every majority-party senator, including most freshmen, has been assured of a subcommittee chairmanship. Rules changes and pressures from the membership have made subcommittee chairmanships available to almost half of the House Democrats as well.

Further changes in rules and practice have made desirable committee and subcommittee assignments more widely available, have increased and dispersed staff resources, and, by increasing the autonomy and authority of subcommittees, have greatly enhanced their value as mechanisms for issue and policy development. In short, the congressional committee system, characterized by particularism and fragmented power, in recent years has become *more* fragmented but in ways that are highly serviceable to individual members desiring a base for self-promotion and a piece of policy "turf." How serviceable the trend is for the policymaking capacities of Congress as a whole is, however, a more complicated question.

COMMITTEES AS A CORRECTIVE TO CONGRESSIONAL INDIVIDUALISM

As we have seen, congressional committees fill the policymaking vacuum left by the absence of strong, cohesive parties. Moreover, the dominance of congressional committees in policymaking is highly functional for the electoral and power needs of individual members. From the first, however, committees have been regarded not simply as an organizational form appropriate to large and diffuse assemblies such as the U.S. House and Senate, but as a means of overcoming some of the decisionmaking difficulties such assemblies experience.

Henry Clay, Speaker intermittently from 1811 to 1825, first brought committees to a dominant role in the conduct of House business. Although he was constrained by the necessity of including spokesmen for numerous blocs on key committees, his delegation of decisionmaking to these sublegislatures still represented "a functional adaptation to the early Congress's incapacity to organize itself for effective policymaking by majorities."[8] While the committee system reflects congressional decentralization and the aspirations of individual members, it also represents a corrective to congressional individualism. The committee system is a means of bringing expertise and attention to bear on congressional tasks in a more concerted fashion than the free enterprise of scattered members could be expected to accomplish.

As one observes legislators scrambling for subcommittee chairs and liberalizing the rules of participation, it is easy to assume that they want as much policymaking "action" as they can get and that the committee-subcommittee system simply accommodates their desires. This assumption, however, seriously underestimates the independent impact the committee system has on their priorities and their behavior. As Mayhew has pointed out, the quest for re-election often leads members to no more than superficial stabs at policymaking; a desire to "claim credit" will awaken interest only in those few measures most directly related to the constituency, while "position taking" generally requires only the publicizing of an issue, not any serious attempt to do anything about it.[9] In other words, members will often need incentives beyond the desire for public approval and electoral success if they are to undertake the arduous tasks of policy development and oversight of the executive. One House freshman makes clear that one of the reasons for his extensive labors on the Commerce Subcommittee on Oversight is *not* the electoral payoff: "My work hasn't gotten much play back in the district."[10] Even in a highly visible issue like health, the electoral rewards are slim. As another member notes: "Very few people back in the district know anything about the work I do on that subcommittee."

Why, then, do members engage in serious legislative work? Many, in fact, do not. Congress contains many members who concentrate on constituent service, self-promotion, and the taking of well-publicized stands on issues — what Speaker Rayburn liked to call "show horse" behavior. Such members may be re-elected by large margins, and recently several notorious examples have gained "promotion" from House to Senate.[11] But they are unlikely to gain that power and prestige within the governmental establishment that many legislators covet. This desire for a reputation in the Washington community provides a crucial motivation for the serious engagement of policy problems. The committee system channels these desires for leverage and status into activity that serves the *institution's* needs and builds its policymaking capacities. Members who do not pull their weight are apt to feel the disapproval of fellow committee members, and most members understand quite well that to slough off as a sub-committee chairman is to gain an unfavorable reputation as a lightweight.

In other systems legislators are induced to do serious work by the prospect of promotion and preferment within the party or the government. In the American setting, where these structures have less to offer, the committee system represents an alternative incentive-producing mechanism indigenous to the legislature. Without committees, American legislators would have many fewer inducements to, and opportunities for, serious legislative and oversight activity. Committees thus provide an important corrective to what analysts like Mayhew regard as the natural tendencies of the system. Members who wish to influence the direction of policy and/or to enhance their standing and leverage in Washington find in committee work the prescribed and often quite promising means to these objectives.

Although committees stimulate legislative efforts, those efforts are still likely to reflect the fragmentation and particularism discussed earlier. The committees handling agriculture, maritime, or other policies are generally populated by members with a particular stake in these programs, and they are often able to write their bills without paying much attention to conflicting objectives or broader impacts. Thus the aggregate congressional output is apt to appear uncoordinated, unbalanced in favor of those interests that have a firm footing in the committee system, extravagant (since each committee is authorizing programs it favors and is usually taking little account of overall spending levels), and vulnerable to delay and obstruction in areas of conflict. These characteristics of congressional policymaking are often at the root of legislative-executive conflict. Because rampant particularism is apt to lead to successful challenges by the executive, concern in Congress is excited as well. Hence the need arises for a second "corrective," not only to the undisciplined impulses of individual members, but also to the policy they produce once in harness. The committees, the major element of the "solution" in the first instance, become part of the problem in the second.

It is common to contrast the "centrifugal" force represented by congressional committees to the "centripetal" force of party leadership.[12] Indeed, the parties and executive leadership are critically important in setting priorities, resolving conflicts, overcoming procedural obstacles, and mobilizing majorities — all functions that a particularistic, fragmented assembly is likely to find problematic. But here, too, committees comprise part of the solution.

Appropriations and Budget Committees

The House and Senate formed their modern appropriations committees in the early twenties, reversing a process whereby jurisdiction over key appropriations bills had been parceled out to numerous legislative committees. Since then, any program authorized by these committees has had to undergo a second scrutiny by the appropriations panels to determine the level at which it would be funded. The power and reach of the appropriations committees has made them highly sought after by members who wish to ensure adequate funding for one program or another and who value the bargaining leverage such a position provides. But the appropriations committees, especially in the House, have also cast themselves in key *institutional* roles as guardians of the budget and protectors of Congress against its own (and the executive's) enthusiasms.

Richard Fenno has found one key "strategic premise" to dominate House Appropriations deliberations: "reduce executive budget requests."[13] Committee members are socialized to adhere to this norm of fiscal austerity. They understand that those who "fit" tend to fare better on the committee. Moreover, most House members feel that they have a collective stake in the power and fiscal control exercised by the committee. This sets up a certain tension; members feel less strongly about this collective stake when it is their programs that are being cut. Therefore, Fenno finds appropriations members holding a second strategic premise in tension with the first: "provide adequate funding for executive programs." In view of their own political stakes and the expectations of their colleagues, appropriations members cannot push their budget-tightening, control functions too far. Nevertheless, they still see themselves as protecting Congress's institutional credibility and the coherence of its policy product — and most members, in granting the appropriations committees extraordinary deference, have proved willing to underwrite such a role.

Appropriations has its limits as a control device. The norm of budget-cutting can easily become indiscriminate, particularly when thousands of complex items must be dealt with quickly and resources for program evaluation are limited. Nor is the appropriations process immune to the fragmentation and particularism that characterizes the committee system generally. In both houses the appropriations committees have become, in effect, holding companies for 13 largely autonomous subcommittees, and in areas like health, public works, and defense, norms of fiscal austerity have tended to give way to those of client and constituent service. Moreover, such control as the appropriations committees might have exercised has been sapped by "backdoor spending" techniques such as the granting of fixed entitlements to beneficiaries and of contract and borrowing authority. By fiscal 1974 only some 44 percent of the budget could be directly controlled by the appropriations committees on an annual basis. And appropriations at best covers only half the fiscal picture; the intake side is controlled by separate revenue committees — Ways and Means in the House and Finance in the Senate. Yet any effort at fiscal control clearly requires coordination of taxing and spending policy.

It was a recognition of these deficiencies of appropriations as a control device, as well as the immediate challenge represented by President Nixon's impoundments and his accusations that Congress was irresponsible and free-spending, that led Congress to pass the Budget and Impoundment Control Act of 1974. New budget committees were formed in both houses with responsibility for setting targets to guide other committees as they passed individual authorization, appropriation, and tax bills. The new committees also had responsibility for setting binding spending and revenue totals at the end of the budget-making cycle. A Congressional Budget Office was established to give Congress a capacity for budget and policy analysis comparable to that of the executive branch.

The budget committees must still operate in a context of fragmented power. They lack specific budget and tax writing authority and are dependent on other committees for the estimates and projections they make. Close observers, however, have noted a constraining effect on the legislative committees, both in the way they organize and justify their activities and in a reduced degree of deference to client groups.[14] The appropriations committees that seemingly had the most power to lose to the new units were partially reconciled by the Budget Act's limitations on impoundment and backdoor spending. Particularly in the Senate, the Appropriations Committee found in the new procedures a means of coordinating its own subcommittee operations. It is too early to pronounce the budget committees a permanent and authoritative congressional fixture. Certainly, the House has displayed an unwillingness to see Budget evolve into a power center comparable to Appropriations. But members have proved responsive to the argument that Congress as an institution has a stake in these new control mechanisms and have generally sustained the budget committees on the floor.

The Rules and Ways and Means Committees

Two additional House committees have also performed important control functions: Rules, and Ways and Means. These committees, however, have less independence and power than they used to. The Rules Committee, which schedules and structures the consideration of measures on the House floor, was an important arm of the Speaker in the period of strong party leadership that preceded the revolt against Speaker Joseph Cannon in 1910. The committee subsequently emerged as a power in its own right. After Conservative Coalition members gained a majority on the committee in the late thirties, it frequently exercised its control functions in a way that conflicted with the Democratic party leadership. Recent years have seen major turnovers in Rules Committee membership and leadership, and rules changes have returned to the Speaker the power to name the committee's Democratic members. As a result, Rules has emerged as a "new arm of [the] leadership in a decentralized House."[15] But if party and Rules Committee functions have been brought once again into harmony, the latter can still be of considerable importance in resolving jurisdictional problems, providing feedback to the committees and an inducement to trim their sails, and preparing the way for orderly and consensual decisions on the floor.

The Ways and Means Committee has traditionally ranked with Appropriations and Rules in power and prestige and, like them, has been deferred to by the membership as a guardian of the House's institutional interests. As Mayhew points out, Ways and Means, in effect, "is hired to put a damper on particularism in tax and tariff matters and to protect what members call the 'actuarial soundness' of the social security program."[16] This deference has not been rooted merely in a desire to protect the House's place in the system; Ways and Means, after all, writes the law in areas that are important to every representative, and from 1911 until 1974 Ways and Means Democrats also controlled their party's committee assignments in the House. In recent years, as members have become less convinced that the power and autonomy of Ways and Means were in fact serving their interests, they have proved willing to weaken its control functions for the sake of greater openness and responsiveness. Emboldened by Chairman Wilbur Mills's involvement in a sex-alcohol scandal, the Democratic Caucus proceeded in the 94th Congress to enlarge the committee from 25 to 37 members and to remove the Democrats' committee-assignment functions.[17] These and earlier rules changes, together with membership turnover and the accession of a less authoritative chairman, have made Ways and Means a more diverse and accessible committee, but they have also reduced the committee's capability to develop a united front and to keep its bills intact on the floor.

The powerful role that the old Ways and Means Committee played in mobilizing the House was dramatically demonstrated in 1970 and 1971 as it steered the Nixon administration's controversial welfare reform bills to passage (both bills died in the Senate Finance Committee, where conflict was sharper and less controlled). It would be too simple to blame the failure of the Carter administration's analogous bill in the House in 1978 to the decline of Ways and Means's cohesion and capacity to mobilize, but this much can be said: the support and the clout of Ways and Means were major assets for the Nixon administration, assets that the Carter administration would have found immensely valuable in its welfare and energy battles had they been available eight years later.

Ways and Means's reduced capacity was not limited to isolated instances. While committee bills were subjected to an average of 25 roll calls in the 91st-93rd Congresses, the average figure jumped to 96 in the 94th and 95th Congresses. Floor votes went against the chairman's preferences only six times in the 1969-74 period (8 percent of all votes), but the chairman was reversed 33 times in 1975-78 (17 percent of all votes). Ways and Means, compared to other committees, still commands considerable deference.[18] But the trend is unmistakable: challenges to Ways and Means have become more frequent and more often successful. Given the committee's past role, this represents a decline in the House's capacity to counter particularism and the fragmentation of power.

Summary

Our discussion of the Appropriations, Budget, Rules, and Ways and Means Committees suggests that, while the committee system mirrors congressional fragmentation, particularism, and individualism, it also represents a corrective of sorts to these organizational characteristics. The corrective mechanisms are themselves rather dispersed and subject to centrifugal pressures; nor are they effective to a degree that would satisfy the advocate of parliamentary or party government. But committees represent not only a device for spreading power and servicing the needs of members, but also a means by which Congress partially overcomes its policymaking disabilities and difficulties. Realistic attempts to increase the coherence of Congress's policy product must therefore look beyond the standard remedies of party and executive control to ways of building on the committee system's strengths and altering its operations from within. The House Select Committee on Committees' attempt in 1974 to recast jurisdictional boundaries and Speaker Tip O'Neill's appointment in 1977 of intercommittee ad hoc groups to process energy and welfare legislation represent two not altogether auspicious attempts in this direction.[19]

DIFFERENCES AMONG COMMITTEES: THE POLICY IMPACT

Thus far we have explored the reasons for the persistence of committees as the dominant organizational form in Congress and have asked how these structures are related to the institution's general ability to make public policy. As Richard Fenno has stressed, however, congressional committees not only *matter;* they also *differ* in ways that have a considerable impact on the decisions they make and the authority they are able to muster.[20] Any account of congressional policymaking that attains any degree of specificity is bound to explore not only the effects of a committee-centered organizational structure in general, but also the dimensions along which committees and their policy roles systematically vary. Our task in the space remaining is to indicate which aspects of committee life should be examined if we want to understand the kind of policy they produce.

Committees are collections of individuals who bring different goals, values, identifications, and skills to their committee roles; the performance of a committee may in part be seen as a function of these characteristics of its membership. According to Fenno, one of three broad "member goals" predominates on many House committees and shapes their respective policy roles: gaining influence in the House, helping constituents and thereby insuring re-election, and mak- . ing good public policy. For example, the Appropriations Committee's willingness to hold the line on spending and its determination to guard the power of the purse may be explained in terms of its members' orientation toward power in the House; the Interior Committee's determination "to secure House passage of all constituency-supported, member-sponsored bills" is rooted, by contrast, in the predominance of constituent-service orientations among its membership.[21]

While such goals undoubtedly influence members' initial choice of a committee and continue to influence their behavior after they are seated, they are often too general to explain many of the policymaking tendencies and trends that committees display. For example, Ways and Means's recent tendency to report more, and more controversial, legislation may reflect a shift in emphasis from the cultivation of power in the House to the making of "good public policy." But both goals have been important all along; more decisive may have been shifts in membership views of what *constitutes* "good public policy" and in preferred strategies for accommodating the parent chamber. The recent performance of oversight on the House Government Operations Committee, "more aggressive and wider in scope than previously," is more plausibly explained by increases in member liberalism and activism than by any turnabout in general member goals.[22] The Senate Commerce Committee is also impossible to categorize in terms of any one dominant member objective; the recent dampening of consumer and environmental protection initiatives on the committee is less indicative of any shift in its eclectic mix of member goals than of the replacement of several of its liberal activists with different kinds of members.

These examples point up the difficulty of pigeonholing committees according to Fenno's criteria. A richer account of member characteristics is needed if one is to account for legislative performance. Clearly important is *ideology,* the members' beliefs about the proper role of government and desirable goals for public policy. Equally decisive can be the members' *legislative orientations* — the degrees of initiative and activism they are willing to undertake or support. Members' *ties* and *identifications* can exert a powerful influence on both the frequency and content of their policymaking efforts. Finally, the particular *purposes* and *skills* of individual members and groups of members must be taken into account as a critical determinant of what committees undertake. These multifarious member characteristics are not as elusive or as difficult to generalize about as it might seem. Often committees attract members with similar constituency ties or ideological inclinations, and committee life itself can foster common goals and orientations. In any event, analysis of this sort is necessary if we are to understand committee performance.

The characteristics of committee and subcommittee leaders can have a particularly important policy impact. The dispersion of power in Congress and the degree of autonomy enjoyed by committee and subcommittee chairs places a great many people in a position to translate their objectives more or less directly into policy proposals and public law. This autonomy, to be sure, is not what it once was. Recent congressional history contains numerous examples of leaders who were deposed and prospective leaders who were denied their slots because they were judged hostile to the interests of a caucus or committee majority. The denial of subcommittee chairs to several senior representatives in 1979 suggests, in fact, that members are becoming more willing to violate seniority not simply in cases of extreme autocracy or misconduct but also where "one candidate's views are closer to them than the others."[23] Still, most committee and subcommittee leaders can be expected to retain their slots and to enjoy a great deal of latitude in implementing their own priorities and preferences. Several recent examples of leader-induced change leave little doubt that much of what is done on committees is a function of their leaders' goals and skills. Senate Commerce Committee activism was reduced upon Howard Cannon's accession to the chairmanship in the 95th Congress, and a broadening of the Judiciary Committee's agenda came with Edward Kennedy's chairmanship in the 96th.[24]

At the subcommittee level the effect can be even more profound. For example, in 1975 House Commerce Democrats replaced Harley Staggers (D-W.Va.) with John Moss (D-Calif.), an unusually active and aggressive member, as chairman of the Oversight and Investigations Subcommittee. A series of major alterations in the subcommittee's product and performance, including heightened levels of activity and increased attention to highly controversial health and energy issues, followed this leadership change:

> By far the most important factor in altering the [subcommittee's] role was the selection of John Moss as chairman. Rules changes

made it possible for committee Democrats to make a deliberate choice for the position, and they increased the autonomy and resources Moss enjoyed after he won. But the "reforms" themselves would have had little impact on performance had the swing vote on that seventh ballot gone to Staggers.[25]

The characteristics of a committee's staff also affect significantly its policy role. The past decade has erased many of the disparities that once existed in the size and expertise of committee staffs. As recently as 1964, Harry Byrd ran the Senate Finance Committee with one professional staff member, but those days are gone forever. In 1960 all congressional committees and subcommittees taken together employed fewer than 1,000 persons; by 1977 the total was well over 3,000. Committee aides are more likely now to have specialized experience and training, and less likely to be purely patronage appointees.[26] More significant differences remain with respect to the distribution of staff resources within committees. Here too some of the disparities have been reduced: rules changes have generally assured House subcommittees of sizable staffs and of independence from the full committee chairmen in appointing them and directing their work, while Senate rules now provide junior members with personal aides to cover their committee responsibilities. But the Senate still has several committees where the chairman virtually monopolizes staff resources, and in both houses there are some committee staffs so decentralized as to make an efficient division of labor impossible and the full committee practically bereft of expertise.

Staffs also vary in their partisanship, which affects both their accessibility and the kind of services they render. While most committees have established the separate majority and minority staffs authorized by the Legislative Reorganization Act of 1970, the degree of cooperation between them varies widely. And the House Appropriations and Budget committees and the armed services and ethics committees in both houses have maintained the tradition of a "nonpolitical" bipartisan staff.

Finally, the orientations of committee staffers toward their work influence the number and kinds of projects their committees undertake. While these orientations are often prescribed by committee leaders, and their impact is dependent on the members' receptivity to or sufferance of staff efforts, in many cases staff have considerable discretion in the handling of issues. How they define their job has an independent impact on what their mentors are able or inclined to do. This is all the more true as staffs get larger and the legislative workload increases. Staff orientations often approximate what might be termed "professional" and "entrepreneurial" syndromes, the former stressing the "neutral" provision of expertise, the latter the active stimulation of initiatives.[27] The activist role of the Senate Commerce

Committee in consumer affairs from 1965 to 1976 is a classic example of the impact a politically skilled entrepreneurial staff can have, while the Joint Committee on Internal Revenue Taxation staff, which serves the revenue committees in both houses, demonstrates the kind of credibility and clout — albeit with some limits on policy innovation — a group of experts adhering to the norms of "neutral competence" can provide. The continuing debate over how assertive and "political" the Congressional Budget Office staff should be suggests that, while such orientations will rarely be found in unmixed form, very real policymaking strengths and liabilities can come with a tilt in either direction.

ORGANIZATIONAL VARIATIONS

In exploring the policy impact of various characteristics of a committee's members and staff, we have already encountered the committee as an organization. We need to know, not simply person-for-person, who wants or aspires to what, but how roles are distributed, resources deployed, and decisionmaking controlled. Only then will we understand whose goals and preferences are likely to matter and what kind of policy leadership the committee as a whole will be able to muster. In this section two of the most important organizational variables will be considered: the degree and style of partisanship and the way power and resources are allocated via the subcommittee system.

Partisanship

The level of partisan cooperation on a committee depends on a number of factors: the ideological complexion and range of iden-tifications of the membership, the extent to which policies under the committee's jurisdiction are the objects of partisan conflict, and the styles and preferences of the full committee and subcommittee chairmen and ranking minority members.[28] Partisan cooperation gen-erally has some advantages for both sides. For the majority it means a reduced likelihood of sniping or obstruction in committee and on the floor; for the minority, a chance to contribute to key decisions at an earlier point. In areas of sharp partisan division, however, the costs of cooperation may be judged too high — the possibility of a restricted agenda or diluted policy content for the majority or of co-optation for the minority. Trade-offs in committee may develop between the "strength" of policy content and the probability of con-sensual approval; both are likely to be influenced by the extent and character of the committee's partisanship.

Subcommittee System

Recent congressional reform has focused on the subcommittee system. As already noted, subcommittee proliferation has spread authority, visibility, and resources around in both chambers; the major legislative committees had spawned an average of nine subunits by the mid-seventies. In the Senate, however, proliferation occurred later, was less formalized and standardized by rules changes, and resulted in more serious overextensions of members. With 100 members populating 174 Senate and joint committee subunits, the average senator in 1976 served on 14.3 subcommittees. Senators originally sought more accessible subcommittee positions, but they came to perceive a personal and institutional stake in a more manageable workload. Amendments reorganizing the Senate committee system in 1977 effected a modest retrenchment, reducing the 31 Senate and joint committees to 25, marginally adjusting jurisdictions, prohibiting any senator from chairing more than three committees and subcommittees (after 1978), and limiting senators to eight subcommittee memberships (three on any one committee).

Table 7-1 suggests some of the ways committees have responded to these changes. Commerce and Judiciary consolidated their subcommittees, while Human Resources, Banking, and Judiciary reduced the size of the subunits and/or forced members to choose among them.

Particularly interesting is the effect on Labor and Human Resources (formerly Labor and Public Welfare), traditionally one of Congress's most decentralized committees. Most Human Resources members are liberal activists who want a hand in many of the policy areas under the committee's jurisdiction. Each of them was on an average of 7.5 Labor and Public Welfare subcommittees before the reorganization; desirable subcommittees like Health, Education, and Employment were virtually coextensive with the full committee in their membership. The reorganization reduced the number of Labor and Human Resources subcommittees from 11 to 8, but most subcommittee chairmen were naturally reluctant to have their empires abolished or merged. This meant that most members had to drop more than half of their subcommittee slots and that the full committee became the only place where they had a crack at many of their former policy areas. Full committee markups thus became more serious affairs, the number of hearings held by the full committee began to increase, and Chairman Harrison Williams (D-N.J.) gained support for his efforts to build up the full committee's staff capacity.

Figure 7-1 gives a comparative picture of the rate and degree of decentralization on several House and Senate committees. The indicator chosen, days of hearings held at the subcommittee level,

Table 7-1 Changes in Senate Committees Before and After the Reorganization Amendments of 1977

COMMITTEES*	Number		SUBCOMMITTEES Average Size		Average Number of Assignments Per Member	
	94th Cong.	95th Cong.	94th Cong.	95th Cong.	94th Cong.	95th Cong.
Agriculture	6	7	8.0	7.3	3.7	2.9
Armed Services	9	8	7.2	7.9	4.1	3.0
Banking	8	8	8.0	5.5	4.9	2.9
Commerce	13	6	9.5	8.3	6.1	2.9
Energy	6	5	8.8	10.0	3.8	2.9
Finance	11	10	6.5	5.4	4.2	3.0
Foreign Relations	9	9	6.3	5.0	3.4	3.0
Human Resources	11	8	10.3	5.6	7.5	3.0
Judiciary	15	10	6.9	5.1	6.8	3.0
Public Works	6	6	8.2	7.0	3.7	3.0

*Many committees changed their names between the 94th and 95th Congresses: Agriculture and Forestry became Agriculture, Nutrition and Forestry; Commerce became Commerce, Science and Transportation; Interior and Insular Affairs became Energy and Natural Resources; Labor and Public Welfare became Human Resources; and Public Works became Environment and Public Works. The names of the Armed Services; Banking, Housing and Urban Affairs; Finance; Foreign Relations; and Judiciary Committees remained the same.

tells more about the processes of publicizing, information-gathering, and oversight than it does about the later stages of policy development. Nevertheless, the picture of the relative dispersal of authority and resources is a roughly accurate one. The House patterns, which were as diverse as the Senate's 15 years ago, have become more uniform. This change reflects the impact of rules that mandated the creation of subcommittees and guaranteed them a great deal of autonomy. Because the chairman and most committee members on Ways and Means are reluctant to delegate responsibility for major tax bills, these crucial items continue to be handled at the full committee level. But most House members most of the time perceive that they have a strong stake in committee decentralization, and pressures for the dispersal of authority and resources show few signs of abatement.

In the smaller and more flexibly organized Senate, members are less anxious to grasp at every available shred of subcommittee power and more apt to suffer the effects of overextension. Chamber rules and members' attitudes give Senate chairmen more flexibility than their House counterparts in determining their committees' working arrangements. As Figure 7-1 suggests, Senate committees continue to show considerable variation along the centralization-decentralization continuum. A decisive chairman still can effect a partial reversal of the parceling out of committee functions, as William Proxmire (D-Wis.) showed upon taking the Banking, Housing, and Urban Affairs helm in the 94th Congress and as Edward Kennedy (D-Mass.) demonstrated upon assuming the Judiciary Committee chair in the 96th. The new Senate rules restricting subcommittee memberships have further strengthened the hand of chairmen who wish to handle more business at the full committee level, although in their capacities as subcommittee leaders, members can be relied upon to resist the more extreme forms of consolidation.

Committees thus continue to differ, particularly in the Senate, in their degree of centralization, and these differences have an impact on policymaking. Decentralization usually increases the number of members who are able to play a substantial policy role and heightens the committee's overall quantity of activity. After the Ways and Means Committee formed subcommittees in 1974, the number of hearings held jumped by 148 percent, from 103 days in the 93rd Congress to 255 in the 94th. Increases at the later legislative stages were smaller but nonetheless impressive: from 45 to 96 committee reports (113 percent compared to an 8 percent increase in the House as a whole) and from 34 to 49 public laws enacted (a 44 percent increase compared to a 10 percent decrease in the House).

Decentralization also influences policy content: subcommittee autonomy normally reinforces the tendency of committees like Interior and Agriculture uncritically to service clientele groups, and it permits

Figure 7-1   Percentage of Days of Hearings Held at Subcommittee Level (1965-1978),* Selected Committees, 89th-95th Congresses

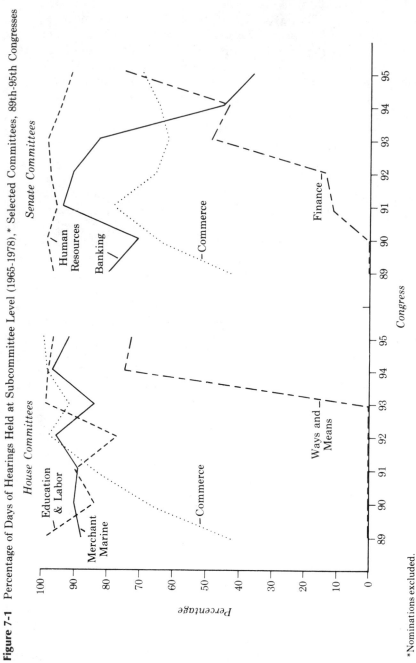

*Nominations excluded.

SOURCE: Computed from legislative calendars and other committee documents.

enthusiasts of various sorts to write their single-minded preferences into Congress's working drafts. The extent to which their particularism is modified, or their "strong" bills are diluted, will partially depend on the kind of review that is exercised at the full committee level. Such a retention of full committee authority can also increase a committee's capacity to bring a refined and credible proposal to the floor. One House Commerce member, reflecting on that committee's consolidation of subcommittee prerogatives after some resistance from Chairman Harley Staggers, makes it clear that, under the circumstances, the committee's effectiveness has increased as subcommittee heads have assumed more responsibility for the management of legislation. But he adds:

> The right chairman could play an important role in coordinating and refining what the subcommittees produce. There's also a need for a tempering role, so we don't waste lots of time coming out with something that the subcommittee members are all excited about but which really doesn't have a chance. I think a number of members would welcome such a role; we're pretty frustrated with the slipshod way things are handled in full committee now.

It is impossible to predict the substantive policy effects of decentralization in a given situation without some knowledge of to *whom* the authority and resources are being given. It could actually mean a dampening of initiative, as House Commerce Democrats recognized in denying the Consumer Affairs subcommittee chair to hardline conservative David Satterfield (D-Va.) in 1977. The House's Select Committee on Committees was correct when it suggested in 1974 that the designation of separate oversight subcommittees would ordinarily have a stimulative effect; members would be given tools and incentives, in terms of their desire for reputation and leverage, to build up an active oversight operation. Here, too, the Commerce Committee furnishes a pertinent example. The mere existence of resources and authority at the subcommittee level had only limited effect as long as Harley Staggers chaired the oversight subcommittee; it remained for John Moss to take full advantage of the entrepreneurial opportunities the situation offered.[29] Although the intentions and ties of congressional members and leaders are the major factors influencing Congress's policy product, committee organization plays a crucial role in facilitating or deflecting, stimulating or discouraging, their efforts.

THE POLICYMAKING ENVIRONMENT

Policy is influenced not only by the patterns of a committee's internal life but by the external forces that impinge on its operation. The committee's "sociology" shapes the pursuits of its members in many ways; the legislator must become a part of ongoing, institutionalized processes, and the gaining of acceptance and effectiveness requires a measure of cooperation and conformity. But committees, even the prestigious control committees of the House, can hardly be seen as insulated, self-contained organizations. They are buffeted continually by organized interests, governmental agencies, and other political forces, and their roles are often determined by how the politicians that comprise them respond to the opportunities and perils that the environment offers.

Fenno has examined four clusters of "outsiders" — members of the parent chamber, the executive branch, clientele groups, and the political parties — who are likely to have "an interest in committee behavior coupled with a capacity to influence such behavior."[30] Different outside influences predominate on different committees and are reflected in their respective policy roles. For example, the House Foreign Affairs Committee, which operates in an area where the executive traditionally dominates and the Senate tends to monopolize congressional prerogatives, generally displays a reactive policy role that has little independence about it. Education and Labor, by contrast, is a committee that various and contending elements — group, party, executive, congressional — seek to influence. The prominence of organized labor and educational groups has influenced who seeks membership on the committee and how they direct their efforts once they get there. But environmental crossfire makes many such undertakings vulnerable; both the content and the success rate of Education and Labor bills are very sensitive to presidential support and to the number of liberal Democrats in the House.[31]

One can also think of the environmental influences of a committee as a set of incentives and constraints that derive from the character of the policy the committee handles. Exactly which cluster of outsiders is able to command the attention of a committee may be less important than certain characteristics of the policy terrain that make involvement appear profitable or costly to the prospective policymaker. Committees seldom exploit all of their jurisdictional possibilities with equal enthusiasm. While our emphasis thus far has been on how certain characteristics of a congressional committee may standardize its behavior across a range of policy areas, it is also true that a single committee may construe its responsibilities differently in different areas. The Commerce committees, for example, have staked out an innovative role and advanced positions in areas like consumer protection and major disease research, while in surface transportation and communications regulation they have traditionally assumed policy leadership reluctantly and with difficulty. To account for such differences within and between committees, one needs to understand how the policy environment looks to committee members and leaders. What is it that attracts, discourages, or constrains their involvement?[32]

Table 7-2 Policy areas handled by the House and Senate Commerce Committees categorized according to the degree of public salience and conflict they are perceived to entail

| *Public* | *Level of Conflict* | | |
Salience	High	Medium	Low
High	health care delivery and environmental protection	most consumer protection measures	medical research
Medium	coordination of transportation modes	AMTRAK; coastal zone development	tourism promotion
Low	communications and transportation regulation	merchant marine subsidies; aviation promotion	oceanographic and fisheries research

Table 7-2 illustrates how several policy areas within the jurisdiction of the House and/or Senate Commerce Committees can be classified on two critical dimensions: the degree of *conflict* they entail and the *public salience* members perceive them to possess. Members wishing to gain visibility and a reputation for policy leadership find issues in the high-salience, low-conflict cells uniquely attractive, while they ordinarily avoid as unrewarding and perilous those issues that tend toward the lower left-hand cells (low-salience, high-conflict).

Other areas offer more ambiguous incentives. As constituency-servers, legislators are drawn to those distributive policies that fall, by and large, under the low-conflict, low-salience designation, but they are increasingly unlikely to see such service as greatly enhancing their public or in-house reputation. The lure of public salience may overcome the perils of conflict, leading members into high-salience, high-conflict areas like health care delivery and environmental protection, but the result can be politically costly. The difficulties that an assembly structured like the Congress presents to such broad-gauged initiatives represent an added disincentive to serious effort.

Thus may some of the environmental conditions that committees face and that influence their propensity to take up particular policy questions be identified. These conditions also influence the content of a committee's policy moves. The presence of public salience, for example, may dampen particularism (i.e., the tendency to defer to the best-organized clientele groups) even as it enhances an issue's attractiveness. Thus as aviation deregulation became a more salient public issue, it became both more likely that members would try to get "up front" on the question and less likely that they would take their cues solely from the scheduled airlines. Similarly, the presence of conflict may trigger the often-noted congressional tendency to recast redistributive and regulatory measures in some sort of positive-sum form. For example, the first draft of the Communications Act "rewrite" by Communications Subcommittee Chairman Lionel Van Deerlin (D-Calif.) contained numerous plums — unlimited license terms for local stations, for example, and a development fund for public broadcasting — designed (vainly, as it turned out) to head off the crossfire among contending interests that otherwise was sure to sink the proposal.

These examples also show that the situational conditions a committee confronts are not immutable; unpromising issues can become more attractive, and vice versa. Moreover, members can do a great deal to *prompt* such movement. Policy entrepreneurship is not simply a matter of responding to favorable conditions but involves the active building of salience and tempering of conflict. Of course, members are not absolutely bound by these conditions; their purposes and interests may lead them to idiosyncratic applications of the profit calculations we have imputed to them or to the abandonment of such calculations altogether in a given instance. The delineation of the incentives and constraints offered by the policy environment does not offer a determinate picture of committee behavior. It merely shows, given the normal desires for re-election and political influence, what sorts of issues are likely to attract committee attention most readily.

CONCLUSION

The impact of committees on the congressional policy process can be examined at two levels. The committee system as a whole both reflects and reinforces congressional particularism and fragmentation; its persistence can be understood in terms of the weakness of alternative organizational forces and the "fit" between the committee system and the re-election and power needs of individual members. Committee government gives Congress important strengths in policymaking. It insures attention to constituency-based needs and interests and provides a forum for the publicizing of a wide assortment of problems and proposals, converting the energies and ambitions of its members into institutionally useful activities. On the other hand, committee government often contributes to the difficulty Congress has in acting in high-conflict areas or in achieving overall fiscal and policy coordination.

The power granted to the "control" committees, the reliance on the president for priority-setting and political mobilization, and the strengthening of party leadership and caucus authority can all be seen as correctives, not always compatible with one another, to the shortcomings and excesses of committee government. But other "reforms" have reinforced the system's basic fragmentation and particularism. A large-scale organizational reversal seems unlikely, for the present system — whatever its shortcomings from an institutional perspective — gives most members a strong stake in its continuation.

To this general view must be added an examination of committees in their particularity, for Congress's policy product reflects not only the strengths, weaknesses, and biases imparted by the system as a whole, but also the differences that individual committees display as they develop lives of their own. Of prime importance are the purposes, ideologies, and identifications that members bring to the committee and the nature of the policy environment they face — the threats of opposition or pre-emption from influential groups and agencies, the prospects for support and alliance, the profits and costs of involvement as determined by levels of conflict and public salience. To this basic delineation of member and environmental characteristics must be added an understanding of the committee as an organization with its own ethos, leadership style, level and style of partisanship, and internal allocation of authority and resources. It is these factors that mediate and shape the efforts of individual members and thus help determine what the committee as a collectivity finally produces.

NOTES

1. Bruce I. Oppenheimer, "Congress and the New Obstructionism: Developing an Energy Policy," in this volume.
2. Woodrow Wilson, *Congressional Government* (New York: Houghton Mifflin Co., 1913), p. 78.
3. "Distributive policies are characterized by the ease with which they can be disaggregated and dispensed unit by small unit, each unit more or less in isolation from other units and from any general rule." Theodore Lowi, "American Business, Public Policy, Case-Studies, and Political Theory," *World Politics,* 16 (July 1964): 690.
4. See David E. Price, *Who Makes the Laws?* (Cambridge: Schenkman Publishing Co., 1972), pp. 2-6. For a summary account of the division of labor on 13 major bills, see pp. 289-297.
5. See the discussion in David R. Mayhew, *Congress: The Electoral Connection* (New Haven: Yale University Press, 1974), pp. 17-38.
6. Ibid., pp. 49-77.
7. See "A New Old Guard Has Come Forward in the House," *National Journal,* August 13, 1977, pp. 1264-1269; and "Freshmen in the Senate Being Seen — and Heard," ibid., March 17, 1979, pp. 439-443.
8. James Sterling Young, *The Washington Community, 1800-1828* (New York: Harcourt, Brace & World, 1966), pp. 132-133, 151.
9. Mayhew, *Congress,* pp. 110-125.
10. This and subsequent quotations are from personal interviews with Commerce Committee members.

11. For one example see Albert R. Hunt, "The 'Show Horse': Rep. Pressler Works Hard to Create Image, Not to Create Laws," *Wall Street Journal,* May 20, 1977, p. 1; and the reply by Representative Pressler in the Sioux Falls *Argus-Leader,* May 25, 1977.

12. Stephen K. Bailey, *Congress in the Seventies* (New York: St. Martin's Press, 1970), chaps. 4-5.

13. Richard F. Fenno, Jr., *Congressmen in Committees* (Boston: Little, Brown & Co., 1973), pp. 48-49.

14. See Joel Havemann, *Congress and the Budget* (Bloomington: Indiana University Press, 1978), pp. 131-133, 163-173; and John W. Ellwood and James A. Thurber, "The Politics of the Congressional Budget Process Re-examined," in this volume.

15. See Bruce Oppenheimer's account in *Congress Reconsidered,* 1st ed., edited by Lawrence C. Dodd and Bruce I. Oppenheimer (New York: Praeger Publishers, 1977), chap. 5.

16. Mayhew, *Congress,* pp. 154-155.

17. See Catherine Rudder's account in *Congress Reconsidered,* 1st ed., chap. 6.

18. For comparative data across several House and Senate committees for the period 1969-1974, see David E. Price, *Policymaking in Congressional Committees: The Impact of "Environmental" Factors* (Tucson: University of Arizona Press, 1979), p. 38.

19. For an account of the select committee's efforts, see Roger H. Davidson and Walter J. Oleszek, *Congress Against Itself* (Bloomington: Indiana University Press, 1977) and Davidson, "Two Avenues of Change: House and Senate Committee Reorganization," in this volume.

20. Fenno, *Congressmen in Committees,* pp. xiii-xv.

21. Ibid, pp. 1-14, 47-49, 57-59.

22. See Norman J. Ornstein and David W. Rohde, "Shifting Forces, Changing Rules, and Political Outcomes: The Impact of Congressional Change on Four House Committees," in *New Perspectives on the House of Representatives,* 3rd ed., edited by Robert L. Peabody and Nelson W. Polsby (Chicago: Rand McNally & Co., 1977), pp. 198, 249.

23. "New Setbacks for House Seniority System," *Congressional Quarterly Weekly Report,* February 3, 1979, p. 183.

24. The early months of the 96th Congress — marked by resistance on the part of a number of Judiciary members and aides to the plans and tactics of Kennedy and his staff, and a general wariness of new initiatives at a time of public disillusion with active government — also pointed up some of the *limitations* of leadership. See "What Happened to Judiciary?" *National Journal,* April 21, 1979, p. 653. On Commerce, see "The Cautious Approach of Cannon's Commerce Committee," ibid., May 27, 1978, pp. 846-850.

25. David E. Price, "The Impact of Reform: The House Commerce Subcommittee on Oversight and Investigations," in *Legislative Reform: The Policy Impact,* ed. Leroy N. Rieselbach, (Lexington, Mass.: Lexington Books, 1978), pp. 153-154.

26. See Susan Webb Hammond, "Congressional Change and Reform: Staffing the Congress," in ibid., pp. 185, 187 and "Growing Staff System on Hill Forces Changes in Congress," *Congressional Quarterly Weekly Report,* November 24, 1979, pp. 2631-2646.

27. For a comparison of the House and Senate Commerce Committees of the 92nd Congress on this dimension, see David E. Price et al., *The Commerce Committees* (New York: Grossman, 1975), pp. 22-41.

28. For a discussion of the factors making for overall similarities and marginal (but consequential) differences in partisanship between House-Senate counterpart committees in two instances — Commerce, and Education and Labor/Labor and Public Welfare, see ibid., pp. 50-55; Price, *Who Makes the Laws?*, pp. 261-264, 273-277; and Fenno, *Congressmen in Committees,* pp. 83-87, 174-177.
29. Price, "Impact of Reform," pp. 133, 153-155.
30. Fenno, *Congressmen in Committees,* p. 15.
31. Ibid., pp. 30-35, 226-242.
32. This discussion is adapted from Price, *Policymaking in Congressional Committees.*

8

Coalition Politics in the House of Representatives

David W. Brady and Charles S. Bullock, III

One of the main functions of the United States Congress is legitimating or enacting public policies. In order for any bill to become law, majorities in the House of Representatives and the Senate must approve the legislation. In most Western European legislatures the process of building majorities for a particular piece of legislation is dominated by political parties. In the British House of Commons, for example, members of the majority Conservative Party vote together to pass bills approved by the Conservative cabinet. When all members (or 90 percent or more) of the same party vote alike against the other party (or parties), it is called a party vote. As such, party voting simplifies the leaders' task of building majorities for legitimating public policies.

COALITIONS IN CONGRESS

The United States House of Representatives stands out from other western parliamentary bodies because of its low levels of party voting. Building majorities in the House has become a constant search for coalitions capable of governing. Thus the House majority leadership cannot count on a consistent Democratic majority to pass pro-labor, pro-agricultural assistance, and pro-consumer affairs legislation. Precisely because party voting in the U.S. House is low, different coalitions arise on different issues. As a result, the House has spawned a large number of member groups or caucuses that must be put together in order to pass legislation.

Table 8-1 shows levels of party voting (measured by a majority of one party voting against a majority of the other party) from 1932 to 1978. The results clearly indicate the decline in party voting over this 46-year period. The high point of cohesive party action occurred from 1932 to 1936 during the New Deal era, which was precipitated by the Great Depression. Since 1937, however, party as a base of agreement for congressional majorities to govern has declined. In the absence of cohesive party majorities, conflicts over policy take place within the congressional parties, splitting them into factions that have to be put together before Congress can make decisions. Thus, in a very basic sense, politics in Congress is coalitional in nature. Much of the substance of public policy in the United States is the result of the bargains and compromises necessary to build majority coalitions in the U.S. House of Representatives. In this paper we examine the oldest and most influential coalition in the House: the Conservative Coalition.

THE CONSERVATIVE COALITION

For more than 40 years liberals have blamed a combination of Southern Democrats and Republicans for defeating progressive policy.[1]

Table 8-1 Party Voting in the House, 1932-1978

Year Elected	Congress	Percentage Majority Versus Majority*	Year Elected	Congress	Percentage Majority Versus Majority
1932	73rd	70.6	1956	85th	49.2
1934	74th	59.9	1958	86th	52.8
1936	75th	63.9	1960	87th	48.8
1938	76th	71.4	1962	88th	51.7
1940	77th	41.5	1964	89th	47.1
1942	78th	49.4	1966	90th	35.8
1944	79th	48.1	1968	91st	28.2
1946	80th	44.8	1970	92nd	32.9
1948	81st	50.9	1972	93rd	36.2
1950	82nd	64.1	1974	94th	40.8
1952	83rd	44.9	1976	95th	36.7
1954	84th	42.3			

* Percentage of recorded votes in which a majority of one party voted in opposition to a majority of the other party.

Political scientist John Manley quotes from a 1939 speech by Senator Claude Pepper (D-Fla.) in which he damned the "willful alliance" that was thwarting the fulfillment of Franklin Roosevelt's 1936 campaign promises for social reform.[2] The persistence of the Conservative Coalition is recognized by Congressional Quarterly, which since 1957 has regularly reported the frequency with which members of Congress have voted with the Conservative Coalition on roll calls that pitted a majority of the Republicans and Southern Democrats against a majority of Northern Democrats. One of the most striking features about the influential and long-lived coalition is that it meets almost none of the procedural or organizational criteria for coalition building. There are no whips, no formal leaders, no inducements to members in the form of choice committee assignments or patronage. In fact, in its organizational heyday in the late 1950s, the Conservative Coalition organization consisted of short meetings between "Judge" Howard Smith (D-Va.), Chairman of the House Rules Committee, and Joe Martin (R-Mass.), the Minority Leader.[3] Interviews with strong supporters of the coalition indicated that the coalition was "an understanding between Southern Democrats and Republicans about certain issues." One respected southerner said he (Joe Waggonner, D-La.) didn't line up the votes. "They were already lined up. . . . Southern Democrats and Republicans think more alike. They are both conservative."

How then are we to understand a voting bloc that has persisted for about 40 years and is commonly referred to as a coalition when it meets few, if any, of the criteria for a formal coalition? In this paper we argue that the CC is best understood as a voting alliance functioning to block liberal legislation. Since its goal is to *block* certain legislation, it need not formally organize as do House coalitions desiring to *pass* legislation. The major factor accounting for the voting behavior is convenience. On certain issues many Southern Democrats are conservative and vote with a majority of Republicans.

We shall systematically explore the origins of the coalition — when it began and its pattern of activity — as well as determine over time the types of issues on which it has been active. In the final section we examine some correlates of the coalition's activity and success.

Structure

To understand the blocking, or convenience, nature of the Conservative Coalition, it is useful to compare it with the Democratic Study Group (DSG). In contrast with the DSG, which has a staff of 18, offices in the House Longworth Building, a whip organization, and publishes weekly summaries of legislation scheduled for House debate, the CC, despite its much longer presence on Capitol Hill, has not formalized the relationship between its Democratic and Republican components or among its rank and file members.

Manley's research supports the contention of Judge Smith and Joe Martin that strategy planning and contacts were carried out by a few Republicans and Southern Democratic leaders who could then influence the votes of the rank and file.[4] Our interviews with members serving since Smith and Martin left Congress in 1967 indicated that there is less coordination today; no southerner has assumed Smith's leadership position, and consequently no one is able to speak for Southern Democrats. Instead, coalition strategy may now be set by southerners and Republicans on the committees that handle the legislation. These members may then give voting cues to those who turn to them for advice.

Why has the Conservative Coalition never formalized its relationships? A basic reason is probably a hesitancy among both Southern Democrats and Republicans to embrace publicly across party lines. While party loyalty is a loose constraint on behavior, it has strong symbolic value as an abstract principle when not related to a specific policy issue. Thus Randall Ripley reports that most representatives profess strong partisan ties. As one Southern Democrat acknowledged, "I go through great throes when I cannot go along with my party. It is not easy to vote against your party."[5]

While differences in partisan affiliation are important, other factors also explain the lack of organization of the CC as a whole and of its contingent of Southern Democrats. A number of reasons can be suggested to differentiate the ability of the CC to function as a blocking coalition in contrast with the need for a formal structure evinced by the DSG and other positive House coalitions.

Differences in objectives is the major reason. The Conservative Coalition has generally been interested in preventing change while other coalitions have sought to enact new policies. Because of the number of decision points at which a proposed program can be defeated or diluted, the CC need triumph only once to block change. To pass new legislation, proponents must be successful at several stages and before different groups — subcommittees, full committees, the Rules Committee, the Committee of the Whole, on the floor of the House, at the conference committee, and again on the floor. The need to control the outcome at various points creates an inducement for more extensive coordination and planning than is faced by conservative opponents. Conservatives can operate more like guerrillas who need win only one battle in order to prevent the advance of the liberals. For example, as Richard Fenno has shown, conservatives delayed federal aid to public schools for years by controlling the outcome at various decision points.[6] Since one conservative victory usually will kill any chance of a program being enacted until the next Congress, it will be less necessary to fashion majorities at several points in the legislative process.

Other factors help account for the coalition's lack of organization. In the past, Southern Democrats had better attendance records on the floor than northerners. Consequently, southerners had less need for an organization that could facilitate maximum presence on the floor. One important reason for creation of the DSG was the need to encourage liberal attendance at sessions of the Committee of the Whole, as political scientists Arthur Stevens, Arthur Miller, and Thomas Mann point out:

> They [liberals] tended to represent competitive districts; hence instead of spending their time on the floor, they often were engaged in performance of constituent services or in public relations activities. Thus conservative forces had an advantage simply as a result of the people on the floor.[7]

Conservatives have had less need for information supplementing that disseminated by the leadership than have liberals. Until recently, southerners have held a disproportionate number of the committee chairmanships, especially the most prestigious ones. Occupying these important leadership positions has given them access to the information networks, so that the voting cues that were given by informed members tended to have a conservative bias.[8] Therefore, another reason behind the founding of the Democratic Study Group — the need for an independent source of information — was not present among conservatives.

Finally, the operating style of the conservatives may be less amenable to an organizational structure. The traditionally less competitive districts represented by Southern Democrats could —at least until recently — be won by politicians who practiced a very personal style of campaigning.[9] In more competitive areas, incumbents are more likely to have had to work with a campaign or party organization to get elected. Therefore, Northern Democrats find working within the framework of an organization like the DSG more compatible than do southerners who are used to operating alone in politics. However, of the above explanations the dominant factor is that the coalition's objective is to block legislation.

In summary, Southern Democrats share certain policy preferences with Republicans. The overriding goal is to maintain the status quo in the face of liberal policy innovations. Southern Democrats and Republicans have voted against much of this legislation and in doing so were labeled the Conservative Coalition. This pattern of activity is in contradistinction to the activity of groups like the Democratic Study Group that must organize to build winning majorities at each stage of the congressional policy process.

Origins

Establishing the exact date of the Conservative Coalition's appearance in the House has been a matter of speculation by political scientists, historians, and members of Congress. There is agreement that by the late 1930s it was an active force in Congress.[10] Prior to the New Deal there were, of course, some roll calls on which the coalition voting pattern would occur.

Because of the informal nature of the CC we cannot date it by determining when its leaders first met to discuss strategy. An alternative is to determine, from 1925 to the present, the percentage of times in each session of the House that the coalition was active. The use of these percentages also permits determination of the ebb and flow of coalition activity over time.

Table 8-2 shows the proportion of House coalition activity by session of Congress from 1925 to 1978 (69th-95th Congresses). A rise in coalition activity beginning in the 75th Congress (1937-39) with relatively high levels of activity continuing thereafter is evident. Coalition activity as a percent of all roll calls increases linearly from 4.3 percent (74th Congress) to 22.1 in the 79th Congress (1945-46). In the 76th Congress, coalition activity approaches 10 percent and after that never again falls below 10 percent for a Congress. Thus the 75th Congress (1937-39) appears to be the origin of the Conservative Coalition.[11]

The increase in coalition voting in 1937 coincides with the proposal for the Fair Labor Standards Act and the National Housing Act.

Table 8-2 House Conservative Coalition Activity by Congress, 69th-95th

Year Elected	Congress	Percent Active by Congress	Year Elected	Congress	Percent Active by Congress
1924	69th	3.5	1952	83rd	17.0
1926	70th	1.4	1954	84th	10.1
1928	71st	5.8	1956	85th	16.1
1930	72nd	4.9	1958	86th	19.4
1932	73rd	2.1	1960	87th	20.8
1934	74th	4.3	1962	88th	16.4
1936	75th	7.6	1964	89th	20.3
1938	76th	9.3	1966	90th	22.0
1940	77th	12.5	1968	91st	23.9
1942	78th	21.8	1970	92nd	27.9
1944	79th	22.1	1972	93rd	23.8
1946	80th	19.6	1974	94th	24.7
1948	81st	16.4	1976	95th	20.8
1950	82nd	24.9			

V. O. Key has suggested that the coalition first emerged to fight federal support for organized labor.[12] Labor legislation was a natural place for anti-New Deal Republicans and Southern Democrats to join in opposition to Roosevelt and the Northern Democrats.[13] The common ground was an interest in maintaining low labor costs. At the constituency level the bulwarks of both contingents of the coalition were businessmen, bankers, merchants, and others wanting low wages. Unions tended not to support Republicans in the North and were viewed as a disruptive influence by Democrats in the South.

Table 8-2 also reveals changing patterns of activity. Coalition activity began during Roosevelt's second term, peaked during Roosevelt's third term, and continued high through Truman's presidency. During the 78th to 82nd Congresses, the average level of activity was 21 percent, only once falling appreciably below 20 percent.

In contrast, during Eisenhower's two terms the coalition was active on 20 percent of the roll calls only twice; the average was 15.6 percent. The Kennedy-Johnson era saw a resurgence of coalition activity, much of it in opposition to Great Society programs. This resurgence persisted. Only once from the 88th to the 95th Congress did activity fall below 20 percent; the average was 22.9 percent.

It is possible to interpret the data from the 1930s in terms of the liberalness of presidential programs. Early in the New Deal, measures to remedy the effects of the Depression were strongly supported. During the second stage of the New Deal, however, activity of the coalition emerged to thwart liberal measures on "education, social welfare, public housing, immigration, taxes, labor antitrust, civil rights, public works and resource development," in the words of Representative Frank Thompson (D-N.J.).[14] Throughout the rest of the New Deal-Fair Deal era, the coalition continued to challenge Roosevelt and later Truman's more liberal policies. Eisenhower's election brought to the White House a moderately conservative Republican who worked well with Southern Democratic congressional leaders, resulting in less need to oppose liberal presidential proposals on the floor. Coalition activity increased during the Kennedy administration as a response to the increase in liberal legislation brought to the floor. Richard Nixon's presidency did not cause a drop in coalition activity comparable to that of the Eisenhower presidency, but as Manley points out, the election of Nixon was the coalition's first opportunity to attempt to check the deluge of liberal legislation passed by the 89th Congress.[15]

Issues

Since the basis for the voting alliance is a shared conservative ideology, it is useful to determine the issue areas on which the CC has been active. In defining issue areas special emphasis is placed on coordinating results with the analysis of issue domains performed by Aage Clausen and Barbara Sinclair.[16] Sinclair's analysis covers the House's shifting policy agenda from the 69th to the 76th Congress. Clausen covers the House from the 83rd through the 88th Congress. These studies provide a reasonably clear picture of the majority policy dimensions in Congress from 1926 to 1964. Although their purposes differ from ours, it is possible to match our findings to theirs. In this section roll call votes over the 1937 to 1978 period are analyzed to determine the issue areas in which coalition activity was high.

The roll call analysis showed the coalition active at one time or another in the following dimensions: agricultural assistance, social welfare, civil rights, foreign policy, and labor legislation. The two issue areas most directly comparable to our studies are agricultural assistance and social welfare.

The social welfare dimension refers to "a relatively direct intercession of the government on behalf of the individual cushioning him against jolts administered by the economy. . . ."[17] This dimension emerges in the 78th Congress as increasing numbers of southerners who had responded to the crisis of the Great Depression by supporting New Deal welfare innovations broke with their party. Sinclair's analysis of social welfare roll calls also finds evidence of this split, although she places it one Congress later.[18]

The civil rights dimension is dominated by questions concerning equal treatment of blacks and other minorities. This issue dimension was of obvious concern to Southern Democrats interested in perpetuating segregationist policies. Republicans often supported Southern Democrats on these votes, especially when they felt that too much government activism would result if the federal government had to enforce equality. Suffice it to say that since 1937 the coalition often has been active on legislation concerning civil rights.

Labor is a particularly important issue area because it gave rise to the Conservative Coalition. Clausen includes it in the social welfare dimension, but in our analysis labor is a separate issue until the 79th House.[19] Recent work by Sinclair indicates that from the 75th to 79th Congresses labor legislation was a distinct dimension from social welfare votes.[20] The labor and nonlabor dimensions merge when the regional voting pattern that had characterized the labor dimension extended to the nonlabor dimension. Labor legislation refers to attempts to have government support organized labor.

The foreign policy issue area includes all roll calls on foreign aid, participation in international organizations, and military aid to foreign nations. The principal difference between this dimension and Clausen's "International Involvement" domain is that foreign trade, defense, and presidential doctrines do not occur regularly enough to be included. Southern Democrats may vote with Republicans on

Table 8-3 House Conservative Coalition Activity in Five Issue Areas, 1937-1976

Congress Year	75th 1937	76th 1939	77th 1941	78th 1943	79th 1945	80th 1947	81st 1949	82nd 1951	83rd 1953	84th 1955	85th 1957	86th 1959	87th 1961	88th 1963	89th 1965	90th 1967	91st 1969	92nd 1971	93rd 1973	94th 1975
Labor†	*	*	*	*																
Agricultural Assistance					*	*		*												
Civil Liberties	*				*	*	*	*	*	*	*	*	*	*	*	*	*	*	*	*
Social Welfare				*	*	*	*	*	*	*	*	*	*	*	*	*	*	*	*	*
Foreign Policy											*	*	*	*	*	*	*	*	*	*

* Indicates the presence of the issue cluster.
† In 1945 Labor merges into Social Welfare dimension.

matters like funding the Organization of American States, but they do not vote together against Northern Democrats on foreign trade and defense measures. On the basis of this difference, we have called this dimension foreign policy rather than using Clausen's term. The direction of the coalition's voting pattern was and is restraint in dealing with other nations and international organizations and against "loose" immigration policies.

In sum, at various times between 1937 and 1976 the Conservative Coalition actively opposed legislation supporting labor unions, social welfare, and civil liberties. In addition, the coalition was active on foreign policy and agriculture assistance measures. Table 8-3 shows the pattern of House coalition activity over time for each of the five issue dimensions.

The issue dimensions that dominate coalition activity are clearly civil rights and social welfare. Foreign policy, as we have defined the issue, appears with Eisenhower's presidency and continues to be important. Labor was a separate policy area from 1937 to 1945 but thereafter is absorbed into the social welfare area. The three issue areas identified by us in the 86th and 87th Congresses — civil liberties, social welfare, and foreign policy — coincide closely with ones on which Northern and Southern Democrats were substantially divided in W. Wayne Shannon's analysis.[21]

Agricultural assistance — legislation designed to subsidize farmers — provides an interesting footnote to our thesis regarding convenience as the basis for the coalition's activity. In the 78th, 79th, 80th, and 82nd Houses, Midwestern Republicans joined Southern Democrats to support farm subsidies. Republican support was prompted by the conditions surrounding price supports during and after the Second World War. During the war, price supports were above parity levels to encourage farm production, a policy supported by the American Farm Bureau Federation. However, from 1943 to 1945 urban Democrats voted for lower and more flexible price supports. The combination of factors resulted in roll call votes meeting Conservative Coalition criteria. Since World War II, farm policy has flip-flopped between lower, flexible supports and above parity supports. Until 1953, Republicans joined Southern Democrats in favor of higher supports. Ultimately, the AFBF switched its position and in the 1950s came to favor a more market-oriented policy (lower supports). Since the AFBF's policy switch, very few agricultural roll calls have featured Conservative Coalition voting patterns.

Our analysis of CC origins and levels of activity shows that the coalition originated on the labor issue where Southern Democrats and Republicans shared the same interest, and that over time other issue areas came to be viewed in terms of shared interests. Therefore, it is safe to conclude that the Conservative Coalition has been an important facet of the congressional policy process for more than 40 years.

Activity and Success

We have argued that the Conservative Coalition is essentially a voting alliance to block liberal legislation. Determining whether this thesis is correct entails examining correlates of both the coalition's floor activity and its success levels.

Activity. Since the CC is issue based and has as its primary objective preventing the adoption or expansion of liberal programs, it need succeed in only one of two arenas: in committee or on the floor. If coalition supporters are well-organized in committee, then they can prevent undesirable legislation from reaching the floor or else modify it to make it acceptable. If they are unable to shape the legislation to their liking in committee, the CC may succeed in defeating or amending it before the full House. In short, the coalition may either block or change legislation before it reaches the floor; its control of committees would therefore be related to activity rates. Or the coalition could vote against liberal legislation on the floor itself; and in that case the coalition's numerical strength would be related to its activity rates.

The organizational variables that measure the coalition's ability to prevent legislation from reaching the floor are 1) the proportion of the standing committees on which Southern Democrats are chairmen or ranking minority members, and 2) the number of southerners chairing or serving as the ranking minority member on the chamber's three most prestigious committees: Appropriations, Rules, and Ways and Means. Shannon observes that, "There can be no doubt at all that the committee-seniority system greatly amplifies the effects of Southern Democratic dissidence."[22] Another study points to Southern Democrat-Republican control of the most powerful committees as critical to Conservative Coalition influence in the House.[23]

During much of the period studied, the Rules Committee was a largely autonomous body that could prevent the movement of legislation to the floor or to conference committees. Certainly, prior to the 87th Congress, a conservative voting alliance operating on Rules succeeded in preventing floor consideration of certain liberal programs. Appropriations offers a chance to limit programs that the coalition failed to check during the authorization process. The third committee, Ways and Means, served as the Democrats' committee on committees prior to 1975 as well as handling all aspects of tax legislation. This base made it one of the most influential committees of the House.

The coalition's floor strength is measured by determining the proportion of House Democrats who are from the North and the proportion of Republicans and Southern Democrats in the House. The first measure taps the strength of the coalition's floor opposition, while the second taps the floor strength of the coalition itself.

We will test alternate notions about CC activity. On the one hand, if committee and subcommittee markup sessions are places where the coalition may succeed and thereby avoid a floor fight, then we would expect a negative relationship (correlation) between Southern Democratic strength at the committee level and coalition floor activity. We might further anticipate that when southerners constitute a large share of the Democrats' House contingent or when Republican House strength is high, then Northern Democrats, realizing that they are unlikely to win floor votes, may not push proposals opposed by the Conservative Coalition. Such a situation would result in a negative relationship (correlation) between the coalition strength and frequency of CC activity and a positive relationship between Northern Democratic strength and CC floor activity. Support for these propositions would indicate greater organization than we expect for the Conservative Coalition.

The alternative perspective suggests that because of a lack of organization, potential coalition strength will not dissuade Northern Democrats from bringing issues to floor votes. Although northern liberals may be defeated in committee and recognize that they have little hope of floor success, they may demand a roll call either on the off chance that they may defeat the unorganized CC or to create a record on which the Democratic party, particularly its presidential wing, can run in the future. James Sundquist provides a number of examples in which Northern Democratic failures during the Eisenhower years laid the groundwork for the programs that formed the heart of the Kennedy-Johnson presidencies.[24] Our expectation is that neither the measures of Southern Democratic committee strength nor the measures of coalition floor strength will be strongly related to CC activity.

Table 8-4 depicts the correlates (Pearson) of CC floor activity from its emergence in the 75th Congress through the 94th Congress. The correlation coefficients can vary from -1.0 to $+1.0$; the higher the value, the stronger the relationship. Table 8-4 indicates that none of the measures is strongly related to coalition activity. Of the two measures of southern committee control, only the weaker one ($r = -.11$) is in the direction anticipated if southern influence on committees reduces the necessity of the coalition to become active on the floor. Thus there is little support for the hypothesis that when southerners chair committees they prevent issues coming to the floor in such a way as to challenge conservative preferences.

Table 8-4 Relationship Between the Conservative Coalition's Committee and Floor Strength in the House and Levels of Coalition Activity, 75th-95th Congresses

	Activity**
Southern Democrats Chairing 3 Most Prestigious Committees* (%)	.25
Committees Chaired by Southern Democrats (%)	−.11
Northern Democrats + All Democrats	.11
Coalition Strength	.27

 * The Appropriations, Rules, and Ways and Means Committees.
** The numbers are Pearsonian Product Moment Correlations.

Is the coalition more active when northerners constitute a relatively greater share of the House Democratic contingent? Measures of floor strength point to only a weak correlation, (r = −.11). However, a stronger correlate is the size of the coalition in the House, (r = −.24). This indicates that activity increases somewhat when the coalition is strong. However, since none of the correlations are at the .5 level or above, we can conclude that coalition activity is relatively independent of such factors as southern control of committees or coalition floor strength.[25] Coalition activity cannot be explained as simply a product of the coalition's potential for internal organization and power. Moreover, there is only weak evidence that the coalition's potential voting strength is related to floor activity. When we consider the variables for both Northern Democratic and coalition strength, a possible inference is that liberals are more likely to push their proposals to a floor vote when their position in the House is weak than when their position in the party is strong.

Success. In order to win, the coalition must have a majority of those present and voting. Thus, while being active entails opposition only, winning means majority building, which depends on such factors as electoral results and politicking for votes. In this section we measure CC success in terms of coalition activity: How often did it win when active?

An overview of the coalition's success shows that from 1939 to 1956, the coalition won almost all of the roll calls on which Southern Democrats and Republicans opposed Northern Democrats. The success rate during this period falls below 80 percent only once, and the average is 92.4 percent. After 1956 the percent winning rises above 90 only once, and there are five sessions where the percent winning falls below 50. Moreover, the average percent winning after 1956 is only 61.2, a 31.2 percentage point decline.

Further analyses of patterns of coalition winning in the House show that from 1937 (76th Congress) to 1956 (84th Congress) the coalition always won over 80 percent of the time; the break point occurs in the 85th (1957-58) and 86th (1959-60) Congresses when the coalition's success rate falls to as low as 36 percent. This is interesting because it coincides with electoral gains by liberal Northern Democrats and the formation of the Democratic Study Group. The results of further analysis of coalition winning patterns indicate that the DSG's perception of conservative strength in the House was correct: the coalition *had* successfully blocked liberal legislation for over 20 years and for liberals to circumvent the coalition's strength, they would have to get organized. The only other sharp break in the coalition's success rate in the House occurs in the 89th (1965-66) Congress when it hit an all-time low as a result of Lyndon Johnson's landslide presidential victory over Barry Goldwater. It is interesting to note that the 89th Congress passed the most liberal legislation since the early days of the New Deal.

Coalition success prior to 1956 was high in part because Northern Democrats lacked organization, and majorities in the House were slim. In fact, the only two Houses since 1930 where the Republicans were in the majority occur during this period. Since 1958, when Democrats gained more than 50 seats, Democratic majorities have been larger. Common sense dictates that as the size of the coalition forces decreases so too does their ability to win.

Both activity levels and success rates of the CC vary over time. Sometimes coalition activity is high, but the success rate is low. For example, during the 89th Congress the level of activity in the House was over 20 percent, but the success rate was only about one for every four contested roll calls. On the other hand, during the 83rd Congress the activity level was only 17 percent, but the success rate was 100. In order to analyze these various combinations of activity and success, we looked at the proportion of *all* House roll calls that were won by the coalition. This serves as a measure of the coalition's overall significance in shaping floor decisions.

From 1938 to 1944 the coalition was increasingly important in determining House decisions, with a winning percentage growing from 3 percent to 26 percent of all roll calls. The decade 1943-53 is the high point of the coalition's overall significance, with the coalition winning 21.6 percent of all roll calls. However, beginning in 1954 and continuing through 1966, the coalition's influence was at its nadir. Only once — in 1961 — did the coalition win more than 20 percent of the votes. The CC was active throughout this period but not as successful on the floor. The low point was the 89th Congress when the coalition's overall success in the House was only 6 percent. During the last biennium of the Johnson presidency and the Nixon-

Ford era, there was a recovery in CC strength that peaked at 26 percent in 1971. For the other nine years the range was from 12 to 8 percent.

We turn now to correlates of success. Potential correlates are the measures used previously of the coalition's ability to prevent liberal legislation (Table 8-4) — Southern Democrats chairing the three most prestigious committees and the number of all committees chaired by Southern Democrats — and two measures of the potential strength of the coalition's opposition — the size of the Northern Democratic faction in the House and its cohesion on CC roll calls.[26] The reasons for using the committee positions of Southern Democrats as an independent variable have already been given. The argument for using Northern Democrats' size and cohesion is that when this bloc is numerous and cohesive, as in 1958 and 1964, the coalition's success rate declined. Both size and cohesion are expected to be negatively related to CC success. We hypothesize that the coalition's internal committee strength will not be strongly related to its success; the CC is a voting alliance that is not always sufficiently organized to prohibit liberal legislation from reaching the floor.

Table 8-5 shows that Southern Democrats' committee strength is not related to coalition success. In fact, both measures are negatively related to success rates slightly. In contrast, the number of Northern Democrats is highly correlated with CC success rates while the relationship between Northern Democratic cohesion and CC success is significant and in the hypothesized direction. These data support the contention that coalition success largely depends on electoral results. When elections bring more Northern Democrats to the House, the coalition's chances of success decrease and the amount of liberal legislation passed increases.

The results of the analysis of both CC activity and success point clearly to an interpretation of the CC as a blocking alliance rather

Table 8-5   Correlates of House Conservative Coalition Success, 75th-94th Congresses

	Roll Call Victories as a Percent of	
	Roll Calls on Which Coalition Was Active	*All Roll Calls*
Southern Democrats Chairing 3 Most Prestigious Committees	−.02	−.09
Committees Chaired by Southern Democrats	−.18	−.21
Number of Northern Democrats	−.67	−.56
Cohesion of Northern Democrats	−.36	−.28

than a formal coalition. CC control of the internal resources of the House was not related to either floor activity or success. This means that it did not control access to the floor via committee decisions nor did such control affect outcomes. The dominant correlate of CC success on votes was the number of Northern Democrats elected. Therefore, floor success is not determined by the coalition's ability to build formal majorities, but rather by the numerical strength of their opposition. And, of course, it is the U.S. electorate that determines through elections the numerical strength of both the coalition and Northern Democrats.

IMPLICATIONS AND SUMMARY

The Conservative Coalition is best understood as a voting alliance based on convenience with one primary goal: to block liberal legislation. The origins, fluctuations, and correlates of activity and success of the CC reveal the coalition to be an ideological aggregation mobilized by certain types of issues, particularly civil rights and social welfare. Since the CC has essentially a defensive strategy of retarding policy change, it functions largely on the basis of voting cues and lacks the structure generally associated with a formal coalition. This strategy is in distinct contrast to that of the Democratic Study Group. The DSG is concerned with inducing liberal changes, and it must formally organize if it is to succeed in Congress.

Understanding how the Conservative Coalition works furthers our understanding of the House of Representatives as a whole. The voting alliance begun in 1937 between Southern Democrats and Republicans has greatly reduced the ability of the majority Democratic party to function as a governing party. Since Southern Democrats often cross party lines to vote with Republicans, party leaders are faced with the task of putting together shifting coalitions in order to pass legislation. Thus the more active the conservative voting alliance is, the lower the levels of party voting in the House.

The decline of party strength in the House has contributed greatly to the formation of caucuses and groupings in the House that further complicate the ability of the majority to govern.[27] Observers have pointed to the recent emergence of frost belt/sun belt voting alliances, and Kevin Phillips writes of the Balkanization of America.[28] In addition to these broad regional alliances, partisan and nonpartisan caucuses have formed — usually around a narrow interest. By the late 1970s numerous nonpartisan House groups had sprung up: the Congressional Black Caucus, New England Congressional Caucus, Congressional Rural Caucus, Congressional Clearinghouse on Women's Rights, the Women's Caucus, the Blue Collar Caucus, and the Hispanic Caucus. Moreover, within the parties themselves splinter groups emerged: the liberal

Democratic Study Group, the moderate to conservative Democratic Research Organization, the centrist United Democrats of Congress, the liberal to moderate Republican Wednesday group, and the conservative Republican Study Committee. The proliferation of these and other groups is eloquent testimony to the weakened status and strength of party in the U.S. House of Representatives.

The broadest conclusion that we can draw from this study of the conservative voting alliance is that the Conservative Coalition paved the way, by its success, for other internal groups to affect the legislative process. In fact, its success was so significant that it helped generate its liberal counterpart, the Democratic Study Group. Moreover, the conservative voting alliance's early and continued success helped to make congressional government coalition government.

NOTES

1. In computing Conservative Coalition support scores Congressional Quarterly considers these 13 states to be homes for Southern Democrats: Alabama, Arkansas, Florida, Georgia, Kentucky, Louisiana, Mississippi, North Carolina, Oklahoma, South Carolina, Tennessee, Texas, and Virginia. Throughout this paper we use the same definition for Southern Democrats.
2. John Manley, "The Conservative Coalition," *American Behavioral Scientist,* 17 (November-December 1973): 225.
3. Ibid., pp. 233, 234.
4. Joseph W. Martin, *My First Fifty Years in Politics* (New York: McGraw-Hill Book Co., 1960), pp. 84-86.
5. Randall Ripley, *Party Leaders in the House of Representatives,* (Washington, D.C.: Brookings Institution, 1967), p. 143.
6. Richard F. Fenno, Jr., "The House of Representatives and Federal Aid to Education," in *New Perspectives on the House of Representatives,* 2nd ed., edited by Robert L. Peabody and Nelson W. Polsby (Chicago: Rand McNally & Co., 1969), pp. 281-323.
7. Arthur Stevens, Arthur Miller, and Thomas Mann, "Mobilization of Liberal Strength in the House, 1955-1970," *American Political Science Review,* 68 (June 1974): 667-681.
8. Donald Matthews and James Stimson, "The Decision Making Approach to the Study of Legislative Behavior" (Paper presented at the annual meeting of the American Political Science Association, New York, New York, September 1969).
9. Richard F. Fenno, Jr., "U.S. House Members in Their Constituencies," *American Political Science Review,* 71 (September 1977): 883-918; Charles Bullock and Catherine Rudder, "The Case of the Right Wing Urologist: The Seventh District of Georgia," in *The Making of Congressmen,* ed. Alan Clem (North Scituate, Mass.: Duxbury Press, 1976), pp. 55-92.
10. V. O. Key, *Southern Politics* (New York: Vintage Books, 1949); Manley, "The Conservative Coalition"; James T. Patterson, *Congressional Conservatism and the New Deal* (Lexington, Kentucky: University of Kentucky Press, 1967).
11. In addition to the percentages shown, we calculated both discontinuity coefficients and utilized the single Mood test to determine Conservative Coalition origin. Both tests gave us 1937 as the date of origin.

12. Key, *Southern Politics.*
13. Barbara Sinclair, "Party Realignment and the Transformation of the Political Agenda," *American Political Science Review* 71 (September 1977): 940-954.
14. Manley, "The Conservative Coalition," p. 230.
15. Ibid., pp. 242-244.
16. Aage Clausen, *How Congressmen Decide: A Policy Focus* (New York: St. Martin's Press, 1973); and Sinclair, "Party Realignment."
17. Clausen, *How Congressmen Decide*, p. 46.
18. Sinclair, "Party Realignment."
19. Clausen, *How Congressmen Decide.*
20. Sinclair, "Party Realignment."
21. W. Wayne Shannon, *Party, Constituency and Congressional Voting* (Baton Rouge: Louisiana State University Press, 1968), pp. 111-114.
22. Ibid., p. 173.
23. John Donovan, *The Policy Makers* (New York: Pegasus, 1970); Paul Lenchner, "The Conservative Coalition: Toward Clearing the Confusion," *Public Affairs Forum* (March 1975): 5-9.
24. James Sundquist, *Politics and Policy* (Washington, D.C.: Brookings Institution, 1968).
25. We also correlated floor activity with a dummy variable for the party of the president. The small r of −.16 indicated a weak relationship between having a Republican in the White House and greater Conservative Coalition activity. Correlations between the presidential party variable and the two measures of floor success were even weaker.
26. This latter measure is determined by calculating the Rice Index of Cohesion for each Conservative Coalition roll call in a session and summing these roll calls and then dividing by the total number of roll calls.
27. David Brady, Joseph Cooper, and Patricia Hurley, "The Decline of Party Strength in the House," *Legislative Studies Quarterly* (August 1979).
28. Kevin Phillips, "The Balkanization of American Politics," *Harpers* (May 1978): 37-47.

9

Congressional Caucuses and the Politics of Representation

Burdett A. Loomis

Congresswoman Jane McRodriquez, a freshman Republican representative from Nahant, Mass., is showing signs of exhaustion. She arrived on the Hill this past January determined to do right by her constituents and by her interest in ecological problems, especially those of the nation's ports and harbors. She was assigned, like any average representative, to two House committees and five subcommittees, none of which had much to do with her special concerns. But she soon discovered a "port caucus" — an informal meeting group of congressmen interested in boats, docks and sludge. She joined. She also joined the congresswomen's caucus, as a matter of personal pride, and the New England caucus — and the suburban caucus, and the ecology caucus, and the new members' caucus, and the Republican conference and (thanks to her mixed heritage) both the Spanish caucus and the Irish caucus. She now attends seventeen caucus meetings a week, and hasn't had her hair done in three months.[1]

This fictional and puckish description introduced a *Newsweek* article ("A Balkan Congress") on caucuses. The article, while amusing, was a fount of misinformation that points up the elusive character of many of these recently organized informal groups in the House. Although almost 40 such groups exist in various forms, their significance is difficult to judge because their focus is frequently limited to a narrow range of issues affecting, for example, textiles or shipbuilding or New England. At the same time, the mere formation of numerous nonofficial groups or caucuses may be instructive for understanding the contemporary Congress.

HISTORICAL DEVELOPMENT

Traditionally, informal groups of House members have served to alleviate some of the problems in making this large and unwieldy body do its work.[2] State and city delegations, friendship cliques, regional groupings, and social organizations have all existed as forces in the legislative process. After making major gains in the 1958 congressional elections, liberal Democrats formed the Democratic Study Group (DSG) and ushered in, albeit unknowingly, a new era for nonofficial groups in the House. During the 1960s two more such groups were organized: the Republican moderates' Wednesday Group and the antiwar Members of Congress for Peace through Law (MCPL). The floodgates opened in the 1970s: 12 black members of the House formed the Congressional Black Caucus (CBC) in 1971; nine more groups were organized by 1975; and more than 20 more have followed suit since 1976. The Senate, a smaller and less formal body, has been slower to develop caucuses; however, many senators do belong to those groups that welcome members from both chambers.

The proliferation of informal House groups is undeniable. Members have joined caucuses in droves, and many have taken on activist caucus roles. Representative Charlie Rose (D-N.C.), for example, has helped to found several informal groups, most notably the Congressional Clearinghouse on the Future, the Forum on Regulation, and the Congressional Rural Caucus.

Although it is too early to draw any full-blown conclusions about the significance of caucuses, their formation does provide an excellent vantage point for observing the relationship between the actions of individual members and change in the Congress as an institution, especially as a representative body. Criticisms of congressional unresponsiveness and inefficiency have grown increasingly numerous and insistent in recent years.[3] Neither the demands of the executive, the requests of the public, nor the presence of clear policy problems have proved successful in moving the Congress to action. (The delay between the 1973 Arab oil embargo and final passage of a national energy policy in 1978 is a case in point.) At the same time, especially in the House, incumbents have generally enjoyed clear sailing in their re-election bids, regardless of their party ties or the tides of national politics. Why this anomaly? Although the reasons are varied, the basic explanation is that individual members can prove themselves responsive to the needs of their constituents by providing services and claiming credit for numerous substantive and symbolic actions.[4]

In short, while the institution may be woefully unresponsive, the members can act very responsively in their casework and on specific district-related policy problems; the evaluation of congressional responsiveness depends upon whether the body as a whole or the individual member is considered. Examining informal congressional groups or caucuses may give us some insight into both the dearth of institutional responsiveness and the ability of the member to appear extremely responsive.

Writing about the member/institution relationship, David W. Rohde and Kenneth Shepsle have observed:

> Individual behavior . . . is motivated by "goals" or objectives," but is channeled by extant institutional practices; extant institutional practices, however, have only limited immunity to the contagious frustration of individual goals unrealized.[5]

Prior to 1958 and 1959 and the formation of the Democratic Study Group, "extant institutional practices" did not include the development of organized subgroups outside the party-committee structure. The "contagious frustration" of the 1950s Democratic liberals resulted in a change in institutional practices; likewise, the moderate GOP Wednesday Group and the Members of Congress for Peace through Law served the interests of members frustrated over policies, either within their own party or the Congress as a whole. Although the Congress established and nurtured these three caucuses a decade ago, there was no rush to form others.

During the past 10 years various "reforms" have been directed at easing the frustrations of junior House members. More subcommittee chairs have become available, "power" committees have expanded their memberships, decisionmaking in the Democratic Caucus has grown more democratic, and staff resources have increased dramatically. Yet in the wake of this dispersion of power, many members possessed the incentives either to organize or join caucuses.[6] Caucuses proliferated during the 94th-96th Congresses (1975-80) — from 8 in 1973 to almost 40 in 1980.[7]

Again, the institution-individual nexus is important. As Arthur Stevens, Arthur Miller, and Thomas Mann note in their discussion of the Democratic Study Group's formation in the late 1950s:

> Institutional arrangements devised for collective decision-making often result in biases for certain interests at the cost of others.[8]

Numerous groups of members have perceived biases in the institution's structure of collective decisionmaking and have acted to counter those biases. These members have acted adaptively to provide avenues for pursuing their own interests. More importantly, the caucuses have served, as Richard Fenno points out, "to strengthen a congressional strength" — that is, to make the representational side of the congressional job even more predominant.[9]

The consequences of organizing a Steel Caucus, a Port Caucus, or a Suburban Caucus are to formalize more fully the already strong representational tendencies of the Congress and to weaken further the ability of the legislative branch to act responsively toward society-wide problems that affect substantial numbers of particular interests.

NONOFFICIAL GROUPS: A COMPOSITE PORTRAIT

The roster of nonofficial groups listed in Table 9-1 illustrates the diversity of interests that have organized within the Congress.[10] Although two of the earliest groups (the Democratic Study Group and the Wednesday Group) were partisan and oriented toward broad approaches to policy and congressional activity, the more recently established caucuses tend to be bipartisan and interested in specific issues. Such a trend does not imply that single-issue politics has come to dominate these groups or the Congress as a whole, but it does mean that most caucuses have organized around sets of issues (for example, the Rural Caucus and the Textile Caucus) or a particular point of view that affects a wide range of issues (for example, the regional "lens" of the New England Caucus).

The great majority of the nonofficial groups circulate information. Some use elaborate weekly reports; others rely on word-of-mouth. At least intermittently, most groups engage in intrachamber lobbying. One notable exception is the Environmental Study Conference, which relies solely on its credibility as a reliable information source to wield its influence.

Caucuses vary widely in their staffing patterns. Several groups employ between 7 and 20 paid staffers, complemented by numerous interns. Conversely, about half the groups have neither paid staff nor separate offices; in these instances personal aides provide caucus coordination, often as a regular part of their duties for an activist member. Between the extremes of a fairly large staff that occupies extensive office space and a nonexistent staff, there is a third pattern — a minimal operation where one to three staffers serve as group coordinators, organizers, researchers, and publicists. In these circumstances much of the staff's work involves keeping the caucus (and thus the paid help) afloat. Basic services, such as providing relevant information, must be maintained, while the aides continually seek financial sustenance by soliciting members' clerk-hire funds for staff salaries. Because the services provided by all but the few well-staffed caucuses are not substantial, the amount and scope of most caucuses' activities are severely limited. It is the members themselves, therefore, who must make most of the groups effective.

We will examine four different caucuses: the Congressional Black Caucus, the Northeast-Midwest Congressional Coalition, the New

Table 9-1   "Nonofficial" Groups in the Congress as of January 1979

	Bicameral?	Membership[1]	Issue Focus[2]	Group Bond[3]	Paid Staff?	Funding Sources[4]	Qualified as Legislative Support Agency[5]
House Partisan Groups							
Democrats							
Democratic Study Group	No	Vol.	B	Ideol.	20	O,D,S,C,	Yes
Democratic Research Organization	No	Vol.	B	Ideol.	3	D,C	Yes
United Democrats of Congress	No	Vol.	B	Mixed	No	—	Yes
94th Caucus	No	Inclus.	B	Class	1	C	Yes
Congressional Hispanic Caucus	No	Inclus.	B	Demog.	3	O	Yes
95th Caucus	No	Inclus.	B	Class	1	C	Yes
Republicans							
Wednesday Group	No	Vol.	B	Ideol.	3	C	Yes
Republican Study Committee	No	Vol.	B	Ideol.	15	C,D,S	No
95th Republican Club	No	Inclus.	B	Class	No	—	No
96th Republicans	No	Inclus.	B	Class	No		No
Bipartisan Groups							
Congressional Black Caucus	No	Inclus.	F	Demog.	7	O,C	Yes
New England Congressional Caucus	No	Inclus.	F	Region	3	O,C	Yes
Northeast-Midwest Congressional Coalition	Yes*	Inclus.	F	Region	8	O,C	Yes
Congressional Rural Caucus	No	Vol.	F	Issue Set	2	O,C	Yes
Blue Collar Caucus	No	Vol.	F	Occup'n.	No	—	No
Congresswomen's Caucus	No	Inclus.	F	Demog.	1	C	Yes
House Congressional Steel Caucus	Yes*	Vol.	S	Issue	No	—	Yes
Ad Hoc Congressional Committee for Irish Affairs	No	Vol.	S	Issue	No	—	No
Congressional Suburban Caucus	No	Vol.	F	Geog.	No	D	Yes

	Senate counterpart*	Membership[1]	Type[2]	Group bond[3]	Staff	Funding[4]	LSO designation[5]
Textile Caucus	No	Vol.	S	Issue	1	C,D	Yes
Conference of Great Lakes Congressmen	No	Inclus.	F	Geog.	No	—	No
Congressional Ad Hoc Monitoring Group on South Africa	No	Vol.	S	Issue	No	—	No
Metropolitan Area Caucus	No	Inclus.	F	Geog.	No	—	No
House Ocean Policy Advisory Committee	No	Vol.	F	Issue Set	No	—	No
House Fair Employment Practices Committee	No	N.A.	F	Issue Set	No	—	Yes
Congressional Port Caucus	No	Vol.	S	Issue	1	C	No
Congressional Shipbuilding Coalition	No	Vol.	S	Issue	No	—	No
Members of Congress for Peace Through Law	Yes	Vol.	F	Issue Set	7	O,C,D	Yes
Coalition for Peace Through Strength	Yes	Vol.	F	Issue Set	Yes†	O	No
Environmental Study Conference	Yes	Vol.	F	Issue Set	9	C,D	Yes
Congressional Clearinghouse on the Future	Yes	Vol.	B	Issue Set	3	C	Yes
Solar Coalition	Yes	Vol.	F	Issue Set	Yes†	O	No
High Altitude Coalition	Yes	Vol.	F	Issue Set/Geog.	No	—	No
Congressional Clearinghouse on Women's Rights	Yes	Vol.	F	Issue Set	1	C	No
Forum on Regulation	Yes	Vol.	F	Issue Set	No	—	No
Vietnam Era Veterans in Congress	Yes	Inclus.	F	Issue Set	No	—	No

† Allied with outside groups that provide staff.

* Separate counterpart groups exist in Senate.

[1] Voluntary membership = elective, by any member; Inclusive membership = all members included of a given category.

[2] B = Broad; F = Focused; S = Single-Issue

[3] The group bond can be a variety of different factors: ideology, demography, geographical feature or region, a single issue, a set of issues, occupation, congressional class.

[4] C = Clerk-hire; D = Dues; S = Subscriptions; O = Outside

[5] House Administration Committee designation as legislative support group (96th Congress, 1979).

Members' Caucus, and the Steel Caucus. They vary greatly in partisanship, publicity, size, structure, activity, and goals, but are similar in their representation of identifiable interests that some members see as slighted by the existing institutional arrangements of the Congress.

The Congressional Black Caucus: Symbol and Substance

Although most caucuses seek to represent their interests by "acting for" them in various ways, some groups seek to represent interests by "standing for" them, either descriptively or symbolically.[11] Because the composition of the U.S. Congress does not accurately reflect the composition of the U.S. population, the small numbers of women and minority members in Congress are frequently cast as symbolic representatives of much larger constituencies.[12]

Although congresswomen have formed a caucus and a clearinghouse group, it is the Congressional Black Caucus (CBC) that best illustrates the possibilities of symbolic representation through a nonofficial group. As former CBC chairman Charles Rangel (D-N.Y.) stated in rejecting the application of Fortney (Pete) Stark (D-Cal.), a white member of the House with numerous black constituents:

> The Caucus symbolizes black political development in this country. We feel that maintaining this symbolism is critical at this juncture in our development.[13]

Rangel's statement echoed the sentiments of other congressional blacks, who saw the "representatives in Congress [as] . . . the logical groups to assume national leadership among the more than 1,500 black elected officials in the entire country."[14] With the 1978 defeat of Senator Edward Brooke (R-Mass.), this claim takes on special meaning. The symbolic role of leadership among black elected officials has propelled such individuals as Rangel and Representative John Conyers (D-Mich.) into the national spotlight as prominent black spokesmen.

More recently, black House members have sought to increase their internal congressional power in policymaking, moving toward a more substantive approach to representation by attempting to influence policy aggressively. Nevertheless, even with a paid staff of seven, an impressive budget (more than $200,000 annually from a fund-raising dinner), and considerable sympathy from Democratic leaders in and out of the House, the CBC remains most successful as a symbolic focus for many national black concerns.

Herein lies a serious problem for the CBC. Unless it does more than merely act symbolically, unless it produces substantive policy results in areas such as unemployment and social programs, the CBC risks losing some of its legitimacy — a setback that would seriously impair subsequent attempts to exert legislative leverage and/or national black political leadership. Such is the precarious position of many caucuses, continually needing to justify their existence if they are to survive. The attraction of providing symbolic representation and the appearance of accomplishment is as important to caucuses as to individual members who continually claim credit or take policy positions that often have little substantive impact.[15]

The Northeast-Midwest Congressional Coalition: Large Numbers, Broad Interests

The Northeast-Midwest Congressional Coalition (originally named the Northeast-Midwest Economic Advancement Coalition and hereafter simply referred to as the coalition), with its 213 bipartisan House members, appears to be very different from the CBC, with its 13 Democrats. Yet their caucus organizations have some striking similarities in terms of budgets (more than $200,000), staff, and goals and in their efforts to redirect the flow of federal benefits toward certain types of districts. The coalition's greatest asset, and most profound difference from the CBC, is its numerical strength; with 213 members, a near majority in the House, the coalition can wield tremendous leverage on any issue that enjoys wide internal group support, such as the regional distribution of federal largesse.

Like many newer congressional caucuses, the coalition, formed in 1976, emphasizes particular issue concerns and downplays partisanship. Under the auspices of its founder and former chairman, Massachusetts Democrat Michael Harrington, and its Republican Co-chairman Frank Horton (N.Y.),[16] the coalition has sought to represent the Northeast-Midwest interests both by exercising political clout (through its numbers) and by developing a regionally-oriented policy perspective for the systematic analysis of federal programs.

The structure of the coalition reflects these dual goals of exercising immediate influence on important regional issues (aid to New York City, for example) and "helping to re-define the self-interest" of the region's elected representatives.[17] Following IRS rules, the coalition acts as a lobbying force, with two staff members paid from members' clerk-hire funds; the Northeast-Midwest Institute (located in the same office) is "a private, nonprofit research center . . . funded by grants from state governments and private foundations."[18] The coalition, with a core of member-activists and a staff director, lobbies on specific regional issues and has produced a respectable legislative record in such policy areas as community development funding and federal procurement policy. The institute, on the other hand, has adopted an educational role, producing analyses designed to imbue members with a regional perspective on policy matters. Such reports as "Proposed Military Base Realignments: The Regional Impact" and "A Regional

Analysis of Four Natural Gas Price Alternatives" illustrate the institute's educational bent.

The impact of the coalition/institute is difficult to assess, especially
in terms of the institute's educational objectives. Although there has
been an increase in regional thinking in the House, the extent to
which this is a product of the coalition's work is unclear. More
evident of the coalition's strength is the united front it has presented
on those issues the staff and the 31-member steering committee regard
as important. On a broad regional issue such as rewriting the community development funding formula, coalition members voted 189-
4 to support an advantageous version; even on the controversial loan
guarantees to New York City, the Northeast-Midwest members voted
favorably by a 4-1 margin.

Such focused in-House lobbying both inside and outside the caucus
may constitute an effective new force in congressional voting. Kingdon
notes that contacts among members are especially important in floor
decisionmaking;[19] caucuses make these contacts more orderly and
systematic. Nevertheless, the coalition's bipartisan membership poses
substantial difficulties in choosing specific issues to rally around.
Regional perspectives must compete with partisan, ideological, and
constituency views. Although coalition activists and staff see some
splintering as inevitable, further exposure to regional policy perspectives
will produce agreement over a widening range of issues, they believe.

In sum, the Northeast-Midwest Coalition/Institute seeks to change
the way the House processes policy, adding a layer of regional representation to the institutionalized role of the member in his or
her district. During an era of shrinking federal support, such a development seems natural. However, to the extent the coalition (and
its "Sunbelt" adversaries) are successful, increasing numbers of policies
will be perceived as redistributive, and the Congress will encounter
more obstacles in making coherent policy decisions, no matter how
the coalition or any given caucus fares.[20]

The New Members' Caucus: Representation and Adaptation

If representativeness is the major theme of caucus development,
adaptation is its minor refrain. Caucuses provide bits of recognition
and potential power to their activists — frequently junior members
who do not yet chair subcommittees (or serve as ranking members).
Although some senior members have become more active recently,
younger members remain disproportionately involved in caucus work.
The New Members' Caucus is entirely comprised of junior members.
It was established in the wake of the large 1974 Democratic gains
(75 House seats) and provides the most striking example of combining
representation with adaptation.[21]

Newly arrived members frequently form loose, socially-oriented organizations that usually disband at the end of their freshman term. The Democratic members of the class of 1974, with limited financial and staff help provided by outside sources, quickly created a skeletal organization in November 1974, prior to the December party caucus. This grouping metamorphosed into the New Members' Caucus (NMC) of the 94th Congress and has since maintained its staff and office, but changed its name to the 94th Caucus — leaving the NMC designation as its legacy to the freshman Democratic organization in each succeeding Congress. In 1979, five years after its founding, the 94th Caucus/NMC (hereafter, the NMC) abandoned most of its formal structure. By that time, however, 27 members of the class of 1974 held subcommittee chairs, and 13 served on exclusive committees. Thus of the 56 remaining Democrats first elected in 1974, 40 (71 percent) held substantial pieces of turf. The caucus had lost much of its importance to the individual members.

As an organization, the NMC was typical of many House caucuses. It occupied unenviable (but free) office space and employed a single aide (formerly two). Membership in the group remains automatic to all those Democrats first elected in the 94th Congress, but participation among those eligible is uneven; a core of perhaps 20 members was fairly active during the 96th Congress.

Numerical Strength. When the members of the class of 1974 came to Washington, they faced an institution that was more open to influence by freshman than at any time in this century. The new members had one great asset — numbers (75) — and one substantial need — information. The New Members' Caucus provided a "reference point" for many freshmen through which they could use the power of their numbers and act to channel information among themselves.

Even three years after the original caucus successes, when the freshman helped depose three senior chairmen (and save a fourth — Wayne Hays)[22], a close observer of the NMC noted that "numbers were still very important in keeping the class together on some specific issues, and in getting responsiveness from people they want to deal with." Obtaining responsiveness may be the key here. The class of 1974 has not shown consistent block voting strength on a variety of issues, but from the beginning the new members could command attention by the threat of using their numbers. This was especially effective in the House Democratic Caucus, where the class of 1974 held more than one-fourth of all votes. One former caucus chairman described the initial experience of the NMC in dealing with the House establishment:

> When we've acted together it's made a difference. Take the chairmanship thing. We first sent a letter to each chairman asking that

they come to one of our meetings and talk a little bit about their committee. To a person, we got back polite notes saying no — *so,* we then sent a second letter saying we were going to vote *en masse* against any chairman who didn't come. They all came. Even Hebert (from Louisiana), who showed up the day before the Super Bowl in New Orleans.

To summarize, the considerable numbers of the new members did prove useful for caucus chairmen to use as a "big stick" in obtaining the attention of the House and its power centers and, to an extent, the Carter administration. Nevertheless, although it developed a whip system, the caucus has shied away from trying to influence members' votes save on a few reform-related issues. The activist core of the NMC realized that the common policy interests of a class are extremely limited; to push very far in one policy direction or another would almost surely cause an open rupture and a total loss of influence.

Information Source. If freshman Democrats in the House were long on numbers in the 94th Congress, they were short on information, especially in many national policy areas. As a group they rejected an "apprenticeship" role, yet they could not act effectively on the range of issues they were interested in.[23] The NMC served to fill their information needs admirably. Initially, weekly sessions on specific issues were held, and freshmen exchanged information that they had found useful in their committee or subcommittee work. As one member commented about these exchanges, "We talk to each other, depend on each other . . . I've learned a lot from the other members." While the formal and informal exchange of information among NMC members remained important, the caucus leadership has increasingly sought cabinet officers and House leaders to address the group, often on general policy matters. The caucus leverage as a large group continued to pay dividends in obtaining information, if not action.

As the new members became more sophisticated, so too did the information presented and exchanged. Even after three years of congressional experience, the 94th freshmen continued to use the NMC and its functions as information conduits, in large part due to the activists' mutual trust in each other's presentations. Members claimed to profit from a series of campaign-related meetings in 1976 organized by Nevada's Jim Santini, and caucus president Fred Richmond from New York organized a "Friends of the Class of 1974" fund-raiser, from which many new members received some contributions. Even after their superlative 1976 showing (only two losses in 75 races), the caucus members remained nervous — exchanging campaign-related information on Carter administration policies as well as more conventional campaigning strategies.[24]

Aside from re-election, power, and policy considerations, the NMC also gives many of its members a great sense of togetherness, which provides a solid foundation for the exchange of policy-related information. Those active in the caucus are good friends and are generally policy entrepreneurs, although labeling them "liberals" would miss the mark.[25] As a recent class president put it:

> There is incredible camaraderie in the class ... [but] I couldn't think of a more nonideological group.[26]

The members do realize the limits to their organized efforts, but the NMC has become one mechanism for them to use in adapting to the disadvantages and obstacles they necessarily confront. For new members facing a fractionalized House with few clear sources of power, the caucus offered opportunities to cope with unfamiliar policies, obtain some power, enhance their re-election chances, and establish strong friendships. As one thoughtful freshman concluded:

> The primary purpose, and its best contribution, was simply to give us psychological security and reinforcement. We talked with each other, shared the original ups and downs, exchanged gossip about senior members.... But *it was the organization that provided us with a formal way to do it.* Without it, it would just be a matter of accident and superficial contacts.

Representation. Hannah Pitkin describes representation as "acting in the interest of the represented, in a manner responsive to them."[27] There are problems, however, in asserting that the NMC is a vehicle of representation: Who are their constituents? What interests do they respond to? The class of 1974 has not acted with great unity in most policy areas; coming from widely differing individual districts, there is little reason to expect them to. When their initial 1975 Democratic Caucus triumphs were not followed by subsequent victories, many voices, both inside the class and out, spoke knowingly that the 75 freshmen Democrats had been swamped by the tides of politics as usual within the House.

Even the new members themselves downplayed their ability to act effectively and responsively. As one activist pessimistically observed after his first six months in the House:

> I was very involved at the beginning, and — I must say — am damn proud of what we accomplished. But just as there is a season for all things, so I think the NMC has accomplished its goals and, basically, outlived its usefulness.

Another activist noted that "anyone who thought the freshmen would be doing anything together beyond the first month was mistaken."[28]

Although most conventional measures of ideology have not shown members of the class of 1974 to be especially distinctive, this has not been true across the board. They were highly unified in their response to what they perceived as inchoate but strong skepticism about government among their constituents. This response resulted in efforts to reform Congress and make it a more open institution. Typical of this reform orientation was the new Democrats' divergence from their senior party members on the issue of public financing of congressional elections. While senior Democrats voted 56-125 against such an amendment in 1976, the freshmen favored it 51-27.[29] This issue remains a strong unifying force for NMC activists, and it is one of the few policy items the caucus leadership has tried to push. In the March 1978 defeat of a campaign finance amendment rule, the caucus members voted 68-3 in favor of public funding for House elections, while their Democratic colleagues supported the rule (and the leadership) only 130-66.

Simply illustrating caucus support for reform does not demonstrate any kind of representational linkage between a skeptical public and the NMC. We can see, however, that the members of the class of 1974 feel they are different from any previous class — that they are in some sense a "new breed" ushered into office in the wake of the Watergate scandal. One moderate, not especially active in the NMC, felt that there was indeed a new assessment of responsibilities:

> I think there is less careerism around here — new members are less likely to settle into a rut. And there is more emphasis on ethical standards. Take Home Rule (for the District of Columbia) for example. A lot of older members were against it. . . . One of them came up to me and said, "You were in a state legislature; you know how a city can treat the legislators — give them all kinds of trouble." What it really was was that we were giving the District the power to make us act like normal people.

The member saw the class as "acting for" the District residents. More generally, the NMC activists often see themselves representing forces of change, especially in making the institutions more democratic. As one policy-oriented activist, a past NMC president, commented:

> I can't speak for the Class of '70, but the last two elections [1972 and 1974] have produced a "new member," more oriented toward institutional change. And I don't identify with the institution, and I don't think most of them do either. And I hope they never will.

In not identifying with the institution of the House, this member wanted to emphasize his continuing identification with the people who sent him and his peers to Congress. He sought to avoid placing institutional loyalty above representing his constituents and other interests he felt important, many of which relate back to the reform-oriented electoral surge that initially ushered the class of 1974 into office.

The House Congressional Steel Caucus: The Single-Interest Group

The Black Caucus, the Northeast-Midwest Congressional Coalition, and the New Members' Caucus all pursue various specific policy interests, but their attention is likely to be divided among any number of possible issue areas. The Steel Caucus is different. Like the Textile Caucus, the Steel Caucus serves a single economic interest — albeit a broad one — that cuts across party, ideological and regional lines. The group's 170-strong membership (from 37 states) illustrates the industry's breadth of impact — beyond the basic steel-making firms to mining, manufacturing, transportation and other related enterprises.

Most of the time the Steel Caucus is dormant, but when steel interests are threatened the caucus mobilizes quickly to serve as an in-House lobby. The Steel Caucus had some success in the 96th Congress in pressuring the Carter administration to support the industry by implementing certain modestly protectionist policies oriented toward automatically increasing tariffs if certain triggering prices were reached by foreign steel manufacturers. In the long run, however, the group may be most successful in monitoring steel-related policymaking across a wide range of congressional arenas. In short, the caucus performs much the same job as many industry lobbyists; it watches the government and gathers information that is valuable to its interests.[30]

Perhaps the Steel Caucus's greatest service has been to make many members of Congress aware of the steel-related interests in their districts. Thus the tendency of these members to act to represent the steel industry is increased, even for those whose districts are only marginally affected by federal steel policies.

CONCLUSION

In large part, the history of the House of Representatives has been a struggle to mold a coherent policy making instrument out of a large and disparate collectivity. It has been, one might say, a struggle of the general versus the particular, in which the particular seems the more powerful force.[31]

In light of the recent proliferation of informal groups in the House, the appropriate response to this observation by Roger Davidson and Walter Oleszek seems to be, "Amen." Caucuses have generally formed because members are frustrated with the institution's arrangements for making certain types of policy; the organizational decentralization and dispersion of power provide incentives for circumventing normal policymaking bodies such as committees, subcommittees, and parties. Yet the net result of creating a host of caucuses is to increase the House's fragmentation and to increase the body's responsiveness to particular interests.

Each of the caucuses considered here in its own way seeks to affect policymaking favorably for relatively specific interests. Their methods differ somewhat, ranging from the largely symbolic efforts of the Congressional Black Caucus to the occasional clout of the Steel Caucus to the educational/lobbying combination of the Midwest-Northeast Coalition/Institute. To survive, caucuses must continue to offer tangible benefits to their members; information, publicity, positions of some power, and political leverage are all important assets to members who formally represent only one constituency of 435.

To summarize, as with such other developments as subcommittee reform and the members' increased office perquisites, the proliferation of caucuses illustrates the shoring up of particularistic forces in the House. Coalitions among caucuses are likely to be short-lived, bringing members together only on given matters. And while members decry the increase in single-issue politics, they have only to consider their own behavior. From the Textile Caucus to the Port Caucus to the Hispanic Caucus to all the groups discussed here, particularism is alive and well in the House of Representatives.

NOTES

1. "A Balkan Congress," *Newsweek,* November 14, 1977.
2. The work on informal groupings of House members, while excellent in some instances, has been spotty at best in providing a comprehensive view of this aspect of the House. A few of the central works include: Leo Snowiss, "Congressional Recruitment and Representation," *American Political Science Review* 60 (1966): 627-639; Alan Fiellin, "The Functions of Informal Groups: A State Delegation," *Journal of Politics* 24 (1962): 72-91; Barbara Deckard, "State Party Delegations in the U.S. House of Representatives: A Comparative Study of Group Cohesion," *Journal of Politics,* 34 (1972): 199-222; Arthur G. Stevens, Jr., Arthur H. Miller, and Thomas E. Mann, "Mobilization of Liberal Strength in the House, 1955-1970: The Democratic Study Group," *American Political Science Review* 68 (1974): 667-681; John Manley, "The Conservative Coalition in Congress," *American Behavioral Scientist* 17 (1973): 223-247; Donald Matthews and James Stimson, "Decision-Making in the U.S. House of Representatives," in *Political Decision-Making,* ed. Sidney Ulmer (Cincinnati: Van Nostrand, 1970); and John Kingdon, *Congressmen's Voting Decisions* (New York: Harper & Row, 1973).
3. Possible citations here are endless. One coherent if hyperbolic, critical analysis can be found in Morris Fiorina's *Congress: Keystone of the Washington Establishment* (New Haven: Yale University Press, 1977).
4. See Heinz Eulau and Paul D. Karps, "The Puzzle of Representation: Specifying Components of Responsiveness," *Legislative Studies Quarterly* 2 (August 1977): 53-85.
5. David W. Rohde and Kenneth Shepsle, "Taking Stock of Congressional Research: The New Institutionalism" (Paper delivered at the annual meeting of the Midwest Political Science Association, Chicago, Illinois, April 1978).
6. The notion of incentives as factors in interest group formation is discussed by Robert Salisbury in "An Exchange Theory of Interest Groups," *Midwest Journal of Political Science* 13 (February 1969): 1-32. His ideas of entrepreneurial behavior and multiple incentives seem applicable to group development within the legislature as well.

7. Paul Rundquist, "Formal and Informal Congressional Groups," mimeographed (Washington, D.C.: Congressional Research Service, October 30, 1978). He lists 36 House or bicameral groups. There has been some fluctuation since then, including the formation of the Sunbelt, Tourist, and Balanced Budget Caucuses in the House.
8. Stevens, Miller, and Mann, "Mobilization of Liberal Strength," p. 667.
9. See Richard F. Fenno, Jr., "Strengthening a Congressional Strength," in *Congress Reconsidered*, 1st ed., edited by Lawrence C. Dodd and Bruce I. Oppenheimer (New York: Praeger Publishers, 1977).
10. For a discussion of the difficulties of labeling nonofficial groups, see Louis S. Maisel, "Information and Decision-Making in House Offices," in *Congress at Work*, ed. Joseph Cooper and G. Calvin MacKenzie (Austin: University of Texas Press), forthcoming.
11. For further elucidation of the differences in representational styles and substance, see Hannah Pitkin, *The Concept of Representation* (Berkeley: University of California Press, 1967), p. 60.
12. Ibid., p. 84. See also Charles P. Henry, "Legitimizing Race in Congressional Politics," *American Politics Quarterly* (April 1977): 149-176; and John F. Schwartz and Lee Ridgeway, "Black Representation in Congress: An Examination of the 1971 House of Representatives," unpublished.
13. Henry, "Legitimizing Race," p. 172.
14. Ibid., p. 149.
15. In this sense, caucuses may act much like individual members. See David R. Mayhew, *Congress: The Electoral Connection* (New Haven: Yale University Press, 1974), p. 77.
16. Representative Robert W. Edgar (D-Pa.) succeeded Harrington, who retired from the House at the end of the 95th Congress, as chairman .
17. From a March 1978 interview with a Northeast-Midwest Institute staff member.
18. Rundquist, "Formal and Informal Congressional Groups."
19. Kingdon, *Congressmen's Voting Decisions*, p. 216.
20. For a useful introductory discussion concerning perceptions of policies in redistributive (and other) ways, see Jerrold E. Schneider, *Ideological Coalitions in Congress* (Westport, Connecticut: Greenwood Press, 1979), pp. 31-33.
21. Several authors have recently discussed adaptation in the congressional context; see Roger H. Davidson and Walter J. Oleszek, "Adaptation and Consolidation: Structural Innovation in the U.S. House of Representatives," *Legislative Studies Quarterly*, vol. I, no. 1 (February 1976): 37-65; and Joseph Cooper, "Congress in Organizational Perspective," in *Congress Reconsidered*, 1st ed., pp. 140-149.
22. A challenge to Hays at the start of the 94th Congress was turned back in large part by the vote of new members.
23. Burdett Loomis, "Freshmen Democrats in the 94th Congress: Actions in and Reactions to a Changing House" (Paper delivered at the annual meeting of the Midwest Political Science Association, Chicago, Illinois, April 1977).
24. The class of 1974 received some serious setbacks in the 1978 elections; seven of their members lost re-election. Nevertheless, the "new members" in the 94th Congress constituted a larger single class of Democrats in the House — 61 of 276 — than in the 95th or 96th Congresses.
25. The term "policy entrepreneur" is used by Eric Uslaner in describing some of the new members. See "Policy Entrepreneurs and Amateur Democrats in the House of Representatives," in *Legislative Reform: Its Policy*

Impact, ed. Leroy N. Rieselbach (Lexington, Massachusetts: Lexington Books, 1978).

26. The 1974 class's average ADA score declined markedly during the four years following the 1974 election. In 1975, 54 percent of the freshmen scored 80 or above on ADA ratings, compared to 38 percent of all Democrats. By 1978, only 21 percent of the 1974 freshmen scored that high, compared to 16 percent of all Democrats. The class of 1974 might not have begun as nonideological, but it quickly retrenched, in line with the movement of many of the more senior Democrats.

27. Pitkin, *Concept of Representation,* p. 209.

28. *Congressional Quarterly Weekly Report,* August 2, 1975, p. 1675.

29. New Members' Caucus mimeo, April 15, 1976.

30. See Lewis Anthony Dexter, *How Organizations Are Represented in Washington* (Indianapolis: Bobbs-Merrill Co., 1969), p. 79.

31. Roger H. Davidson and Walter J. Oleszek, *Congress Against Itself* (Bloomington: Indiana University Press, 1977).

10

Agenda and Alignment Change: The House of Representatives, 1925-1978

Barbara Sinclair

Although congressional voting behavior has been studied extensively, the emphasis has been static rather than dynamic, that is, research has shown us "snapshots" of one policy area at one point in time, rather than change over time.[1] This study examines three aspects of change: change in political agenda, change in policy outputs, and alignment change. Our purpose is to describe such change over the half century from 1925 through 1978.

By the political agenda, we mean the set of problems and policy proposals being seriously debated by the attentive public and by policymakers and the terms of that debate. The political agenda consists of the set of issues at the center of controversy at a given time. *Agenda change* can be said to have occurred when new problems are perceived, when new solutions to existing problems are proposed, or when the terms of the debate, that is, the basis of the division between the "sides," change significantly.

Policy change occurs during every Congress but is usually incremental; it is aimed at a problem on which a previous body of legislation exists, and its approach to the problem is similar to that embodied in existing legislation. Occasionally, however, Congress will pass legislation dealing with a major problem on which the federal government has not acted previously or legislation that approaches an old problem in a radically new way. It is such nonincremental legislation that represents true policy change.

In this study *voting alignments* are characterized in terms of party and region. Analyses of recent Congresses have shown these variables to be of major importance in describing members' voting behavior. We are interested in whether the influence of these factors varies over time.

THE ISSUE DOMAINS

In order to discuss congressional alignments over a half-century period, a schema for classifying votes into a limited number of issue categories is needed. It would be impossible to study individually the thousands of roll calls taken. We shall use an issue categorization developed by Aage Clausen in his work on the Congresses of the 1950s and early 1960s.[2] Since the period he studied is approximately in the middle of that covered here, his classification is appropriate.

The four policy domains of Clausen's that will be used here are government management of the economy, social welfare, civil liberties, and international involvement. The government management category centers on legislation dealing with the economy and the nation's resources. Examples are business regulation, public works, conservation and environmental legislation, monetary and fiscal policy, and the overall level of governmental spending. In contrast, the social welfare domain includes legislation designed to aid the individual more directly. Aid to education, public housing, and labor legislation are examples. The civil liberties category includes civil rights for blacks and such issues as subversive activities regulation and federal criminal justice procedures. The international involvement domain includes all nondomestic policy questions.

For an issue classification to be useful, it must not only make substantive sense, but the votes included in a given category must evoke similar voting alignments. After roll calls were categorized into the issue domains, a procedure to select those that evoked similar alignments was employed.[3] Usually a large proportion of the roll calls met the test for inclusion into the resulting issue scale or dimension. Each member of the House was then given a score on each issue dimension in each of the Congresses in which he served. The score was simply the percentage of the roll calls included in the dimension on which he took a position that would popularly be called liberal. For example, a high score on the social welfare dimension indicates the member voted in favor of establishing and expanding various social welfare programs.

THE GREAT DEPRESSION AND THE TRANSFORMATION OF THE POLITICAL AGENDA, 1925-1938

In 1925 the Republicans had been the majority party in the country for several generations. This dominance was reflected in a Republican president and a heavily Republican Congress. In the House of Representatives elected in 1936, however, Democrats outnumbered Republicans by more than three to one. Subsequent elections reinforced the Democrats' position during this period as the nation's majority party. By 1938 Franklin Roosevelt had twice been elected to the presidency by landslide margins, and Democrats had controlled the Congress since 1931.

Government Management

The Great Depression precipitated this party realignment and led to a transformation in the policy agenda. Only one of the four issue dimensions — government management — was found in the pre-depression Congresses. It appears in each of the Congresses from 1925 through 1938, and in each case voting is along party lines.

Although alignments remained stable, the content of the dimension and the terms of the debate changed radically with the coming of the New Deal. In the pre-New Deal Congresses the extent of pro- or anti-big business sentiment to some extent distinguished the parties, but neither party advocated an activist federal role in regulating or managing the economy. With the 73rd Congress (1933-34) the government management dimension became a New Deal dimension; a high score indicated the member voted for the creation of the TVA, for the invalidation of the gold standards clause, for the Reciprocal Trade Agreements Act, and for the Securities Exchange Act. In the 74th and the 75th Congresses the government management dimension included roll calls on Roosevelt's "soak the rich" tax bill, the regulation of public utility holding companies, and extending the time in which the president could further devalue the dollar.

By and large, the bills included in the government management dimension represented an activist federal government philosophy. Voting in the House on these measures was highly partisan. Thus, while the content of the measures included in the dimension changed with the coming of the New Deal, the gross voting response did not. A much greater ideological distance between the parties resulted. The Democrats clearly supported an activist position. As Table 10-1 indicates, the average Democrat's support for the party position on the major government management dimension is higher after 1930 than in the less ideologically charged years that preceded.

Table 10-1   Government Management and Social Welfare Support Scores, 1925-1938 (In Percentages)

	Democrats			Republicans		
	All	North-east	Solid South	All	North-east	West North Central
Government Management						
1925-30	84.8	75.6	88.6	9.9	4.0	14.8
1931-38	91.3	90.3	94.2	10.1	4.6	23.3
Social Welfare						
1929-38	91.0	93.3	92.9	8.9	4.3	13.7
1938 Fair Labor Standards Act	77.8	99.0	39.2	43.5	46.1	39.8

Despite the strong relationship between party and vote on the government management dimension, certain regional differences within the parties appear.[4] Southern Democrats tend to be more supportive of the party position than their northeastern party colleagues, although the differences after 1930 are slight. Within the Republican party the progressive heritage of many representatives from the West North Central area shows up in their willingness to defect from the party position, while northeasterners are the conservative mainstay of the Republican party.

Social Welfare

The origins of the welfare state are popularly associated with the New Deal. Prior to the depression, legislation designed to help the individual relatively directly was not completely without precedent in American history. Some labor legislation was on the books; veterans' pensions and other social services for certain classes of veterans had a relatively long history; and, in the early 1920s, legislation concerning maternal and infant health needs was passed. Nevertheless, direct help to individuals was generally not considered within the province of legitimate federal action at that time.

During the 1925-38 period the social welfare dimension first appears in the 71st Congress (1929-30). Roll calls on a veterans' pension bill and on providing additional hospital facilities for veterans are included. More clearly related to the depression are roll calls on taking a census of unemployment and on the use of federal funds for relief. Firmly opposed to a federal "dole," President Hoover favored relying upon private charity to alleviate the misery caused by widespread unemployment. The Democrats read their gains in the midterm election as a mandate, and in the 72nd Congress Speaker John Nance Garner proposed a several billion dollar relief bill. Democratic control of the House and Hoover's statement that the bill was "the most gigantic pork barrel ever proposed . . . an unexampled raid on the public treasury,"[5] helped ensure that the measure would be perceived in partisan terms. The struggle over relief spending dominates the social welfare dimension during the New Deal 73rd-75th Congresses. While in the 71st and 72nd debate centered around whether the federal government should provide direct relief, in the later Congresses the controversy concerned the dollar level.

Most of the relief programs were temporary, but during the 74th Congress (1935-36) two major permanent programs were passed: the Social Security Act and the Wagner Labor Relations Act. In terms of the expansion of federal responsibility for the welfare of the individual, this legislation represented truly nonincremental change, yet both passed with relative ease. During the 75th Congress two more clearly nonincremental programs were passed: the Housing Act of 1937, which committed the federal government for the first time to a long-range program of public housing for low-income families, and the Fair Labor Standards Act, the first federal wages and hours bill. Passage of the second act was especially difficult because it evoked a very different alignment from that characteristic of the major social welfare dimension.

As Table 10-1 shows, voting on the major social welfare dimension was partisan at its inception and remained so during this period. Democrats were highly supportive; there is little regional variation and no tendency for the South to be less supportive than other segments of the party. While the average support level of Republicans is low, support does vary along regional lines with West North Central Republicans being the most consistently deviant regional grouping.

The roll calls on the Fair Labor Standards Act did not evoke the same alignments as the major social welfare dimension. The bill split the Democrats along North-South lines; Southern Democrats were much less supportive of the party position than their northern colleagues. The 1937 housing bill also split the Democrats along North-South lines, though the division was less deep. Just under 60 percent of Democrats from the Solid South supported the bill on final passage compared with 94.9 percent of Democrats from other regions.

The regional split on the Fair Labor Standards Act had an economic foundation. Southerners feared that a nationwide minimum wage would nullify their region's advantage in attracting industry. For the same reason northeastern Republicans, usually very conservative, supported the bill. The much less intense southern opposition to the housing bill stemmed from the southerners' belief that the program would aid large northern cities primarily and offered little to rural areas.

During the New Deal most Democrats were highly supportive of most social welfare legislation. By the 75th Congress (1937-38), however, the beginnings of the regional split that was to become so pronounced in later years were evident. On these two nonincremental bills, both of which were perceived as benefiting urban industrial areas, the rural South defected from the party position.

Clearly, the new agenda was the product of the Great Depression. Faced with economic collapse and widespread misery, the public demanded government action. When President Hoover did not respond, a Democratic president and Congress were swept into office by landslide margins. In attempting to cope with the emergency, Congress passed numerous innovative bills that immensely expanded the scope of government responsibility. Voting on most of this legislation was heavily partisan. Consequently, interparty membership replacement was crucial for policy change.

EXPANSION OF THE POLITICAL AGENDA: CIVIL LIBERTIES AND INTERNATIONAL INVOLVEMENT, 1937-1952

The late 1930s saw the development of two new issue dimensions: civil liberties and international involvement. The origins of both are traceable to changes in the political environment. Because the Democratic coalition that emerged from the New Deal realignment included northern blacks, civil rights inevitably entered the political agenda. Roosevelt, keenly aware of the party-splitting potential of the issue, kept his distance from civil rights legislative proposals, but Democratic representatives from the northeast felt no such compunction.[6] Blacks were now a part of their voting constituency, and a modicum of attention had to be paid to their demands.

Civil Liberties

Civil liberties becomes an element of the House agenda in the 75th Congress (1937-38) when the first antilynching bill passed the House. The 76th House again passed an antilynching bill, and from 1942 through 1949 the House passed five bills barring the poll tax as a voting requirement. None of this legislation survived the Senate; the filibuster proved to be an insurmountable barrier for civil rights forces to overcome.[7] Although civil rights was the dominant component of the civil liberties dimension, also included were roll calls on subversive activities legislation.

Table 10-2 Civil Liberties Support Scores, 1937-1950 (In Percentages)

	Democrats		Republicans
All	*North*	*Solid South*	*All*
49.1	84.8	6.4	80.3

The North-South split within the Democratic party on the civil liberties dimension is not surprising. Southern Democrats were bitterly opposed to civil rights legislation. In contrast, Republicans were highly cohesive and supportive, as Table 10-2 indicates.

International Involvement

During most of the 1930s the United States was preoccupied with domestic concerns. Not until the 76th Congress (1939-40) does a substantial cluster of roll calls appear that warrants the international involvement designation. This scale consists mostly of roll calls on the Neutrality Act but also includes several roll calls on the draft and on defense appropriations. From 1939 on, international involvement is a continuing element of the House agenda. In content, the 77th scale is similar to that found in the 76th but also includes lend-lease. The 78th and 79th scales include, as a major component, roll calls on funds for the United Nations Relief and Rehabilitation Administration. From the 80th through the 82nd, the scales are dominated by roll calls on the Marshall Plan, aid to Greece and Turkey, mutual security legislation, aid to Korea, and other foreign aid issues.

As Table 10-3 shows, the level of Republican support for international involvement varies, but the deep split in the party along coastal versus interior lines is relatively constant. A secular change in Democratic voting alignments is evident. Democrats from the Solid South, the most supportive regional grouping in the 1939-42 period, move to being distinctly the least supportive grouping from 1949 on.

The impact of world events can be clearly seen on the origin and development of the international involvement dimension in the 1939-52 period. The dimension developed in response to the situation in Europe. During most of the 1930s Congress concentrated its time and attention on the domestic scene; large majorities supported a hands-off policy towards Europe. Not until 1939 did a majority become convinced that the conflict in Europe required a change in U.S. policy. Even then the majorities were party-based and were frequently very narrow. Not until Pearl Harbor did a consensus develop.

Table 10-3   International Involvement Support Scores, 1939-1952 (In Percentages)

| | Democrats | | | | Republicans | | |
	All	North	Solid South		All	North-east	Pacific	Interior
1939-42	87.9	79.7	96.7		24.9	40.5	41.1	11.7
1943-48	90.4	88.4	90.3		61.3	84.4	79.7	43.4
1949-52	84.9	94.0	72.1		33.2	49.8	41.4	19.6

During the war years, party differences on foreign policy issues were few and much less deep. Although Democrats provided greater support than Republicans for the administration's aid program, most measures drew support from Republican majorities. A hot war did not seem the time to oppose the president's foreign policy. Bipartisanship in foreign policy voting continued during the 80th Congress. The Cold War was taking shape, and the first Republican congressional majority since the 1920s was not inclined to defeat President Truman's foreign policy proposals and thereby risk winning a reputation for irresponsibility. When the Democrats regained control in the 81st Congress, the influence of party on foreign policy voting increased. By then, a bipartisan consensus on the containment policy and on presidential supremacy in the foreign policy area was firmly established. Congressional conflict had been largely narrowed to the details of the foreign aid pattern.

Constituency attitudes, in addition to the influence of world events and of partisan control of the Congress, seem to have influenced voting on the international involvement dimension. During the pre-Pearl Harbor period southerners were consistently most favorable toward the adoption by the United States of an activist role in helping the allies; the public in the midwest and Great Plains was least favorable.[8] This pattern of opinion was roughly reflected in congressional voting in the prewar period. Southern Democrats were most supportive of international involvement; interior Republicans the least.

The coastal-interior split within the Republican party was evident throughout the 1939-52 period. Regional culture — the greater parochialism and isolation from world events of the small town and rural people of the interior regions — has frequently been offered as an explanation for this split.[9] Certainly its persistence suggests that it is rooted in constituency differences.

How is the decline in southern Democratic support on international involvement to be explained? It can be argued that, from the point of view of southern representatives and quite likely of their constituency elites, the issues changed. Charles Lerche contends that southerners have always supported a strong national defense, have believed the U.S. should pursue clear-cut victory in wars, cold or hot; and opposed "giveaways" to countries not sufficiently grateful and subservient.[10] By the early 1950s the foreign aid program began to look less and less like a temporary emergency measure; to many southerners it began to appear increasingly like a "giveaway" for which the U.S. received no real return.

The late 1930s saw a further expansion of the political agenda. Unlike the issues that dominated the earlier part of the decade, the new issues deeply split the parties along regional lines. The cohesive party-line voting of the New Deal era was not extended to the new issues that activated intraparty constituency differences.

RETURN TO NORMAL POLITICS: GOVERNMENT MANAGEMENT AND SOCIAL WELFARE, 1939-1952

The sense of urgency that had fueled the New Deal had largely dissipated by the late 1930s. Numerous reforms had been passed; the economy, while still not fully recovered, was no longer in danger of total collapse. After Pearl Harbor the war overshadowed all other problems. War production brought prosperity and thus eroded any remaining impetus toward further domestic reform.

Although the Democrats were clearly the majority party during the 1939-52 period, the huge congressional majorities of the New Deal were a thing of the past. Republicans made big gains in House seats in the 1938 and 1942 elections and in 1946 won control. The conditions for further nonincremental policy change were absent and a return to normal politics was to be expected.

From 1939 to 1952 there were no significant agenda changes in the social welfare or government management areas. Controversy centered primarily around the issues that had come to the fore during the New Deal, and policy change was incremental. The permanence of the New Deal reforms became clear when the Republican-controlled 80th Congress made no real attempt to repeal them. A number of the New Deal programs were even expanded during this period, but no new departures were made.

Although the policy agenda remained stable, voting alignments changed. On both the social welfare and the government management dimensions, a North-South split developed within the Democratic party. Democrats from the Solid South, who had been the most supportive segment of their party during the New Deal, became by the mid-1940s the least supportive group by far. Republican voting patterns also changed. On government management, West North Central Republicans no longer defected from the party position, and party cohesion increased. On social welfare, northeasterners, the most conservative regional grouping within the Republican party in the late 1920s and 1930s, became the most supportive group by the early 1950s. West North Central Republicans followed the opposite path, and by the late 1940s the once insurgent Midwest had become the center of Republican orthodoxy, as Table 10-4 indicates.

The North-South split in the Democratic party is so familiar to political scientists that they have largely been blind to the need to explain it. The reasons for the development of the split, however, are far from self-evident. Southern representatives' high support for New Deal programs in the 1930s was consonant with public opinion in the South. Opinion surveys from the 1930s and early 1940s show southerners to be the regional grouping most supportive of New Deal programs.[11] If, during the late 1940s and early 1950s, southern public opinion had swung sharply right, the increased conservatism of southern representatives could be explained as a response to constituency opinion change. Surveys indicate, however, that, except on race, there were no significant regional attitude differences on domestic issues during those years.

The explanation seems to lie in the change in political atmosphere generally and in a change in the southern economy coupled with the special character of southern politics. Public opinion polls show an overall decline in support for further policy departures in the late 1930s.[12] Many people, mass as well as elite, perceived the emergency to be over and believed additional change to be unnecessary. When

Table 10-4 Government Management and Social Welfare Support Scores, 1939-1952 (In Percentages)

	Democrats			Republicans		
	All	*North*	*Solid South*	*All*	*North- east*	*West North Central*
Government Management						
1939-42	89.0	88.6	89.5	10.2	12.3	9.6
1943-52	78.8	88.0	69.1	12.7	7.4	14.0
Social Welfare						
1939-44*	86.7	93.9	80.9	10.6	9.7	13.3
1945-52	67.0	87.0	45.6	17.1	21.2	13.8

*The 77th Congress dimension is excluded from the means because it evoked a deviant alignment pattern.

the war brought prosperity, those whose support for the New Deal rested upon the emergency argument could see little rationale for further policy innovation. Equally important, prosperity probably brought a decline in the saliency of domestic politics.

In the postwar years the South began to industrialize. We know that industrializing elites tend to be strongly opposed to government intervention of the sort supported by liberals in the post-New Deal years.[13] When the forces of industrialization were added to the older agrarian conservatism, the remnants of agrarian radicalism in the South were largely extinguished. Southern elites in the postwar years had a heavily conservative cast.

If these developments are considered in the light of the special character of southern politics, an explanation for the North-South split begins to emerge. The low level of political participation in the South gave elites in the area greater influence than in the rest of the country. When the saliency of politics to the mass public drops, elite influence should be further magnified. The lack of a rich organizational life in the South — particularly the absence of unions — limited the avenues of expression for those opposed to the economic elite. In many northern districts, a supportive coalition could be based upon blue collar workers and union leaders. In the South this was not possible.

The difference in interest between agrarian and industrializing areas on the one hand and industrialized areas on the other may explain the changing alignments within the Republican party. The key factor according to Everett Ladd is "the essential harmony between the thrust of the New Deal and the conditions of advanced industrialism."[14] By the late 1940s northeastern Republicans seem to have realized that the New Deal's social welfare programs were a force for stability in their heavily industrialized area, and their opposition softened. Northeasterners then became the most deviant section of the Republican party on social welfare.

As the aftershocks of realignment gave way to a period of normal politics, policy change became incremental once again, and the high party cohesion characteristic of the height of the New Deal was replaced with party fragmentation along regional lines. By the early 1950s the pre-realignment voting patterns had been completely transformed.

FROM POLITICAL QUIESCENCE TO POLICY ACTIVISM: DOMESTIC POLICY CHANGE, 1953-1968

The 1952 elections ended 20 years of Democratic control of the presidency and 24 years of Democratic control of the Congress. The shift in partisan control did not, however, signal a basic change in policy direction. In the fight for the presidential nomination, the moderate wing of the Republican party had emerged victorious. Republican majorities in the House and Senate were narrow. If dreams of "repealing" the New Deal still lurked in some Republican hearts, political reality militated against their expression.

When Democrats regained control of the Congress in the 1954 elections, the Democratic party was fairly evenly divided between an increasingly conservative southern wing and the northern liberals. Not until the recession sharply increased the Democratic majority in the 1958 elections did the northern wing gain a clear numerical preponderance. Even then, their committee positions gave southerners power out of proportion to their still very considerable numbers.

The 1950s saw few burning issues that involved large numbers of people. Two wars followed by general prosperity led to a period of low saliency politics. By the mid-1950s the Cold War had become routine. Public pressure for domestic policy departures was minimal. In only one area — civil rights — did a popular movement demanding change emerge in the 1950s.

Presidential candidate John Kennedy promised to "get the country moving again," and with his election eight years of divided control ended. Although Kennedy's winning margin was small and the Democrats lost seats in the Congress, their majority was nevertheless substantial. The president himself and the northern wing of the party were committed to change. Signs that the political quiescence of the 1950s was a thing of the past became increasingly evident. The civil rights movement gained momentum and attracted widespread public notice. In late 1960, 46 percent of a national sample said that the new president and Congress should "do more to end segregation."[15]

The assassination of Kennedy brought into office the first southern president since the Civil War. Lyndon Baines Johnson soon made it clear that his dedication to civil rights was at least equal to that of his predecessor. When the right wing of the Republican party captured the presidential nomination, a Democratic landslide followed. Barry Goldwater did make inroads in the South, however. Several Deep South states elected Republicans to the House for the first time.

Civil Liberties

Civil liberties was the first of the issue areas to change significantly. When the Supreme Court in 1954 outlawed school segregation, a grass-roots civil rights movement began to develop, and the Congress came under increasing pressure to pass civil rights legislation. The

House passed a civil rights bill in 1956, but it was not until 1957 that Congress enacted the first civil rights legislation since the post-Civil War Reconstruction period. In 1960, a second bill was passed. Although important symbolically, this legislation was quite weak. During the Johnson administration three much stronger bills were enacted: the 1964 Civil Rights Act, the 1965 Voting Rights Act, and the 1968 Open Housing Act. In terms of the problems attacked, the remedies proposed, and their social and political impact, these bills represented truly nonincremental policy change.

As Table 10-5 shows, from 1953 to 1968 the civil liberties dimension continued to split the Democrats deeply along North-South lines, although northern Democratic support dropped in the mid- to late sixties. Republican support on the dimension decreased, and the party divided along regional lines. The first drop in Republican support occurred in the mid-1950s and was not due to defections on civil rights. Also included in the dimension during the late 1950s are votes on bills attempting to curb the power of the Supreme Court; many Republicans joined the Southern Democrats on these roll calls. As the antiwar movement became prominent during the mid-1960s, bills aimed at curbing such protests drew heavy support from Republicans; Republican support for civil rights legislation also decreased. Open housing and school busing were matters directly affecting the Republicans' white, middle-class constituents, and the mail from home was sharply opposed. Thus, as the thrust of the civil rights bills changed, so did the Republican voting response.

Social Welfare

The quiescent 1950s were followed in the 1960s by a burst of nonincremental policy change in the social welfare area as well. Aid to education was finally enacted in 1965 and Medicare, long a dream of liberals, was passed. The passage of the antipoverty program in 1964 signaled an even more significant departure. Social welfare programs from the New Deal through the early 1960s were aimed at helping the non-rich majority. In the mid-1960s the emphasis shifted to programs intended to aid the poor minority directly.

The new issues gave rise to high intensity politics. The regional split within each party, dating back to the 1940s and continuing during the 1950s, intensified in the 1960s. Northeastern Republicans provided higher support for social welfare than Democrats from the Solid South.

Government Management

When compared with the policy innovation that occurred in the civil rights and social welfare areas, activity in the government man-

Table 10-5   Domestic Policy Support Scores, 1953-1968 (In Percentages)

| | Democrats | | | Republicans | | |
	All	North	Solid South	All	North-east	Other*
Civil Liberties						
1955-56	53.1	98.1	.7	89.0	94.4	91.0
1957-64	54.8	86.3	9.2	50.9	62.5	46.4
1965-68	51.9	73.1	10.5	33.9	50.6	32.1
Social Welfare						
1953-60	71.5	93.5	42.2	32.7	43.4	27.1
1961-68	76.6	95.4	33.6**	33.3	55.0	22.6
Government Management						
1953-60	85.3	91.7	77.1	13.2	13.0	12.9
1961-64	85.5	92.1	73.5	19.3	25.5	16.0
1965-68	84.2	92.0	65.3	15.3	25.6	11.7

*Republicans from the Solid South are exluded from mean civil liberties scores.
**The 88th Congress score is excluded as it is atypically high and obscures the pattern.

agement area during the Kennedy-Johnson administrations is much less dramatic. While a number of new programs were enacted — most notably area redevelopment — most of the issues debated had been around since the 1940s and 1950s: federal spending levels, the pros and cons of deficit spending as an antirecession measure, the role of the federal government in power facilities development, and the structure of the tax code.

Although the political agenda remained stable from the 1950s to the 1960s, voting alignments changed. The North-South split within the Democratic party, which had moderated during the 1950s, intensified, especially in the 89th and 90th Congresses. During the 1950s the Republican party was quite cohesive on the government management dimension. In the 1960s the party began to split along regional lines; by the mid-1960s northeasterners were considerably more supportive than Republicans from other areas.

The Activist Sixties

Peace, growing affluence, and the lack of dramatic issues led to low saliency politics in the 1950s. The early 1960s saw an increase in political interest.[16] The civil rights movement and the Kennedy personality both seem to have contributed to the increase. The trauma of John Kennedy's assassination probably focused public attention on Washington even more.

The 1964 presidential election campaign further transformed the complexion of American politics. Not only was Republican candidate Barry Goldwater perceived as trigger-happy and opposed to federal action on civil rights, but he also questioned the post-New Deal consensus on domestic policy. Offered clear alternatives, the electorate made its choice unmistakably clear. A Democratic landslide of a magnitude unequaled since the New Deal was the result.

The political environment of the 1960s had transformed the American electorate. The average mid-1960s voter, when compared with his mid-1950s counterpart, was more interested in politics; his attitude set came closer to constituting a consistent ideology; and he was more likely to base his vote on his ideology.[17]

These changes in the political environment were conducive to policy change. The more attentive public clearly favored civil rights legislation and such social welfare programs as aid to education and Medicare.[18] To the extent data are available, they indicate that such preferences do not represent a major change in attitudes since the 1950s. What did change was the extent to which politics was salient to the average voter. If members of Congress perceive their constituents to be attentive, they are more likely to feel constrained by constituency preferences.

A change in political climate, due in part to the civil rights movement, led to a change in the political agenda; and the changed climate together with the new issues increased the salience of politics. The result was the first cluster of nonincremental domestic policy changes since the New Deal.

The events of the early 1960s did not affect the North and the South in the same way. Southerners became more conservative relative to the rest of the country on domestic social and economic issues.[19] In the 1950s they held distinctive attitudes only on race-related questions, but during the following decade the region began to diverge from the North across the whole spectrum of domestic issues. While southerners were becoming more conservative, north-easterners were becoming more liberal. Polls from the 1940s and 1950s show northeasterners to be more tolerant on civil liberties issues than the public as a whole. In the 1960s they continued to be the most liberal section on civil rights and became more liberal than the inhabitants of other sections on social and economic policy issues as well.[20] The constituency signals that eastern Republicans received were more likely than previously to point toward support for at least some of the measures proposed by Kennedy and Johnson.

The changes in voting behavior during the 1960s are consonant with changes in public opinion in the Northeast and the South. Especially in a period of high intensity politics, members of Congress will reflect the general thrust of constituency opinion in their voting behavior.

INTERNATIONAL INVOLVEMENT, 1952-1976

From 1952 to 1968, foreign aid dominated the international involvement agenda in the House. Although the foreign policy consensus that had kept other issues off the voting agenda began to break down in the mid-1960s, the House leadership during the Johnson presidency kept most anti-Vietnam War measures from coming to the floor.

From 1969 to 1976, two distinct clusters of international involvement roll calls appear in each Congress. One set is very similar in content to the international involvement dimension found in earlier Congresses. It consists mostly of roll calls on foreign aid bills. The other includes numerous votes directly related to the Vietnam War but also roll calls on cutting Department of Defense appropriations, on cutting funds for a wide variety of weapons systems (the antiballistic missile, nerve gas, and the B-1 bomber for example), on barring aid to Chile and other dictatorships, on overseas troop cuts, on prohibiting the importation of Rhodesian chrome, and on barring the Ford administration from becoming involved in Angola. This dimension will be labeled foreign and defense policy reorientation.[21] Certainly those members who supported these departures were challenging basic precepts of American foreign and defense policy.

The House displayed limited enthusiasm for a thorough reorientation of U.S. foreign and defense policy. As Table 10-6 indicates, no segment of the Republican party showed much support, although northeasterners were somewhat less opposed than members from other areas. Solid South Democrats were also firmly opposed, and Northern Democrats were split.

The overwhelming Republican opposition and the divisions within the Democratic party account for the failure of many of the proposals aimed at a basic reorientation of foreign and defense policy. The defeat of many of the more drastic proposals does not, however, mean that policy remained unchanged. The change in agenda was followed by policy change. Funds for the Indochina war were eventually cut off, some cuts in defense spending were made, and Congress refused to let the Ford administration get involved in Angola.

On the reorientation dimension, congressional voting behavior roughly corresponded to constituency opinion. In the population, Democrats after 1968 were somewhat more likely to be doves than Republicans; northeasterners were distinctly more dovish than inhabitants of other sections. On questions concerning defense spending and U.S.

Table 10-6 Foreign and Defense Policy Reorientation Support Scores, 1969-1976 (In Percentages)

All Members	Democrats			Republicans			
	All	*Solid South*	*North*	*All*	*North-east*	*Pacific*	*Interior**
36.7	49.3	66.3	18.1	18.4	29.0	15.8	17.4

*Republicans from the Solid South are excluded.

relations with communist countries, southerners were especially inclined to take a hard line.[22]

Public opinion was, however, ambivalent. Americans wanted to get out of Vietnam, but to do so with honor; as a result, public opinion swung erratically from dovish to hawkish and back again.[23] Not until 1971 did a stable majority in favor of relatively rapid withdrawal develop.

Certainly, the general public's growing disillusionment with the war in Southeast Asia had an important effect on policy decisions. In terms of support for a more general reorientation of foreign and defense policy, however, it seems likely that the attitudes of members of the House and those of their active supporters were the primary voting cues. The antiwar movement that favored such a reorientation was predominantly liberal, middle-class, and urban in composition. Members of the House who represented districts in which these elements were important and who themselves shared these characteristics were most likely to favor a reorientation of American foreign and defense policy.

Voting behavior on the traditional international involvement dimension did not change during the period from 1949 to 1976. During the Truman presidency, Democrats split along North-South lines and Republicans along coastal versus interior lines. A similar alignment pattern characterized the Nixon-Ford years. The only secular change apparent is the increased opposition of Republicans from the Pacific states.

Although the form of the alignment remained stable, support levels varied depending upon the party affiliation of the president, as the support scores for the 1949-76 period depicted in Table 10-7 indicate. Members of each party gave higher support to a president of their own party than to one from the opposition. Thus, on foreign aid — a program without a domestic constituency yet one not highly salient to most constituents — the president does influence voting behavior.

Table 10-7 Presidential Influence on International Involvement Support Scores, 1949-1976 (In Percentages)

President	Democrats			Republicans			
	All	North	Solid South	All	North-east	Pacific	Interior*
Truman, 1949-52	84.9	94.0	72.1	33.2	49.8	41.4	19.6
Eisenhower, 1953-60	69.0	88.3	41.2	60.8	87.3	74.3	41.0
Kennedy-Johnson, 1961-68	77.1	92.2	47.2	39.6	63.5	39.4	29.4
Nixon-Ford, 1969-76	63.9	78.9	36.2	51.8	73.4	52.6	49.5

*Republicans from the Solid South are excluded.

DOMESTIC POLITICS IN A TIME OF TURMOIL, 1969-1976

When the public sends a strong and clear signal, the Congress usually responds. During the 1969-76 period the public's signals, as indicated by opinion polls and election returns, lacked that clear thrust. In 1968 Richard Nixon was elected president, and George Wallace received 13.5 percent of the popular vote; in 1972 Nixon was re-elected by a landslide. Yet the elections of 1968 through 1974 returned heavily Democratic majorities to the Congress.

The concerns of the public were not difficult to discern — Vietnam, crime and lawlessness, race, pollution, inflation, and unemployment.[24] But on many of these issues both liberals and conservatives could claim, with equal justification or lack of it, a mandate for their approach. Under such circumstances one would expect policy change also to lack a clear thrust.

Neither the civil liberties nor the social welfare agenda changed significantly during these years. By and large, controversy, which was frequently intense, centered around the issues that came to the fore during the 1960s, and congressional liberals concentrated on preserving previous gains against attacks from conservative presidents. Table 10-8 shows that on both dimensions Republicans from the Northeast continued to be more supportive than members from other areas. Within the Democratic party the familiar North-South split narrowed somewhat after 1972. To a considerable extent this narrowing was due to membership replacement. The large southern Democratic freshman classes elected in 1972 and 1974 were much more supportive on both civil liberties and social welfare than their more senior regional colleagues. As the race issue declined in salience in the South, districts that were similar demographically to those represented by Northern

Democrats began to elect representatives who voted more like Northern Democrats.

Stagflation, the Arab oil embargo, and the environmental and consumer movements did bring about a major change in the government management agenda. But only in the environmental area were public signals both strong and clear, and only in that area was agenda change accompanied by nonincremental policy change. The 1970 Clean Air Act, the single most important piece of environmental legislation during this period, not only attempted to attain its goals through regulation, rather than the subsidies that had been the primary mechanism in earlier environmental legislation; it also contained "technology-forcing" provisions, provisions that set standards above what was thought to be feasible with present technology. The Arab oil embargo, however, ended the period of easy victories. As attention shifted to the need for increased energy production, environmentalists were forced onto the defensive.

As the focus of government management legislation shifted, so did voting alignments. The distance between the parties decreased as the support of Solid South Democrats plummeted and that of northeastern Republicans increased. This change in alignments can be linked to constituency interests. Environmental and consumer protection legislation had its greatest appeal to the affluent in the industrialized areas.[25] In industrializing areas, however, elites and often the general population as well objected to such regulations. Energy policy pitted producer against consumer interests. Thus, northeastern Republicans representing affluent constituents in a heavily industrialized and non-oil-producing area moved toward the Democratic

Table 10-8 Domestic Policy Support Scores, 1969-1976 (In Percentages)

| | Democrats | | | Republicans | | |
	All	North	Solid South	All	North-east	Other*
Civil Liberties						
1969-72	54.6	75.5	15.3	27.2	39.2	26.9
1973-76	63.6	78.1	33.3	31.3	45.3	32.9
Social Welfare						
1969-72	79.4	94.8	46.7	33.3	50.0	28.3
1973-76	79.6	91.0	55.0	32.4	52.2	26.2
Government Management						
1969-76	70.5	83.1	45.3	24.6	39.2	19.5

*Republicans from the Solid South are excluded from mean civil liberties scores.

pole on the government management dimension, and Solid South Democrats representing an oil-producing and a still industrializing area moved to the Republican pole.

CONGRESSIONAL ALIGNMENTS DURING THE EARLY CARTER YEARS, 1977-1978

Jimmy Carter's election to the presidency in 1976 did not coincide with a change in political agenda. The state of the economy continued as the problem of primary concern to most Americans. The Carter administration emphasized the passage of an energy program as its top domestic priority.

Domestic policy change was incremental. In response to the high unemployment rate, Congress passed an economic stimulus program. Strip mining legislation was finally enacted. After a long struggle an energy program passed, but it had little relationship to the one originally requested by Carter. Neither labor nor blacks — two important components of the Democratic coalition — fared well. Common situs picketing legislation and labor law reform were defeated. Before passage, the Humphrey-Hawkins full employment bill was watered down to the point of meaninglessness.

By and large, voting alignments were very similar to those characteristic of the Nixon-Ford years; in the domestic area the only significant change was the splitting of the government management dimension into the two scales shown in Table 10-9. One is dominated by roll calls on energy and environmental legislation and is quite clearly a continuation of the 1970s government management dimension. The second government management scale includes roll calls on economic stimulus programs, debt limit increases and budget resolutions, the Humphrey-Hawkins bill, and the Kemp amendment to the tax bill — an amendment that would have drastically cut taxes.

The two scales elicit quite similar voting alignments. The second, however, splits each of the parties to a much lesser extent than do the other government management scales in the 1970s. Alignments are, in fact, quite similar to those characterizing the government management dimension in the 1960s. The heavier party component to voting alignments on this scale is probably due to the Democratic recapture of the presidency. Democrats from all regions appear to be willing to follow party lines on those issues considered by the congressional leadership and the president to be crucial to the party program, so long as constituency interests are not fundamentally compromised. On issues eliciting strong constituency interests, however, defections from the party occurred. Unfortunately for the president and the leadership, on many of the most crucial issues such as

Table 10-9 95th Congress Support Scores by Party and Region, 1977-1978 (In Percentages)

	Democrats			Republicans		
	All	*North*	*Solid South*	*All*	*North-east*	*Other*
Social Welfare	78.3	89.4	52.1	27.2	46.9	21.7
Civil Liberties	64.7	77.4	36.5	21.4	35.9	20.8*
Government Management						
Dimension	72.3	83.9	47.2	24.1	41.0	19.4
New scale	81.7	88.5	65.2	16.7	27.4	13.6
International Involvement						
Aid	70.1	82.8	44.3	39.8	62.2	33.6
Reorientation	54.1	67.9	24.9	18.7	32.0	15.0
Hard-line	62.4	74.9	35.7	23.4	38.1	19.1

*Republicans from the Solid South are excluded.

energy, Democrats from the South and, to a lesser extent, border and mountain Democrats continued to defect massively from the party position.

In the international involvement area a new scale also appears. As the reorientation dimension represented a challenge from the left to the hard-line foreign and defense policy of Republican presidents, changes in the debate could be anticipated with the advent of the Carter presidency. Carter attempted to incorporate some elements of the new perspective into his foreign policy. His human rights policy, in selected instances, led him to cut off or diminish aid to right-wing dictatorships. He took a somewhat tougher stance on the B-1 bomber; his requirement that the military justify this expensive new weapons systems led to the decision against production. Carter's foreign policy infuriated hard-liners in the Congress while not going far enough to satisfy those committed to a true reorientation of U.S. foreign and defense policy.

The new scale represents a hard-line challenge to Carter's foreign policy. Prominent were votes on a number of amendments placing restrictions on the countries to which U.S. aid could go; the named countries were mostly communist or left-leaning ones, and the aim was to restrict the president's discretion. Attempts to restrict the president's discretion with respect to the Panama Canal treaties and the pull-out of U.S. troops from Korea are included, as are roll calls on the bill reimposing an embargo on Rhodesian chrome, several votes on the neutron bomb and on restoring money for the nuclear aircraft carrier, and several attempts to increase defense spending above the level requested by Carter.

Table 10-9 shows voting alignments on the scale that incorporates this hard-line threat to the Carter policy as well as alignments on the foreign aid scale. The regional splits within the parties are similar on both scales. Within the Democratic party, northerners were more supportive of Carter than southerners; within the Republican party, northeasterners were more supportive than their colleagues from other areas. The levels of support on the two scales are, however, very different. Northeastern Republicans as a group were a part of the right-wing attack on the Carter policy. Northern Democrats were split; their support of Carter's policies against attack from the right was considerably lower than their support on the foreign aid scale, which itself was significantly below the support Northern Democrats gave Kennedy and Johnson on foreign aid.

With reason, Carter complained about the difficulty of building majority coalitions in the foreign and defense policy area. Foreign and defense policy is no longer beyond debate. Consequently, presidential dominance has been greatly reduced. Unlike his Republican predecessors, Carter faced challenges from both the left and the right.

An alteration in partisan control of the presidency when unaccompanied by a change in the political environment is unlikely to result in major policy change. By and large, the early Carter years saw continuity in the political agenda; incremental policy change; and, with the exceptions noted, relatively stable voting alignments.

CONCLUSION

Several important generalizations can be drawn from the policy and alignment changes described in the preceding pages. Significant change in the political agenda is usually linked to change in the broader political environment; such change is not generated within the Congress. For example, the Great Depression led to a fundamental change in the domestic policy agenda. The change in the composition of the Democratic party during the New Deal thrust civil rights onto the agenda in the late 1930s. The environmental and consumer movements and the Arab oil embargo in the 1970s strongly influenced the domestic policy agenda. In the foreign affairs area, the worsening situation in Europe in the late 1930s thrust foreign policy to the center of the agenda, and during the 1960s the Vietnam War led to a major change in the foreign policy agenda.

How the political agenda is set explains why significant agenda change is always the result of environmental stimuli of considerable magnitude. The competition to place items on the agenda is intense;

there are always more problems that someone perceives to be important than the government can possibly handle. At any given point in time the agenda consists of the problems considered important by those with enough political clout to persuade a significant proportion of decisionmakers to share their concerns. For the agenda to change, such powerful groups must alter their priorities, or new groups must become sufficiently potent to influence the agenda. Only a significant change in the political environment is likely to produce such alterations.

Because the barriers are even greater, truly nonincremental policy change is rarer than agenda change. In the domestic area, two clusters of clearly nonincremental policy change occurred from 1925 to 1978. Both the New Deal Congresses and the 89th Congress (1965-66) were preceded by landslide elections that produced heavy interparty membership turnover, and in both cases the majorities that passed the policy departures were primarily party-based. Yet landslide elections do not necessarily lead to nonincremental policy change. The environmental stimulus must be present. If it is, policy change may occur without a major change in party balance. Thus, the 1964 Civil Rights Act and the antipoverty program were passed before the 1964 election. It is important to remember, however, that the 88th Congress that passed these measures had a substantial Democratic majority and that the president was of the same party. It seems, then, that united control of the Congress and the presidency and a substantial congressional majority, as well as an environmental stimulus, are necessary for nonincremental policy change.

Alignment change is frequently but not always associated with agenda change. The environmental stimulus that precipitates agenda change is also likely to alter the representative's voting calculus. As the issues at the center of controversy change, the signals received from the member's constituency may also change.

Although the evidence is far from complete, the single most important influence upon a representative's general voting thrust appears to be his or her constituency. It seems likely, however, that it is not the whole geographical constituency to which the member attends but that segment that supports him electorally. Party voting is, at least in part, due to similar interests among the supportive constituencies of members of the same party. Thus, Democratic unity during the New Deal was due to the common plight of the members' districts and the resulting clear need to do something about the depression. When Southern Democrats during the post-World War II years saw continuation of the reform thrust as a threat to rapid industrialization in the South, the party split. Conversely, many eastern Republicans began to defect from their party's conservative position on social welfare as it became clear that some social welfare programs were in the interest of their supportive constituencies. The high saliency issues of the 1960s further divided the regional groups within each party. The increasing conservativism of the southern populace and the growing liberalism of northeasterners was reflected in congressional voting alignments. The 1970s saw some of the highly divisive civil rights and social welfare issues fade in saliency. As a result, the Democratic split on these issues narrowed. The newly prominent energy and environmental legislation, however, pitted industrialized against industrializing areas and split both parties.

NOTES

1. See Herbert Asher and Herbert Weisberg, "Voting Change in Congress," *American Journal of Political Science* 22 (May 1978): 391-425.
2. Aage Clausen, *How Congressmen Decide* (New York: St. Martin's Press, 1973). Clausen's agricultural assistance domain is not discussed here for lack of space.
3. For a description of the methodology and a more detailed analysis, see Barbara Sinclair, "Party Realignment and the Transformation of the Political Agenda: The House of Representatives, 1925-1938," *American Political Science Review* 71 (September 1977): 940-953; Sinclair, "The Policy Consequences of Party Realignment — Social Welfare Legislation in the House of Representatives, 1933-1954," ibid., 22 (February 1978): 83-105; Sinclair, "From Party Voting to Regional Fragmentation: The House of Representatives, 1933-1956," *American Politics Quarterly* 6 (April 1978): 125-146.
4. The regional categorization used is that of the Survey Research Center.
5. E. Pendleton Herring, "First Session of the 72nd Congress," *American Political Science Review* 26 (October 1932): 869-872.
6. Frank Freidel, *F.D.R. and the South* (Baton Rouge: Louisiana State University Press, 1965), pp. 71-102.
7. No civil rights legislation gets to the floor of the House in either the 82nd or 83rd Congress, and the civil liberties dimension does not appear in either Congress.
8. Alfred Hero, *The Southerner and World Affairs* (Baton Rouge: Louisiana State University Press, 1965), pp. 91-103.
9. Leroy Rieselbach, *The Roots of Isolationism* (Indianapolis: Bobbs-Merrill Co., 1966), pp. 16-17.
10. Charles Lerche, *The Uncertain South* (Chicago: Quadrangle, 1964), p. 262.
11. Everett Ladd and Charles Hadley, *Transformations of the American Party System* (New York: W. W. Norton & Co., 1975), pp. 131-132.
12. Hadley Cantril, ed., *Public Opinion, 1935-1946* (Princeton: Princeton University Press, 1951), pp. 978-979.
13. Ladd, *American Party System,* pp. 138-139.
14. Ibid., p. 141.
15. George Gallup, *The Gallup Poll: Public Opinion, 1935-1971,* vol. 3 (New York: Random House, 1972), p. 1700.
16. Norman Nie, Sidney Verba, and John Petrocik, *The Changing American Voter* (Cambridge: Harvard University Press, 1976), pp. 271-273.

17. Ibid., especially chaps. 8 and 10.
18. James L. Sundquist, *Politics and Policy* (Washington, D.C.: The Brookings Institution, 1968), pp. 441-452, 484-489.
19. Ladd, *American Party System,* p. 168.
20. Ibid., pp. 168-172.
21. See Aage Clausen and Carl Van Horn, "The Congressional Response to a Decade of Change: 1963-1972," *Journal of Politics* 39 (August 1977): 624-666.
22. Gallup, *Public Opinion, 1935-1971,* pp. 2125, 2223 and Ladd, *American Party System,* p. 170.
23. William Watts and Lloyd Free, *State of the Nation* (New York: Universe Books, 1972), pp. 194-198.
24. Nie, Verba, and Petrocik, *Changing American Voter,* p. 103 and Gallup Opinion Index, 1973-1976.
25. Louis Harris, *The Anguish of Change* (New York: W. W. Norton & Co., 1973), pp. 99-118.

11

The Politics of the Congressional Budget Process Re-examined

John W. Ellwood and James A. Thurber

In 1974 Congress was charged with a new mission: to fit isolated revenue and expenditure decisions into a logical, coherent process that would treat the federal budget as a rational whole. The Budget and Impoundment Control Act of 1974 has not been enthusiastically implemented by the congressional leadership, committee chairmen, interest groups, or the president and executive branch, but it has survived. The new budget process created a framework within which Congress can determine expenditures, budgetary priorities, revenue, and debt. It allows Congress to "balance the budget," if it wants; to set its own budgetary prerogatives; and to highlight the relationship between receipts and expenditures. The nature and implementation of the congressional budget process since its enactment raise a number of interesting issues of concern to students of Congress and American public policymaking.

There is an intrinsic interest in the process itself. How does it work? What new institutions were created by the reform, and what new requirements did it impose on traditional units of Congress

For additional analysis see "The New Congressional Budget Process: The Hows and Whys of House-Senate Differences," in *Congress Reconsidered*, 1st ed., edited by Lawrence C. Dodd and Bruce I. Oppenheimer (New York: Praeger Publishers, 1977), pp. 163-192.

and the executive branch? Other basic questions are related to enactment of the reform. Why was it enacted? Where did the support for the new budget process come from?

Beyond this intrinsic interest, however, a study of the implementation of the new budget process sheds light on questions with important consequences for the future. Is the new budget process working? Will it lead to changes in congressional behavior and ultimately in congressional spending policy?

The procedures call for modification of the behavior patterns of nearly every unit of Congress: appropriations committees, revenue committees, and authorizing committees, as well as party leadership. These behavioral changes will necessarily alter the power relationships among the pre-existing institutions as they in turn modify their behavior to take account of the new process and institutions. Therefore, the new budget process also presents the student of Congress with a case study that will be useful in determining (1) what changes in power relationships take place among existing units of the House and the Senate, (2) how existing units of Congress modify their behavior to take account of new units and the requirements of a new process, and (3) how a new committee seeks to build its own power base within a pre-existing legislative body.

The budget process is also of special interest to students of congressional committees. The budget committee is unique among major committees of the House. Fourteen of its 25 members must be from specific committees or leadership positions, and it alone has a rotating membership. In the House the operation of the new budget process during the first year and a half of its existence was so different from that of the Senate, as well as from usual House patterns, as to warrant serious attention.

This chapter is divided into six sections: (1) a description of reasons for the enactment of the new process; (2) a review of how the process works; (3) an examination of the differences between the House and Senate budget process; (4) a tentative explanation of these differences; (5) a discussion of the impoundment process; and (6) the future of the congressional budget process.

REASONS FOR ENACTMENT

The Budget and Impoundment Control Act of 1974 (P.L. 93-344) worked its way through the legislative process in only two years — a remarkably short period for such a sweeping and complex piece of legislation — and was passed by overwhelming majorities: 75-0 in the Senate, 401-6 in the House. The ease with which the act passed Congress reflects the power of the forces and factors that had coalesced behind the reform in the early 1970s.

Traditionally, the "history of budget" in Congress was that of war between the parts and the whole.[1] Each year Congress would take the president's total budget, chop it up into small pieces, and parcel them out among committees and subcommittees that would work on them with little regard for the impact their particular changes might have on the whole. Indeed, few within Congress were even aware of the emerging totals.

Before the budget process was reformed, jurisdiction over the various spending programs was scattered among numerous committees. While the executive branch experienced a series of reforms designed to concentrate policy- and budget-making authority in a central office — formerly the Bureau of the Budget and now the Office of Management and Budget — the congressional budgetary process became merely the sum of a series of isolated, competing, and unrelated actions. Even the many appropriations subcommittees could claim annual authority over only 44 percent of all federal expenditures.[2] Large entitlements such as social security expenditures were controlled by the tax-writing committees. Authorizing committees also gained control over large sums by granting agencies the authority to contract in advance of appropriations or to borrow from the public. This process was found wanting by different groups for the following reasons.

Fear of Rise in Spending and Deficits

From 1956 to 1974, federal outlays increased more than 500 percent, rising from $70.5 billion in fiscal year 1956 to $394.2 billion in fiscal year 1974. Even measured in constant dollars, federal spending more than doubled. At the same time, the federal government ran a deficit in 16 years of this 20-year period. The total federal debt, while declining as a percentage of the gross national product, increased by about $350 billion.

Conservatives, joined by increasing numbers of moderates and liberals, were alarmed by this rapid growth of federal spending and the ever-increasing number and size of deficits. Large segments of the public and Congress advocated the new budget process as a means to limit federal spending, which many viewed as "out of control." Even after enactment of a congressional budgeting process, however, controlling federal spending continues to be a major concern in the 1980s.

Lack of Control in the Appropriations Process

Budget control, of course, can have another meaning besides the ability to limit or decrease spending. One can speak of the congressional budget process being out of control in the sense that Congress finds itself without the mechanisms to work its budgetary will through the appropriations process, regardless of whether that will is in the direction of decreased or increased federal expenditures. Used in this sense, the lack of congressional control was evidenced by the increasing percentage of expenditures that could not be altered without changing the basic authorizing statute, by the fact that less than half of the budget was subject to annual appropriations, and by the inability of Congress to meet its own budgetary deadlines.

Before the reform about 75 percent of the budget was considered "relatively uncontrollable under existing law,"[3] and because of back-door spending measures only about 44 percent of the budget in fiscal 1974 could be directly controlled by the appropriations committees on an annual basis. The rise in permanent budget authority (resulting in most part from the various forms of back-door spending) led to a diminished relationship between congressional budgetary decisions in any given year and the actual outlays of that year.

This inability to control large amounts of federal spending was exacerbated by the timing of budgetary decisions. Appropriations bills were rarely completed by the beginning of the fiscal year, causing many federal agencies to operate on continuing resolutions. Before the new process, not one appropriation bill since 1968 was enacted before the beginning of the fiscal year. Supporters of reform sought to impose deadline and jurisdictional limitations that would increase the power of the appropriations committees and at the same time force them to meet deadlines for reporting out bills.

Need to Control Priorities

Since World War II, Congress has usually been able to avoid making difficult priority choices concerning the federal budget. The rapid growth of the economy has allowed it to resolve conflicts between competing interests by giving most parties larger amounts, if not larger percentages, of the federal budget. This is not to say that the pre-reform congressional budgetary process was not able to change priorities. In fact, over the last 20 years the percentages of the budget allotted to defense and to aid to individuals have roughly reversed. However, the reduction in defense spending (as a percentage of the budget) was accomplished without reducing the amount of money being spent on national security.

As political and economic factors eliminated the "fiscal dividend" that had been promised for the 1970s, it became clear that hard either/or choices would have to be made, choices that could not be avoided by increasing the size of the pie. Those who recognized this prospect felt that congressional budgetary reform was needed in order to unify the disaggregated budgetary process and to create a mechanism for making the hard priority decisions.

Need to Control Fiscal Policy

Because the traditional budgetary process involved a series of isolated, unrelated decisions, Congress had no way to set fiscal policy — that is, the proper level of economic stimulus or restraint that should be exercised through the federal budget.

Some members, mostly conservatives, felt that if representatives and senators were forced to vote on the deficit or surplus, the tendency toward larger and larger deficits would be reversed. To this extent, they saw the vote not as a way to exercise fiscal policy, but as a means to limit spending. Other members, however, saw a need for a vote on the overall deficit or surplus so that Congress would have the capability to challenge the executive branch's dominance of the setting of fiscal policy.

Need to Reassert Institutional Authority

Information. Congress's lack of budgetary information was well known. Since the Office of Management and Budget — part of the executive office of the president — was the only federal budget body, Congress was frequently forced to rely on the president for the information needed to review and oversee the president's budget. Naturally, presidents of both political parties tended to forward information favorable to their policy choices and priorities.

It became an axiom among members that Congress would never be able to assert its proper budgetary role unless it could begin to right the imbalance of information and expertise that existed in favor of the executive branch. Many supporters of reform felt that the creation of new institutions that specialized in budgetary matters would bring this about.

Impoundment. Fresh from his landslide re-election in 1972, President Nixon decided to launch a public relations campaign to reduce the growth of federal spending and to assert his own budgetary priorities by branding Congress as "fiscally irresponsible." Only partially successful in reducing spending through his recommendations and the use of the veto, Nixon attempted to increase his power by expanding his use of impoundment — the refusal to spend funds provided by Congress.

Nixon's use of impoundment began early in his administration but intensified in November 1972 with the impoundment of $9 billion in clean-water funds and in December of that year with the termination of many agricultural programs. In January 1973 the fiscal 1974 budget was presented. It contained an eight-page table listing program reductions the president planned to make. Only 6 out of 109 items were listed as requiring congressional approval; other changes were to be made by presidential fiat. An examination one year later showed that the president had been able to achieve most of his stated reductions.[4]

This unprecedented use of impoundment was a constitutional as well as a political challenge to Congress. By challenging Congress's institutional integrity, Nixon created a coalition supporting budget reform made up of those who wanted to reassert legislative authority over budget making and those who simply opposed his economic policies. This coalition not only advocated budget reform to help check the power of the presidency and to help reassert Congress's constitutional power of the purse, but it also supported reform to refute Nixon's claim that Congress was fiscally irresponsible.

The stage for congressional budget reform was set when different groups in Congress realized changing the status quo was in their best interests. Along issue lines, conservatives sought a new institutional system that would force the membership to limit the growth of federal spending and balance the budget. Members of the appropriations committees sought a new system that would increase the percentage of the budget under their control. Members, in general, sought a new system that would reinstitute the power of the Congress over spending. Long-term academic advocates of congressional budget reform, through their allies on the Hill, sought a system that would give Congress a means to make priority decisions and set fiscal policy. Finally, Democrats, reacting to the Nixon administration's economic policies and the increasing use of impoundment to frustrate congressional will, supported the reform. It gave them a means to reassert their policies; furthermore, failure to do so would have been politically damaging. Given the conflicting expectations that led to passage of budget reform, one could expect the long-term acceptance of the new budget process to be very difficult.

CONGRESSIONAL RESPONSE: CHARACTERISTICS OF THE BUDGET AND IMPOUNDMENT CONTROL ACT

The congressional response to these internal and external pressures for reform was the Budget and Impoundment Control Act of 1974, signed into law on July 19, 1974. The reform movement started in earnest in 1972 with the creation of the Joint Study Committee on Budget, which was charged with examining the budgetary process for the purpose of improving decisionmaking procedures. The budget reform that emerged was an overlay to the old budgetary process; the existing structure of Congress was not altered. The reform created new House and Senate budget committees, the Congressional Budget Office (a full-time professional staff for analytical studies), a complex set of budgetary procedures, a timetable for budgetary actions, a change in the fiscal year, requirements for standardized budget terminology and information for the president's budget, and provisions for controlling presidential impoundments.

Committees

The House and Senate budget committees created under the act must report at least two concurrent resolutions on the budget each year, analyze the impact of existing and proposed programs on budgetary outlays, and oversee the operations of the Congressional Budget Office. The Senate Budget Committee consists of 20 members selected by the Democratic and Republican conferences. The 25 members of the House Budget Committee are drawn from the Appropriations Committee (5 members), Ways and Means Committee (5 members), the leadership (4 members), and from the Democrats (17) and Republicans (8) as a whole.

The staff of the House committee consists of approximately 62 professionals and 19 support personnel. Because of the rotating nature of committee membership, an early decision was made by the committee's first chairman, Al Ullman (D-Ore.), and its first staff director, Walter Kravitz, to hire a staff with a great deal of programmatic expertise. As a consequence, the initial staff of the House Budget Committee had relatively little Hill experience. In addition, the lack of subcommittee staff and the small size of the partisan core staff have meant that committee members have had to rely on the core staff for support.[5]

The Senate Budget Committee has a larger staff than its House counterpart, approximately 57 professionals and 34 support personnel. However, under the Senate arrangement, each member of the committee is allowed to hire two staff persons — one professional and one support. As compared to their counterparts on the HBC, the staff of the SBC has had less programmatic and budgetary but more political experience. They also tend to be younger. In this respect, they follow the traditional House/Senate staffing patterns.[6]

Analytic Support

In addition to the quality of their staffs, the performance of the budget committees will depend on their support from the third element of the new budgetary triad, the Congressional Budget Office (CBO). The CBO is the major analytical and informational component of the budget reform. Its first director, Dr. Alice M. Rivlin, was appointed to a four-year term by the Speaker of the House and the president pro tem of the Senate, upon the recommendations of the two budget committees. The CBO has been given broad, analytical responsibilities. These fall into three general categories: (1)

monitoring the economy and estimating its impact on the budget, (2) improving the flow and quality of budgetary information, and (3) analyzing the costs and effects of alternative budgetary choices.

New Process Timetable

The new congressional budgetary process sets October 1 as the beginning of the fiscal year. On November 10 the president must submit a current services budget, and on the fifteenth day after Congress meets he must submit his budget.[7] Congress must adopt at least two concurrent resolutions: one on or before May 15 (before revenue and expenditures bills have been passed) and the other by September 15 (after action has been taken on all appropriations bills), as Table 11-1 indicates.

It is possible to break this timetable down into four general stages: (1) information gathering, analysis, preparation, and submission of congressional budget by Congressional Budget Office and budget committees (November 10 to April 15); (2) debate on and adoption of congressional budget by both houses and establishment of national spending priorities (April 15 to May 15); (3) enactment of spending bills (May 15 to early September); (4) reassessment of spending, revenue, and debt requirements in second budget resolution; enactment of reconciliation bill (September 15 to September 25).

Table 11-1 Congressional Budget Timetable

Deadline	Action to Be Completed
November 10	Current services budget received
January 18*	President's budget received
March 15	Advice and data from all congressional committees to budget committees
April 1	CBO reports to budget committees
April 15	Budget committees report out first budget resolution
May 15	Congressional committees report new authorizing legislation
May 15	Congress completes action on first budget resolution
Labor Day +7**	Congress completes action on all spending bills
September 15	Congress completes action on second budget resolution
September 25	Congress completes action on reconciliation bill
October 1	Fiscal year begins

* Or fifteen days after Congress convenes.
** Seven days after Labor Day.

SOURCE: U.S., Congress, Senate, Committee on the Budget, *Congressional Budget Reform*, 93rd Cong., 2nd sess., March 4, 1975, p. 70.

HOUSE AND SENATE DIFFERENCES

By 1980, the "new" procedures and institutions under the Congressional Budget and Impoundment Act had been in place for six budget cycles. House-Senate differences during this period have been examined by several scholars.[8] These studies generally concur that the budget process in the House has been characterized by a high degree of partisanship and a relatively "weak" budget committee. The opposite appears to be true in the Senate, with a high degree of bipartisanship existing within a potentially strong Senate Budget Committee. There is much less agreement, however, as to whether (and how) these differences affect the substance of budgeting in the Senate and the House.

Committees

The House and Senate budget committees have many similarities and some significant differences. The Senate Budget Committee, unlike its House counterpart, has joint jurisdiction over the waivers of and bills to amend the congressional budget act. It also has been granted joint jurisdiction with the Senate Appropriations Committee and relevant authorizing committees over deferrals and rescissions. The most important differences between the committees, however, are in terms of the nature and tenure of their membership. The 20 members of the Senate Budget Committee (up from an original 16) are not restricted in any way, and tenure on the committee is not limited. Because of the difficulty in attracting new members to the committee, however, the Senate rule that a member can serve on only two major committees continues to be waived.

Most existing studies of the process point to the lack of comparative advantage of budget committee service in either House. Neither committee has developed to the point where service on it dramatically increases a member's influence (the chairmen excepted) in the Congress. Unlike Appropriations, Ways and Means, or Finance membership, service on the budget committees does not provide an opportunity to service constituency groups or program clientele. At this point the budget committees remain gatekeepers with little power. Finally, neither budget committee has standing subcommittees. Although the core staff of both committees is very large, the average committee member is provided with only one professional staff assistant. Thus to choose a budget committee assignment over another committee will result in the loss of potential staff.

Partisanship

The scholarly work in print is based on data from the first three years of the new budget process. Studies of the process found

House activity dominated by extreme partisanship and Senate actions characterized by unusual bipartisanship.[9] These patterns have continued over the first five years of implementation.

Voting on budget resolutions in the House Budget Committee and on the floor of the House has been characterized by extreme cohesion among Republicans. This can be seen by examining Rice Cohesion Indexes of votes on budget resolutions in Table 11-3.[10] Table 11-2 contains average party cohesion scores for those roll call votes in the Senate and House budget committees in which the parties were in opposition. Table 11-3 provides the same data for roll call votes on the floor of the House and Senate.

The first pattern that emerges is one of continued high cohesion in Republican voting in the House Budget Committee and low party cohesion for Senate Republicans both on the committee and on the floor. Lance LeLoup's finding that all major votes in the HBC were partisan (a majority of Democrats on the opposite side of issues from a majority of the Republicans) is confirmed over the entire five-year period.

In the Senate Budget Committee, with the exception of Republican roll call votes during the first year of the process, the cohesion of both parties follows the traditional moderate partisanship pattern. On votes to report out budget resolutions, the SBC Republican voting pattern has been more bipartisan than the scores in Table 11-2 would indicate, with at least two-thirds supporting the resolution. In the House Budget Committee, on the other hand, with the exception of a single case where two Republicans voted to report out the first First Concurrent Resolution on the Budget so that the process would not fail its first test, not a single Republican has voted in favor of reporting out a budget resolution.

Table 11-2 Party Cohesion Scores for House and Senate Budget Committee Roll Calls in which Parties Were in Opposition

| | 94th Congress | | 95th Congress | | 96th Congress |
	1st sess. FY 1976	2nd sess. FY 1977	1st sess. FY 1978	2nd sess. FY 1979	1st sess. FY 1980
House Budget					
Committee	(N=6)	(N=12)	(N=33)	(N=33)	(N=41)
Democrats	46.2	60.4	60.2	63.6	49.0
Republicans	91.6	100.0	79.6	84.4	93.8
Senate Budget					
Committee	(N=23)	(N=27)	(N=30)	(N=38)	(N=80)
Democrats	45.4	39.6	55.6	44.4	50.2
Republicans	75.8	52.8	44.0	43.0	57.8

Table 11-3   Party Cohesion Scores for Floor Roll Calls on Budget Resolutions in which Parties Were in Opposition

	94th Congress		95th Congress		96th Congress
	1st sess. FY 1976	2nd sess. FY 1977	1st sess. FY 1978	2nd sess. FY 1979	1st sess. FY 1980
All Roll Calls					
House	(N=9)	(N=9)	N=20)	(N=18)	(N=32)
Democrats	52.3	54.1	45.3	39.8	48.7
Republicans	81.4	73.3	75.5	73.6	66.4
Senate	(N=4)	(N=4)	(N=10)	(N=11)	(N=21)
Democrats	77.3	57.4	59.5	57.9	56.5
Republicans	13.9	14.1	17.8	16.5	34.4
Roll Calls Directed at a					
Single Program or Function					
House	(N=0)	(N=4)	(N=11)	(N=7)	(N=16)
Democrats	—	43.5	32.7	21.3	43.8
Republicans	—	69.4	67.6	54.2	54.0
Senate	(N=0)	(N=1)	(N=4)	(N=5)	(N=7)
Democrats	—	5.8	57.8	49.7	50.6
Republicans	—	29.4	17.1	11.4	23.5
Roll Calls Directed at					
Allocation or Stabilization Policy					
House	(N=9)	(N=5)	(N=9)	(N=11)	(N=16)
Democrats	52.3	68.6	64.2	51.7	53.6
Republicans	81.4	77.1	87.4	85.9	78.9
Senate	(N=4)	(N=3)	(N=6)	(N=6)	(N=14)
Democrats	77.3	74.5	60.7	64.8	59.4
Republicans	13.9	8.9	18.2	20.7	39.8

Initially, it might appear from the average cohesion scales in Table 11-3 that Republican cohesion on floor votes on budget resolutions in the House is slowly declining. What actually appears to be occurring, however, is an increasing number of symbolic roll call votes on the floor of the House to add or reduce budget authority and/or outlays for a single program. These roll calls are separated from those that are associated with potential changes in fiscal policy or reallocation of budget priorities. Republican cohesion on roll calls associated with proposals aimed at line-item changes is less than the 67.2 average Republican score that Julius Turner and Edward Schneier found in 14 selected congressional sessions from 1921 through 1967.[11] The average Republican cohesion scores for roll calls on proposals to modify the fiscal policy or interbudget function priorities of budget resolutions, on the other hand, remain high during the five-year period.

Table 11-4 Comparisons of Budget Committee Members with All Members of the House and Senate by Party, Using Selected Interest Groups and Congressional Quarterly Voting Studies

	94th Congress 2nd sess. FY 1977	95th Congress 1st sess. FY 1978	95th Congress 2nd sess. FY 1979	96th Congress 1st sess. FY 1980
Democrats				
Senate				
ADA	− 8.1	7.5	4.4	− 3.7
COPE	3.5	1.2	2.7	− 2.0
Conservative				
Coalition	2.6	5.1	4.3	− 0.3
Party Unity	7.3	7.6	3.5	− 4.5
Presidential Support	0.6	2.6	− 0.8	− 3.3
House				
ADA	− 3.6	− 5.5	14.9	13.7
COPE	− 5.6	− 4.1	2.2	8.9
Conservative				
Coalition	− 4.4	− 1.5	12.0	9.7
Party Unity	− 2.4	− 1.5	8.9	8.7
Presidential Support	− 5.1	− 4.2	6.8	9.6
Republicans				
Senate				
ADA	19.0	18.5	10.1	3.4
COPE	14.0	11.8	8.5	5.2
Conservative				
Coalition	17.7	7.4	7.7	3.2
Party Unity	8.0	4.9	6.2	0.4
Presidential Support	12.5	7.0	8.6	0.3
House				
ADA	14.5	8.2	9.2	5.3
COPE	14.7	11.9	7.8	6.2
Conservative				
Coalition	21.9	21.3	11.6	13.2
Party Unity	21.5	23.0	9.3	11.6
Presidential Support	13.0	23.9	2.9	2.2

NOTE: The numbers represent the difference between a given budget committee group and their representative party members in the House or Senate. Positive scores for Republicans indicate that Republican budget committee members are more conservative or partisan than all Republicans. Positive scores for Democrats indicate that Democratic budget committee members are more conservative or partisan than all Democrats.

Membership

During the first four years of the new process, the leadership of each party in each House recruited members for the budget committees. This was necessary in the Senate because of the few rewards of such membership. In the House, recruitment was also carried out to make sure that the Democrats and Republicans on the House Budget Committee accurately reflected their party's views.

Table 11-4 sets out the differences in average scores of two interest groups, Americans for Democratic Action (ADA) and the AFL-CIO Committee on Political Education (COPE), and three Congressional Quarterly voting studies between budget committee members and their political party compatriots in the House and Senate. Republicans on both the House and Senate budget committees appear to be more conservative and more partisan than other party members within their House. While it is dangerous to use these types of indexes to compare members of the House and the Senate, a consistent pattern does emerge of greater partisanship in the House — generally and among House Republicans. Thus, although Senate Budget Committee Republicans appear from the data in Table 11-4 to be more conservative and partisan than all Senate Republicans, they are probably less conservative and partisan than House Budget Committee Republicans.

Senate Budget Committee Democrats appear to be a fair sample of all Senate Democrats during the first four years of the process. The mix of House Budget Committee Democrats, on the other hand, significantly changed at the beginning of the 95th Congress. As indicated in Table 11-4, during the 94th Congress HBC Democrats were, as a group, slightly less liberal and partisan than all House Democrats. LeLoup and Allen Schick report that when it became obvious to the Democratic leadership that all Republicans on the HBC would oppose any budget resolution that contained a significant deficit (and the deficits during these years were very large due to the effects of the 1974-75 recession), conservative Democrats on the committee were replaced by liberal loyalists.[12] At the beginning of the 95th Congress, eight Democrats with average ADA and ACA (Americans for Constitutional Action) scores for the 94th Congress of 45.0 and 32.4 were replaced by eight others with scores of 83.5 and 9.[13] The shift this caused in the Democratic majority of the House Budget Committee is readily apparent in Table 11-4.

Relationships to Other Congressional Actors

The Senate Budget Committee has sought to increase its influence over policy by becoming a powerful committee vis-à-vis other Senate committees. To accomplish this end it has liberally interpreted its mandate in the budget act and engaged in confrontations on the floor of the Senate. Former Chairman Edmund S. Muskie (D-Maine) and ranking minority member Henry Bellmon (R-Okla.) followed an aggressive strategy of opposing legislation on the floor of the Senate that they felt was not included within the targets, ceilings, or floors of the budget resolutions. This strategy is likely to change dramatically under the new chairman, Pete V. Domenici (R-N.M.), who has strong conservative policy preferences.

All chairmen of the House Budget Committee, on the other hand, have avoided floor confrontations. They have sought to meet with committee chairmen informally when they and the House Budget Committee felt that a particular piece of legislation was not included in a resolution. This cautious strategy is a reflection of the desire on the part of House Budget Committee members to avoid dictating to other House committees. Most often this caution is expressed in a desire not to "break faith" with the other committees — particularly the authorizing committees — of the House. When in early 1980 the HBC deviated from the conciliatory strategy and attempted to "balance" the Fiscal Year 1981 budget against the will of committee chairmen, it was opposed by a majority of them on the floor.

These two approaches caused a several month delay in the final passage of the Second Concurrent Resolution for Fiscal Year 1980. For the first time the Senate Budget Committee succeeded in invoking the budget act's reconciliation provision. Under this provision the Congress can order one or more of its committees to report out legislation within a certain time limit that would have a specified dollar effect. First in the Democratic Caucus and then on the floor of the Senate, the Senate Budget Committee confronted seven Senate committees and won a commitment that they would report out legislation that, in total, would reduce anticipated budget authority and outlays by $3.6 billion.

The House Budget Committee rejected as too extreme the use of the reconciliation provision. The HBC's strategy was to negotiate promises from several authorizing committees of the House that they would try to report out "legislative savings" to save some $5 billion. The leaders of the HBC took the position that to go along with invoking reconciliation after the committee had reached agreements on legislative savings would be to "break faith" with the other committees of the House. This was the first important test of the reconciliation process in 1979. The budget committees in the past have always set their spending targets high enough to avoid the embarrassment of breaking the ultimate spending ceilings that were arrived at simply by adding the appropriations actions between May 15 and September 15. Former Chairman Muskie said of the 1979 reconciliation process, "all the committees resent the budget process and they might gang up. But if the committees adopt the attitude that this is trespassing on their areas, then they ought to repeal the budget process."[14]

The Decisionmaking Process in Committee

The two budget committees have followed very different decisionmaking processes in putting together their concurrent resolutions. First, it is important to remember that in an effort to avoid jurisdictional conflict between the budget and revenue and appropriations committees, the new budget process called for early flexible spending and revenue targets and final firm ceilings applied to 16 (now 19) functional categories of the budget. The appropriations committees would establish budget authority for approximately 1,100 appropriations accounts between May 15 (targets) and September 15 (ceilings) and the budget resolutions were to operate at a much higher level of aggregation.

However, in order to determine whether a given bill will exceed a target, it is necessary for the budget committees to have some idea of the specific makeup of what is included in each functional category. This creates a quandary: the budget committees must operate to avoid jurisdictional conflict with the appropriations committees and must operate at a high level of aggregation, but that high level of aggregation. During budget resolution bill markups, members of islation to determine whether the targets are about to be broken.

The House Budget Committee has chosen to put together budget resolutions at a very low level of aggregation, most often at the appropriations account level. On the other hand, the Senate Budget Committee, at least publicly, has operated at a much higher level of aggregation. During budget resolution bill markups, members of the Senate Budget Committee frequently suggest spending levels for an entire function, leaving the decision as to how much money each program within that function will receive up to the Appropriations Committee. This leads to the second major difference in the decisionmaking process of the two committees: the use of the "chairman's mark" by the House Budget Committee.

So far, HBC chairmen have presented a suggested budget resolution — called a chairman's mark — as a starting point for committee debate at each markup. The chairman's mark is very specific. It consists of the president's budget level for each function and any changes recommended by the chairman and/or the Democratic Caucus. Because these changes are mostly at the appropriations account level, it is possible to create an appropriations account level budget from the chairman's mark. Amendments to the chairman's mark within the House Budget Committee are also made at the appropriations account level. Thus, the budget resolutions that are reported out of the House Budget Committee can easily be broken down to a very low level of aggregation. Budget votes in the House almost always are close, with liberals disgruntled over military expenditures and conservatives concerned about spending for social programs. The

House chairman's mark is always a compromise between ideological camps. Chairman Ernest F. Hollings (D-S.C.), Muskie's successor in 1980, did not provide a chairman's mark for the Senate Budget Committee's deliberations. Rather, the budget was taken up subfunction by subfunction (referred to as "Missions"). Senators moved to adopt a given spending level for entire subfunctions.

Third, the decisionmaking processes of the two committees differ in that the House Budget Committee continues to use the president's budget as the baseline from which alternatives are measured, whereas the Senate Budget Committee uses as its baseline either the current law budget (what this year's budget would be like next year if there were no policy changes and only those programs that were indexed by law were inflated) or the current policy budget (what this year's budget would be like next year if there were no policy changes and all programs were inflated, unless such action was specifically prohibited by law).

Fourth, the Senate Budget Committee markups and the Senate votes on budget resolutions contain targets for four years beyond the upcoming fiscal year. Such multiyear targeting has been rejected so far by the House Budget Committee as being politically unacceptable. The SBC, on the other hand, sees multiyear targeting as a way to influence the authorizing committees of the Senate.

WHY THE PROCESS DIFFERS

Over the past several years three hypotheses have been put forward to explain why the budget process differs in the House and Senate. For simplicity's sake they can be labeled the personality hypothesis, the political hypothesis, and the institutional hypothesis.

Personality Hypothesis

Many actors in the congressional budget process see the political backgrounds and personalities of the chairmen and ranking minority members of the two budget committees as the major factors contributing to the differences we have described. Both Edmund Muskie and Henry Bellmon were the first candidates of their political parties to win the governorships of Maine and Oklahoma in this century. In addition, both Muskie and Bellmon, as governor, had to work with a legislature dominated by the opposition party. Proponents of the personality hypothesis therefore conclude that Muskie and Bellmon made an ideal team for bipartisan cooperation. Thus, when Muskie left the committee in early 1980 and Bellmon retired at the end of the 96th Congress, changes in this bipartisan cooperation were expected.

This hypothesis also points to the partisan background of Representative Delbert Latta (R-Ohio), the ranking minority member of the House Budget Committee, as a major factor behind the heightened partisanship that characterizes the process in the House. Latta is much more conservative than previous ranking minority members. He was rated by the ACA at 100 percent in 1976, 88.1 percent in 1977, 89 percent in 1978, and 92 percent in 1979.

Political Hypothesis

The second hypothesis points to the makeup of the budget committees as the main force behind the differences. According to this view, Muskie when he was chairman had no choice but to develop a bipartisan relationship with ranking minority member Bellmon after it quickly became evident that the liberal Democrats did not have enough votes to control the Senate Budget Committee. In the case of the House, the political hypothesis would hold that as soon as it became evident that the Republicans viewed votes on the size of the deficit and the allocation of budgetary resources as major symbolic issues that could divide the parties, the Democrats did the logical thing: they modified the membership of the House Budget Committee to guarantee a working majority.

It follows from these first two hypotheses that the extreme partisanship of the budget process in the House and the unusual bipartisanship of the process in the Senate are both unstable. Schick, for example, expects budgeting in the Senate to become more partisan and budgeting in the House to become less partisan with membership turnover.[15]

Institutional Hypothesis

Finally, major differences in the new budget processes of the House and Senate could result from the relative differences in power, within their respective bodies, of the House and Senate budget committees. The power of the two committees differ in quantity and kind because of the restrictions on membership and tenure that apply to the House but not to the Senate Budget Committee.

The stature of members within Congress is largely determined by the power they gain through their committee assignments. Because of the tenure limitation, it is impossible for representatives to build a career around service on the House Budget Committee. Since representatives have only one major committee assignment, members of House Budget, when faced with a conflict, will give their time, effort, and loyalty to the duties and viewpoints associated with their major committee assignment. Thus, when there is a clash between the interests of the House Budget Committee and those of their main committee, HBC members will side with the position of their major committee.

In contrast to this pattern, senators on the Senate Budget Committee can identify their membership on that committee with their power and stature in the Senate. As the Senate Budget Committee becomes more powerful, they become more powerful. A similar alternative is not open to members of the House committee. This career opportunity also means that SBC members realize that their power in the Senate will be associated with the rise in stature and power of the committee. Therefore, it is in the interest of SBC members to see to it that the budget resolutions reported out by the committee are successfully defended from amendment and passed on the Senate floor. This motivation of self-interest goes a long way toward explaining the bipartisan nature of Senate Budget Committee proceedings.

For example, during the markup of the fiscal year 1976 First Concurrent Resolution, Chairman Muskie and other liberal Democrats on the committee ended up on the losing side in 14 out of 27 votes. In these votes Muskie and other liberals tried unsuccessfully to reduce expenditures for defense and to increase expenditures for stimulative programs to fight the ongoing recession. But having lost their fight in committee, all these liberals supported the resolution on the floor of the Senate. Moreover, Chairman Muskie opposed amendments on the Senate floor that would have had the same effect as those that he proposed, and which were defeated, in committee.

The same pattern emerged among the SBC Republicans. In the 1976 debate over whether to recommit the military construction authorization bill to conference, the Senate Budget Committee's position was supported by Senator Bellmon and three of the other five Republicans on the committee. In the past, these senators had established strong pro-military positions, but in this case they supported their committee and voted against higher defense authorizations.

This self-interest motivation does not exist for the members of the House Budget Committee. Republicans, not having the votes to determine the nature of the resolution in committee, have no stake in supporting the resolution when it comes to the floor. Thus House Budget Committee membership has no effect on the roll call behavior of its members.

All of the above leads to the hypothesis that the House Budget Committee, compared with its Senate counterpart, is in a relatively weak position within its House. This weakness has had a major impact on the degrees of partisanship, decisionmaking styles, and strategies followed by the chairmen and members of the two committees.

The major strength of the institutional hypothesis is that, of the three explanations, it alone can explain the House-Senate differences in decisionmaking processes, styles, and strategies as well as the differences in the degree of partisanship.

CONGRESSIONAL CONTROL OF IMPOUNDMENTS

A major last minute addition to the budget reform act was Title X, which provides procedures for controlling presidential impoundments and thus gives Congress significantly more power over the president in the budget process. It confronts the problem of presidential impoundment directly. The authors of the budget reform felt it was necessary to control the president's power to impound funds if they were to have a rational budget process. Enacting the budget reform without limiting presidential impoundments would have been futile. This fear was expressed by Representative Richard Bolling (D-Mo.), a member of the committee that drafted the act:

> It makes no sense for Congress to establish new procedures for the appropriation of funds if the President can override the will of Congress by means of impoundment. At the same time, the methods used to control presidential impoundments must be reasonable and appropriate. They should neither deny the President the capability to manage the Executive branch nor impose upon Congress the burden of redoing its previous decision.[16]

One of the prime motivations behind the addition of the impoundment control provisions in the budget reform act was President Nixon's confrontational budgetary politics and his perceived abuse of presidential power. Nixon most often chose to confront Congress rather than take the path of accommodation. As his troubles grew over the Vietnam War and Watergate, Nixon publicly castigated Congress as "big spenders" and "fiscally irresponsible" in an unprecedented political challenge to Congress. As a symbolic expression of an attempt to control Congress, Nixon impounded in January 1974 almost $9 billion of water treatment plant construction funds, a popular "pork barrel" and environmental improvement program. He seldom consulted congressional leaders with respect to his impoundments, unlike previous presidents who sought accommodation. Presidential impoundments have existed since President Thomas Jefferson, but until the Nixon presidency, a minority president had not challenged a majority Congress in quite such a public and embarrassing way. Nixon made a public symbolic claim of constitutional power to impound funds.

To check future presidential actions of this kind, Congress gave itself the authority under the provisions of Title X to review and control presidential impoundments in two ways: if the president wants to withhold funds for 12 months or less, he must inform Congress; if he wants to do away with funding for a program completely, he must receive permission from Congress.

The impoundment control provision in the budget act originated as a House-Senate compromise from previously proposed anti-impoundment legislation. Impoundments were defined either as *rescissions* (to cancel budget authority completely) or *deferrals* (to delay budget authority up to 12 months). Funds may be rescinded when the president decides the budget authority is not required to fulfill the objectives of a program, when he wants to terminate a program, or when the appropriated money for a program is not to be obligated. The president must send a rescission message to Congress and both houses must approve it by majority vote within 45 days of continuous session, or the proposed canceled funds must be spent. The president must also notify Congress of any delay in obligating budget authority, a deferral. Either house may overturn the deferral message by passing an "impoundment resolution" by simple majority in one body at any time. There is no time limit on overturning deferrals as there is with the passage of rescissions. Obviously, passing rescissions is much more difficult for the president than retaining deferrals. The president must persuade Congress to act on rescissions, which is always more problematic than using delaying tactics to retain deferrals. Having to define two types of impoundments protects congressional power over the integrity of the budget and gives the executive branch some administrative discretion.

The ease with which deferrals are sustained and the difficulty with which rescissions are approved is reflected in Table 11-5, which shows the approval rate for both types of impoundments from fiscal year 1976, the first year of implementation, through fiscal year 1980. Success of presidential deferrals has been consistently high: 96 percent in 1976 and 98 percent in the transition quarter, 99 percent in 1977, 99 percent in 1978, 63 percent in 1979, and 86 percent in 1980. Congress must sustain a deferral of funds, and it is difficult to get members to take action unless there is a crisis or strong, widespread pressure to do so. This is unlikely to occur with respect to deferrals. They are sustained unless Congress acts.

Rescissions are much more difficult to approve. They are proposals to terminate a program, not just delay the expenditure of funds for a short period of time. It takes pressure from the president to move rescissions; a majority in the House and Senate must act affirmatively on the rescission message within 45 days, or the funds must be released. The lack of success in approving presidential rescission impoundments again reveals how difficult it is for Congress to take an affirmative action, but in this case the initiative must come from the executive rather than the Congress. The approval rate for rescissions has generally been very low: 4 percent in 1976, no approvals in the transition quarter, 37 percent in 1977, 46 percent in 1978, 80 percent in 1979, and no approvals in 1980. The 1979

Table 11-5 Congressional Approval of Rescissions and Deferrals (In Millions of Dollars)

	FY 1976	Transition Quarter	FY 1977	FY 1978	FY 1979	FY 1980
Rescissions						
Proposed	$3,328.7	$253.3	$1,926.9	$1,290.1	$ 908.7	$ 1,618.1
Approved	138.3 (4%)	0.0 (0%)	711.6 (37%)	593.7 (46%)	723.6 (80%)	0.0 (0%)
Deferrals						
Reported	8,775.3	338.6	7,484.4	4,966.8	4,685.3	10,523.6
Sustained	8,396.9 (96%)	333.9 (98%)	7,458.8 (99%)	4,910.3 (99%)	2,946.0 (63%)	9,003.6 (86%)

SOURCE: Office of Management and Budget, "Cumulative Reports on Rescissions and Deferrals" (1976, Transition Quarter, 1977, 1978, 1980), unpublished memoranda.

high success rate of 80 percent probably reflected the "balance the budget" mood of Congress, but it was not extended to 1980.

Title X of the Budget and Impoundment Control Act of 1974 must be deemed one of the most successful components of the entire budget act. The president can no longer revoke spending authority permanently without a majority vote in both the House and Senate in his favor. By a simple majority vote, either chamber can force the president to spend funds immediately that he has withheld temporarily. This has given Congress new power in the budgetary process. However, viewed from the presidential perspective, Title X is potentially an item veto for the president. It has not been used in that manner (to the disappointment of many in the executive branch), probably because many realize that an item veto would be unconstitutional. According to Jerome Miles, a department budget official, many in the executive branch thought that, ". . . by isolating individual items — items which have little merit on their own — a large number of marginal programs and projects could be eliminated from the budget. This has not happened and probably will not."[17]

In conclusion, Congress has taken a major step toward protecting its institutional prerogative against perceived presidential abuses of the budgetary process through the impoundment control provisions of the budget reform. The new impoundment control process has worked smoothly and has had a significant impact on the pre-1974 trend toward centralization of budget power in the presidency.

THE FUTURE OF THE CONGRESSIONAL BUDGET PROCESS

Although many of the early supporters of the new congressional budget process expected it to end federal deficits and slow federal expenditure growth, its main accomplishments have been normative and procedural rather than substantive. Procedural reforms — such as the new budget process — can lead to changes in policy output by increasing the level and quality of budgetary information available to decisionmakers and voters, by requiring decisionmakers to make explicit choices on all major budgetary questions, by re-allocating power among decisionmakers, or by limiting the discretion of decisionmakers on budgetary questions.

The first alternative has been the underlying principle of the major U.S. budgetary reforms in this century. In 1912, arguing for the reforms that were eventually enacted as the Budget and Accounting Act of 1921, President William Howard Taft stated, "The constitutional purpose of a budget is to make government responsive to public opinion and responsible for its acts."[18] For budgets to provide voters with the necessary information so that they can judge their government's actions, they must satisfy "such fundamental standards as visibility, clarity, explicitness, and comprehensiveness."[19] The new congressional budget process provides this information by requiring that elected officials record their positions on the major questions answered in every federal budget.

Some proponents of the 1974 reform believed that requiring legislators to look at the budget as a whole would change attitudes toward public spending. This does not appear to have occurred in the aggregate. There is some evidence, however, of a dramatic dropoff in the creation of new entitlements since the implementation of the act. The potential impact of information is most evident when it is lacking. During the 1970s, real growth in transfer payments to individuals was balanced to some extent by a relative decline in defense expenditures. Given the current climate of uncertainty over Soviet intentions, information on "how much is enough" for defense is lacking. In such an atmosphere, it is not surprising that substantial increases in defense outlays are being seriously considered.

The budget act is silent about redistributing power within the Congress. Clearly, many of the congressional actors who supported the passage of the act did so under the assumption that it would increase or maintain the relative power of their committee(s). Given that spending norms vary by committee, one way to control expenditure growth is to increase the power of those committees that are dominated by conservatives. For years, the appropriations committees saw themselves as the guardians of the public purse. Over the last decade and a half, they have slowly abandoned this role. Allen Schick points out, in fact, that the requirement that all committees of each house report their budgetary needs to their respective budget committee by March 15 of each year has turned the traditional guardians into claimants.

The aggressive strategy of the Senate Budget Committee could eventually make it the new guardian of the national purse. But for it to achieve this role, it will have to win power from existing committees. A theoretical case can be made that in the short run the bargaining approach of the House Budget Committee will be just as effective as the series of institutional conflicts engaged in by the Senate Budget Committee. Such an hypothesis would follow from the assumption that congressional decisionmakers are more flexible prior to the point at which they have to take a public stand. The House Budget Committee's strategy of exploiting the bargaining patterns of the Congress thus turns many potential conflicts into nondecisions.

Yet there are real limitations to this House strategy. From the beginning of the current wave of budget reform, House leaders have been anxious to limit the power of the House Budget Committee. They feared the creation of a super committee. But, by making the HBC so weak, they limited its potential for becoming the new guardian. Having done so, they are now turning to more complicated formulations in the form of expenditure limitations, as the new guardian. It is significant that while none of the Democratic members of the Senate Budget Committee are actually supporting the current movement to limit legislators' discretion over expenditures, the two major bills before the House are authored by the House Budget Committee's chairman and one of its most powerful Democratic members. Moreover, in the discussion of what to do about limiting expenditure growth, no one has proposed strengthening the budget committees, especially the House Budget Committee.

The major impact of budget reform on public policy is yet to be determined and difficult to calculate considering the complexity of many "environmental" factors, although fears that the reform would primarily help conservatives in opposing spending for social programs while giving military spending the upper hand appear not to be realized. Nor is there evidence of a major change in priorities toward more social spending in the budget as a result of the new process. However, some observers believe the reform has forced some prioritization of major new program initiatives — that is, consideration of trade-offs between programs of marginal value and new program initiatives. Others argue it has made Congress too cost conscious, thus killing new programs such as national health insurance.

The reform has given committees and members better tools for evaluating new programmatic demands and economic trends. It has given Congress more control over presidential impoundments. The new process highlights macroeconomic and macrobudgetary trade-offs. The issues are more visible, so they can be more readily contested by individuals and groups. However, it is unlikely the process itself will be the initiator of programmatic changes; it is more likely that initiatives will continue to come from members of Congress, committees, party leaders, executive branch agencies, the president, interest groups, and the public. The congressional budget process is working and here to stay.

NOTES

1. This phrase is attributable to Allen Schick of the Congressional Research Service. See Allen Schick, *Congress and Money: Budgeting, Spending, and Taxing* (Washington, D.C.: The Urban Institute, 1980). See also Joel Havemann, *Congress and the Budget* (Bloomington: Indiana University Press, 1978). For an excellent discussion of the traditional budgetary procedures in the House, see Richard F. Fenno, Jr., *The Power of the Purse* (Boston: Little, Brown & Co., 1966). See also Aaron Wildavsky, *The Politics of the Budgetary Process,* 2nd ed. (Boston: Little, Brown & Co., 1974).

2. U.S., Congress, Senate, Committee on the Budget, *Congressional Budget Reform*, 93rd Cong., 2nd sess., March 4, 1975, p. 3.

3. For a discussion of controllables, see *The Budget of the United States Government, Fiscal Year 1977* (Washington, D.C.: U.S. Government Printing Office, 1977), pp. 6-10.

4. See Dennis M. Sherman, "Impoundment Reporting by the Office of Management and Budget: A Preliminary Analysis," *Congressional Research Service*, January 7, 1974, printed in *Congressional Record* (daily edition), January 29, 1974, p. S66.

5. Interview with Walter Kravitz, Congressional Reseach Service, November 28, 1975.

6. See Harrison W. Fox and Susan Hammond, "The Growth of Congressional Staffs," in *Congress against the President*, ed. Harvey C. Mansfield, Sr. (New York: Praeger Publishers, 1975), pp. 112-124.

7. Section 605(a) of the Congressional Budget and Impoundment Control Act of 1974 defines the current services budget as "the estimated outlays and proposed budget authority which would be included in the Budget . . . for the ensuing fiscal year if all programs and activities were carried on during such ensuing fiscal year at the same level as the fiscal year in progress and without policy changes in such programs and activities."

8. See John W. Ellwood and James A. Thurber, "The New Congressional Budget Process: The Hows and Whys of House-Senate Differences," in *Congress Reconsidered*, 1st ed., edited by Lawrence C. Dodd and Bruce I. Oppenheimer (New York: Praeger Publishers, 1977), pp. 163-192; Ellwood and Thurber, "The New Congressional Budget Process: Its Causes, Consequences, and Possible Success," in *The Impact of Legislative Reform*, ed. Susan Welch and John Peters (New York: Praeger Publishers, 1979); Havemann, *Congress and the Budget;* Lance T. LeLoup, "Process vs. Policy: The U.S. House Budget Committee," *Legislative Studies Quarterly*, 4 (May 1979): 227-254; and Schick, *Congress and Money.*

9. For a fuller discussion on this point, see John W. Ellwood and James A. Thurber, "The New Congressional Budget Process: Its Causes, Consequences, and Possible Success" (Paper delivered at the Symposium on Legislative Reform and Public Policy, University of Nebraska, Lincoln, March 11-12, 1976).

10. The Rice Index of Cohesion is used. See Lee F. Anderson, Meredith W. Watts, Jr., and Allen R. Wilcox, *Legislative Roll-Call Analysis* (Evanston, Ill.: Northwestern University Press, 1966), pp. 32-33. According to Anderson, Watts, and Wilcox: "For the purposes of the index, Rice defined cohesion as the extent to which the distribution of votes on a legislative roll call deviates from the distribution that would be expected if all influences operated in a random fashion. The argument states that, if one hundred votes were cast in a purely random manner, they would distribute themselves equally on both sides of the issue, i.e., 50 'yeas' to 50 'nays.' This instance is defined as the case of minimum cohesion and is assigned the index value of 0. The opposite extreme occurs when all members vote on the same side of an issue — that is considered complete cohesion and is assigned the index value of 100. The index is thus established as having a range from 0 to 100. Intermediate values in this range are determined by the degree to which the percentage 'yea' vote deviates from 50.0 in either direction, toward 0.0 or toward 100.0. For example, when 75 percent vote 'yea' on an issue, there is a 25/50 or 50 percent departure from 0 cohesion toward complete cohesion, the index is 50.0."

11. Julius Turner, *Party and Constituency: Pressures on Congress,* rev. ed., edited by Edward V. Schneier (Baltimore: Johns Hopkins University Press, 1970), p. 20.
12. See Lance T. LeLoup, "Budgeting in the Senate" (Paper delivered at the annual meeting of the Midwest Political Science Association, Chicago, Illinois, April 20, 1979); Schick, *Congress and Money.*
13. See LeLoup, "Process vs. Policy."
14. *Washington Post,* August 27, 1979, p. A-7.
15. See Schick, *Congress and Money.*
16. U.S., Congress, House, *Congressional Record,* June 18, 1974, p. H5182.
17. Jerome A. Miles, "The Congressional Budget and Impoundment Control Act: A Departmental Budget Officer's View," *Bureaucrat,* 5 (January 1977): 391-404.
18. William Howard Taft, *The President and His Powers* (New York: Columbia University Press, 1967), p. 137.
19. Ibid.

III

Congress, the Executive
and
Public Policy

12

Congress and the New Obstructionism: Developing an Energy Program

Bruce I. Oppenheimer

Since the Arab oil embargo of November 1973, it has been common to read about the failure of Congress to develop national energy policy or to hear criticisms of its inability to expedite a variety of legislative proposals. These comments have been offered by noted newspaper columnists, by three presidents of the United States, and by members of the House and Senate themselves. Although the purposes of those critics may have varied, few could claim that there was not a substantial grain of truth in their analyses. Others, however, argue that we really should not expect more from Congress. Congress's efforts to grapple with energy policy were doomed because of "endemic weaknesses" of the institution, they claim. James. L. Sundquist has summarized the institutional problems of Congress under four concepts: parochialism, irresponsibility, sluggishness, and amateurism.[1] Again there is certainly some merit in his conclusion:

> Congress remains organized to deal with narrow problems but not with broad ones. . . . It can, for instance, devise policies affecting energy but not a national energy policy.[2]

Ironically, however, by the time the 1980 election arrived, Congress had indeed enacted what could fairly be described as a national energy policy. It had not been an easy task, but the major issues that required resolution for an integrated national energy policy had been addressed. These included decisions on the pricing of oil, the pricing of natural gas, a tax on windfall profits, automobile mileage standards, and commitment of government resources to the development of alternative energy sources (particularly synthetic fuels), as well as a variety of related issues. Certainly some energy issues lingered, and new ones would arise. But most of the key issues that had been on the agenda since shortly after the embargo had been resolved.[3]

In order to develop a better understanding of congressional efforts to enact energy policy in particular and public policy in general, three central questions will be addressed in this essay. First, why did it take six to seven years before most of the key energy issues were finally resolved? Second, how was Congress able to resolve these issues at all? And third, what were the costs involved in Congress's failure to reach some consensus on the issues more quickly?

I contend that the reasons for congressional slowness on energy policy stem largely from the unanticipated consequences of internal congressional reforms of the 1970s rather than from the innate sluggishness of legislative institutions in the twentieth century. In fact, several facets of energy policy and changes in the decisionmaking structure of Congress lead one to expect it to respond more quickly than it did. As we shall see, much of the delay in the passage of energy policy by the Congress resulted from new sources of obstructionism within the House and Senate. These forces made the mobilization of majorities to enact legislative policy more difficult than ever before. As a result of these reforms, it became easier for a small number of House or Senate members — at times even a single member — to prevent the respective bodies from having the opportunity to make decisions on energy issues, to choose among alternatives. Moreover, this "new obstructionism," unlike the obstructionism of conservative committee chairs in the 1950s and 1960s, was a tool available to a large number of members.

Given the new obstructionism, what Congress has accomplished in the resolution of energy issues is rather remarkable. Why, by 1980, did the United States have something that fairly could be described as a national energy policy? How was the new obstructionism overcome? What types of resources were used, and why were significant successes achieved?

In the last section of this essay, the question of costs will be addressed from two particular perspectives. What were the policy costs of delay, and what were the spill-over costs from the excessive use of leadership resources to resolve the key energy issues? Of necessity, the evaluation of these costs will be somewhat speculative. Nevertheless, it is an important task. Unless some attempt is made to estimate these costs, an evaluation of Congress's effectiveness in enacting energy policy or public policy generally cannot be achieved.

WHY SO SLOW?

Aside from the innate slowness of the congressional process, other reasons are often offered to explain Congress's failure to enact energy policy more quickly in the 1970s. A common reason given is that there was a lack of consensus about what that policy should be and that Congress remained closely divided on the key questions. Clearly, a split existed between those who viewed solutions to energy issues in terms of production encouragement and those who favored conservation approaches. The former viewed decontrol of oil and gas pricing as crucial to increased domestic production; the latter argued that the controlled prices were already sufficiently high to encourage production and efforts instead were needed to discourage consumption and to prevent energy companies from making "windfall" profits.

In addition, both sides had substantial support. Many of the votes taken on energy issues in the various committees and on the House and Senate floor were close. In 1975 Representative Robert Krueger (D-Texas) offered a proposal for gradual decontrol of oil prices. The Krueger proposal was first narrowly adopted in the Energy and Power Subcommittee of the Interstate and Foreign Commerce Committee, then defeated by a single vote in the full committee, and finally lost as an amendment on the House floor by a vote of 202-220. Close divisions can also be seen in the Senate where the Energy and National Resources Committee was divided 9-9 on the Pearson-Bentsen proposal to deregulate natural gas prices.[4] The closeness of the divisions clearly exacerbated the problem.

Another reason offered for the failure of Congress to enact a national energy program more quickly is the ineffectiveness of presidential and congressional leadership. President Carter in particular bore the bulk of the criticism. These leadership failures were often blamed on Carter's inexperience and lack of skill in dealing with Congress. Undoubtedly, there is some truth to these notions. However, it was during his first nine months in office, when story after story of White House ineptitude in dealing with Congress surfaced, that Carter achieved one major congressional success: his energy program was marshaled through the House of Representatives, albeit with Speaker O'Neill's assistance.

Perhaps most importantly, if there were reasons to expect a slow congressional response to the need to develop energy policy, there were also reasons to expect the Congress to act quickly. First, despite its tendency toward sluggishness, Congress has demonstrated the capacity to respond quickly during times of emergency.[5] And although there were substantial lulls in the emergency status of energy policy once the embargo ended, it was always on a "front burner." Second, consensus may be slow to develop on closely divided issues. But six to seven years is a long time to wait for reasonable individuals to make the necessary compromises. Finally, during the 1970s Congress did much to try and reassert its policymaking role and move closer to equal status with the executive branch. Professional staffs for members and committees were increased. Congressional research arms like the Congressional Research Service and the General Accounting Office were strengthened, and the Congressional Budget Office was established.[6] Congress took on a new posture of activism — more bills, more subcommittees, more hearings, more witnesses, more hours in session, more votes.[7]

A major feature of the reforms was the further decentralization or "pluralization" of congressional decisionmaking through the development of subcommittee government. Organization theorists, as well as congressional reformers, expected the reforms would breathe new life into the policymaking capacities of the institution. As David E. Price hypothesized in his book on Senate committees:

> Consider, for example, James Q. Wilson's and James D. Barber's speculations as to the general effects of organizational "pluralization." When the number of "organizationally defined sub-units" is great, so the reasoning goes, the system's capacity for innovation will be increased: the interests of the organization's members will become more sharply focused and more intense, sub-units will feel a greater need to justify their existence and to enhance their role, and they will probably enjoy a reduced degree of supervision and less rigidly defined jurisdictions. The result will be not only an increased tendency to generate policy, but also a greater likelihood that the proposals will be "radical," due to the specialization and intensity of concern of those devising them. At this point, the argument continues, a reverse effect may set in. For pluralization will also give rise to malcoordination and conflict, and hence to veto, clearance, and bargaining procedures. The result in the long run may thus be the adoption of a lesser number of proposals, less radical in character.[8]

There were additional reasons to expect Congress to act quickly despite its failure to do so during the 93rd Congress immediately following the embargo. As the 94th Congress began, observers were optimistic that results would be forthcoming. The election had produced the expected Democratic landslide, increasing the party's House majority to 2:1 (nearly as large as that of the productive 89th Congress during the Johnson administration). Many of the newly elected members were thought to be liberals with unified policy goals. Congressional preoccupation with impeachment had subsided, and President Ford needed to build a record in the two years prior to the 1976 election. Most reforms were in place, including changes in the composition of the House Ways and Means Committee, previously a major stumbling block for energy tax legislation.

But the results proved disappointing. The 94th Congress left the major component issues of a national energy policy unresolved. If the usual explanations of congressional failure to enact policy do not suffice, and if there were reasons to expect Congress to abandon its sluggishness, what additional explanation can be offered for the delay?

The Basis of the New Obstructionism in the House

At least one scholar, Charles O. Jones, was skeptical about the effects of these reforms. In his essay "Will Reform Change Congress?" he concluded:

> The central point to emphasize is that we cannot yet be certain of the effects of the "revolutionary" reforms on congressional performance. It is simply too soon to tell whether procedural, organizational, and personnel changes have increased responsiveness, promoted access and deliberation, and facilitated reaching conclusions in law making.[9]

My research on energy policy clearly indicates that Jones's words of caution were well-founded. From my analysis of House action on two major pieces of energy legislation in 1975, an energy tax bill (HR 6860) and an energy conservation bill (HR 7014), I have concluded that there are five major reasons for the failure of the House to develop energy policy during the 94th Congress.[10]

First, the leadership, especially the Speaker, found its powers insufficient to cope with the new forces of decentralization — committee and subcommittee chairs, members, and staff. Despite its best efforts, it could not mobilize the House to make decisions on energy policy. Thus, the energy policy recommendations of a leadership task force at the start of the 94th Congress had to be dispersed to the appropriate committees and subcommittees without sufficient resources to ensure that the committees would act or report legislation in a timely fashion. Nor could the leadership, despite assistance from a cooperative Rules Committee in scheduling floor consideration of legislation, exert enough influence during the 94th Congress to merge the interrelated energy tax and conservation bills. Opponents of the merger could use the decentralized process to delay and thus prevent the merger.

Second, the reforms weakened committee chairs, making them more vulnerable to the demands of any group among their committee's Democratic members. Committee chairs could no longer deliver their members; rather, it appears that the members could deliver the chairs.

To show their effectiveness, committee and subcommittee chairs became more diligent than ever in protecting their jurisdictions. As various energy proposals were announced, chairs worked to capture the appropriate piece for their committees or subcommittees. During the 94th Congress, House members learned to take advantage of this to delay or defeat legislation, by getting chairs to raise jurisdictional issues. For example, Ways and Means opponents of oil price decontrol pressured former Ways and Means Chairman Al Ullman (D-Ore.) to oppose the Krueger amendment to the Commerce Committee's energy bill when it was offered on the House floor. The opponents argued that the amendment, which tied decontrol to the enactment of a windfall profits tax, encroached on the prerogatives of Ways and Means to write tax legislation. In fact, these opponents knew that merger of the decontrol and windfall tax issues would assist passage of decontrol.

In addition, weakened chairs lost much of their ability to mobilize support to enact legislation. In March 1975 Ullman tried to build a consensus around energy proposals of his own. Although the reception of the program was positive at first, it soon became apparent that the consensus among Ullman's own party members on Ways and Means was a weak one.[11] With each week that passed Ullman had to retreat further, and his proposals were either weakened, defeated or deferred.[12] Comparable limitations on the ability to lead, to build majorities, and to establish consensus faced other committee and subcommittee chairs as well. Even when Democratic chairs arranged compromises with the Ford administration, they lacked the resources to make these compromises work. To the degree that the Ford administration, or later the Carter administration, desired a compromise, it had to bargain with individual committee members — not just the chairs. Removing the ability of committee chairs to delay and defeat, as it existed in the fifties and sixties, also removed the influence needed to mobilize and facilitate.

Third, reforms designed to make the Ways and Means Committee more active and responsive to the Democratic House majority actually opened up new avenues for obstruction and delay. The expansion of the Ways and Means Committee from 25 to 37 members, the loss of committee assignment responsibilities for its Democratic members, and new restrictions on use of a closed rule to limit floor amendments significantly diminished the ability of the committee to write energy tax legislation and to achieve passage on the floor.[13]

Every Ways and Means member I interviewed claimed the larger membership made consensus-building more difficult. The committee was badly divided in marking up and reporting the energy tax bill (HR 6860) in 1975, and those divisions continued on the floor. With a modified rule for floor consideration, it required nearly two weeks to complete floor action. Roll call votes were taken on 20 amendments, and the bill was stripped of its key provisions. The reforms produced many of the intended goals, but they undercut the ability of Ways and Means to work at developing consensus in committee and left decisions to be made through floor votes, not compromise. In the environment of a re-election oriented House membership, energy tax increase, whether desirable or not, could not survive.

Fourth, reforms opened up new avenues for obstruction and delay that were often as effective as those used by conservative committee chairs in the fifties and sixties and had the appearance of being legitimate rather than arbitrary. The growth of subcommittee power established new potential for delay as well as a new layer for activity. Extended hearings and markups delayed reporting the energy conservation bill back to the full Commerce Committee until May 14, and it was not until June 24 that the committee completed its work. By that time the House had already completed action on the energy tax bill, and so the opportunity for merger of the two was lost; precisely what those opposed to oil price decontrol desired.

The reforms also made consideration of legislation a more time-consuming process since they produced greater equality among House members than had previously existed and allowed junior members to become more active in subcommittee, committee, and floor proceedings. On the 1975 Commerce Committee energy conservation bill 32 roll call votes were taken and 23 amendments were offered. Some members used the new freedom to unravel, delay, and defeat legislation.

Jurisdictional disputes, actual or contrived, served to further delay legislation and distract attention from the substantive issues. This problem was particularly great with energy legislation because it cut across normal committee and subcommittee jurisdictions. The most explicit use of jurisdictional disputes to derail legislation occurred in the efforts to defeat oil price decontrol. In simplified terms, jurisdictional claims were used to undermine the merger of the oil pricing and windfall profits tax issues during the 94th Congress.

Fifth, the failure of the House to consolidate energy jurisdiction primarily in a single committee, as recommended in the Bolling reform proposals of 1974, meant that consideration of energy legislation remained divided among a range of committees and subcommittees. The House therefore never had the opportunity to consider energy legislation in a comprehensive manner in 1975 and 1976. Although some legislation was passed, the key interrelated issues remained largely unsettled.[14]

As we have seen, the new obstructionism in the House can be attributed to insufficient leadership powers to cope with the forces of decentralization, weakened committee chairs, a weakened Ways and Means Committee, reforms that enabled further delay of legislation in committee and on the floor, and the failure to restructure committee jurisdictions. We shall now consider obstructionism in the Senate.

Obstructionism Spreads to the Senate

Originally I thought that these findings did not apply to the Senate. In part this was because the House had proven to be the major hurdle for energy legislation during the period of my earlier research. But activities in the Senate from late 1977 to 1980 indicate that many of the same findings in a general sense do apply to the Senate. To a large extent they had not been evident previously because the Senate did not need to obstruct as long as the House performed that function (or dysfunction). Thus, similar problems arose in the Senate only after a first wave of obstructionism was overcome in the House. For example, once the Carter energy plan passed the House in July 1977, it quickly became plagued in the Senate with similar difficulties. Despite the fact that committee jurisdiction over energy legislation is better consolidated in the Senate than in the House, the Carter program was first split in two. The tax portion was referred to the Finance Committee and the remainder to the Energy and Natural Resources Committee. The Energy Committee then divided its share into four separate pieces of legislation and agreed to consult with five other standing Senate committees on various aspects of the legislation.

On the natural gas portion of the program, the Senate leadership failed to break the Energy Committee's 9-9 tie vote; settled for reporting the bill without recommendation; suffered through a post cloture filibuster on the bill by junior senators Howard Metzenbaum (D-Ohio) and James Abourezk (D-S.D.), which required all-night sessions, 14 days of debate, and 128 roll call votes; and then appointed all 18 members of the Energy Committee, including the filibuster partners, as conferees. Not surprisingly, they continued to be deadlocked 9-9 well into 1978.[15]

Similarly, the decision to divide the Carter program into a series of bills in the Senate meant that they could be attacked on the floor in a piecemeal approach, undercutting the integrative nature of the program. The Senate may have lacked the jurisdictional squabbles of the House, but opponents of various parts of the program gained definite advantages from attacking, amending, and holding hostage separate parts of the program. Until hours before the adjournment of the 95th Congress, Senate opponents of the Carter program from both the political left and the right worked to delay Senate floor consideration of the conference report on the energy tax bill.

These efforts were designed to prevent the House from considering the conference report on the combined bills in a single vote, which it could not do unless the Senate passed the tax conference report. (The other conference reports in the package had already passed the Senate separately.) The opponents hoped to force the House to take a separate vote on the natural gas conference report because they believed it could be defeated on a separate vote but not as part of a package.

Although the reforms in the Senate were less specific and extensive than in the House, the effects were similar. Decentralization of decisionmaking, democratization of internal procedures, and increased equality among the members had costs as well as benefits. As the examples above illustrate, Senate leadership had great difficulty in mobilizing the membership and resolving deadlocks. Democratization gave members new resources for delay as well as new freedom to act. The capacity to obstruct was available to junior senators as well as senior. And when the leadership tried to undercut the obstructors — former Majority Leader Byrd's tactics in cutting off the post cloture filibuster on the natural gas bill — the efforts at ending obstruction, rather than the efforts of the obstructionists, were criticized as arbitrary. This analysis is not meant to support a return to House and Senate operations of the 1950s when committee chairs possessed substantially more resources than most members. Rather it is intended to show that decentralization and dispersion of the internal workings of the two bodies opened new avenues for obstruction.

Features of the New Obstructionism

Holding Legislation "Hostage." During the period from late 1977 to 1980 several other features of the new obstructionism have become evident. First, many members of Congress felt they had the capacity to hold legislation hostage. Some of the more visible examples of this have already been mentioned, such as the 1977 post cloture filibuster by two junior senators on the natural gas bill. However, the capacity of individual House and Senate members to play the role of hijacker was nowhere more crucial than during the conference committee deliberations on the Carter energy program, particularly on the natural gas portion. At first, the Senate natural gas conferees were blocked from even negotiating with the House conferees. The Senate-passed Pearson-Bentsen amendment provided for the gradual deregulation of natural gas prices. This position was favored by nine of the Senate conferees and opposed by nine of them. They could not agree on a position on which to bargain with the House conferees, the House having voted to retain price controls on interstate gas, extend them to intrastate gas, and allow certain price increases.

Although informal meetings were held in late November and December 1977, little progress was made. When Senator J. Bennett Johnston (D-La.) offered a compromise after Congress had adjourned for the first session, it met with disastrous results. Although Johnston worked with leading House Democratic conferees on the compromise, his fellow Senate conferees defeated it, 16-2, foreshadowing what was to come.

By March 1978 it appeared a compromise allowing for deregulation by 1985 had been reached. Five members on each side of the natural gas issue supported the compromise, and the Senate conferees approved it, 10-7. Then, by a slim 13-12 margin, the House conferees accepted the compromise with an amendment. (This indicated a loss of three antideregulation House conferees without any gain from the prederegulation side.) Senator Pete Domenici (R-N.M.), one of the 10 supporting the compromise, threatened to withdraw his support in reaction to the House amendment, and Senator Abourezk, an opponent of the compromise, threatened to filibuster any plan that allowed for deregulation.[16] Once again a compromise unraveled.

In late April a group of House and Senate conferees and Secretary of Energy James Schlesinger seemingly had worked out a new natural gas compromise, but now 2 of the 13 House conferees who had accepted the March compromise, Henry Reuss (D-Wis.) and James Corman (D-Cal.), objected to the new agreement. Reuss reportedly felt it was too generous and would assist separate passage of the crude oil equalization tax that he opposed, and Corman wanted to insure a strong crude oil tax if he were to support the new compromise.[17] Obviously, to win Reuss back would mean losing Corman and vice versa. A 13-12 majority in March became a 12-13 minority in April.

This required bargaining with yet another hostage holder, Joe Waggonner (D-La.), who had problems with the extension of price controls to intrastate natural gas. By mid-May a compromise was finally worked out allowing for increases in the ceiling prices of intrastate gas. Waggonner provided the deciding vote among the House conferees, and the Senate conferees accepted the new agreement. All that remained was for the staff to draft the proper language. But when the final language was presented to the conferees in August, three House and two Senate conferees who had supported the May compromise refused to sign the report, again holding the legislation hostage.[18] Although some claimed that the formal language did not reflect what they thought had been agreed to in May, others held out on related issues. For example, Louisianians Senator Johnston and Representative Waggonner, in the interests of a Louisiana pipeline company, became concerned with a Federal Energy Regulatory Commission case involving allocation of natural gas in intrastate markets.

Thirteen votes were reassembled on the House side only after Corman and Charles Rangel (D-N.Y.), who had not agreed to the May compromise, replaced Reuss and Waggonner. President Carter reassured Corman and Rangel that the poor would be given protection from large increases in energy prices. On the Senate side Domenici and James McClure (R-Idaho) agreed to rejoin those supporting the report, thus providing a majority. Afterwards, however, McClure revealed that his support for the report was gained in return for President Carter softening his position on the breeder nuclear reactor.[19]

There were "hostage holding" episodes throughout the 1974-80 period when Congress was trying to develop energy legislation. The kidnappers or hijackers were liberals, conservatives, and moderates; Democrats and Republicans; senior members and junior members. Moreover, their motives were not all the same. But whatever the motives, they undercut the process of mobilization and served the cause of those truly involved in obstructing the congressional process.

The Appearance of Legitimacy. A second feature of the new obstructionism, the appearance of legitimacy, also deserves elaboration. It is this appearance of being legitimate rather than arbitrary that both distinguishes the obstructionism of the 1970s from that of earlier periods and makes it so difficult to counter. In large part the obstructionism that occurred during the efforts to enact energy legislation was under the guise of protecting the rights of individual members. This included protecting the "rights" of members on committees and subcommittees with energy jurisdictions, fighting any efforts to limit the offering of floor amendments or the ability of members to speak on the floor, objecting to private meetings among conferees, and establishing large conference committees to insure broad representation.

Obstructionists took advantage of the increased equality among members and the more democratic operations within Congress to prevent the House and the Senate from having the option to choose among legislative policy alternatives. Jurisdictional protection meant that obstructors could prevent interrelated parts of energy policy from being considered in conjunction. Efforts to adopt restrictive rules for floor debate in the House or to cut off dilatory amendments and filibusters in the Senate were met by charges of "gag" rule and arbitrary leadership. Yet open procedures were used by obstructors to delay (with lengthy debate and numerous floor votes), to unravel (through a bits-and-pieces amending process), and to distract attention from the main issues at hand. Moreoever, the obstructionists found they had willing and often unwilling accomplices among the many newer members anxious to showcase their abilities.

Clearly this new obstructionism was hard to counteract. The autocratic committee chairs of the fifties and sixties were easy to identify. The members knew of their efforts to delay and defeat liberal legislation like civil rights, aid to education, and Medicare, and they were clearly described by the press as obstructionists. But it is far harder to see, for example, that someone arguing against restrictions on the offering of House floor amendments is trying to obstruct. Similarly, free and largely unlimited debate in the Senate is seemingly desirable. Yet openness of activities, equality among members, and internally democratic procedures often serve as facades for obstruction.

Obstructive Work Atmosphere. There is one final aspect of the new obstructionism that deserves brief mention. The work atmosphere of the reformed Congress of the 1970s may, in itself, generate obstructionism. The demands placed on House and Senate members by constituents, staff, and colleagues; by an ever expanding range of complex issues; by the proliferation of meetings, hearings, and roll call votes; and by a growing number of contacts from interest groups creates increased strain on the members.[20] Time for members to sit down, deliberate, and negotiate with each other over policy differences is scarce. Under these circumstances, obstructionism may serve as the easiest way for a member to feel successful. The delivering of impassioned floor speeches, the offering of bits-and-pieces amendments, and the casting of large numbers of roll call votes is far easier than reflecting on the complexities of policy alternatives, developing integrative legislative alternatives, and working out the tough compromises in committee instead of leaving everything to the floor.

HOW WAS OBSTRUCTIONISM OVERCOME?

Given the potency of the new obstructionism and the way it was applied in the decisionmaking on energy legislation, it is not difficult to understand why resolution of major energy issues took so long. What is perhaps harder to comprehend is how these issues were resolved at all and why the component parts of a national energy policy are now in place. As an examination of two efforts to undercut the forces of obstruction will illustrate, overcoming obstructionism required extensive use of leadership resources, skill, timing, and some luck.

The Ad Hoc Select Committee on Energy

After numerous failures to resolve major energy issues during the 94th Congress, many obstacles faced the new House Speaker,

Tip O'Neill, and the new Majority Leader, Jim Wright, if they were to prevent a repeat performance in the 95th. Despite the election of a Democratic president, they still had to cope with the forces of obstruction in a decentralized House: competing committee and subcommittee jurisdictions; weak chairs eager to protect jurisdictions; a process that allowed for new sources of delay; and the potential unraveling of legislation once it reached the floor. Crucial to coping with these difficulties was the leadership's decision to establish the Ad Hoc Select Committee on Energy and, more importantly, its care in designing the committee.

A number of key decisions were made in the establishment of the ad hoc committee. First was the realization that it could not supersede committees and subcommittees having energy jurisdictions. The new leadership was not strong enough to make enemies of every member with a jurisdictional stake in energy legislation. It was decided instead to refer parts of the energy program being prepared by the Carter administration to the appropriate standing committees first and then to allow the ad hoc committee to have secondary jurisdiction over all the pieces of the package. Moreover, the membership of the ad hoc committee would include key members of the committees with original jurisdiction. This gave the process a sense of legitimacy. Use of the committee system itself served to undercut objections of the relevant committee chairs.

Second, giving the ad hoc committee the opportunity to work on all the pieces of the program after the standing committees had finished with the separate parts enabled it to serve as a mechanism for putting the pieces back together. The legislation could then be sent to the floor as a package. In addition, the procedure allowed the ad hoc committee to serve as a safety valve. It could review the decisions of the standing committees, resolve remaining jurisdictional disputes, and protect the program against the parochialism of various committees and subcommittees.[21] Thus, if the committee system pulled the programs apart — the fate that met the leadership task force efforts in 1975 — the leadership retained the ability to put it back together.

Third, Speaker O'Neill, after considerable discussion with other members and advisors, placed a deadline on the standing committees for reporting their parts of the package. If they did not meet the deadline, the ad hoc committee would assume responsibility for the legislation. This requirement successfully undercut members' ability to use the decentralized committee and subcommittee process for delay. The committee chairs complained about meeting the 60-day deadline, but except for one committee that reported a day late, all conformed to the timetable.

Finally, the leadership skillfully chose the ad hoc committee members. In some cases O'Neill had no choice. The chairs of committees and subcommittees with important energy jurisdictions had to be appointed. But the leadership succeeded in appointing members who were broadly representative of the House in terms of geography and standing, committee representation, and range of opinions on energy matters. As one observer concluded, "Even given the controversial nature of energy proposals, if this group could approve a program, chances were good that it would pass the House."[22] And that is precisely how the leadership wanted it to appear. In fact, the Speaker and the Majority Leader had stacked the ad hoc committee to insure that they could count on 21 of the 40 members in crucial situations.[23] Thus, they limited the chances that the ad hoc committee could be used against them as an additional weapon of obstruction.

Although the ad hoc committee may not have been the most efficient mechanism to deal with the problem, it undercut some of the obstructionism that had handicapped the previous efforts of the House to develop energy legislation. It allowed the House to work in a timely fashion. It enabled key compromises to be hammered out instead leaving everything for the floor. It meant that the House could legislate an entire package at once, not just one piece at a time. Furthermore, careful coordination between the ad hoc committee and the Rules Committee allowed for the design of a rule that kept the package from unraveling on the House floor.

These efforts to undercut obstructionism were extraordinary, however. The leadership used its resources extensively and with unusual skill. Both the leadership and the administration were new, which gave them one-time advantages with House members. In addition, some luck was required for the program to survive the House. Yet even under these optimal circumstances, the victory was narrow.

Passage of Synthetic Fuels Legislation

Many of the features that spurred House passage of the Carter energy proposals in 1977 also were essential ingredients in the passage of synthetic fuels legislation two years later. The 368-25 floor vote in favor of synthetic fuels legislation in 1979 does not reflect the true difficulty involved.

When synthetic fuels legislation first reached the House floor in 1975, it was part of the conference report on the ERDA authorization bill. The House bill had not contained a synthetic fuels provision, thus avoiding a potential jurisdictional nightmare among competing House committees. Nevertheless, a coalition of liberals and conservatives voted 263-140 to strike a $6 billion loan guarantee section for synthetic fuels from the conference report. When synthetic fuels legislation was revived in 1976, the jurisdictional conflict reappeared in full. The legislation was referred to four committees: Science and Technology; Interstate and Foreign Commerce; Banking, Currency and Housing; and Ways and Means. Although each committee reported legislation, they were in substantial disagreement, and the legislation was not brought to the floor. Only when Science and Technology Chairman Olin Teague (D-Texas) threatened to delay floor activity at the end of the session, did the Rules Committee grant a rule providing for floor consideration of synthetic fuels. The Ford administration, the AFL-CIO, and the U.S. Chamber of Commerce backed Teague's compromise proposal calling for $3.5 billion in loan guarantees and $500 million in price supports, but the rule was rejected on the House floor by a one-vote margin.[24]

Growing gasoline lines in the spring of 1979 set in motion another attempt to get synthetic fuels through the House. William Moorhead (D-Pa.), chairman of the Economic Stabilization Subcommittee of the House Banking Committee, suggested to a caucus of Democrats on his subcommittee that the Defense Production Act might be used as a new vehicle for synthetic fuels. The legislation was drawn purposely to avoid jurisdictional disputes. Because the price supports section was limited to fuels purchased only for defense, the Commerce Committee could not claim jurisdiction. No research was included, thus keeping it away from Science and Technology. And finally there were no tax provisions involved at first, precluding the Ways and Means Committee. The bill called for the Defense Department to buy the synthetic fuels equivalent of 500,000 barrels of oil by 1985 and authorized federal loans and loan guarantees to achieve this goal. The legislation was reported out of committee on June 3 and passed the House in an expanded form on June 26.[25]

Those voting against the rule to consider synthetic fuels in 1976 who were still in the House in 1979 split 111-15 in favor of the Moorhead bill. The success in overcoming obstructionism with synthetic fuels was considerably more one-sided than with the ad hoc committee in 1977. Nevertheless, without an understanding of how jurisdictional disputes could be used to obstruct, Moorhead's skill in designing the legislation, long gasoline lines, and a little luck, synthetic fuels might easily have met the same fate in the House in 1979 as it had previously.

It was only under circumstances such as those surrounding passage of Carter's energy proposals in 1977 and synthetic fuels legislation in 1979 that the new obstructionism could be nullified and the Congress given the opportunity to choose among policy alternatives. Nevertheless, one may rightly claim that these two cases do not represent the optimum in legislative policy decisionmaking or even close to it.

According to some, the House overreacted to past obstruction in passing the synthetic fuels bill and did so without a careful consideration of its design, costs, and benefits. It is also important to realize that the costs of the new obstructionism have been substantial: the development of a national energy policy was delayed.

WHAT WERE THE COSTS?

Although I have been studying the efforts of Congress to develop a national energy policy since the late 1973 oil embargo, I have become fully aware of the costs the new obstructionism has generated only recently. With the resolution of many major energy issues in 1978, 1979, and 1980, I realized that these issues and their solutions were already part of the policy agenda back in 1974. At various points, provisions reasonably close to those finally agreed to had been available. But political actors on all sides of these issues successfully prevented the Congress from building consensus, arranging compromises, and having the opportunity to choose among alternative packages. Without the resources of the new obstructionism, many of these issues might well have been resolved from two to four years sooner than they were.

If one accepts this point of view, or even accepts the notion that chances for conflict resolution were seriously hampered, then one can reasonably estimate some of the costs incurred. The most obvious of these costs is that, like the legislation itself, the goals of energy legislation were significantly delayed. The programs finally enacted are projected, among other things, to increase the domestic production of oil and gas, to stimulate the development of new energy sources and forms, to encourage conservation of energy, and to decrease dependence on foreign energy sources. If one believes the programs will be successful, then the costs of delay are evident. However, even if one believes the programs will not achieve these goals in any significant way, then we have been denied the opportunity to see that they would not work. And that too is a cost. At a far more speculative level one might wish to ponder the effects on inflation in the 1980s of the failure of the United States to develop a national energy policy in the mid-1970s.

Energy producers and consumers have also borne the costs of these delays because of the unpredictability they created. With Congress unable to reach decisions on the pricing and taxing of oil and natural gas, on outer continental shelf legislation, and on the financial commitment of the government to a synthetic fuels program, corporate and personal energy decisions were also delayed. For example, knowing that natural gas pricing will be deregulated by 1985 (and in the interim, price increases of defined amounts will be allowed) may not have pleased natural gas producers who favored immediate deregulation, but it provided a far more predictable environment in which to plan for exploration than one where it was not known whether regulated prices would exist indefinitely or whether there would be immediate deregulation.

There have also been costs to the internal workings of Congress on other issues of public policy. To enact major energy legislation has required that the House and Senate leadership use their resources to the fullest in mobilizing majorities. Having used these resources, the leadership has discovered that they may not regenerate very quickly. Thus, for example, the members whom Speaker O'Neill persuaded to support provisions of the Carter energy package in 1977 established credits with him. As other issues developed in the 95th Congress, such as key votes on labor legislation, many of them were immune from leadership persuasion. They could correctly claim, "I helped you earlier on energy, but I can't this time."

At a broader level the failure of government, and particularly of the Congress, to develop an energy policy may have affected the confidence of citizens in the government's ability to respond to crises. If one believes that the energy situation in the United States is "the moral equivalent of war," as President Carter claimed, then one expects government institutions to respond with a minimum of delay. When government institutions do not respond quickly to the crisis, one can assume that there was no crisis or that the government is not operating effectively. In either case confidence in government is undermined. These costs have already been realized. But it is important to understand that the new obstructionism has not just affected congressional decisionmaking on energy policy. Few major areas of legislative policymaking have been immune. A detailed analysis of the progress in legislative policy ranging from health care and tax reform legislation to agriculture and public works would in all likelihood produce similar findings.

Much of the blame for the lack of results has been placed on Presidents Ford and Carter and their inability to deal effectively with Congress. One could not deny that they share in the responsibility. However, on balance it must be noted that they faced a "reformed" Congress in which increased activity masked new opportunities to obstruct.

There are likely to be future costs to the new obstructionism as it affects energy policy in the United States. Although most of the major legislation has now been enacted, the passing of laws does not necessarily end obstructionism. Just as the process was dispersed among many committees and subcommittees for the consideration of energy legislation, so has the legislative oversight of energy programs also been left dispersed.[26] This provides the opportunity for the forces of obstruction to tear at the implementation of the programs in a piecemeal manner. The failure of the House again in 1980 to consolidate committee jurisdiction on energy matters as recommended by the Patterson Committee leaves the door open to this second and far less visible form of obstruction.

CONCLUSION

Unfortunately, this essay cannot end on an optimistic note. The study of energy legislation illustrates that the congressional process in recent years has not been functioning very effectively. The power of the House and Senate still exists largely in a negative sense. Programs can be delayed and defeated far more easily than they can be developed and enacted. This situation prevails despite the best efforts of reformers to improve Congress's policymaking capacities and to reduce the opportunity for obstruction. Thus, we find at the beginning of the 1980s a Congress with more subcommittees, more professional staff, more research tools, more hearings, more roll call votes, and more openness, than a decade before. No longer do committee chairs have the same ability to obstruct the course of legislation in an arbitrary manner. Junior members now have an important role to play in the process and no longer need to serve a lengthy apprenticeship. Party organizations have been activated and strengthened. In fact, most of the agenda of internal congressional reformers of the late 1950s were finally achieved by the mid-1970s.

But it is equally clear that many of the consequences of these reforms were not anticipated. The reforms not only increased the potential for legislative activity, but they also increased the potential sources of obstruction. What we may have is a Congress that is more active but less productive.

Moreover, the new obstructionism is more difficult to confront. The obstructors are harder to identify, and many members serve the cause of obstructionism unwittingly. Those wishing to obstruct may vary from one issue to another. Thus, there are few clear "villains." Furthermore, many members reap personal benefits from engaging in activities that serve the cause of obstructionism. Members who give floor speeches, offer amendments, protect the jurisdictional claims of their committees and subcommittees, or stand firmly behind particular interest group positions often do so for positive reasons. Individually, they rarely serve to obstruct the process through those activities, but collectively, when members engage in these activities with little institutional or self-constraint, obstruction may often result.

Solutions to the new obstructionism are not easily developed or implemented. Certainly a return to the distribution of influence that existed prior to the reforms is not desirable. One answer is to give the party leadership sufficient control over the operation of the House and Senate to place limits on the activities of the members. But House and Senate leaders have discovered that opposition mounts quickly when they try to constrain their party members. Recent efforts in this direction, such as the proposal of the Patterson Committee to consolidate energy jurisdiction in a separate standing committee, have been unsuccessful. At best, the House Democratic leadership has had some success in using the Rules Committee to limit floor amendments on complex legislation. Normally the adoption of each restrictive rule, however, meets substantial floor opposition and charges of being an undemocratic "gag" rule. In general, members are reluctant to accept institutional constraints on their independence.

A second approach to dealing with the new obstructionism would require that self-restraint be part of the socialization process for members. There is little evidence that this is included in what new members learn. In fact, the formal orientation sessions for new members offer advice that works against the development of self-restraint.

Finally, there is the somewhat perverse notion that when the operation of the House and Senate gets sufficiently unmanageable adjustments can and will be made. For example, in reaction to the Abourezk and Metzenbaum filibuster during the 1977 natural gas debate, the Senate changed its rules to restrict the post cloture filibuster. But questions remain regarding the effectiveness of this approach. How unmanageable must the situation get before changes are made? Will the changes cope with the basic problem or only its most undesirable symptoms? And lastly, what costs will be incurred while we wait?

NOTES

1. James L. Sundquist, "Congress and the President: Enemies or Partners?" in *Congress Reconsidered,* 1st ed., edited by Lawrence C. Dodd and Bruce I. Oppenheimer (New York: Praeger Publishers, 1977), pp. 222-243.
2. Ibid., p. 240.
3. One major energy issue remained unresolved at the end of the 96th Congress. It involved the creation of an Energy Mobilization Board designed to provide energy projects with a fast track through the bureaucracy. The House and Senate passed differing forms of the legislation. When the conference report reached the House floor in June 1980, it was rejected by a 232-131 vote.
4. The Pearson-Bentsen proposal, named for its authors, Senators James Pearson (R-Kan.) and Lloyd Bentsen (D-Texas), first passed the Senate

in the 94th Congress as part of the merger of an emergency natural gas bill and a natural gas deregulation bill. It provided for the gradual deregulation of natural gas prices. The House, however, defeated a similar provision when it was offered as a floor amendment. In the 95th Congress the two senators offered a modified version of their original proposal.

5. Many examples of quick congressional action have occurred during emergency international crises such as wars and military actions. But even in domestic areas, legislation — relating to dock and rail strikes, for example — has passed within days of being introduced. Over a longer time span the classic cases of Franklin Roosevelt's 100 days and the Johnson 89th Congress show how expeditiously Congress can act when time considerations or emergencies exist.

6. For a discussion of the activities of these resource agencies of Congress, see Lawrence C. Dodd and Richard L. Schott, *Congress and the Administrative State* (New York: John Wiley & Sons, 1979), pp. 248-262.

7. See Lawrence C. Dodd and Bruce I. Oppenheimer, "The House in Transition," in this volume.

8. David E. Price, *Who Makes the Laws?* (Cambridge, Mass.: Schenkman Publishing Co., 1972), p. 14.

9. Charles O. Jones, "Will Reform Change Congress?" in *Congress Reconsidered,* 1st ed., pp. 255-256.

10. Bruce I. Oppenheimer, "Policy Effects of U.S. House Reform: Decentralization and the Capacity to Resolve Energy Issues," in *Legislative Studies Quarterly,* vol. V, no. 1 (February 1980): 5-30.

11. See Tom Wicker, "Energy Plan in Sight," *The New York Times,* March 4, 1975, and Joseph Kraft, "Developing an Energy Program," *The Washington Post,* March 4, 1980.

12. For example, Ullman's proposed increase in the gasoline tax began at $.40/gal. and eroded in several stages to $.03/gal. with a potential increase of another $.20/gal. depending on gasoline use. His excise tax on inefficient automobiles was weakened, and a tax credit for efficient ones was defeated. Finally, Ullman's proposal for a windfall profits tax was deferred.

13. For analyses of the Ways and Means Committees' operation before the reforms, see John F. Manley, *The Politics of Finance* (Boston: Little, Brown & Co., 1970); and after the reforms see Catherine E. Rudder, "The Policy Impact of Reform on the Committee on Ways and Means," in *Legislative Reform: The Policy Impact,* ed. Leroy N. Rieselbach (Lexington, Mass.: Lexington Books, 1978), pp. 73-89.

14. Oppenheimer, "Policy Effects of House Reform," pp. 10-18.

15. The tie continued until the death of Senator Lee Metcalf (D-Mont.) on January 12, 1978. The Democratic Senate leadership then decided to expand the Energy and Natural Resources Committee to 19 members in order to avoid future tie votes. But neither of the two members added following Metcalf's death was allowed to participate as a conferee.

16. *Congressional Quarterly Weekly Report,* March 3, 1978, p. 743.

17. Ibid., April 29, 1978, p. 1039.

18. Included in this group were Representatives Henry Reuss (D-Wis.), Joe Waggonner (D-La.) and Charles Wilson (D-Texas), and Senators J. Bennett Johnston (D-La.), James McClure (R-Idaho), Mark Hatfield (R-Ore.), and Pete Domenici (R-N.M.).

19. The McClure announcement upset former Senate Minority Leader Howard Baker (R-Tenn.), who had substantial interest in keeping the breeder reactor program for his home state. This moved Baker more clearly with the opponents of the natural gas compromise.

20. For a discussion of the effects of stress and strain on Congress, see Joseph Cooper, "Congress in Organizational Perspective," in *Congress Reconsidered,* 1st ed., pp. 140-159.
21. David J. Vogler provides a careful analysis of the use of ad hoc committees, including the Ad Hoc Select Committee on Energy, in "The Rise of Ad Hoc Committees in the House of Representatives" (Paper delivered at the annual meeting of the American Political Science Association, New York, New York, August 31-September 3, 1978).
22. Charles O. Jones, "Congress and the Making of Energy Policy," in *New Dimensions to Energy Policy,* ed. Robert Lawrence (Lexington, Mass.: Lexington Books, 1980), pp. 168-169.
23. For example, the leadership appointed Charles Wilson instead of Robert Krueger as one of the Texans on the ad hoc committee because it was perceived that Wilson would be more open to compromise and leadership influence. This was done despite Krueger's extensive work on energy legislation in the 94th Congress.
24. *Congressional Quarterly Weekly Report,* September 25, 1976.
25. The bill was amended on the House floor by former Majority Leader Jim Wright (D-Texas) to raise the goal to two million barrels by 1990 and to increase the price support from two to three billion dollars.
26. See Dodd and Schott, *Congress and the Administrative State,* p. 219.

13

Executive-Congressional Conflict in Foreign Policy: Explaining It, Coping with It

I. M. Destler

Throughout most of the postwar period, the general attitude of foreign policy-minded Americans toward congressional influence could be summarized in four words: "the less, the better." As one careful critique of the academic literature put it, presidents were seen as "formulating bold and forward-looking new policies for the nation, while an unimaginative Congress . . . appeared to be hindering those efforts and defending parochial interests."[1] Practitioners shared this attitude. Even the Chairman of the Senate Foreign Relations Committee, J. William Fulbright (D-Ark.), wondered in 1961 whether congressional influence on foreign policy was not greater than the country could afford. He found it:

> highly unlikely that we can successfully execute a long-range program for the taming, or containing, of today's aggressive and revolutionary forces by continuing to leave vast and vital decision-making powers in the hands of a decentralized, independent-minded, and largely parochial-minded body of legislators. The Congress, as Woodrow Wilson put it, is a "disintegrated ministry," a jealous center of power with a built-in antagonism for the Executive.[2]

After all this, of course, came Vietnam. Beginning around 1965, senators like Fulbright led the foreign policy community to a rediscovery of the value of checks on executive power.[3] After Richard Nixon ordered U.S. troops into Cambodia in 1970, 13 executive-oriented Harvard scholars made a pilgrimage to Capitol Hill to endorse congressional actions against the president, expressing what one of them termed a "dramatic shift in views I have held long and deeply with regard to the efficacy of Congressional action designed to restrain presidential discretion in national security affairs."[4] Years of struggle led to action in 1973 — the War Powers Resolution establishing a more explicit congressional role in the commitment of American troops overseas and the prohibition on further U.S. bombing of Indochina. Then hard upon Vietnam came Watergate, where millions of Americans again looked to the Congress to deliver them from what executive power had wrought. Building on this momentum, the Congress of the seventies moved effectively into a range of issues — linking improved U.S.-Soviet trade relations to free emigration of Soviet Jews; embargoing arms aid to Turkey after its invasion of Cyprus; prohibiting clandestine U.S. involvement in Angola. And Congress also established new procedural vehicles for policy influence, including the right of legislative veto on executive arms sales and import relief decisions.[5]

Yet as the decade ended, much of the bloom had left the congressional rose.[6] It had taken an enormous Carter administration effort to get the "parochial-minded" Senate to ratify the Panama Canal treaties in 1978 and to get the even more parochial House to pass implementing legislation. In 1979 the Congress approved the comprehensive multilateral trade agreements submitted by the president, but his SALT II treaty met a decidedly hostile reception, even though it (like the trade package) was the product of seven years of negotiation, most of it under the Nixon and Ford administrations.[7] Once again, the question was whether the United States could operate effectively in the international arena if its legislature tied the executive's hands or rewrote painfully negotiated accords. The Soviet invasion of Afghanistan followed the SALT II stalemate, causing Carter to shelve the treaty, at least temporarily; it also brought strengthened demands that congressional restrictions on executive flexibility be eased, so that the United States could compete more effectively in the geopolitical arena.

In significant part, this flowing and ebbing of congressional standing is a function of two factors: substantive preferences and the presence or absence of crisis. Many who write on such matters are moderate liberals in orientation; hence some shift back to an executive orientation was predictable once Vietnam was behind us and the White House returned to Democratic hands. Conversely, Senator Barry Goldwater (R-Ariz.) — who opposed the War Powers Resolution as an intrusion on needed presidential authority — went to court in December 1978 arguing that it was unconstitutional for President Carter to withdraw the United States from its security treaty with Taiwan without congressional assent. The second factor, crisis, usually reinforces presidential power and the argument that the president needs the flexibility to respond — hence the rise in Carter's standing in the polls in early 1980.

But the deeper cause of executive-congressional conflict is a core political-procedural dilemma. Americans want two things that often prove incompatible in practice: *democratic government* (involving ongoing competition among a range of U.S. interests and perspectives) and *effective foreign policy* (which requires settling on specific goals and pursuing them consistently). To reconcile these competing needs insofar as they can be reconciled, the framers of the Constitution established, in Richard Neustadt's apt phrase, a government of "separated institutions sharing powers."[8]

It is an oversimplification to say that the executive represents policy coherence in any pure sense or that the legislature is a pure decentralized democracy. The Congress, or portions thereof, can take purposive decisions as happened on Indochina and Watergate in 1973 and 1974. The executive is typically divided in opinion and interest. Moreover, most foreign policy issues do not involve a substantive struggle between the executive and Congress in that simple sense; rather, the typical pattern is policy advocates in one branch working with allies in the other against executive and legislative officials with opposing views. But the executive and the Congress are "separated institutions." These two primary decision arenas in American foreign policy have distinct characters.

In general, the genius of Congress is democracy, diversity, debate. Often Congress nurtures creativity. Nelson Polsby describes the Senate as "a great incubator of policy innovation in the American system," and Alton Frye emphasizes the "policy entrepreneurship" role.[9] The executive, by contrast, offers the hierarchy and concentrated formal authority that make coherent policy execution at least possible. What Alexander Hamilton called "energy in the executive" is particularly important to the conduct of foreign policy.[10] In periods when the United States is conducting an activist foreign policy — the case since 1940 — there is a need for "decision, activity, secrecy, and dispatch" which only the president and his senior advisers can supply.[11]

Because executive-congressional conflict reflects a deep tension among core values, it has no simple solution. Yet it demands deeper analysis, both for those seeking to understand conflict and those responsible for coping with it in the executive-legislative arena. The place to begin, of course, is the Constitution, which gives both the president and the Congress authorities that influence policy on particular issues. Conflict results from differing views about policy goals or means and efforts to advance those views by employing these authorities. The two branches do not come to the battle equally armed, however. The executive generally has the initiative. One reason is that the president has particular constitutional powers in foreign policy: to negotiate treaties, to command the armed forces, and to appoint and receive ambassadors. Conflict arises when senators and representatives seek to use congressional powers — over appropriations, general legislation, treaties, appointments — to control or constrain the president and the executive in their exercise of foreign policy discretion.

SOURCES OF CONFLICT

But when and why do members do this? Why does conflict arise at some times and not others, on some issues and not others? For insights one must examine what motivates members of Congress and executive officials in their dealings with each other. Such an examination should also shed light on some common prescriptions for conflict management. Executive-congressional consultation, for example, can help prepare the way on issues likely to involve congressional action. But how consistent is such consultation with other demands on those at both ends of Pennsylvania Avenue? Similarly, while strengthening the foreign policy staff of members of Congress may add to congressional expertise and raise the level of executive-congressional dialogue, it also adds new actors to the foreign policy process, actors with their own interests in policy engagement.

To analyze congressional (and executive) motivations, it is useful to consider four overlapping sources of foreign policy conflict on current issues: (1) *persistent substantive orientations* on Capitol Hill that diverge from those of the president and his senior advisers; (2) the *electoral political interests* of individual senators and representatives; (3) the *institutional characteristics of Congress;* and (4) the *expansion and proliferation of congressional staffs.*

Substantive Differences

The obvious place to begin is with differing opinions about policy content. Many senators and representatives have serious views about the substance of American foreign policy. These views often differ substantially from the preferred policies of the president and his senior advisers. To the degree that legislators are committed to these views, they are likely to employ their constitutional and statutory authorities to make them prevail. And those who specialize in international issues tend to have particular substantive interests. Richard Fenno's comparative study of House committees finds that members of Foreign Affairs usually sought to join because of commitment to "good public policy," whereas members of other committees were more likely to stress other goals such as "influence within the House" or "re-election."[12]

If a viewpoint becomes widely shared and persists over a period of years, it can become particularly influential. A dramatic example is the consensus that developed against the Vietnam War, a consensus that not only produced the War Powers Resolution and the Indochina bombing ban, but also led to a subsequent prohibition against U.S. involvement in the Angolan civil war. Congressional opinion since 1975 has become more conservative than that of the administration on political-military issues, as in the fifties and early sixties. This is one reason why Carter's SALT II treaty got such a cool Senate reception, and why the hardening of his foreign policy after the Soviet invasion of Afghanistan was generally welcomed on Capitol Hill.

Another way that substantive views in Congress make themselves felt is more idiosyncratic — through "pockets of conviction" linked to energy, persistence, and political skill. The impact of Senator Henry Jackson (D-Wash.) on strategic arms policy is one major example; others include the role of Senator Edward Kennedy (D-Mass.) on refugee issues and of former Representative Donald Fraser (D-Minn.) on development aid. Such personal efforts usually require a committee or subcommittee power base. And they are effective, often, because they are exceptional. Most senators and representatives lack the time or the interest to give foreign policy issues this kind of sustained attention. Thus those who do can have disproportionate impact, both on the actions of Congress and those of the executive branch.

Electoral Interests

A second source of conflict is the electoral pressures on senators and representatives. Not only must they worry about overall U.S. policies, but also about their own visible role in the policy process and how the public perceives their stands. Most want to be re-elected; a substantial minority aspires to broader-constituency public offices (some representatives to the Senate, some senators to the White House). In David Mayhew's persuasive formulation, these electoral needs drive legislators to concentrate on three types of activity affecting how they appear to their constituents: credit claiming, advertising (of one's name), and position taking on public issues (to strengthen identification with stances favored in the legislator's support coalition).[13] Foreign Relations is one of the Senate's most prestigious committees not so much because of its legislative power — which is comparatively modest — but because it offers a "bully pulpit" for members to gain visibility and reputation on international issues.

In credit claiming, advertising, and position taking activities, a senator or representative's primary stake is not in how overall U.S. policies actually turn out; what matters instead is what the member appears to be saying and doing about them. In 1979 presidential aspirant Howard Baker (R-Tenn.), whose support of the Panama treaties as Senate Minority Leader exposed him to right-wing attack, took a strong anti-SALT II position in order to recoup and looked forward to the Senate floor debate — aborted because of Afghanistan — to publicize his position. In some instances it may even be in a senator's interest *not* to win on an issue because then he takes on responsibility and risks being blamed if the policy fails. Henry Jackson, for example, won congressional support and reluctant Ford administration acquiescence in his proposal to link trade concessions to Soviet policies on Jewish emigration.[14] When Russia renounced the bilateral trade agreement and emigration declined, Jackson was vulnerable to charges that his amendment had been impractical and counterproductive.

An example of presidential awareness of members' thurst for the public limelight was President Eisenhower's hope in the 1950s that former Ohio Senator John Bricker could be induced, through creation of some sort of "Bricker Commission," to put aside his widely supported amendment to restrict presidential treaty-making power. The president was convinced that "all Bricker wants is something big in public with his name on it."[15] In 1978 junior senator Dennis DeConcini (D-Ariz.) won at least temporary notoriety by conditioning his support of the Panama treaties on a reservation declaring the U.S. right to "the use of military force in Panama" to keep the canal open after it went under Panamanian control. This condition triggered a predictable uproar in Panama and almost led to its rejection of the treaties; only after a compensating Senate reservation reiterated U.S. "adherence to the principle of non-intervention" did Panamanian President Omar Torrijos agree to final ratification.[16]

Linked to legislators' electoral interests is their need to respond to interest groups. Industries seek protection from imports. A strong, attentive Jewish constituency and a newly emergent Greek-American lobby seek to affect Middle Eastern and Mediterranean policy. On noneconomic international issues, such pressures are less important than on most domestic issues. Legislators need not always accede to such pressure, especially where countervailing forces exist, but they must respond to them in some way. And on issues like the

Carter energy program, a matter of domestic economic regulation with considerable foreign policy import, legislators may find that the need to cope with pressures and counterpressures is what most drives their decision.

Legislators are also influenced by partisan party loyalties. It seldom pays for an administration to define a controversial foreign policy issue in partisan terms; this is likely to lose more votes than it gains. And party loyalties are a weakening influence on congressional voting behavior. But there remains some predisposition to support a president of one's own party, as evidenced by differing alignments on foreign aid legislation under Democratic and Republican presidents.[17] Moreover, legislators must be sensitive to party sentiment in order to avert primary challenges or to bolster their prospects for winning nominations for "higher" office. Senate and House party leaders must retain the confidence of their party colleagues. In his handling of Panama and SALT, for example, Senate Majority Leader Robert C. Byrd moved very cautiously, relating the substance and timing of his personal policy statements to the evolving Senate mood.

Institutional Factors

A separate source of executive-congressional conflict is the particular features of Congress as a policy-influencing institution. One such feature is the unsuitability of congressional "handles" to the conduct of day-to-day foreign policy. Congress can, of course, prevail on any single issue through its lawmaking and appropriations powers. In this sense Senator Fulbright was correct in concluding that "It was not a lack of power which prevented the Congress from ending the war in Indochina," because "Congress had the means, through its control of appropriations, to compel an early or immediate end. . . ."[18] But Congress could not legislate a more nuanced approach, such as a particular negotiating strategy, to terminate a war. Nor can it for other issues. The money power has practical limitations because, as Thomas Schelling observed more than a decade ago, most major foreign policy choices are of the "non-budgetary sort."[19] Relations with particular countries are comprised of a stream of day-to-day decisions and communications; inevitably these involve executive discretion.

In the fifties a freshman Republican representative asked President Eisenhower which committee he should join — Foreign Affairs or Ways and Means. Eisenhower advised the latter, noting that "on taxes Ways and Means was king, but that on foreign relations he was."[20] A key reason is that taxes can be controlled by legislation establishing rules of general applicability, and executive discretion — while it does exist — is usually limited in this area. Congress can also limit executive foreign policy discretion by establishing binding rules (e.g., a requirement imposed in 1974 that 70 percent of food aid must go to the neediest nations), and by fixing policy toward specific countries on specific issues (e.g., embargoing arms sales to Turkey that same year). But the policy costs can be severe; rules often outlast the circumstances justifying their creation. A law that restored balance to U.S. food aid allocations in 1974 and 1975 helped to distort them in 1976, when more grain was poured into Bangladesh despite overloaded ports and storage capacity.[21] And the Turkey prohibition locked the United States into an unproductive and potentially damaging policy stalemate when the Ankara government responded in kind. Congress responded by lifting the embargo in 1978.

Legislators often recognize that discretion is desirable in principle, of course. But in practice they are not the ones who get to exercise it, and administration officials — faced with their own sets of pressures — may well employ their discretion to get around what Congress intends. The response on the Hill may then be to tighten the rules. This is particularly likely in periods like the last several years when trust between the two branches is low.

A related problem with congressional handles on foreign policy is that legislative action is *public* action. It may often be desirable that U.S. pressure be exercised more discreetly — a "quiet" suspension of arms sales, for example, or low-key representations on human rights. But again, this involves executive action, and to the degree that such pressure is being applied discreetly, members of Congress cannot be sure that it is really being exerted seriously at all.

Another institutional source of conflict is the decentralization of congressional policymaking power, which is rooted in the formal equality and separate constituencies of members. Combined with the weakness of national parties, these alone give individual members considerable leeway in what they *say* about policy issues. Often conflicting or counterproductive signals overseas are the result, as illustrated when Panamanians heard on live radio how certain senators characterized their country and their national leader.

More significant in generating conflict, however, is the dispersion of actual influence over issues. This is the product, in part, of a series of internal reforms dating from the 1910 revolt against Speaker Joe Cannon but accelerating sharply in the early 1970s. Procedural democracy and subcommittee proliferation have weakened committee chairmen. As partial compensation, there have been gains in the strength of the party leaders, whose direct role in shaping the specific substance of legislation traditionally has been much less than their influence over floor scheduling and over members' committee assignments.[22] But on key votes administration lobbyists generally work to deliver the votes themselves rather than expecting leaders to do so.

Negotiating with 100 or 435. individuals is not a simple task, but today an administration needs to deal directly with an increasing number of members. Complicating the task is the weakening of party and ideological ties, and the lack of a broad-based national foreign policy consensus. Thus the Carter administration had to mobilize votes issue by issue during the 95th Congress. In the United States Senate, it won five major foreign policy-related victories in 1978: Panama, arms sales to the Mideast, lifting the Turkey embargo, the energy program, and foreign assistance. Just 11 senators said "yes" on all five, and only one was consistently opposed.

The Proliferation of Congressional Staffs

Finally, executive-congressional conflict arises from the increased role of foreign policy staff aides on Capitol Hill. Between 1947 and 1976 the number of personal and committee staff members increased more than fivefold.[23] Only a minority of the personal staff members handles substantive issues, and only a minority of these handles international matters. But expansion in these categories has at least paralleled the total increase. Between 1968 and 1978, for example, the number of staff aides listed in the privately published *Congressional Staff Directory* as serving on the four major foreign policy/national defense committees more than tripled — from 89 to 274. And in 1975 junior senators on these and other committees were given additional funds to hire people to support them in their committee work. Today most senators have at least one foreign policy specialist on their personal staffs — something that was very rare as recently as 15 years ago.

Staff aides provide members of Congress with close-at-hand expertise, which strengthens their capacity to engage knowledgeably on issues. One recent treatment dubbed them "the New Equalizers."[24] But staff aides also reflect and probably exacerbate the decentralization of the Congress because in most cases their power springs from a relationship with a single legislator. This is true by definition for personal staffs. It is usually also true for committee aides, since without the confidence of an important committee member they tend to be limited to routine functions. This does not mean, however, that the interest of each aide is identical to that of his or her legislative patron. Indeed, as legislators' schedules become more burdened, as the number of staff members increases, substantive and political communication between legislator and aide becomes progressively more difficult. The legislator has less feel for the nuances of "his" issues; aides have, out of necessity, considerably greater freedom in day-to-day action, and this makes them independently influential actors. Overburdened legislators tend increasingly to deal substantively with one another through their staffs, making the Congress a less collegial place than it was 15 or 25 years ago.

Do staff aides use their influence to mediate interbranch conflict or to generate it? Obviously, they do both. Foreign policy experts on Capitol Hill who speak the same language as executive branch officials certainly can facilitate compromise on particular issues, though sometimes at the cost of pushing the legislator a bit to one side — he doesn't always "speak the same language" or have the time to learn it. Substantive staffs can also provide a capacity for advance planning. In 1977, for example, pro-SALT Senate aides organized interchanges with executive branch counterparts on strategic arms control. This was followed by a similar effort by their bosses; a group of 17 senators began meeting semimonthly in the office of Majority Whip Alan Cranston (D-Calif.) to prepare for the anticipated ratification debate.

But often staff members are not so much objective analysts as conduits for information packaged by special interests. As one of the best informed analysts of staff politics concludes, "Congress has become just as incapable of evaluating the biases in the information from its own staffs as it has from sources outside Congress." [25] Moreover, staff members have strong stakes in generating new proposals that challenge executive policies; there is a "web of self-interest binding Members and their staffs to the fate of 'their' common programs: Members want bills with their names on them; the staff wants to 'cast a shadow.'" [26] Henry Jackson's amendments on Soviet trade and strategic arms were vehicles not just for the senator but for his influential national security aide, Richard Perle, as well. In fact, a staff member typically has much stronger stakes in pushing any particular proposal than does his boss since the legislator will have a number of policy aides and a number of initiatives pending.

Ultimately, of course, a staff member's impact is limited by the willingness of his or her boss to become involved in particular substantive issues. But usually staff pressure is toward increasing such involvement. This generates more executive-congressional conflict, for better and for worse. As a result, activist staffs often increase the workload of members of Congress, though one frequent argument for staffs is that they help relieve that burden.

MANAGING CONFLICT

Ideally, suggestions for coping with executive-congressional foreign policy conflict would be preceded by some statement of what the optimal level of conflict is. In practice, this seems impossible. Substantively, the answer varies with one's degree of satisfaction with prevailing policies. Politically and procedurally, one can point to a range of advantages and disadvantages of executive-congressional conflict, but there is no easy formula to aggregate them.

Congress fuels decentralization in American foreign policymaking, thereby contributing to innovation and policy entrepreneurship. Conflict raises the level of public consciousness about issues, generates information, and often brings to prominence previously neglected interests. The threat of a congressional rebuff may constrain the executive in the short run, but it also may make policy more soundly based in the longer run, for this threat forces the executive into a more active public explication of its policies and helps limit the gap between those policies and public understanding and preferences.

Sometimes diplomatic benefits accrue from executive-congressional conflict. Panama certainly conceded more because of the need for Senate ratification, and more than once a "threat" of unfavorable congressional action has induced Japan to make trade concessions. Last but not least, policy conflict helps to protect us from arbitrary government power.

But executive-congressional conflict can also do serious damage to foreign policy. One detrimental byproduct is *tactical inflexibility*. The more an administration is hemmed in by congressional restrictions, the less it can pursue subtle policies or conduct delicate negotiations with particular countries and regions. Another negative byproduct is *policy unpredictability*. Foreign officials increasingly respond to U.S. diplomats: "Ah yes, no doubt that is your government's intention, but what will Congress do?"[27] Such uncertainty undermines presidential credibility and U.S. diplomatic credibility generally. It is one thing to be constrained by a Congress whose will one knows or can reasonably predict. In 1967 Lyndon Johnson could check quietly with former Senate Armed Services Chairman Richard Russell (D-Ga.) on how far he should commit the United States to reversion of Okinawa to Japan; when the chairman counseled caution, Johnson could limit himself to moderate steps without advertising his impotence. But it is quite another matter to get comparably authoritative signals today.

These consequences of executive-congressional conflict are part of the enormous larger problem of achieving purposive and coherent foreign policies, such as are necessary to make headway on urgent world problems like arms control and international economic recovery.[28] My judgment is that the pendulum swung too far in the seventies, that the policy costs of conflict and decentralization became too great. Others will disagree. In any case, prescriptions for conflict management must respond to its sources, and each of the *roots* of conflict analyzed earlier suggests *routes* to its resolution that can be pursued by official "conflict managers": the leaders of both branches, but primarily the president and his senior foreign policy aides.

Dealing with Substantive Differences

If conflict arises from differing substantive policy preferences, policy leaders have three options: they can *adjust* by acceding to, or compromising with, opposing views; they can seek to *persuade* others to change their views; or they can seek to *override* their adversaries by mobilizing a winning coalition against them. In practice, leaders often employ some combination of all three.

Adjustment can be tactical or strategic. In the first instance, a concession is made on a detail without changing the central policy thrust, as when the Carter administration accepted several Senate amendments and reservations to the Panama treaties. The hope was that these token modifications would prove tolerable to Panama and win Senate ratification votes in Washington. A strategic adjustment involves something larger, an administration substantially changing its policy because of domestic constraints, or shelving a particular goal because it cannot win congressional acceptance or is unwilling to invest the political capital required to get it. An example of the first was the Vietnam policy shift begun in 1968 after the Tet offensive; an earlier example of the second was the deferral of serious China policy moves until "the second Kennedy administration."[29] Even if one prefers the president's goals to those of his adversaries, strategic adjustment is often very desirable. Better to devote one's energies to goals that are domestically sustainable than to begin with a sweeping set of initiatives, only to see most of them undermined by domestic strife.

Persuasion can be direct, through substantive communication with the legislators themselves, or indirect, through efforts to change public or elite opinion and thus the weight of arguments legislators read in the press and hear from their constituents. On Panama, the Carter administration launched a nationwide campaign of persuasion to counter broad public unhappiness with the treaties and balance the intense grassroots lobbying by treaty adversaries. It was generally believed that at least two-thirds of the Senate was willing to support ratification if the public political risks could be reduced. On SALT, by contrast, substantive skepticism was more entrenched in the Congress and portions of the national security community than in the nation at large.

A final option for policy leaders in dealing with substantive differences is to override their adversaries. When executive initiative is involved, this may mean simply going ahead with an action on the calculation that Congress won't later reverse it. Or if the issue is before the legislature, it means outvoting those whose support cannot be won at acceptable cost. (In some cases, of course, the prospect of being outvoted will make legislators more amenable to substantive bargaining.)

Coping With Political Interests

To the degree that substantive lines are clearly drawn and views are deeply held, policy conflict is a zero-sum game: one cannot simultaneously ratify the treaties and keep the "American Canal in Panama." But since policy actors have other, nonsubstantive interests, understanding these interests offers a route to conflict management that allows leaders to win substantive gains by helping legislators get nonsubstantive benefits. The political needs of senators and representatives can be understood and recognized as legitimate, rather than condemned. Leaders can seek ways of responding to these interests to build support for their policies.

If politicians depend on self-advertising and credit-claiming, then leaders can consider credit-sharing. Rather than portraying policy gains as the achievement of a few lonely individuals, as Nixon and Kissinger were wont to do, an administration can share the limelight with legislative leaders whose support is important to its goals. The classic example is the role of Senate Majority Leader Arthur Vandenberg from 1947 to 1949. Dean Acheson's description of the process is still worth quoting:

> Arthur Vandenberg . . . was born to lead a reluctant opposition into support of governmental proposals that he came to believe were in the national interest. . . . One of Vandenberg's stratagems was to enact publicly his conversion to a proposal, his change of attitude, a kind of political transubstantiation. The method was to go through a period of public doubt and skepticism; then find a comparatively minor flaw in the proposal, pounce upon it, and make much of it; in due course propose a change, always the Vandenberg amendment. Then, and only then, could it be given to his followers as true doctrine worthy of all men to be received. . . . [The stratagem's] strength lay in the genuineness of his belief in each step.[30]

And, Acheson goes on to explain, the Truman administration happily supported Vandenberg's formula for marrying his political interest to the administration's foreign policies.

Similarly, the Carter administration needed Majority Leader Byrd and Minority Leader Baker on Panama and wisely shared credit with them. Each enacted publicly his conversion to the treaties in a way that underscored the importance of his role. But because power in today's Senate is less centralized, meeting leaders' political interests is not enough. Thus more than 40 senators — with administration encouragement — went to Panama to see for themselves. And no less than 78 cosponsored the Byrd-Baker "leadership amendments" that incorporated in the treaty language concessions that Torrijos had made on the interpretation of U.S. defense rights.

This credit-sharing strategy, however, did not leave room for individual legislative entrepreneurship. When Senator DeConcini made acceptance of his reservation declaring U.S. rights to "the use of military force in Panama" the condition for his vote in favor of the treaties, the Carter administration was faced with a difficult choice. Still needing three or four votes, it may have compounded this difficulty by negotiating with DeConcini alone, rather than also engaging the leverage of Senate leaders.[31]

Another way that leaders can help legislators cope with politically difficult issues is to take some of the heat for them. Both Byrd and Baker played this role on Panama, and Byrd sought to do so on SALT II. Such a role can be particularly valuable on issues where there is strong interest group pressure. One of the reasons why Carter's special trade representative, Robert Strauss, quickly became popular on Capitol Hill was that he was perceived as coping very adroitly with industry pressures, thus shielding legislators from their full force. And Strauss's office was an institution Congress had established for that precise purpose. Executive lobbyists can also help by seeing to it that before an issue comes up for a vote a sympathetic legislator hears from important interests in support of his (and the administration's) position. For example, when Ford administration officials wanted to get Byrd to play an active role in moving the Trade Act of 1974 to enactment, they persuaded the United Mine Workers to cable him that they found the bill acceptable.[32]

A similar rule applies to ethnic and other specific interest groups. The more key executive officials are on good working terms with them and can maintain their understanding and basic confidence, the less they are likely to press legislators to override administration actions. To the degree such groups have strong substantive views, it may be very difficult to maintain that confidence while pursuing policies that they oppose. Middle East policy supplies the most obvious contemporary example.

Institutional Problems: The Limits of Consultation and Centralization

Congressional foreign policy leverage depends ultimately on handles that are blunt instruments — cutting off funds, rejecting or amending painfully negotiated treaties. The costs to foreign policy of actually employing these instruments are often severe, and this is recognized on both ends of Pennsylvania Avenue. One executive approach to this problem, pursued with particular frequency in the Nixon administration, is to try to put this monkey squarely on congressional shoulders. If the executive puts forward a fait accompli (bombing Cambodia or promising credits and Most-Favored Nation status to Russia), Congress cannot reverse the decision without publicly repudiating administration policy generally and thus undercutting "American commitments." This might be called the "chicken" approach to executive-congressional relations; it seems founded on the belief that even if Congress is not in on the policy takeoffs, a majority will not wish to risk being blamed for crash landings. All administrations pursue this course to some degree, but it has proved decreasingly effective as the presumption of executive rightness in foreign policy has weakened.

The alternative prescription, almost universally supported, is consultation among executive and legislative leaders as policies are taking shape.[33] This approach enables congressional views to be incorporated more smoothly and continuously. At its best, consultation offers a trade. Legislators get earlier entrée to issues and some degree of influence over them in return for some commitment to mobilize congressional backing for the policies that emerge; they advise as well as consent. Executive leaders give up some of their autonomy in exchange for strengthening the political base for their policies and reducing the dangers of being blind-sided on the Hill. Such consultation sometimes involves actual congressional involvement in negotiations: 26 senators, for example, went to Geneva in 1977 and 1978 as official advisers to the SALT II negotiating team.

But in practice consultation can quickly become complicated. One obvious problem is who should consult with whom. Close consultation can only work among a fairly limited number of people; otherwise, it becomes too cumbersome and too public. But whom does one choose in Congress? If the leaders of the chamber and/or the relevant committees can speak reliably for the Congress on a given issue, that is fine. Scrupulous detailed consultation with the Senate Finance and House Ways and Means Committees, for example, preceded formal Carter submission of his proposed Trade Agreements Act of 1979 and led directly to its overwhelming enactment. But Senate Foreign Relations was not comparably representative of the Senate on SALT. Nor is it always clear who represents the executive. Senior House International Relations Committee members protested in June 1978 that Carter administration divisions had generated confusion "as to what is U.S. policy on such issues as Soviet-American relations and Africa." [34] They weren't sure who, within the executive, could authoritatively consult with them.

There are other problems with consultation. Theoretically, an administration does not simply co-opt congressional leaders but allows them real policy influence. But if the president and his senior advisers cannot convey a clear and consistent sense of where they want to go and some political credibility concerning their ability to get there, they will discourage those inclined to cooperate and encourage those inclined to challenge. An administration may find that its genuine efforts to share information and influence win not cooperation but contempt.

Finally, the day-to-day costs of consultation may be greater to politicians than they appear at first glance. One cost is in time and attention — overtaxed resources that legislators must allocate with care. Thus, like busy people everywhere, "their own responsibilities force them to live and operate in the short run." [35] Consequently, legislators are reluctant to give detailed attention to a particular issue until they have to. Not surprisingly, those who consulted with senators on Panama in early 1977 found it difficult to get them to focus on the specifics that became so crucial in early 1978. The same was true on SALT a year later.

Even more important, perhaps, early engagement has costs in limiting political flexibility. Even those who expect ultimately to support particular treaties often find it safer to wait until the texts are completed and the initial political reaction comes in. Moreover, it should be emphasized that executive officials, including the president, may eschew consultations for similar reasons: they may want to maintain their flexibility. It is hard enough to manage an issue with a foreign country and within the executive branch without opening it up to congressional participation as well.

One means of encouraging prior consultation by the executive is the legislative veto. In legislation enacted in 1974 and 1976, Congress subjected certain presidential decisions on trade policy and arms sales to congressional override, thus encouraging the administration to check congressional sentiment before it proceeded. Successive administrations have opposed such provisions as intruding on presidential prerogatives, but they are less constraining than advance prohibitions written into law, and they do less collateral damage because they do not single out particular countries for negative treatment.

Decentralization is another institutional problem of congressional foreign policymaking. Here the counterprescription is obvious: strengthening congressional leadership. As already noted, recent reform has been mainly in the opposite direction, moving power from the committee to the subcommittee and individual member. The weakening of committee chairmen and the strengthening of the House caucus has opened up the possibility of increased power for chamber political leaders. As Bruce Oppenheimer shows in the preceding chapter, Speaker Tip O'Neill was able to expedite energy legislation by creating, in early 1977, an Ad Hoc Select Committee on Energy. The Speaker has also been given new powers over committee assignments and referral of bills. However, as Lawrence Dodd has noted, there is strong tension between congressional desires to maintain power for their institution — which point toward centralization — and members' interests in power for themselves individually — which pull them toward decentralization.[36]

Another means of combating congressional decentralization, in theory at least, would be giving the foreign policy committees greater authority and substantive reach. Ways and Means under Chairman Wilbur Mills provides a possible model — that of screener and broker for the whole House on issues within a broad jurisdiction.[37] The Bolling Committee Report of 1974 sought to move House Foreign Affairs in this direction. The application of this approach to current foreign policy, however, presents numerous problems. First is that of jurisdiction, which passes to Armed Services on military issues and to other substantive committees on most international economic questions. Second, the expanded role would require committees that reasonably reflect the range of views in their parent chambers, whereas Foreign Relations in the Senate and Foreign Affairs in the House tend to attract atypically liberal, internationalist legislators. Third, such a "solution" is dependent on the strength and political style of the chairman. Fourth and most important, many members today would view such a proposal not as a solution but as the sort of problem from which they had at long last freed themselves.

Finally, there is the possibility of establishing a new congressional focal point for foreign policy consultation and integration: the oft-proposed Joint Committee on National Security along the lines of the Joint Economic Committee or Graham Allison and Peter Szanton's proposal for a Committee on Interdependence in each house, without direct legislative authority but drawing its membership from the major standing committees.[38] While such proposals probably wouldn't hurt, it is uncertain how much they would help if the committees lack leverage within the Congress itself, as they certainly would without legislative jurisdiction. Thus, one analyst has argued the need to go further, to establish, by constitutional amendment, a Congressional Security Council empowered to "exercise congressional authority under specified emergency conditions." [39] But others worry that such a body might be too easily co-opted by the president, becoming "an instrument rather than a critic of executive authority." [40]

Since significant centralizing reforms are presently impractical, probably the best route for executive and congressional leaders is to build personal political alliances stretching across a range of issues. If leaders can work systematically and reciprocally to strengthen one another, some centralizing impact may be felt. The most important such alliance in the late seventies was that between the Carter administration and Majority Leader Byrd.

Rationalizing Congressional Staffs

What should be done about congressional staffs? The average level of subject matter competence among congressional foreign policy aides is probably considerably higher than among congressional substantive staff members taken as a whole. But they must respond to similar pressures because they work in the same basic environment.

If the magnitude of staffs generates conflict, one reform would be to reduce staff size. The only practical way to do this would be to cut overall staff funds available to legislators and committees, since the control of each over allocation of its funds will remain pretty near absolute. Another approach, not necessarily inconsistent with the first, is to concentrate on changing the balance among types of staff members to increase the ratio of experienced, nonpartisan substantive professionals to partisan advocates. These professionals would serve on standing committees and be custodians of process as well as experts trusted on both sides of the aisle; they would of course have their own views on issues, but would subordinate these to their primary tasks of supplying expertise and helping manage committee decision processes. Partisan advocates would remain on personal staffs and on investigatory subcommittees, but in reduced numbers. One oft-cited congressional model of staff professionalism is the Joint Committee on Internal Revenue Taxation, which has long supplied high quality, and highly respected, tax expertise for the tax writing committees of the two chambers.[41]

But it is far easier to brainstorm about what roles staff members should play than to make such roles work out in practice. Committee staffs get their authority from their relationships with the key committee members; responding to members' needs may drive staff members toward advocacy roles, whatever reformers might intend. If a staff holds to a nonpartisan, process role, most of the action may well pass to the personal staffs of member senators because the effectiveness of a "neutral" staff supplying expertise and managing process depends on a centralized committee decision process and a relatively strong chairman who values and enforces these staff roles. Thus, decentralization of committees means a decentralized advocacy process among members that fuels staff advocacy in turn.

A final approach to staffing, again not inconsistent with the aforementioned, is to strengthen staff institutions that serve Congress as a whole, in order to expand the quality and quantity of analysis at Congress's disposal. To this end, the Congressional Research Service has been upgraded, the General Accounting Office has moved from a relatively narrow auditing focus to program evaluation, the Congressional Budget Office conducts macroeconomic and budget analyses, and the Office of Technology Assessment studies subjects with important science and technology content.

The problem these institutions face, however, are well-known. Too often they must serve 535 masters, and yet their distance from these masters makes it difficult to establish the relations of trust necessary for involvement in members' urgent current concerns. Consequently, much time is spent on "quickie" drafting of speeches rewritten in the personal offices or putting out reports, often of high quality, that go unread. Because of these problems, these organizations have difficulty attracting and retaining top quality staffs whom legislators will respect and listen to as professionals. And thus they are unable, with the partial exception of the Congressional Budget Office, to supply the sort of visible, integrative analysis that might itself give structure and coherence to congressional debates.

CONCLUSION

Since executive-congressional conflict has multiple causes, there is no convenient single solution. The root of the problem is that Americans want things that are, in practice, contradictory. We agree on the need for coherent and purposive policies, but often disagree very strongly about the content of those policies. And we value our democratic political process in which differing policy goals and means contest.

The foreign policy problem is not to avoid executive-congressional conflict, but to manage it. Certain general remedies — institutionalizing consultation, strengthening staff expertise on Capitol Hill — are difficult to implement or have mixed effects. Others — strengthening leadership institutions — go against recent congressional reform trends. Nevertheless, this essay has tried to suggest, through analysis and illustration, how a better understanding of congressional interests and institutions can help in getting livable resolutions of foreign policy issues.

NOTES

1. Victor C. Johnson, "Congress and Foreign Policy: The House Foreign Affairs and Senate Foreign Relations Committee" (Ph.D. diss., University of Wisconsin, 1975), pp. 33-34.
2. J. William Fulbright, "American Foreign Policy in the 20th Century Under an 18th Century Constitution," *Cornell Law Quarterly*, 47 (Fall 1962): 7.

3. Compare, for example, the above-cited article with "Congress and Foreign Policy" written by J. William Fulbright in July 1974. This later article appeared in the *Report of the Commission on the Organization of the Government for the Conduct of Foreign Policy* (Murphy Commission), Appendix L, June 1975, pp. 58-65.
4. Letter from William M. Capron to Senator Frank Church, quoted in "Eating Crow at Mike's," *Washington Monthly,* September 1970, p. 50.
5. For a detailed description of this "revolution," see Thomas Franck and Edward Weisband, *Foreign Policy by Congress* (New York: Oxford University Press, 1979).
6. There was even a third Fulbright formulation, arguing for "leaving to the executive the necessary flexibility to conduct policy within the broad parameters approved by the legislature." See J. William Fulbright, "The Legislator as Educator," *Foreign Affairs,* (Spring 1979): 726.
7. See I. M. Destler, "Trade Consensus, SALT Stalemate: Congress and Foreign Policy in the Seventies," in *The New Congress,* ed. Thomas Mann and Norman Ornstein (Washington, D.C.: American Enterprise Institute for Public Policy Research, 1981).
8. Richard Neustadt, *Presidential Power* (New York: Signet, 1964), p. 42.
9. Nelson W. Polsby, "Policy Initiation in the American Political System," in *Perspectives on the Presidency,* ed. Aaron Wildavsky (Boston: Little, Brown & Co., 1975), p. 229; Alton Frye, "Congress and President: The Balance Wheels of American Foreign Policy," *Yale Review,* 69 (Autumn 1979): pp. 6-7.
10. *The Federalist,* No. 70, Modern Library edition, p. 454.
11. Ibid., p. 455.
12. Richard F. Fenno, Jr., *Congressmen in Committees* (Little, Brown & Co., 1973), pp. 9-13.
13. David R. Mayhew, *Congress: The Electoral Connection* (New Haven: Yale University Press, 1974), Part I.
14. A detailed account appears in Paula Stern, *Water's Edge: Domestic Politics and the Making of American Foreign Policy* (Westport, Conn.: Greenwood Press, 1979).
15. Emmet John Hughes, *The Ordeal of Power* (New York: Atheneum Publishers, 1963), pp. 143, 144. Eisenhower added: "We talk about the French not being able to govern themselves, and we sit here wrestling with a Bricker Amendment."
16. See I. M. Destler, "Treaty Troubles: Versailles in Reverse," *Foreign Policy* 33 (Winter 1978-79): 45-65.
17. A comparison of relatively close House votes on foreign economic assistance from 1966 to 1977 yields the following. During the Johnson administration, 68 to 78 percent of Democrats voted aye, compared to 29 to 39 percent of Republicans. Under Nixon and Ford, Democratic support dropped to 54 to 67 percent, while Republican support rose to 39 to 59 percent. The two votes examined in the Carter administration show Democratic support at 62 and 70 percent, Republican at 39 and 44 percent.
18. Fulbright, "Congress and Foreign Policy," p. 59.
19. Thomas Schelling, "PPBS and Foreign Affairs," Senate Government Operations Subcommittee on National Security and International Operations, 1968, p. 2.
20. Fenno, *Congressmen in Committees,* p. 30.
21. See I. M. Destler, *Making Foreign Economic Policy* (Washington, D.C.: Brookings Institution, 1980), pp. 77-82.

22. See Randall B. Ripley, "Congressional Party Leadership and the Impact of Congress on Foreign Policy," *Murphy Commission Report,* Appendix L, p. 49.
23. Harrison W. Fox, Jr. and Susan Webb Hammond, *Congressional Staffs: The Invisible Force in American Lawmaking* (New York: The Free Press, 1977), p. 171.
24. Frederick Poole, "Congress v. Kissinger: The New Equalizers," *Washington Monthly,* May 1975, pp. 23-32.
25. Michael J. Malbin, "Congressional Committee Staffs: Who's in Charge Here?" *The Public Interest* (Spring 1977): 19.
26. Ibid, p. 38.
27. John Lehman, *The Executive, Congress and Foreign Policy: Studies of the Nixon Administration* (New York: Praeger Publishers, 1976), p. x.
28. For an extended analysis of the problem of organizing the executive branch for such policies, see I. M. Destler, *President, Bureaucrats, and Foreign Policy* (Princeton, N.J.: Princeton University Press, 1972 and 1974).
29. Roger Hilsman, *To Move a Nation* (New York: Doubleday & Co., 1967), chap. 24.
30. Dean Acheson, *Present at the Creation: My Years at the State Department* (New York: W. W. Norton & Co., 1969), p. 223.
31. Destler, "Treaty Troubles," esp. pp. 60-61.
32. Destler, *Making Foreign Economic Policy,* p. 186. On the executive-congressional relations of trade, see also Robert A. Pastor, *Congress and the Politics of U.S. Foreign Economic Policy: 1929-1976* (Berkeley: University of California Press, 1980), Part II.
33. For a number of proposals to improve executive-congressional consultation, see "Congress and Foreign Policy," *Report of the Special Subcommittee on Investigations of the House Committee on International Relations,* January 2, 1977.
34. Letter of June 7, 1978, to President Jimmy Carter from 14 members of the House International Relations Committee, released by the committee. The committee was renamed "Foreign Affairs" in 1979.
35. Charles O. Jones, "Why Congress Can't Do Policy Analysis," *Policy Analysis* (Spring 1976): 261.
36. Lawrence C. Dodd, "Congress and the Quest for Power," in *Congress Reconsidered,* 1st ed., edited by Lawrence C. Dodd and Bruce I. Oppenheimer (New York: Praeger Publishers, 1977), pp. 289-297.
37. See John F. Manley, *The Politics of Finance* (Boston: Little, Brown & Co., 1970) and Fenno, *Congressmen in Committees.*
38. Graham Allison and Peter Szanton, *Remaking Foreign Policy: The Organizational Connection* (New York: Basic Books, 1976), pp. 110-111.
39. Dodd, "Congress and the Quest for Power," p. 303.
40. Arthur Schlesinger, Jr., "The Role of the President in Foreign Policy," *Murphy Commission Report,* Appendix L, p. 40.
41. Malbin, "Congressional Committee Staffs," pp. 20-25. Malbin puts forward the idea of "dual staffing"; committees might have a "core of nonpartisan professionals on the staff, supplemented by partisan slots controlled by the majority and minority." For his full analysis, see Michael J. Malbin, *Unelected Representatives: Congressional Staff and the Future of Representative Government* (New York: Basic Books, 1980).

14

Congressional Oversight: Structures and Incentives

Morris S. Ogul

Legislative oversight of the bureaucracy involves some of the most complex forms of behavior that Congress undertakes.[1] Oversight — defined as behavior of legislators, individually or collectively, formally or informally, that affects bureaucratic behavior in policy implementation — is less understood than almost any other aspect of congressional behavior. This lack of understanding results in large part from a reliance by political analysts on the "conventional wisdom" about legislative oversight, a wisdom that blinds us to the reality of oversight activity.

LEGISLATIVE OVERSIGHT: THE CONVENTIONAL WISDOM

Like Pavlov's dog, Congress responds to cries for more and better legislative oversight of the bureaucracy by practicing its own form of salivation: Congress provides itself with more staff, increases budgets for committees, buttresses its information collection facilities, and issues itself more detailed instructions to do a better job. With equal predictability, these measures fail to close or even significantly narrow any perceived oversight gap in either its quantitative or qualitative dimensions. And so the pursuit of effective oversight goes on. If the plot seems circular or the theme repetitive, that is because it is. The conventional wisdom of Congress prevails: vote more authority, hire new staff, increase committee budgets, and add to information resources. The conventional wisdom at work can be illustrated by watching Congress prescribe itself invigorating potions through grants of additional authority to oversee.

Legislative Authority

The formal history of legislative oversight is frequently said to begin with Section 136 of the Legislative Reorganization Act of 1946:

> To assist the Congress in appraising the administration of the laws and in developing such amendments or related legislation as it may deem necessary, each standing committee of the Senate and the House of Representatives shall exercise continuous watchfulness of the execution by the administrative agencies concerned of any laws, the subject matter of which is within the jurisdiction of such committee; and, for that purpose, shall study all pertinent reports and data submitted to the Congress by the agencies in the executive branch of the Government.

Congress amended this provision in the Legislative Reorganization Act of 1970, and four years later the House of Representatives modified its rules and procedures concerning oversight, establishing general and special oversight responsibilities for committees and subcommittees. This repeated tinkering with legislative authority suggests continual congressional concern with oversight and dissatisfaction with the performance of the function. The most interesting question about this evolution is: Do additions to legislative authority to oversee affect legislative behavior? Although research on oversight is too scanty to support firm conclusions, the evidence points toward a modest impact of authority on behavior. Most of the approximately 40 members of Congress interviewed during the mid-1960s believed that the Legislative Reorganization Act of 1946 created a full and direct obligation to oversee. In addition, they saw that obligation as appropriate for the Congress. In brief, members believe that systematic oversight *ought* to be conducted.

Why then the continuing gap between expectations and behavior? One possible explanation is that members do not really believe in oversight; they only say that they do. Interviewing suggests that such is not the case. A second reason for the gap between expectations and behavior might lie in the nature of the expectations. The plain but seldom acknowledged fact is that systematic, all-inclusive oversight is simply impossible to perform. No amount of congressional dedication and energy, no conceivable increase in the size of committee staffs, and no boost in committee budgets will enable Congress to oversee policy implementation in a comprehensive and systematic manner. The job is too large for the members and staff to master. A third explanation is that factors other than a general desire to oversee often govern members' behavior. In particular situations, such as when members hold a key position on a committee or subcommittee, they could realistically do something about oversight. But multiple priorities as well as policy preferences influence their decisions, and oversight may not be their major concern.

Committee Staffing

A second recommendation almost guaranteed to emerge from congressional self-examinations is to increase the size of committee staffs. Former Representative Roman Pucinski (D-Ill.) defended this position:

> I am suggesting a substantial increase in committee staffs of professional people because it is becoming abundantly clear that within the framework of our present facilities, more and more the legislative branch of our Government must rely on the executive branch as the basis for information on which to judge legislation.[2]

Legislative reforms tend to reflect this feeling. The 1946 Legislative Reorganization Act stipulated four professional and six clerical staff persons for each committee except for Appropriations. The reorganization act in 1970 called for six professional and six clerical staffers. H. Res. 988, effective in January 1975, set staff size at 18 professional and 12 clerical persons except for two House committees, Appropriations and Budget. The actual size of committee staffs is usually much larger. Figure 14-1 depicts the growth of committee staffs.

The figures are clear but their consequences are not. There is no hard evidence to suggest any strong correlation between the size of committee staffs and the quantity or quality of legislative oversight of the bureaucracy. Members seldom correlate staff size and effectiveness. Interviews of staff persons conducted for the House Select Committee on Committees found that "professional staff people themselves did not feel that, in the main, their own staff operations were too small."[3] A discussion of the rise of congressional committee spending and of the increase in information resources yields the same pattern. In each case, the figures go up but the basic deficiencies in the performance of legislative oversight remain. The conventional wisdom about legislative oversight does not resolve the dilemma of how to get more and better oversight.

THE JUDICIARY COMMITTEE AND CIVIL RIGHTS

The deficiencies of conventional wisdom concerning oversight become even more apparent when we look at committee behavior. The

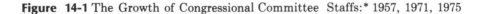

Figure 14-1 The Growth of Congressional Committee Staffs:* 1957, 1971, 1975

Number of Committee Staffers

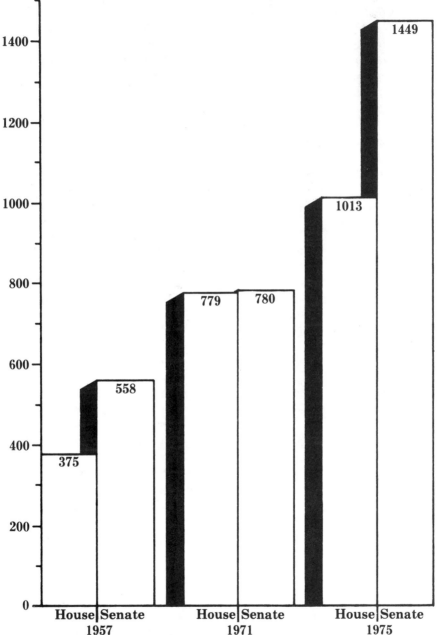

House | Senate
1957

House | Senate
1971

House | Senate
1975

* Includes standing, select, and special committees.

SOURCE: Data presented in Harrison W. Fox, Jr. and Susan Webb Hammond, *Congressional Staffs* (New York: The Free Press, 1977), pp. 169-170.

civil rights oversight activities from 1965 to 1967 of the House Judiciary Committee, especially subcommittee no. 5, the subcommittee that was assigned jurisdiction in this area, provide a good example. The committee suffered no lack of authority to oversee in the area of civil rights. The committee staff was substantial, as both members and staff persons attested:

> The staff is adequate for our activities.
>
> If other staff members were added, they would be drawn toward the current activities of the committee.
>
> More staff is not crucial because if we had more staff and they developed more materials, they would still have to come to us to act.
>
> There is plenty of staff to handle the problems in the civil rights area.[4]

Conventional wisdom would suggest that a committee with full authority, appropriate staffing, and an adequate budget would be an extensive and systematic overseer. Yet analysis reveals a strikingly different picture, one in which almost no formal civil rights oversight was being performed. The major exception might be the school guidelines hearings in 1966. An examination of these hearings is instructive.

Title VI of the 1964 Civil Rights Act permitted the Office of Education to cut off federal funds from programs that discriminated on the basis of race. Section 602 required that:

> Each Federal department and agency which is empowered to extend Federal financial assistance to any program or activity, by way of grant, loan, or contract other than a contract of insurance or guarantee, is authorized and directed to effectuate the provisions of section 601 with respect to such program or activity by issuing rules, regulations, or orders of general applicability which shall be consistent with achievement with the objectives of the statute authorizing the financial assistance in connection with which the action is taken. No such rule, regulation, or order shall become effective unless and until approved by the President. . . .

To implement this provision the Office of Education drew up guidelines in Spring 1965 and again in March 1966. Objections from many southern school districts, relayed through their representatives in Congress, were intense.

The clamor for the repeal or modification of Title VI heightened the demand for congressional oversight activity. The House Rules Committee in late September and early October 1966 held hearings on H. Res. 826, which called for the establishment of a select committee to investigate school guidelines and policies of the Commissioner of Education in school desegregation. Faced with a possible loss of jurisdiction, Judiciary Chairman Emanuel Celler (D-N.Y.), not previously enamored with the idea of civil rights oversight, now promised the Rules Committee a full and fair investigation.

Despite Celler's assurances, the Rules Committee voted to create the select committee provided for in H. Res. 826. Chairman Celler then promised to create a special judiciary subcommittee on civil rights if the Rules Committee, in exchange, would not implement the resolution. Chairman Celler fathered the Subcommittee on Civil Rights in November 1966. Hearings followed quickly in December. These happenings, bizarre in the context of previous committee behavior, were thus explained by committee members:

> We were sort of pushed into it. We were forced into it. We might have lost our jurisdiction if we didn't.

Thus the dual threat of a loss of jurisdiction and of the creation of a select committee not likely to be favorable to desegregation had moved the Judiciary Committee when internal pressures could not.

No report emerged from these 1966 hearings because, as Subcommittee Chairman Byron Rogers (D-Colo.) succinctly put it, "None is needed." Rogers demonstrated a notable lack of enthusiasm for civil rights oversight again the following year in the 90th Congress. "We will probably hold some hearings in this session. If we go into anything, it will probably be school guidelines," Rogers stated. (His subcommittee had been reconstituted as the School Guidelines Subcommittee, but its jurisdiction was still civil rights.) One staff member commented later, "The chairman is not particularly enthusiastic about having more hearings." And no hearings were held in 1967.

With the immediate pressure lessened and attention shifting elsewhere, the school guidelines subcommittee faded away. The Judiciary Committee had made motions toward oversight but only in the face of intense, immediate, and sustained external pressure. In this example of a formal oversight effort, the clear intent was to defuse external pressures rather than to probe and assess administrative conduct.

Formal Versus Informal Oversight

A sparse record of formal oversight from a committee that is highly active in a policy area suggests the possibility that informal oversight may be the prevailing practice. Interview evidence indicates that most members prefer informal methods of oversight where possible. Formal methods are seen as an indication of the breakdown of informal efforts. Only a distinct minority prefers formal methods of oversight as a first tactic.

Judiciary Chairman Celler saw his informal relations with those in charge of civil rights activity in the Justice Department as excellent.

Operationally, this meant that Celler agreed with much of what the Justice Department was doing and *that he was regularly and fully consulted by the department on civil rights matters.* Those Judiciary members who advocated more formal oversight had to persuade a strong and reluctant chairman that their views were correct. Their inability to do so is evidenced in what might be called the Kastenmeier caper.

Representative Robert Kastenmeier (D-Wis.), a member of the full committee and of subcommittee no. 5, advocated the establishment of a special constitutional rights subcommittee to deal with questions of civil liberties and constitutional guarantees. Concerned especially with the implementation of the Voting Rights Act of 1965, he asked Chairman Celler in September 1965 to create a special voting rights subcommittee. Kastenmeier and a few other members wanted a formal mechanism in the Congress for overseeing the implementation of the civil rights bills passed since 1957.

After complicated negotiations, a special ad hoc committee on civil rights that was to report to subcommittee no. 5 emerged in October 1965. The ad hoc subcommittee was to assess the desirability of establishing an oversight subcommittee. According to one committee member, "We were not encouraged to hold hearings." Informal conferences were held over six days with federal officials and with spokesmen for interested groups. Others submitted written statements for the record.

According to one staff member, no verbatim records were kept. Most of the testimony centered around Title VI of the 1964 Civil Rights Act, which provided for the withholding of federal funds under specified circumstances. According to Kastenmeier, "Throughout the conferences, it was the opinion of all parties that an oversight committee be established within the Judiciary Committee."[5] The ad hoc committee presented its report to subcommittee no. 5 in February 1966 and then disbanded. It made these four recommendations:

> *First:* That a subcommittee, existing or special, within the House Judiciary Committee be authorized and directed to attend to matters involving voting and civil rights on a continuing basis.
>
> *Second:* That such subcommittee be authorized to travel within the continental limits of the United States for the purpose of conducting appropriate on-site hearings and/or investigations.
>
> *Third:* That adequate funds for professional staff and for other purposes be obtained for such subcommittee.
>
> *Fourth:* That authority to require the attendance of such witnesses and the production of such books or papers or other documents or vouchers by subpoena or otherwise be obtained for such subcommittee.[6]

Chairman Celler did not implement the ad hoc committee's recommendations unilaterally. He had reportedly taken similar actions in the past but now referred the matter to the full committee, where it lay dormant. One staff member, attempting to explain the absence of a positive committee reaction, stressed the pressures of other business. Many observers were convinced that this explanation provided less than the whole story.

Why did this effort seem to fail despite the support of members who shared the chairman's views on civil rights questions? The answer can be found in some judgments about political efficacy. Chairman Celler, supported by enough members to kill the proposal, had apparently reached two conclusions. First, the net impact of formal oversight would probably be pressure for less enforcement rather than for more effective enforcement. Second, sufficient oversight was being carried on through informal means.

Latent Oversight

Those who accuse Congress of not doing much oversight may be seeing only part of the picture. A committee, while devoting its efforts to legislation and other activities, may be conducting some oversight latently. The presence of latent oversight — that accomplished while another legislative activity is ostensibly being performed — can be ascertained by looking at civil rights activities in the Judiciary Committee. Subcommittee no. 5, in the course of hearings on proposed legislation, latently gave some attention to oversight. The product of their efforts was less than systematic but more than minuscule.

Most subcommittee members and staff persons supported this latent presence:

> We achieve much oversight as we consider legislation. Hearings for legislation are the major instrument for performance of the oversight function on this subcommittee.

But others on the committee saw the formal distinction between legislation and oversight as an accurate reflection of behavior:

> Our big question is legislation. This is what we spend our time on. We are not primarily an oversight committee.

> The Congress hears too little of the widespread activities undertaken under these statutes. Most pertinent data on civil rights are presented in hearings on the current year's proposals.

How much oversight goes on in legislative hearings can only be determined by an examination of the record. A careful reading uncovered enough examples of oversight to merit attention but only enough to modify slightly the earlier generalization about the committee's oversight activities. An analysis of committee oversight —

formal and informal, manifest and latent — provides a more useful and complete picture of oversight than the formal record of investigations alone yields.

Why So Little Oversight?

How did the Judiciary Committee members explain the absence of systematic oversight? Most asserted that the committee was simply too busy legislating to do much overseeing. Some data does build a prima facie case. In the 89th Congress (1965-66) the Judiciary Committee was given responsibility for 35.8 percent of all measures introduced in the House of Representatives.[7] Included were such items as constitutional amendments on presidential inability, voting rights bills, measures proposing assistance for law enforcement agencies, bail reform proposals, and assorted civil rights bills. Subcommittee no. 5 held hearings on 371 bills, including the proposed voting rights act for which there were 13 sessions of hearings, 4 days of subcommittee deliberation, and 11 days of full committee deliberation.[8] On the proposed civil rights bill of 1966, the subcommittee held 10 days of hearings, deliberated on the bill for 6 days, and sent the bill to the full committee, which devoted 9 sessions to it.[9]

The record confirms that the Judiciary Committee was, in fact, extraordinarily busy and productive on civil rights and other questions. The usual excuse offered by members of many committees — we are too busy legislating — did have some validity here. But even on this committee an element of rationalization loomed large. The committee did not oversee very much, partly because of the press of its schedule but mainly because its leadership, firmly in control of events, wanted to limit the scope of oversight efforts.

During this period Chairman Celler was the dominant force on the committee, and he wanted little oversight effort. Why? The reasons were to be found in the interaction between personal, policy, and partisan factors — surely one of the most potent packages conceivable.

Personal Power. Chairman Celler had great respect for Justice Department officials with responsibilities for civil rights matters. They, in turn, consulted him with all the deference due to a powerful patriarch of the House of Representatives who had the added virtue of being the dominant voice on his committee. Consultation here was more than ritualistic. Instead, Celler's views seemed to be given great weight. Sometimes rudeness, slights, and lack of attention provide added incentives to oversee; Celler lacked these spurs to action.

Policy Preferences. If oversight efforts more frequently flow from policy disagreements than from policy consensus, then little oversight was to be expected here. Celler and Justice Department officials basically agreed about what needed to be done and about how to proceed. Moreover, Celler genuinely feared that formal oversight efforts in civil rights might expand the scope of conflict and thus upset existing policy patterns. Because the issues were so volatile, Celler felt that oversight efforts would provide room for segregationists, and others whose views Celler did not share, to jeopardize constructive policy implementation in the Justice Department.

Partisanship. One member of the committee stated the issue succinctly:

> We are of the same political party as the president and, of course, we do not want to do anything to embarrass him unless there is something absolutely wrong with a program.

Thus, another incentive for oversight was removed.

The story seems to have two morals. First, the general obligation to oversee gives way before the specific realities of personal power, policy preferences, and partisan attachment. Second, motivations and incentives do a better job than structures in explaining the conduct of oversight or the absence thereof.

An Afterthought

In February 1971 Chairman Celler assigned jurisdiction for civil rights oversight to subcommittee no. 4. What accounted for a type of action that had been rejected previously? The answer was to be found in new circumstances. The flood of civil rights legislation beginning in 1957 had ended. A Republican administration was perceived by Celler as eroding established civil rights legislation. Celler's personal influence in the Justice Department had diminished.

In 1973, with a new committee chairman, Peter Rodino (D-N.J.), this new pattern persisted. When the Judiciary Committee ended its long-standing practice of having numbered subcommittees at the end of the first session of the 93rd Congress, one of the new units created was the Subcommittee on Civil Rights and Constitutional Rights.

INCENTIVES AND OVERSIGHT

The experience of the Judiciary Committee suggests two conclusions. First, the conventional wisdom concerning oversight provides an inadequate basis for analysis and reform. Second, granted a base of adequate resources — a situation that describes most committees and subcommittees in the Congress — the motivations of members are more central to oversight efforts than are structural factors. Increasing budgets, adding staff members, and gaining new authority may indeed help Congress to oversee more effectively in specific situations, but these acts cannot address the core problems because they ignore a central factor — member motivation and incentives to act. Focusing on member motivation and incentives, however fruitful, leads analysts rapidly into barely explored territory. A brief glance at two topics helps to sort out this incredibly complex problem.

The Multiple Priorities of Members

Each member of Congress is faced with a variety of obligations that are legitimate, important, and demanding of time and energy. In principle, members should be working hard at all of them, but since they do not weigh their obligations equally, they are unlikely to give them equal attention. Because the weights assigned change with status and circumstance, the interests of each member of Congress in oversight will wax and wane despite his or her belief in the importance of performing oversight. When action is perceived to contribute directly and substantially to political survival, it is likely to move toward the top of any member's priority list.[10] Extra incentives to oversee come from problems of direct concern to a member's constituents or from issues that promise political visibility or organizational support. Conversely, problems not seen as closely related to political survival are more difficult to crowd onto the member's schedule. In the choice phrase of one member, "Our schedules are full, but flexible."

In making their choices about what to do, members of Congress will do those things considered important to them at the time. As a result, oversight is frequently neglected. The price of multiple priorities is selective neglect.

Oversight becomes more difficult if most members assign a low priority to a committee's work. The House Post Office and Civil Service Committee (POCS) provides a spectacular example. Examining the committee from 1965 to 1967 from the perspective of conventional wisdom yields an opaque picture. In the years 1965-66 POCS had a staff ranging from 32 to 42 members, and its expenditures in 1965 alone were $147,418.24. Despite this, the overall operations of the committee were in such low repute that in 1973 the House Select Committee on Committees (the Bolling Committee) seriously considered abolishing it altogether. Examining the record of POCS through the lenses of member motivation can considerably clarify one's understanding of its oversight failures.

The low status of POCS in the House guaranteed that few would want to serve on it. In 1965 and 1966 most members of the committee did not want to be there. Two members spoke for their peers:

> I didn't really choose the committee. It was assigned to me.

> I was assigned to this committee. I will get off of it as fast as I can.

Members of the committee left it in droves as soon as seniority permitted. Low initial attractiveness and high turnover meant relatively uninformed and largely indifferent members.

Almost all POCS members were assigned to more than one standing committee, and some 80 percent of these members listed POCS as their second priority. The consequences were predictable. Those who remained on the committee seldom did so because of an intense interest in its subject matter. More particularistic reasons governed their behavior.

On low-status committees, such as this one, subcommittee chairmanships tend to come rather quickly. Some enjoyed their perquisites of power and stayed to maintain them. Others stayed to guard specific interests in their district. Some found the slow pace of the committee appealing. Some were linked to committee-oriented interest groups vital to their re-election. Motivation here for comprehensive or systematic oversight was modest. The close ties of many of the "stayers" to interest groups, primarily postal employee organizations and associations of mail users, provided strong incentives to attend primarily to two aspects of committee jurisdiction: employee wages and benefits and the mail rates of user groups.

Policy Preferences

The relationship between policy preferences and the motivation to oversee is intimate. Interviews across several committees revealed that members of Congress are seldom eager to monitor those executive activities of which they approve. A member who is indifferent to a program seldom presses for oversight. But disagreement on policy provides an important incentive to oversee. Almost all members feel a general obligation to oversee; the behavioral consequences are slight. When that responsibility merges with policy disagreement, oversight is much more likely.

The ties between policy preferences and oversight were spectacularly clear in the Judiciary Committee case study. This committee was an able group; many of its members were vitally interested in civil rights policymaking and administration. Because Chairman Celler approved of what the Justice Department was doing, his committee did very little formal overseeing in the period studied. The absence of oversight could be explained by a simple formula: when policy preferences and the general obligation to oversee lead in differing directions, policy preferences normally prevail as a guide to conduct.

Structures, Resources, and Incentives

Why do so many members of Congress still approach oversight from a structural-resource perspective when the limitations of doing so are clear? The evidence suggests several answers: (1) Members have found that structural and resource changes can have some impact on what they do. (2) Structures and resources are tangible. Something can be done about them. Congress can readily require oversight subcommittees or vote more money for investigations. (3) Motivations are difficult to ascertain and may be politically dangerous to uncover. They are linked in exceedingly complex ways to behavior. They are frequently hard to do a great deal about. (4) Members tend to avoid painful topics especially when the costs of doing anything about them are high and the benefits uncertain. (5) Like all of us, members may not always assess their situation very astutely.

In the past most analysts preferred structural-resource approaches and solutions. But today Bibby, Fenno, Kaiser, Mayhew, Ogul, Price, Scher, Vinyard, and other political scientists recognize the central relevance of motivations and incentives.[11] Translating this relatively recent awareness into analytically fruitful projects is the next major step if research on legislative oversight is to take any great leap forward.[12]

The danger exists, however, of creating new straw men to replace old ones. A focus on incentives should not distract us from the importance of relating individual impact to personal *and* situational factors.[13] Not all members are equal in their abilities, nor are they equally well placed to pursue their interests successfully. Even an intense desire to oversee depends for its fruition on more than the individual member's wants. Individual members conduct very little oversight themselves. Oversight efforts are centered in the committees and subcommittees. Where one is placed in the committee system is a vital element in translating desire into performance. *A focus on the intersections between incentives and structures is imperative.*[14]

Members of Congress do what they do and slight what they slight for reasons that seem persuasive to them. The bases for choice are many. Balancing reasonable requests for time and action is central. Most members feel that they can justify much of what they do in terms that their constituents would find quite acceptable. Most staff members do what their employers, the members of Congress, want them to do. The incentives for conducting more intensive and extensive oversight are great in the abstract and modest in many concrete situations. Any analysis of legislative oversight has to be grounded in this reality.

In the face of imperfect performance, members of Congress still believe in doing a good job at oversight. Concurrently, many members seem comfortable while not doing much to narrow the gap between expectations about oversight and the actual performance of it. Many members are insufficiently dissatisfied with their oversight behavior to feel a strong enough stimulus to alter existing patterns.

How comprehensively Congress could do oversight and how systematic its efforts might be are questions that defy absolute answers. In relative terms, Congress can do more and better oversight. The primary question concerning legislative oversight of bureaucracy is not what Congress can do but what the members, individually and collectively, want to do and how badly they want to do it. Put another way, ask not only what oversight Congress *can* or *should* perform, but also what oversight members *want* to perform.

NOTES

1. For related comments on oversight, see U.S., Congress, Joint Committee on the Organization of Congress, *Organization of Congress,* Hearings pursuant to S. Con. Res. 2, 89th Cong., 1st sess., June 1965, pt. 4: 594; John Culver, *Committee Organization in the House,* Hearings under the authority of H. Res. 132, 93rd Cong., 1st sess., June 1973, vol. 2, p. 17; Theodore J. Lowi, "Congressional Reform: A New Time, Place, and Manner," in *Legislative Politics USA,* ed. Theodore J. Lowi and Randall B. Ripley (Boston: Little, Brown & Co., 1973), p. 371; and Roger Davidson, David Kovenock, and Michael O'Leary, *Congress in Crisis: Politics and Congressional Reform* (Belmont, Calif.: Wadsworth, 1966), p. 174.
2. *Organization of Congress,* August 1965, pt. 9: 1333.
3. Samuel C. Patterson, "Staffing House Committees," in *Committee Organization in the House"* (Paper prepared for the House Select Committee on Committees), vol. 2, p. 675.
4. All unattributed quotations are from interviews conducted by the author. Anonymity to the interviewees is assured.
5. U.S., Congress, House, *Congressional Record,* 89th Cong., 2nd sess., September 21, 1966, pp. 22547-22548 (daily edition).
6. Ibid., p. 22547.
7. U.S., Congress, House, Committee on the Judiciary, *Legislative Calendar, Eighty-Ninth Congress,* p. 9.
8. Ibid., p. 18.
9. Ibid., p. 19.
10. The best discussion of this problem is David R. Mayhew, *Congress: The Electoral Connection* (New Haven, Conn.: Yale University Press, 1974).
11. Richard F. Fenno, Jr., *Congressmen in Committees* (Boston: Little, Brown & Co., 1973); Davidson, Kovenock, and O'Leary, *Congress in Crisis,* p. 174; Mayhew, *Electoral Connection,* pp. 110-140; John F. Bibby, "Committee Characteristics and Legislative Oversight of Administration," *Midwest Journal of Political Science* 10 (February 1966): 78-98; Fred Kaiser, "Oversight of Foreign Policy: The U.S. House Committee on International Relations," *Legislative Studies Quarterly* 2 (August 1977): 255-279; Morris S. Ogul, *Congress Oversees the Bureaucracy* (Pittsburgh: University of Pittsburgh Press, 1976); David E. Price, "The Impact of Reform: The

House Commerce Subcommittee on Oversight and Investigations," in *Legislative Reform,* ed. Leroy N. Rieselbach (Lexington, Mass.: D.C. Heath & Co., Lexington Books, 1978), pp. 133-157; Seymour Scher, "Conditions for Legislative Control," *Journal of Politics* 25 (August 1963): 526-551; Dale Vinyard, "Congressional Checking on Executive Agencies," *Business and Government Review* 11 (September-October 1970): 14-18; Vinyard, "Congressional Committees on Small Business," *Midwest Journal of Political Science* 10 (August 1966): 364-377; Vinyard, "The Congressional Committees on Small Business: Pattern of Legislative Committee-Executive Agency Relations," *Western Political Quarterly* 21 (September 1968): 391-399.

12. A survey of recent research on oversight reveals increasing sensitivity to these problems. For some examples, see Joel D. Aberbach, "Changes in Congressional Oversight," *American Behavioral Scientist* 22 (May/June 1979): 493-515; Lawrence C. Dodd, George C. Shipley, and Philip Diehl, "Patterns of Congressional Committee Surveillance: A Comparative Analysis of the House and Senate, the 80th to 91st Congresses" (Paper delivered at the annual meeting of the Midwest Political Science Association, Chicago, Illinois, April 1978); Harrison W. Fox, Jr., Susan Webb Hammond, and Jeanne Bell Nicholson, "Foresight, Oversight, and Legislative Development: A View of Congressional Policy-Making" (Paper delivered at the annual meeting of the American Political Science Association, Washington, D.C., September 1-4, 1977); John R. Johannes, "Casework as a Technique of U.S. Congressional Oversight," *Legislative Studies Quarterly* 4 (August 1979): 325-351.

13. This point is made especially well by Fred Greenstein, *Personality and Politics* (Chicago: Markham, 1969).

14. Chapter 7 of Ogul, *Congress Oversees the Bureaucracy,* offers additional analysis leading to this conclusion.

15

Congressional Control of the Bureaucracy: A Mismatch of Incentives and Capabilities

Morris P. Fiorina

Recent political commentary contains numerous references to "out of control," "irresponsible," or "runaway" bureaucracy, and already this concern has had important effects. It has stimulated various reform proposals (zero-based budgeting, sunset laws, revenue and spending limits), helped elect Jimmy Carter, and made it increasingly difficult to tell traditional liberals from conservatives. Recent academic commentary also recognizes that the bureaucracy is not well-controlled, perhaps that it cannot *be* well-controlled. Stephen Hess contends that the attempt to manage the bureaucracy — in the sense of overseeing day-to-day bureaucratic operations — is a mistake modern presidents should avoid[1] and advocates instead a presidential role of agenda setting and policy (not managerial) decisionmaking. According to Peter Woll, the emergence of the federal bureaucracy adds a fourth dimension to the constitutional separation of powers.[2] His work attempts to come to grips with the bureaucracy's place in that system. Somewhat earlier Samuel Huntington wrote gloomily of the future of democratic assemblies in a world of large and powerful bureaucratic establishments.[3]

Although well-meaning reformers often construe such theses as justifications for institutional panaceas, such as sunset and sunshine

332

laws, zero-based budgeting, and executive branch reorganization, I doubt that the cited authors were advocating such institutional engineering. It is one thing to note that the bureaucracy is an important branch of the federal government, that it can develop and use political resources, that its expertise gives it an advantage in dealing with other branches of the government; it is quite another to claim that the bureaucracy is out of control. On its face, the claim may appear patently true, but on a deeper level it is mostly false.

WHAT IS CONTROL OF THE BUREAUCRACY?

The bureaucracy is not out of control because the Congress controls the bureaucracy, and the Congress gives us the kind of bureaucracy it wants. If some modern day James Madison were to conceive a plan that would guarantee an efficient, effective, centrally directed bureaucracy, Congress would react with fear and loathing. To be sure, particular members may wish to terminate particular agencies, but if the choice were between the existing bureaucratic world and the utopian bureaucratic world just conjured up, Congress would cast a nearly unanimous vote for the status quo. The parent loves the child, warts and all.

Theoretical and Actual Control

Obviously, I am playing on ambiguities in the concept of "control." First, we must distinguish between *theoretical* (formal or legal) control and *actual* (politically feasible) control. The Constitution divides formal control over the bureaucracy between the president and Congress, and the courts have come to play an important role as well. While nominally the president heads the bulk of the federal apparatus, his practical authority is rather modest. Civil Service and advise and consent requirements circumscribe his appointment powers. The president's personal agency, the Office of Management and Budget (OMB), is indisputably powerful, but once matters escape its clutches and get into the congressional arena, renegade agencies may defy their formal master. Lacking the rifle of the item veto, the president can only threaten the cannon of the general veto, and denizens of Washington can judge when he dares not fire the cannon.

Congress, on the other hand, has the formal power of life and death over the bureaucracy. Congress can abolish an agency or reorganize it, change its jurisdiction or allow its program authority to lapse entirely. Congress can cut its appropriations and conduct embarrassing investigations. A hostile Congress unconcerned about the consequences of its actions could decimate the federal establishment.

Of course, Congress seldom exercises its formal powers. In fact, such seemingly radical ideas as sunset laws and zero-based budgeting are merely attempts to insure that existing congressional powers are used more frequently or at least that their use is contemplated more frequently. As numerous observers have remarked, procedural changes alone are insufficient to increase control over the bureaucracy; to achieve their purpose such changes must also provide incentives to exercise that control.[4]

Coordinated and Uncoordinated Control

There is a second, more important ambiguity in the concept of "control." What kind of control do we want? Control for what? Imagine a naval fleet in which each vessel is under the absolute control of a chief officer. But suppose that these captains themselves are responsible to no higher authority and have no particular interest in communicating with each other. Well-meaning observers who watch such a fleet maneuver might judge the fleet to be out of control. They might even recommend measures intended to enhance control of the fleet's operation. Yet each commanding officer would greet such recommendations with skepticism; looking about his ship he sees no evidence of lack of control.

Like the individual ships in the preceding analogy, the *parts* of the federal bureaucracy typically are well-behaved in the sense that they are responsive to the captains in the congressional committees and subcommittees that determine their fates. But the *whole* of the bureaucracy is out of control, as is Congress.[5]

Thus, the second distinction is that between *coordinated* and *uncoordinated* control, or alternatively, *centralized* and *decentralized* control. When I remark that the Congress controls the bureaucracy, I use the term in the second sense.[6] Congress controls the parts, but there is little overall coordination. Particular congressional committees control the agencies they want to in the manner they want to. But those who address the problem of "control of the bureaucracy" have centralized or coordinated control in mind. How can the disparate parts of the bureaucracy be integrated? How can they be made to work in harness to achieve major policy goals?

The causes and consequences of decentralized control of the bureaucracy constitute the agenda for this essay. In the next section I will consider to what degree the bureaucracy is out of control and what can be done about it. Central to this discussion is a consideration of the incentives of the interested parties: the Congress, the president, the bureaucrats, and the electorate. Who can exert influence? To what end do they wish to do so? What kind of control will result? Answers to these questions provide a basis for speculating about the value of various suggested "reforms." In a nutshell, I will argue that the Congress has the power but not the incentive for coordinated control of the bureaucracy, while the president has the incentive but not the power. This mismatch between the incentives and capabilities of the relevant political actors is at least as important as informational overload, imbalance in expertise, and the internal processes of bureaucracies in explaining the absence of coordinated control of the federal bureaucracy.

MODELS OF COORDINATED CONTROL

New procedures are not necessary to achieve coordinated control over the bureaucracy. All necessary powers now exist. While this claim is hardly original, a review of its basis may prove useful. Models or idealizations of the political order will serve as the vehicle.

A Simple World

Assume that a new president were to take office with a large and reliable congressional majority, a majority that he could depend upon to "rubber stamp" his legislative program and budget. This president would first appoint his people to every executive political post not covered by Civil Service. The president's people at OMB then would make sure that all new proposals by federal agencies were consistent with the administration's grand design. With these steps the future operation of the bureaucracy would be brought under control. Meanwhile, in formulating the budget, OMB could bring existing programs under presidential control by starving those found to be inconsistent with his program or in extreme cases by having Congress abolish agencies and/or programs. By assumption, the Congress approves all such requests as well as the budget and proposed legislation.[7]

In this simple world the bureaucracy could be out of control only because mistakes are made, mistakes of program conception or mistakes in administration. Perhaps there is simply too much new legislation proposed or too little time to review existing programs. Still, such mistakes would be unlikely to persist for very long; rather, old mistakes would be remedied as they became apparent. There would be no chronic cases of out of control programs or agencies; in such a world any outright opposition could be broken. Programs could be abolished, agencies reorganized, executives fired, and civil servants transferred. All this follows from the assumption of a cooperative, compliant Congress.

A More Complicated World

But Congress is not a rubber stamp. Congress makes more than marginal adjustments in the president's program and budget. So, let us assume a more active legislative body. We now presume that the president's budget is submitted to businesslike appropriations and revenue committees, and that his program is submitted to expert legislative committees. But let us also assume that the authorizing committees have jurisdiction over all aspects of a policy question (other than appropriations), that such committees are representative of the membership of the whole chamber, and that the individuals who serve on such committees have as their primary goal the formulation of effective, efficiently implemented national policy. For good measure, let us presume that a powerful party leadership consciously coordinates the work of the authorizing, revenue-raising, and revenue-expending committees, and that individual members heed the party position because they believe in it and/or because their political fortunes are tied to it.

In this more complicated world I submit that again there would be little or no problem with out of control bureaucracy. The president and the Congress would each formulate coherent programs. Undoubtedly, these would differ in some respects, and in compromising the two, some incoherence might result. But the assumption of common affiliation to a cohesive party should exert a reasonably tight constraint on the amount of irrationality that creeps into the process.

The Real World

Ah, the incredulous reader may say, that's just not the U.S. Congress you're describing. Committee jurisdictions are a "crazy quilt." Congress is no place for the compulsively neat person. The national energy policy passed in 1978, for example, was worked over by five different House standing committees, then run through a rarely used ad hoc procedure. Moreover, congressional committees are anything but representative. The westerners head for Interior, farm district representatives for Agriculture, and urban representatives for Education and Labor and Banking and Currency.[8] This self-selection bias is then exacerbated by observance of reciprocity: the country people on Interior will keep their noses out of Housing matters, if the city people on Banking and Currency will do the same for public lands.[9] Suddenly, even common party membership is not sufficient to insure reasonable agreement between the program of the president and the programs of the congressional committees. And the worst is yet to come.

Implicit in the notion of reciprocity is the admission that members of Congress do not have as their primary goal the formulation of good national policy. That is a secondary goal; policy that benefits the district, and thereby re-election chances, is the primary goal. Consider two policy alternatives in some specific area. Policy X provides $100 in net benefits to each of districts 1-400, and costs districts 401-435 $1,000 each. Policy Y provides districts 401-435 with net benefits of $1,000 each but costs districts 1-400 $100 each. In terms of national net benefits the policies rank as follows:

Policy X: (400 x $100) - (35 x $1,000) = $5,000
Policy Y: (35 x $1,000) - (400 x $100) = −$5,000

Understandably, a president might support policy alternatives like X; if you want to make an omelet, you've got to break some eggs. And Congress? Typically, the representatives of districts 401-435 control the committee that chooses between X and Y. By enabling special interest members to gain control of their area of special interest, reciprocity insures that more policies like Y will be chosen than would otherwise be the case. And given that we are a large heterogeneous country, all members are special interest members in some areas. Thus, reciprocity makes it possible for a relatively greater number of policies like Y to defeat policies like X than would be the case under simple majority rule.

When we see a public agency spending inordinate amounts of public funds to pave over certain congressional districts, we are not observing an out of control agency. We are observing an agency that is paying off the members of Congress who nurture it. The federal agencies exist in a symbiotic relationship with the congressional committees and subcommittees to which they report. Of course, not everything an agency does is of concern to its set of relevant members. It purchases freedom in such areas by playing ball in the areas that are of concern. So, part of the agency may be genuinely out of control, but *Congress wants it that way.* It is a necessary cost of maintaining a bureaucracy sufficiently unconstrained (in law and by its nominal leaders) that it is permeable to congressional influence.

What do sunset laws and zero-based budgeting do in such cases? Little, really. Oh, on occasion they might force consideration of some overlooked program that no longer has any conceivable rationale. But the principal effect of such procedural innovations would be to shift more of the burden of proof from Congress to the bureaucracy, and thus make it easier for members to extort favors from the bureaucracy. If that's what we mean by control of the bureaucracy, fine.

The foregoing is a highly simplified argument, one subject to many qualifications, but that does not detract from its essential accuracy. If one is concerned about control of the bureaucracy, the critical questions do not revolve around the legal instruments of control.

These exist and are used regularly. The critical questions revolve around the fact that the Congress and the president do not want to control the bureaucracy for the same ends. The goals of the typical president and the goals of the typical member of Congress differ considerably. Consequently, what they want from the bureaucracy differs. And therein lies the problem.

DIFFERING INCENTIVES FOR CONTROL

Put most simply, the goals of the president lead him to prefer centralized control of the bureaucracy, while the goals of members of Congress lead them to favor decentralized control. Given the Congress's somewhat stronger position than the president's vis-à-vis the instruments of control, decentralized control prevails.

Presidential Goals

What are the goals of the typical president? Re-election comes most immediately to mind, but place in history is a close second. Fortunately for analytical purposes, the two goals often appear to be consistent. The president is the nation's chief official and responsible for major policy directions. Presumably, the president will attain re-election as well as a prominent place in the history books by dealing successfully with important national problems: attaining peace with honor, lowering unemployment, controlling inflation, ending crime in the streets, achieving racial equality.

Naturally, there are times (as former President Nixon so often reminded us) when the short-run bullet must be bitten to achieve long-range goals, times when re-election and place in history pull the president between them (e.g., energy policy circa 1978). But even when his goals are not completely consistent, the president usually desires to accomplish something in the way of broad policy goals. The president will not be content to sit in office and react to each specific problem or situation that arises. And in order to accomplish broad policy goals, the president must control the executive branch. (Many of the Nixon administration's more original shenanigans may be viewed, at least in part, as attempts to harness elements of the federal bureaucracy that were not under control of the administration.) As the representative of all the people, the president desires centralized control of the bureaucracy — whether to construct the national coalition he needs to win re-election or to make the major policy initiatives that will insure his place in history.

Congressional Goals

Members of Congress are in a different situation. Most of them simply wish to stay where they are, although House members are always on the lookout for a stray Senate seat, and numerous senators find personally compelling reasons to offer themselves as presidential candidates. With a few exceptions, place in history is an unrealistic goal for members of Congress. Each representative is a paltry one vote of 435. Unlike the president, a representative cannot credibly claim responsibility for putting the economy back on its feet or healing the wounds of a civil war. At best, several generations may remember him or her as the person who brought several sewage treatment plants to the district. Senators are in a somewhat better position, but even so they are merely one vote of 100, and how many twentieth-century senators can plausibly be said to have achieved a prominent place in history? No, for the member of Congress life is in the here and now. ("Now" is literally "now" for representatives whose lives are organized into two-year cycles.) The primary goal of members is figuring out how to survive the next election.

And survive they do! Since the Second World War about 90 percent of all incumbents have chosen to run for re-election and on average 90 percent of those have succeeded. Moreover, they have been getting even more successful in recent years.[10] How have they managed, given the erosion of traditional partisan sources of support and the increase in public cynicism toward government institutions and incumbents?

The Congressional Role

The key to this puzzle is a mid-century change in the congressional role.[11] As the scope of the federal government has expanded, the federal bureaucracy has enjoyed a concomitant expansion. Citizens in turn "enjoy" more opportunities to interact with their public servants, whether in an effort to take advantage of federal programs or to evade federal regulations. In this situation the member of Congress is ideally situated. Traditionally, if one has problems with the bureacracy, one writes one's representatives in Congress who have a long history of intervening in bureaucratic decisionmaking for the benefit of constituents. With the expansion of federal activity, the member of Congress's role as an intervenor — an ombudsman — has become more important. Objectively, there is a greater demand for members' services, and sensible incumbents have done little or nothing to stem that demand. In fact, some members, particularly the more junior ones, stimulate the demand for ombudsman services, seeing such activities as a means to reach those individuals in their districts who would otherwise oppose them on policy, ideological, or party grounds. In short, members are increasingly de-emphasizing their role as formulators of national policies — a controversial role, after all — and emphasizing their role as ombudsmen who strike fear into the hearts of incompetent or arbitrary bureaucrats.

In turn, citizens increasingly tolerate members' positions on major national policies. What does it matter if one's representative is a conservative or liberal, Republican or Democrat? One vote of 535 can't make much difference. But as subcommittee chairman or ranking minority member, the representative in Congress has been a whiz at getting water treatment plants and mass transit feasibility studies. Moreover, he or she kept the old coke ovens from being shut down by EPA and tracked down umpteen lost social security and veterans' checks. Why give up the incumbent's seniority and experience just because of disagreements about the MX or national health care?

How have members of Congress managed to carry out ombudsman activities so successfully? Simple. Congress has powerful instruments of control over the bureaucracy, and there is ample evidence that the threat of those instruments is seldom far from bureaucratic minds.[12] The effectiveness of those instruments is made all the more real by the establishment and maintenance of the elaborate committee-reciprocity system already mentioned. Members of Congress are given the opportunity to exercise disproportionate influence over segments of the federal bureaucracy that are of special concern to them. If an agency is causing problems for a member's constituents, the member need not organize a coalition of 51 or 218 members to discipline that agency. All that's needed is agreement from a couple of sub-committee colleagues. One can hardly blame an agency for paying special attention to "suggestions" from an interested member of Congress.

The Congress has had a standing committee system for more than 150 years, but the major trend of the twentieth century has been a decentralizing one.[13] The party leadership lost power to the committee leadership, which in turn lost power to the subcommittee leadership. All of this has occurred under the guise of democratic "reforms" to be sure. But we should not forget that the impact has been one of ever-increasing division of the power to control the bureaucracy. The House under Czar Reed (autocratic Speaker of the House, 1889-91, 1895-99) could and probably did exert coordinated control over a small federal executive. The House under Tip O'Neill and 175 subcommittee chairmen still can coordinate the activities of a much larger bureaucratic establishment — but it won't. Reed was willing to lose back-benchers who were forced to support locally unpopular party positions — breaks of the game. Today there are no back-benchers.

CONSEQUENCES OF THE STATUS QUO

The status quo in the last quarter of the twentieth century is not comforting. Citizens increasingly find themselves in contact with

a bureaucratic establishment, often federal or at least federally stimulated. This bureaucratic establishment is somewhat unresponsive
as bureaucracies are wont to be; at times it may be downright ca-
pricious. And every day it seems to extend a little further into citizens'
lives. But whether the bureaucracy is in the right or in the wrong,
citizens know that they can count on one powerful ally in their
attempts to triumph over bureaucratic procedures and/or dictates:
their member of Congress. Increasingly, citizens view members as
powerful, benevolent friends in an ever more threatening, impersonal
world. Citizens receive solace; members of Congress get votes.

Meanwhile, in Washington, Congress maintains a federal bureaucracy deliberately organized to make it permeable to congressional
intervention — not only to the chamber as a whole, but to subgroups
and even individuals. So long as an agency cooperates when members
make specific requests, it is unlikely to suffer long-term losses no
matter how poor its performance. Perversely, the more inefficient
and/or unreasonable its performance, the greater the political resource
it constitutes. It is no great exaggeration to say that if OSHA did
not exist, Congress might find it necessary to invent it.

And the president? He is something of the odd man out. His
personal appointees become the captives of the subgovernments they
were appointed to control.[14] He finds himself circumscribed at every
step. In the first flush of victory, throwing a net around "runaway"
agencies addicted to cement pouring seems like a fine idea. But
then Congress tells him that he can forget about a national energy
policy if he doesn't learn to keep his nose out of where it doesn't
belong. To obtain his goals the *president* must actively use a coordinated bureaucracy to achieve some positive purpose. But to achieve
their goals *members* often can do no more than fend off perceived
bureaucratic assaults on their constituents. This asymmetry would
put the president in a weaker position than Congress even if his
formal control powers were comparable.[15]

The described state of affairs has several important consequences
for the operation of the federal government in the foreseeable future.
First, *in terms of organization and administration,* we can expect
more of what we've got in the way of inefficient, "out of control"
bureaucracy. Congress has no electoral incentive to work toward coordinated control. Quite the opposite is the case. Congress is making
increasing use of instruments that keep the bureaucracy more closely
tied to decentralized congressional control such as the congressional
veto and sunset provisions. I think it is accurate to say that we
are currently experiencing an increase in uncoordinated control and
a decrease in coordinated control. Moreover, the dynamics of current
trends have a self-perpetuating aspect. The more that members of
Congress are perceived as, and elected as, ombudsmen, the greater

their incentive to maintain the status quo, and the greater their reluctance to agree to proposals that would make major changes in the direction of coordinated control.

Second, *in terms of policy,* we can identify certain biases that arise from conflicting presidential and congressional goals. A president may look fondly on proposals to replace the jerry-built structure of income security programs with a guaranteed annual income accomplished entirely through the tax laws. Or perhaps he might contemplate razing the educational grant structure and implementing a voucher system. In theory such programs hold the promise of reducing gaps and conflicts in the existing program structure while requiring fewer administrative procedures and allowing greater individual freedom of choice. They are naturals for presidents on the prowl for places in history.

But members of Congress have a different bias. Even if such massive program shifts resulted in no net changes in their constituents' welfare — admittedly an unlikely possibility — they would decrease the political resource base of members. If benefits are distributed automatically, constituents will expect them as their due and not treat them as the gift of their benevolent representatives in Congress. And if costs are imposed automatically, as with the collection of taxes, fewer citizens will seek the aid of members in efforts to avoid those costs. Of course, one should grant the possibility that the congressional biases are preferable to the presidential biases — as those interests vested in existing programs believe. Weighing biases, unfortunately, is much more difficult than identifying them.[16]

Finally, *in terms of political responsibility,* we can expect continued abdication by the U.S. Congress. In Theodore Lowi's compelling analysis, elected officialdom delegates power to the bureaucracy but provides vague or nonexistent standards for the exercise of that power.[17] Again the persistent theme appears. The bureaucracy can be out of control only because those charged with the responsibility to control it choose not to. Why do they so choose?

Lowi sees the roots of the problem in acceptance of a public philosophy that exalts flexibility over uniformity and dependability, a philosophy that holds that every problem should be bargained and brokered rather than settled according to a fixed rule of law. Perhaps. But why should this philosophy have such a hold on our decisionmakers? Lowi blames a generation of pluralist social scientists who laid the intellectual groundwork in the classrooms of academia. That is rather heavy stuff for a discipline that has been remarkably irrelevant to the conduct of political affairs. Still, ideas may take hold where we least expect.

Perhaps a more plausible explanation lies in the goals held by individual members of Congress. They adopt (or appear to adopt) a public philosophy based on pluralist tenets largely because it rationalizes what their political self-interest dictates. Woll makes the case nicely:

> A major reason for the power of the bureaucracy in policy formulation is the frequent lack of congressional incentives to adhere to the Schechter rule and establish explicit standards for administrative action. This is particularly true in the regulatory realm, an area involving political conflict that legislators often wish to avoid. Congress is always willing to deal *rhetorically* with problems requiring regulation and with the area of regulatory reform, but real decisions on the part of the legislature will undoubtedly raise the ire of powerful pressure groups on one side or the other that are affected by government regulation.[18]

Why take political chances by setting detailed regulations sure to antagonize some political actor or another? Why not require an agency to do the dirty work and then step in to redress the grievances that result from its activities? Let the agency take the blame and the member of Congress the credit. In the end everybody benefits. Members successfully wage their campaigns for re-election. And while popularly vilified, bureaucrats get their rewards in the committee rooms of Congress.

A public philosophy that holds that the bureaucracy should be granted the flexibility to deal with complex issues may seem to be the best way for an assembly of generalists to make public policy in a post-industrial society. But the entire justification of the committee-reciprocity system rests on the specialized expertise it purportedly fosters. Can we have it both ways? Can we *afford* to have it both ways?

THE (UNLIKELY) PROSPECTS FOR ENHANCING COORDINATED CONTROL

Postwar political science has been slow to embrace proposals for change in our federal institutions. For example, prior to the internal fracturing of the congressional seniority system in the early 1970s, professional students of Congress probably were more united in defense of that system than any other subgrouping of the population, save perhaps old members of Congress. And today, campaign "reform" proposals are far more controversial within our ranks than among the informed public. Radicals in our midst charge us with reactionary defense of the status quo, whether as an unconscious by-product of concern with scientific standards or as a conscious result of more sinister motives. Such theories are hardly necessary to explain the antireform bias of our discipline. History provides us with a distressingly long list of reforms that have failed to solve the intended problems, created new ones, and produced unanticipated side-effects. Our hesitancy to support reform reflects our uncertainty about the eventual consequences; often the devil that we know appears preferable to the one that we don't.

In this essay I have expressed skepticism about the consequences of currently fashionable concepts like zero-based budgeting and sunset laws. This skepticism does not imply approval of the existing situation. Procedural reforms like zero-based budgeting and sunset laws are better than nothing, but their impact will probably be marginal rather than major.

Those really serious about coordinated control of the bureaucracy must realize that the lack of such control is inherent in our electoral institutions. Hence they should be prepared to think big. For example, if they were permitted to make a single change in our federal institutions, they should consider replacing the single-member district system with a list system of proportional representation, treating the entire country as a single district. To elaborate, in every election each party would put up a list with a presidential and vice-presidential candidate, 100 senatorial candidates, and 435 representative candidates. Citizens would cast a single vote for the party of their choice. If one party got 55 percent of the vote, it would get the presidency, the first 55 candidates on its senatorial list, and the first 239 candidates on its representative list. The intended salutary impact of such a reform would be to bring the goals of presidents and members of Congress into closer agreement. To a much greater extent than before, both the president and congressional candidates would depend for election and re-election on the party's national record compiled over the same time period.

Of course, major change in the electoral rules is politically improbable and constitutionally almost impossible. Additionally, it might create a multiparty system and numerous other by-products. Changing the electoral system is both the least likely and the most risky of the conceivable alternatives.

A less radical means of bringing congressional and presidential incentives into closer agreement could be accomplished within the existing electoral structure by superimposing a responsible party system on it. I am familiar with the reasons why such a system would not be "good" for the United States.[19] But we had an approximation of such a system in the late nineteenth and early twentieth centuries. Can it be demonstrated that the country is governed better today than it was then? Of course, the question is academic. Those who await a resurgence of responsible party government have a long wait ahead. Party bonds in the electorate are weakening — an irreversible trend in the view of some scholars.[20] And candidates increasingly have divorced themselves from party organizations, an option that owes its attractiveness at least in part to the existence of decentralized control of the bureaucracy.[21] Advocating a responsible party system at this time is akin to advocating a strengthening of the presidency, which is another possibility we might consider.

Who has the incentives to exercise coordinated control of the bureaucracy? The president. Ergo, to increase such control we should consider ways to strengthen his hand vis-à-vis the Congress's. Scholars of the presidency are much like French generals in their capacity to overlearn the lessons of history. After working under Franklin Roosevelt, they spent two decades expounding the virtues of strengthening the presidency. Now, following the tragedy of Vietnam, the revelations of Watergate, and precedents for those excesses, everyone sees great dangers in a strong presidency.[22] A bit more intellectual evenhandedness would be desirable.

At any rate, given recent history and the attitudes formed in reaction to it, advocates of a stronger presidency are unlikely to meet with much success. It is difficult even to sketch the lines along which the presidency might be strengthened. Congress will not give up its existing powers. Thus, if we strengthen the ties between the presidency and the bureaucracy, we are more likely to increase stalemate than coordinated control. Recall too the fundamental asymmetry: to achieve his goals the president must take positive action, whereas members of Congress can do well enough by reacting and blocking.

Finally, we have the unlikely alternative of strengthening the Congress — as an institution, not as an agglomeration of 400 odd subcommittees and committees, amorphous parties, and institutionally weak leaders. The bureaucracy is subject to decentralized control because the Congress itself is so decentralized. Increasingly, the individual members can achieve their primary goals independently of (and even in opposition to) the ends for which the institution was created. As Fenno observes, we see candidates running for Congress by running against Congress.[23] What can we do to harmonize the desires of the individual members for re-election and the integrity of the institution as a democratic, policymaking assembly?

The trick involves making the fate of individual members more dependent on institutional performance and less dependent on their personal efforts.[24] One possible change would be to assign members to committees randomly, for a maximum tenure of, say, four years.[25] This innovation would curb the present practice of allowing members proportionately greater influence in areas of special concern to their districts. It should reduce the number of policies and programs that exploit a large part of the country (e.g., consumers) for the benefit of narrowly based interests (e.g., shoe manufacturers). Less able to play the role of district ombudsmen, members of Congress might have greater incentive to focus on national policy. They could at least hope that if their colleagues did the same, they all might come out okay. Of course, we would have to sacrifice the system of specialization that exists, but that may be a fair price to pay.

In the past, a great deal of imagination has gone into proposals for the reform of Congress. I hope that imagination still exists because, in the final analysis, an out of control bureaucracy reflects an out of control Congress. We might just as well avoid preoccupation with the symptoms and focus directly on the cause.

NOTES

1. Stephen Hess, *Organizing the Presidency* (Washington, D.C.: Brookings Institution, 1976).
2. Peter Woll, *American Bureaucracy,* 2nd ed. (New York: W. W. Norton & Co., 1977).
3. Samuel Huntington, "Congressional Responses to the Twentieth Century," in *The Congress and America's Future,* ed. David Truman (Englewood Cliffs, N.J.: Prentice-Hall, 1965), pp. 5-31.
4. Woll makes this point cogently in Chapter 4. See also Morris Ogul, *Congress Oversees the Bureaucracy* (Pittsburgh: University of Pittsburgh Press, 1976) and Seymour Scher, "Conditions for Legislative Control," *Journal of Politics* 25 (1963): 526-551.
5. For extensive development of this thesis, see Harold Seidman, *Politics, Position, and Power: The Dynamics of Federal Organization* (New York: Oxford University Press, 1975), chap. 2.
6. Francis Rourke has observed that it would be safer to limit this argument to the domestic policymaking bureaucracies. Revelations about recent decades raise doubts that the national security bureaucracies were under control in even the weak, decentralized sense. Rourke's point is well-taken, and no doubt my arguments do apply better to the domestic political scene. Still, one wonders whether the committee masters of the FBI, CIA, DIA, etc. were in fact as ignorant of their charges' activities as it appears from the record. See John Elliff, "Congress and the Intelligence Community," in *Congress Reconsidered*, 1st ed., edited by Lawrence C. Dodd and Bruce I. Oppenheimer (New York: Praeger Publishers, 1977).
7. Presumably, the serious president would also instruct his people to look very hard at entitlement programs, existing and proposed. An uncontrollable budget is hardly a necessary feature of reality.
8. Kenneth Shepsle, *The Giant Jigsaw Puzzle: Democratic Committee Assignments in the House of Representatives* (Chicago: University of Chicago Press, 1978).
9. Classic discussions of reciprocity are found in Donald Matthews, *U.S. Senators and Their World* (New York: W. W. Norton & Co., 1973), pp. 99-101 and Richard Fenno, *The Power of the Purse* (Boston: Little, Brown & Co., 1966), chap. 4. See also Roger Davidson, "Breaking up Those 'Cozy Triangles': An Impossible Dream?" in *Legislative Reform and Public Policy,* ed. Susan Welch and John G. Peters (New York: Praeger Publishers, 1977).
10. See Albert Cover and David Mayhew, "Congressional Dynamics and the Decline of Competitive Congressional Elections," in this volume. There is no indication that electoral fears play any major role in the retirement

upsurge since 1970. On the contrary, there is impressionistic evidence that the service orientation described in the text eventually wears down some representatives: what they feel they must do to hold their seat makes the seat not worth holding.

11. Morris P. Fiorina, *Congress: Keystone of the Washington Establishment* (New Haven: Yale University Press, 1977).

12. Richard Fenno, *Power of the Purse;* Aaron Wildavsky, *The Politics of the Budgetary Process,* 2nd ed. (Boston: Little, Brown & Co., 1974).

13. This statement should be recognized as an interpretation, not an uncontested fact. For an elaboration of the interpretation, see Fiorina, *Congress: Keystone of the Washington Establishment,* chaps. 1 and 7. For a more complex interpretation see Lawrence Dodd, "Congress and the Quest for Power," in *Congress Reconsidered,* 1st ed.

14. Thomas Cronin, *The State of the Presidency* (Boston: Little, Brown & Co., 1975), chap. 7.

15. It might appear that I am contradicting Huntington with this argument. Not so. Huntington claims that in a world in which the legislative initiative has passed to the presidency, *Congress* can exert its power *as an institution* only by acting negatively — by frustrating presidential proposals — which ultimately weakens the institution. In contrast, I am claiming that *members of Congress* can achieve their personal goals by acting negatively. The crucial point is that the personal goals of members bear a rather tenuous relationship to the constitutional purpose of Congress. In this connection see also Dodd, "Congress and the Quest for Power."

16. The time is ripe for a semi-serious revision of the prevailing view in the 1960s that the president was the representative of all the people, the sole custodian of the national interest. Congress, on the other hand, was then considered the stronghold of declining interests — small towns, rural backwaters, the South, etc. For this reason, we were told, the presidency was a more liberal institution than the Congress. See, for example, James MacGregor Burns, *The Deadlock of Democracy* (Englewood Cliffs, N.J.: Prentice-Hall, 1963). Today one could write that the president remains the sole representative of the national interest, and that the Congress remains the stronghold of declining interests — the cities, the Northeast, labor, etc. That is why the presidency is a more conservative institution than the Congress. The point should be obvious. One must be exceedingly careful when talking about the respective policy biases of the presidency and the Congress. Institutional biases need to be distinguished from those that arise from ephemeral constellations of political forces.

17. Theodore Lowi, *The End of Liberalism* (New York: W. W. Norton & Co., 1969).

18. Woll, *American Bureaucracy,* 2nd ed., p. 173. The Schecter rule refers to the 1935 Supreme Court decision *Schecter Poultry Corp. v. United States* in which the conservative court seized on the inadequacy of congressional standards and quidelines to negate a major piece of New Deal legislation.

19. See, for example, Julius Turner, "Responsible Parties: A Dissent from the Floor," *American Political Science Review* 45 (1951): 143-152.

20. Walter Dean Burnham, "Revitalization and Decay: Looking Toward the Third Century of American Electoral Politics," *Journal of Politics* 38 (1976): 146-172.

21. See Morris P. Fiorina, "The Incumbency Factor," *Public Opinion* (September/October 1978): 42-44.

22. For a critical analysis of scholarly writing, see William G. Andrews, "The Presidency, Congress and Constitutional Theory" (Paper delivered at the annual meeting of the American Political Science Association, Chicago, Illinois, September 7-11, 1971). Andrews takes note of the intellectual about-faces occurring even before Watergate. Since Watergate recantations have been running at flood tide.

23. Richard Fenno, "If, As Ralph Nader Says, Congress Is 'the Broken Branch,' How Come We Love Our Congressmen so Much?" *Congress in Change,* ed. Norman Ornstein (New York: Praeger Publishers, 1975), pp. 277-287.

24. Recall that national surveys typically find that 1/2 to 2/3 of the population approve of the performance of their members of Congress, whereas only 1/5 to 1/3 approve of the performance of Congress. The perception of a divergence between individual and collective performance is precisely the problem, although incumbent members understandably wish to maintain that divergent perception.

25. This is the proposal of Michael Nelson, *Washington Monthly,* December 1976.

IV

Congress in the 1980s

16

Congress, the President, and the Crisis of Competence in Government

James L. Sundquist

When President Carter came down from Camp David in July 1979 to talk of a national "malaise" and warn his countrymen that "a crisis of confidence" was "threatening to destroy the social and political fabric of America," he gave his political rivals in both parties an unintended issue. As the campaign got under way in the fall, Ronald Reagan was saying that there was no "failure of the American spirit," only "a failure of our leaders," that the people did not lack confidence in themselves but only in their government. And Senator Kennedy was throwing Carter's words back at him with, "the malaise is not in our people but in our leadership."

The implication, of course, was that confidence could be restored with a change in leadership. But the thesis of this chapter is that the problems of the U.S. government will not be solved by anything so simple as a change in leadership — or a return to office of the incumbent leadership, depending on one's preference. The American governmental system has built-in structural features that have always presented severe difficulties for any president who would provide the sought-after leadership. But deep-seated trends have been, and are, at work that will make effective government even more difficult to attain in the 1980s than it has been in the decade just ended and those that have gone before.

THE CRISIS OF CONFIDENCE

Every poll that has been designed to measure the confidence of the American people in their government has shown a precipitous decline in that confidence since the mid-1960s. No one disputed President Carter on that point. A few figures will illustrate it.

Consider, for instance, the findings of the Center for Political Studies at the University of Michigan, which has asked some questions in identical form and at the same time in each presidential election year. Persons interviewed in its national sample who expressed agreement with five propositions (chosen from a set of answers in a multiple-choice format) can be considered to be alienated from their national government: "you can trust the government in Washington to do what is right . . . only some of the time"; "the government is pretty much run by a few big interests looking out for themselves"; "quite a few of the people running government are a little crooked"; "quite a few of the people running the government don't seem to know what they're doing"; and "people in the government waste a lot of money we pay in taxes." Table 16-1 shows the averages of those who chose these answers.

The same general trend appears in answers to the Louis Harris poll question that asks how much confidence the voters have in "the people in charge of running" various institutions, both governmental and private. The percentage of respondents expressing "a great deal of confidence" has been going down for all institutions. Table 16-2 depicts the percentages for Congress, the executive branch, and what Harris calls nongovernmental primary institutions (an average of the responses on medicine, higher education, organized religion, the military, major companies, the press, and organized labor) as shown in polls taken at various times during the years indicated.

What were the causes? What has made people angry at their government? The polls have not asked that question directly, but they are a rich source of random clues, and anyone who lived through

Table 16-1 Growing Alienation from National Government

Year	Percent expressing alienation
1964	31
1968	40
1972	47
1976	61

SOURCE: Center for Political Studies, University of Michigan.

Table 16-2 Decrease in Confidence in Government and Private Institutions (In Percentages)

Year	Congress	Executive branch	Nongovernmental institutions
1966	42	41	49
1971	19	23	30
1973	29	19	37
1974	18	28	31
1976	9	11	24
1977	16	23	29
1978	10	14	29
1979 (Feb.)	18	17	24

SOURCE: Harris Survey data summarized in *Public Opinion* (January-February 1979): 24 and *Public Opinion* (October-November 1979): 30-31.

the decade can construct from those clues and from experience and observation a list of events that has contributed to bringing the competence and responsiveness of government and its leadership into question. Most lists, surely, would include these: the Vietnam War, ghetto riots, the rise in crime, Watergate and the Nixon resignation, the Agnew scandal, the highest unemployment since the Great Depression, double-digit inflation, the energy crisis and gasoline lines, and setbacks to the United States in world affairs — in Africa, the Middle East, and elsewhere.

The list could be extended, but in any case a succession of adverse events has produced a generalized feeling about government far more negative than was the case 15 or 20 years ago — the malaise about which Carter spoke. There is the general impression that government is wasteful. There is the widely shared conclusion that government efforts to solve problems do not usually work, that ambitious initiatives like the Great Society are bound to fail. There is the pervasive feeling that the government is too intrusive, oppressing people and businesses with regulation that brings more burden than benefit. There is the judgment that government does not deliver on its promises, that after all the talk about cleaning up the "welfare mess," closing tax loopholes, streamlining the bureaucracy, and cutting red tape, things always remain the same. There is the suspicion that government looks out mainly for the rich and the "special interests," and the conviction that politicians are not as honest as they should be; corruption and scandal were supposed to have ended with Nixon and Agnew, but the Carter administration was barely in office when the Bert Lance affair splashed in the headlines and on television news, and the usual quota of Congressmen were caught accepting bribes.

One does not have to share all these negative opinions to reach the essential conclusion: the performance of the government has fallen far short of what the people have expected and have a right to expect. The past 15 years have seen one long string of mistakes, of commission or omission. Some of the events, the politicans in power at the time may claim, were beyond the control of the U.S. government. But opposing politicians are always around to reject any such attempted alibi and exploit the failure — and the public judgment is not likely to be generous. The people expect the government to control events. After all, candidates for office keep promising that it can do so. They go on insisting that elections make a difference. So each time an election does not, it adds to the disillusionment. And that, in turn, appears to be expressed in the decline in voting participation, which was also precipitate in the 1970s — as Carter noted in his July speech.

If all this is the bad news, the good news is that the people have not given up on the American system — not yet, anyway. Pollster Harris asked some questions in September 1978 designed to probe the public's feelings about government itself, as distinct from the people leading it. He identified a series of characteristics that people desire in government, and then asked two questions: "Do we have a government that fits these characteristics?" And "Is it possible to have" such a government? The responses given for some of the characteristics are shown in Table 16-3.

"It is evident," Harris concluded, "that the American people have not given up hope for a better federal government and better people to lead it. In fact, despite the shock waves that have visited

Table 16-3 What Kind of Government Do We Have? (In Percentages)

	Have	*Don't have*	*Possible*	*Not possible*
Almost wholly free of corruption and payoffs	10	84	48	45
Best people are attracted to serve in public life	18	69	68	22
The good of the country is placed above special interests	26	61	76	16
Public officials really care what happens to people	38	48	81	12

SOURCE: The Harris Survey, November 13, 1978.

the public over the past 15 years ... there has never been much evidence that most people have gone sour on the system itself and have finally concluded that it is unworkable." It is equally clear that the people do not believe the government is working. Why then the current disillusionment with government?

A CRISIS OF GOVERNMENTAL COMPETENCE

What is the public conception of a government that works? At a minimum, I suggest, the people expect this much: first, that a candidate for president have a program to address the central problems that concern the people — not necessarily one with all the answers, but at least a philosophy and an approach that give promise of succeeding; second, that the winning candidate then proceed to accomplish the program — again, not in every detail or all at once, but with enough actual achievement to give the public a sense of progress toward the goals that were projected in the campaign. In short, a mandate to lead the country in an indicated direction is sought and given, and then it is expected to be discharged.

That defines the problem of competence in government. What has always existed in the United States is a gap, sometimes narrow and sometimes wide but always present, between the mandate and its execution. The mandate is granted essentially to one person, the president, but it can be executed only through the collaboration of three separate institutions — the president, the Senate, and the House — elected from different constituencies and free to exercise their powers independently. Two-thirds of the senators did not even run in the election that chose the president, and hence have no share in the mandate. And many of those who were elected with the president — even those of his own party — may have little more in common with him than the date of their election. They were chosen by much smaller electorates, and they presented their individual platforms and received their own distinct and perhaps quite different mandates.

So presidents have always had some trouble getting their programs through Congress. The degree of harmony among the Senate, the House, and the executive necessary for more than routine and incremental legislation — except in situations of manifest crisis — is not the rule in the U.S. government; it is the exception. One can identify only a few brief periods in the entire twentieth century when relations were close enough — or presidential leadership strong enough, which is the other way of describing it — to achieve major innovations in controversial areas of public policy. The most notable of these were the first two years of Woodrow Wilson's administration, when the New Freedom was enacted; the first term of Franklin D. Roosevelt, when the New Deal took form; and the first two years of Lyndon Johnson, when the Great Society was founded.

But the prospects for attaining a sufficient degree of unity among president, House, and Senate to enable the government to move forward confidently and energetically to cope with the country's problems are even smaller now than they were in the time of Woodrow Wilson, or Roosevelt, or Johnson. If attaining governmental competence has been always difficult in the past, it will be even more arduous in the future. For in the last decade or two, the political scene has changed profoundly, and the changes all militate against governmental effectiveness.

Four of the trends, all interrelated, affect the government's ability to formulate policy: the disintegration of political parties, the popularization of presidential nominations, the rejection by Congress of presidential leadership, and fragmentation of authority in Congress that prevents its development as an alternative source of policy integration and leadership. A fifth trend is the gradual deterioration of administrative capability. The remainder of the chapter addresses these in turn, and then considers what, if anything, can be done to alleviate the crisis of governmental competence.

PARTY DISINTEGRATION

Political scientists who for generations have pondered the built-in disunity of the U.S. government have generally sought the solution in an institution that the Founding Fathers did not contemplate and that George Washington warned against — the political party. The party, they found, was the "web" or the "bridge" that bound together the separate elements of government. As late as the mid-1960s, the political party was strong enough to serve that purpose when circumstances were favorable. A Democratic president then could lead the Democratic House and Senate majorities for a time because all felt a party bond and a commitment to a party philosophy and program. But in the past 15 years, a process of party disintegration, already under way, has accelerated. By now, the web has lost much of its tensile strength, the bridge its carrying capacity.

One can hardly regret the passing of old-style political machines with their corruption, bossism, and cronyism. Few persons nowadays suggest returning to the "smoke-filled room" as the way of selecting presidents. The new ideal is for open, participatory parties, united by program objectives rather than by patronage. Yet only in a few places do such new-style party organizations have cohesion approaching that of the old machines (and even in those places, their durability has yet to be proved). Consequently, within what are loosely referred to as the Republican and Democratic "parties," the trend has been steadily toward an every-candidate-for-himself kind of campaign.

Today candidates for the House and Senate — sometimes even presidential candidates — refer to the party platform rarely and reserve the right not to be bound by it. The platforms of presidential candidates are whatever they say they are during the campaign, but the candidates speak only for themselves, not for those who share the ticket with them. The latter have their own platforms. So when those who together carried the standard of the victorious party take office, they do not necessarily have a common program or even a shared philosophy.

The political party has been steadily weakening, then, as a force for unifying the separate policymaking elements of government — president, House and Senate — even when all are controlled by the same party. But with the decline of parties and the concomitant rise in independent voting has come a new phenomenon of extraordinary import for governmental competence — divided party control. As voters pay ever less attention to the party label, picking and choosing among candidates (for the presidency, at least) as individuals in a kind of personality contest, straight-ticket voting disappears. In personality contests, because neither party has any inherent advantage, the winners are distributed between them on a random basis. The result in the case of the president and Congress has been for more than two decades what random selection would be expected, mathematically, to dictate. Half the time the country has had divided government, something rarely known in the days of strong party organization and identification. During the 26 years from 1955 through 1980, the Democrats continually controlled Congress, but during 14 of those years the Republicans held the presidency — six years of split control when Dwight Eisenhower was in the White House and all eight years of the Nixon and Ford administrations. The years 1981 and 1982 now see divided government again, with President Reagan confronting a House organized by the Democrats.

At such times, the normal tendency of the U.S. system toward deadlock becomes irresistible. Harmonious collaboration, barring national crisis, is out of the question. The president and those houses of Congress controlled by the opposition are compelled to quarrel. No presidential proposal can be accepted by the legislators without raising the stature of the president as leader. Similarly, no initiative of the opposition in Congress can be approved by the president without conceding wisdom to his enemies. The conflict, bickering, tension, and stalemate that characterized the recent years of divided government were inevitable.

Given the continued predominance of personality as distinct from party voting, the odds are that in the late twentieth century the country will experience significant periods of divided government, with its accompanying incessant conflict, half the time. If that happens, confidence in government can only be damaged further. When the president is constantly denouncing Congress as prodigal and irresponsible, and Congress in turn is rejecting his ideas as fatuous and unworthy, will not the people inevitably come to believe both?

But the bonds of party have proved too weak to bridge the gap between the branches even when the president and the congressional majority are of the same party, as they were between 1977 and 1980. President Carter's first term was not one of the rare historic periods of fruitful collaboration, and the limited legislative output — as in the case of energy — disappointed almost everyone. The effect on public confidence in government has been direct, and disastrous. To the data on public opinion presented above can be added one more item: A *Washington Post* poll in July 1979 found that two-thirds of the sample believed that President Carter and Congress did not work well together. Of those, 86 percent said that lack of cooperation was harmful to the country. They absolved neither Congress nor the president, although they considered the legislature somewhat more at fault.

HAPHAZARD PRESIDENTIAL SELECTION

In all democratic countries, by definition, the people make the final choice among the parties' nominees for national leadership. But only in the United States do the people themselves also make the nominations.

When the state presidential primaries became the mode rather than the exception after 1968, a basic safeguard in the presidential election process was lost. Previously an elite of party leaders performed a screening function. They administered a kind of competence test; they did not always exercise that duty credibly, but they could. More important, however, they could — and did — ensure that no one was nominated who was not acceptable to the preponderance of the party elite as its leader. Even if a candidate swept the limited number of primaries, he could still be rejected, as Senator Estes Kefauver was in 1952. Usually, then, the nominee was an insider in the political system, a person who had established some credentials as a politician or an administrator, or both, of national stature and of demonstrated competence. The party leaders who approved the nomination were then prepared to follow the nominee, and to mobilize the party on his behalf.

Since 1968, all that is changed. There is no screening mechanism. A party's nominee for president now is someone who has been able to devote enough time to shaking hands in the early primary and caucus states and to forming an effective get-out-the-vote organization there, who has raised enough money to put himself on television throughout the primary season, and who has proved to have popular appeal. He may be an outsider to the national political process. He may have no experience in the federal government he seeks to head. He may be a neophyte in dealing with complex issues of foreign relations and the domestic economy. He may be in no sense the natural leader of large and crucial elements of his own party. If elected, he may be a stranger to the people in Congress with whom he has to work, and he may have little sense of how to get along with them. He may have little idea of the kind of talent he needs to help him run the executive branch, and no network of experienced advisers to help him find them. All this was true of Jimmy Carter.

A president may have the capacity to learn fast, as seems to have been the case with Carter — at least in some elements of the job. But that, if true, is pure luck. And in any case, for a country suffering a crisis of governmental competence, it is perilous to devote the first year or two of a new administration to little more than on-the-job training for an inexperienced president and an even more inexperienced entourage, without knowing how much competence will prove to be there when the training period ends.

Without passing judgment on President Carter's personal capacities, about which people differ, this much can be said with certainty: those who may have found this particular president — or those who may find any successor — deficient as a national leader should look with some urgency to the shortcomings of the system that selected him. Jimmy Carter, the outsider, would not have been the nominee in 1976 of an organized political party: he is what can happen when the choice of party leader is taken entirely out of the hands of the party elite and turned over to the people.

In this lottery, some future president could conceivably have all of Jimmy Carter's weaknesses without his strengths. The adverse effect on competence in government — and public confidence, and national malaise — would be immeasurable.

REJECTION OF PRESIDENTIAL LEADERSHIP

The theorists who envisaged the majority political party as the institution that would unify a government of separated powers considered the president as the leader of the party, the natural leader of the government. And this view went beyond the theorists. The public at large has come to look upon presidential leadership as an essential feature of twentieth-century government in the United States. Looking back over history, it is the strong presidents — Washington, Jefferson, Jackson, Lincoln, the two Roosevelts, Wilson — whom Americans revere. The presidents of the nineteenth century who limited themselves by presiding over the executive branch, while letting Congress direct the nation's policy, are forgotten. And just as the public came to expect presidents to be strong leaders, so did the nation's politicians — including those in Congress. Indeed, the modern powerful presidency could not have been created except by Congress. The presidency did not grow by seizing power. Rather, statute after statute — many initiated by Congress itself — bestowed new functions on it.

A series of events converged in the winter of 1972-73, however, to bring executive-legislative relations to a crisis and arouse a wholly new congressional assertiveness. One issue was fiscal policy: President Nixon had humiliated Congress in a struggle over a spending ceiling in the fall; when Congress failed to come up with the budget cuts he demanded, he impounded $9 billion (by the narrowest definition of the term), thus unilaterally repealing laws Congress had enacted. Another issue was the war power, a question that had been long festering: while Congress was in recess, Nixon without consultation intensified the bombing of North Vietnam and mined the port of Haiphong. A third was executive privilege: Nixon was asserting unlimited power to withhold any information from Congress, solely at his own discretion.[1] A fourth was reorganization: Nixon put into effect the basic features of a plan that Congress had explicitly rejected for reorganizing the executive departments.

When the 93rd Congress assembled in January 1973, its members were in a fighting mood. And in the course of a single Congress, in 1973 and 1974, the legislature went a long way toward rectifying the previous six decades or so of continuous decline. As the Watergate scandal closed in on Nixon, Congress took advantage of a collapsing presidency to shift the balance. It did all it could by law to recapture the war power — or at least a partnership role in it — through the War Powers Resolution, enacted over Nixon's veto. It regained control of fiscal policy — the power of the purse — through the Congressional Budget and Impoundment Control Act, accepted by Nixon in one of his final acts in office. (Meanwhile, President Nixon voluntarily discarded his reorganization scheme, and the Supreme Court stripped him of his claimed unlimited right of executive privilege — though it did not define what the limits are.) Beyond those specific statutory monuments of the new assertiveness, the congressional mood expressed itself in many diffuse ways. Both houses officially instructed their committees to exert more effort in overseeing the administration of the laws, and for the first time the legislature looked closely at agencies it had earlier let slip out of sight, including the Central Intelligence Agency. A device that had been used somewhat sparingly, the legislative veto of contemplated administrative action, was extended over a new and wide terrain. And Congress entered a phase of freer intervention in matters of foreign policy.

All these actions enabled a Democratic Congress to assert leadership and control over an executive branch that at the time was in Republican hands. But in 1977, the presidency reverted to the Democrats again. What, then, of the new relationships? In practice, there was a pronounced easing of tensions. Mutual recrimination largely ended. Rather than being under compulsion to try to discredit a president of the opposition party, the congressional majorities found themselves under pressure to make their own president look good; party labels had not lost their meaning altogether, and congressional Democrats had to expect to run on the same ticket with Jimmy Carter in 1980. By the same token, the president had to be conciliatory because he knew he would need the support of all those Democrats in their states and districts. Democrats in both the legislative and executive branches had a political interest in the record on which they all would run.

Nevertheless, the formal balance of power has remained the same as it was when Gerald Ford was president. All the innovations of the 93rd Congress have remained in effect — war powers, budget process, impoundment control, legislative veto, expansion of oversight activities. The aggressive and vastly enlarged congressional staffs that were formed when Congress resolved to reject the leadership of a Republican president and oversee and control executive activities have not been disbanded, and they would find scant joy in working for a passive Congress that followed presidential leadership. Congress shows little tendency toward relinquishing any of its new authority; while moderating the tone, it is not giving up the substance of the new assertiveness.

This would be no problem if Congress had the capacity to set the country's course, as the substitute for presidential leadership. But there are severe limitations on the capability of the legislative branch to develop integrated and coherent policy. If the model of presidential leadership and congressional followership is to be discarded (or suspended), no fully satisfactory alternative model of congressional leadership has yet been designed to take its place. And recent trends within Congress make it even less likely than before that such a model can be devised.

LIMITATIONS ON CONGRESSIONAL LEADERSHIP

Whatever else may be said about it, the executive branch is well organized to prepare a comprehensive and internally consistent governmental program. With its hierarchical structure, it can represent divergent views at the lower levels but blend and reconcile them at higher levels, with a point of decision at the top. Congress, in contrast, had no mechanism for policy integration when its era of resurgence began in 1973. Its policy decisions had traditionally been piecemeal, put forward by separate committees and considered separately, at different times, by two independent houses, without benefit of any controlling philosophy or set of policy objectives for either house, much less for the legislative branch as a whole. That had worked reasonably well, most of the time, because Congress had been willing to look to the president to do the integrating. It could then modify and adapt and adjust the elements of the president's program, without destroying its essential unity. But in the era of the new assertiveness, Congress insists upon a freedom to reject the president's program outright. During the period of divided government that ended in 1977, it did just that, and in future such periods it will surely do so again. Whenever that happens, the government's policymaking process — barring congressional reorganization — will be left without even a coherent body of policy objectives and proposals acceptable as a basis from which to begin.

The competence of the policymaking process depends, then, upon the extent to which Congress, in assuming its new responsibilities, creates new machinery to match. But any effective mechanism for establishing broad policy objectives and developing a coordinated and integrated program to support them would require the delegation of considerable new power to the congressional leadership, or to powerful centralized committees of some kind, and centralization of power runs directly counter to the current temper of Congress. Ever since "Czar" Joseph G. Cannon was dethroned as Speaker in 1910, the trend in the House has been toward dispersal of power, and the trend gathered new force in the 1970s when committee chairmen were stripped of much of their power and the seniority system that protected them was abolished. The same tendencies have been apparent in the Senate. If one characteristic of Congress of the 1970s has been the new assertiveness, another can be called the new individualism. And they are basically incompatible.

Political individualism is both the consequence and the cause of the decay of parties, which was discussed above. As the old-style machines faded away, either the vacuum was filled by new-style, program-oriented party organizations — widely participatory, undisciplined, individualistic — or it was not filled at all. In either case, from this different political milieu came a new kind of candidate, for Congress as well as for other offices. Because these new candidates did not arise through disciplined organizations, they are individualists from the beginning of their political careers. As candidates they were self-selected, self-organized, self-propelled, self-reliant, with no habit of being deferential to the established and the powerful, and they will not be so in Congress, either in committee or on the floor. When there were enough of this type of member in Congress, the nature of the place was bound to change.

"No one can lead men and women who refuse to be led," complained journalist David S. Broder in 1975 in diagnosing the ills of a "floundering" Congress. "The House juniors have overthrown the old power centers. Yet they consistently refuse to heed even those they installed in power." The Democratic Study Group that year found the lowest party unity scores in 20 years.

With so unruly a followership, the tendency of the leadership in both houses has been to avoid trying to impose its will, or at least to choose its fights carefully to avoid risking defeat and exposing its weakness. "I don't twist arms. I shake hands," was Speaker Carl Albert's way of putting it. "The Senate never wanted a leader," observed Senator Edmund S. Muskie, "and it has seldom had one, at least not one in the sense of somebody who could mobilize a majority." "I don't feel pressure to go along with the party position," said Senator Gary Hart, a first-term Democrat from Colorado in 1979. But the party position in the Congress is still either the president's program or none at all. Neither in the House nor the Senate, even in the periods of divided government, has the majority leadership presumed to put forward any alternative program of its own; it has not even made policy pronouncements or assembled a staff that in size or backgrounds would enable it to do so.

Nevertheless, Congress has experimented with a device for policy integration more in the pattern of legislative bodies — the committee. In the important field of fiscal policy, new machinery has been created, a budget committee in each house and a Congressional Budget Office to provide analytical support.

But the precedent of the budget process has not been extended beyond the fiscal field. True, Speaker O'Neill experimented in 1977 with the use of ad hoc committees as integrating devices in two other fields, energy and welfare. They did serve to overcome jurisdictional jealousies and bring forward a legislative product with remarkable dispatch (if only by adopting essentially the administration's program). But this promising device can at best be used only on a limited number of issues in any session. And, lacking the statutory deadlines of the budget process, it does nothing to compel the integration of House and Senate policy. The welfare bill produced by the House ad hoc committee and passed by the House was not even seriously considered in the Senate. And the momentum of the House energy bill was wholly lost in a conference committee deadlock that was not broken until the end of the next session in the following year. Since then, O'Neill has not repeated the experiment.

With no continuing integrative devices except in the field of fiscal policy, Congress cannot prepare a comprehensive program corresponding to that of the president. Given the present state of congressional disorganization, the choice is to have policy, particularly in the areas of national security and foreign affairs, made by the president or not to have a coherent and consistent policy at all. The new assertiveness of Congress without organizational reform to match can only be cause for deep concern. The new assertiveness compounded by the new individualism becomes the new anarchy.

DETERIORATION OF ADMINISTRATIVE COMPETENCE

The discussion thus far has concerned the difficulty of making policy through the legislative process. But the crisis of competence extends to administration also. Getting sound and adequate legislation passed — in the field of energy, say — is only part of the problem. The other part is achieving the legislative goals with faithfulness, dispatch, and equity.

That requires administrative skill at all levels of the executive hierarchy. But it is the top level that is critical, for improvement of administrative skill at the lower levels is one of the responsibilities of top management, which institutes an organization's policies for selecting and upgrading the men and women who make up its staff, and then motivates, directs, and supervises them as they carry out their duties. And at the top levels of the U.S. government, administrative capability has been allowed to decline, over a long period, with a resulting loss of capacity throughout the executive branch.

This is necessarily a subjective judgment because there are no direct measures of administrative capability. But it is a judgment widely shared by the general public. The people clearly see their government as wasteful, inefficient, and "bureaucratic" — a catchall term connoting insensitivity, rigidity, and a devotion to procedure for procedure's sake. Indeed, the title "civil servant," once a term of respect, has been replaced by "bureaucrat," usually uttered as an epithet. An important element in Jimmy Carter's appeal as a candidate in 1976 was his promise to reorganize and simplify the government and eliminate waste. His civil service reform bill was supported with enthusiasm by Congress and the public because he presented it as the way to rid the "bureaucracy" of drones and deadheads. Besides being a campaign issue, administrative capacity is a legislative issue when any measure proposing a new program — national health insurance, for instance — is advanced. "Would you want the *government* to run that?" is always one of the questions asked, and the opposition gains support from the pervasive assumption that if the government takes on responsibility for anything it will bungle it.

But even widespread perceptions can be wrong. A conclusion that the government is in fact administratively weak must rest on other grounds. I rest my own judgment on several rather elementary propositions that, I believe, have been proved through the experience over a long period of many organizations — particularly business organizations, which prize managerial capability — and are generally accepted by them. These propositions are:

First, a person selected for a top administrative or managerial post on the basis of demonstrated administrative or managerial capacity is more likely to possess that capacity than one chosen for other qualities.

Second, a person with administrative or managerial experience is not likely to be a fully effective administrator in an organization highly dissimilar to the one in which the experience was gained until after a period of acclimatization.

Third, a person's administrative or managerial competence improves with experience, not only administrative experience in general but experience in a particular organization, until physical and mental vigor begin to decline.

If these propositions are correct, it is easily demonstrated that the U.S. government has been losing administrative capability because each of the precepts implicit in them has been violated on a growing scale. Except for a few areas of the government that have been the domain of elite organizations — the military, the foreign service, some technical bureaus — management in the U.S. government has been entrusted to a steadily increasing number of political appointees. These are persons who are brought in by each new administration mainly from outside the government, who are chosen primarily for qualities that are distinct from administrative competence — their policy views, the constituencies they represent, the political services they have rendered, and so on — and who, for the most part, do not stay in the government long enough to become skilled governmental managers. Those who do are replaced in any case whenever the White House passes from one party to the other.

The United States is unique in this regard. Other countries severely restrict the number of political appointees placed at the head of executive departments. Those appointees function as policymakers, not as managers; management is the responsibility of a corps of career administrators with long experience, who — though doubtless there are exceptions — have risen to the top on the basis of demonstrated administrative competence. But in the United States the notion that there should be a corps of career governmental administrators who would be politically neutral, serving with equal loyalty whichever party came to power, has never really taken root (again, with the exceptions of the military, foreign service, and technical bureaus). After Andrew Jackson, at least, administrative jobs were seen as patronage, to be distributed as rewards to party organizations. When the civil service system was established, top positions were exempted, and through the years the exempt layer at the top has widened. The process has been called politicization of the civil service; it could also be termed amateurization.

With frequent shifts of party control of the executive branch in the last 30 years, politicization has progressed downward through the administrative levels, and outward from the Washington headquarters to regional and field offices, particularly in agencies administering politically sensitive programs. As it has done so, the ceilings on the aspirations of career civil servants have been lowered. The more enterprising of the careerists have tended to leave; others have tended to avoid responsibility and identification with the party in power. Each incoming administration, finding a career force drained of talent and enterprise, has naturally looked outside. The result has been politicization of more jobs, thus further damaging the career service, which provided the incentive for further politicization, and so on, in a vicious spiral.

No business organization operates that way, or could survive if it did. But management-by-amateurs is now generally accepted as the right way to run the government, taken for granted by politicians and by the general public. Establishing professionalism and continuity in governmental management, on the European model, is not even on the agenda of public issues. But it is difficult to see how the crisis of governmental competence can be overcome without a strong and conscious effort in that direction.

SEARCHING FOR REMEDIES

None of the five interrelated trends discussed in the preceding sections is easily reversed. They arise from fundamental forces within the American political culture and have become more or less established habits of political thought and action. Traumatic historical events can set new forces into motion, which in turn can alter the way people think and act, but between such events existing institutional patterns remain, and solidify. However, the crisis of confidence in government the country is now experiencing may prove to be in itself a traumatic event. The 1980 election surely reflects a popular displeasure with the government's record of performance, yet in denying the Republicans control of all three centers of policymaking — House as well as Senate and presidency — the people did not set up the ideal preconditions for success. If under these circumstances the government continues its record of failure, advocates of more fundamental institutional change will surely gain a growing audience. Even so, consensus on specific remedial measures will be difficult to attain, even if appropriate measures can be conceived.

The Party System

There is no lack, to return to the first trend, of persons who deplore the decline of political parties. Leaders of the two parties would surely like to head stronger organizations, but they have found no way to bring them into being. People do not identify with parties, join them, support them, and believe in them as an end in itself (except, perhaps, in the few places where anachronistic, patronage-oriented machines survive). Parties are embraced, rather, when people see them as useful means toward achieving some desired public policy. Parties have formed, or re-formed, at times when great issues have seized the country and polarized the voters — as the slavery question did in the 1850s, or populism and free silver in the 1890s, or relief of hunger and unemployment in the 1930s. At such times, new parties spring into being or old parties take on new meaning because they become instruments for the achievement of goals about which the voters deeply care. But such powerful issues come and go, and when they have gone the parties begin to lose relevance. The last period of polarization, when the current alignment of the two-party system was shaped, is by now almost half a century past. To young people in particular, what the parties stand for, what the differences are between them, why they matter, even why they exist, has become obscure. Revival, then, depends on something outside the party system itself — some kind of crisis that will arouse the people, polarize them, and impel them to organize politically to attain their ends. In the meantime, advocates of stronger parties can do little more than remain alert to the incidental effects on party organizations of particular legislative measures, specifically those governing elections. Public financing of campaigns, for example, can help or hurt parties, depending on whether the money is disbursed to the party that nominates the candidate or directly to the nominee.

Presidential Selection

Parties would be strengthened, and some of the risk removed from the presidential selection process as well, if the trend toward proliferation of presidential primaries could be reversed. Conceivably, a retrenchment in the primary system could begin spontaneously in the 1980s in reaction to the exhaustion and the expense of the long ordeal that the presidential campaign has become. Such a swing away from the direct primary occurred early in this century; after the initial burst of enthusiasm for the new device during the Progressive Era, some eight states repealed their laws, and others made significant modifications to give the party leadership more control over the choice of convention delegates. But there are few signs now of any such reversal. The voters seem to prefer the primary system. Widespread participation, open decisionmaking, and freedom from "boss control" have become accepted as political ideals. The states that have the primaries like the attention of the media and the business the primaries bring in. The party organizations that would be the natural advocates of a return to less participatory procedures hardly exist to lead any such struggle. And finally, even if some states discarded primaries in favor of choosing delegates through caucuses and conventions, the rules that require the caucuses to be open and to encourage wide participation, and that serve to discourage the selection of uncommitted party leaders as convention delegates, would undoubtedly remain. So the risks inherent in allowing tens of millions of voters, rather than party elites, to choose the presidential nominees are not likely soon to be eliminated.

Presidential Leadership

In contrast to the changes in the party and electoral systems, the breakdown of presidential leadership and the accompanying new assertiveness of Congress are the result not of long-term forces but of a series of events. As the memory of these events fade — if, in other words, presidents continue to behave in the relatively restrained fashion of Gerald Ford and Jimmy Carter and continue to be open and candid with Congress — it is reasonable to expect that the same fundamental forces that brought about the modern strong presidency in the first place will again assert their influence.

That is not to say that the pre-Nixon balance of authority between the branches will be restored — nor should it be. The old norms of presidential dominance and congressional passivity contained dangers that are now clear to everyone, including members of Congress. In any case, the many profound institutional changes made in the 1970s to undergird the legislature's new importance will not be undone;

Congress will not repeal the War Powers Resolution or the Congressional Budget and Impoundment Control Act, nor is it likely to disband the vastly enlarged staffs that enable it to exercise tighter control over the executive and play a greater role in the legislative process.

Yet there can be some retreat. Congress seems already to be identifying what can perhaps be called the excesses of the new assertiveness, and to be modifying them. In particular, the congressional intervention in operational decisions of foreign policy that marked the Ford administration diminished in the Carter period. The tide of legislative veto provisions, on the other hand, may not yet have crested, for Ronald Reagan is the first president who has actually endorsed the device and recommended its extension.

So if one could prescribe unified party control of House, Senate, and presidency, it would not be unreasonable to expect a gradual warming of relations between president and Congress, a restoration of greater trust in presidential leadership, and a resultant reinstatement of the efficiency of the policymaking processes.

Whenever the voters choose divided government, however, Congress — even when the two houses work in harmony — will be little better equipped than it was before its post-1973 resurgence to set the country's course. And when the Congress itself is divided, as in 1981 and 1982, the prospect that it can serve as an alternative source of national leadership is reduced to nil.

Administrative Competence

As for the improvement of administrative capability, any movement toward a remedy would depend upon a higher degree of consensus than now exists as to the nature of the problem. If the analysis offered above were accepted, the way to proceed would be clear enough: the number of politically appointed, amateur managers in the government would be drastically reduced and a professional corps of career administrators would be developed to assume enlarged responsibilities. In essence, the United States would adopt the European model, with a clear distinction between a thin layer of political policymakers at the top and a neutral permanent civil service responsible for implementing the policies. The objective would be to provide each top political appointee — Cabinet member, bureau chief, and so on — with a deputy from the career service who would have the necessary experience and training, the knowledge of how to use the resources of the organization, and the managerial skills to make the policies effective.

But the decision to move in that direction would have to be made by the policymakers themselves, and for every politician in the new administration who would favor an expansion of the role of the career civil service, there will undoubtedly be many who would seek the solution to administrative incompetence by moving in the opposite direction — by supplanting more careerists with transient political appointees.

The Civil Service Reform Act of 1978, however, could conceivably prove to be a turning point in the enhancement of the status and responsibilities of the career civil service, even though it was not presented to Congress and the public as a measure for that purpose. It was put forward, rather, as a means to discipline the government's employees and to bring them, through more flexible systems of rewards and punishments, under tighter control by political executives. And it did nothing to narrow the layers of political appointees at the top of the government's departments and agencies. Nevertheless, it did establish for a trial period a Senior Executive Service, which conceivably could evolve, if it is accepted and continued, into a professional managerial corps on the European pattern. But to move in that direction would require a conscious, deliberate decision to do so, and that would demand what does not now exist — a wide measure of national agreement.

So the crisis of competence in government is not easily resolved. Many of the trends that have brought about the crisis, and intensified it in recent years, have roots deep in the traditions of American political behavior, if not in the constitutional structure itself. To that extent, incompetence is endemic. Yet there are ameliorative measures that can be taken, and taking some may lead to creative thought that may devise still others. What is necessary, first of all, is that those who decry the shortcomings of governmental performance recognize that the fault does not necessarily lie in the individuals who happen to occupy the White House or sit in Congress, and replacing them with other individuals will not necessarily help. Severe institutional and structural problems must be addressed. Only when acceptance of that proposition is wide enough will a concerted attack upon those problems be possible.

NOTE

1. "Statement About Executive Privilege, March 12, 1973," *Public Papers of the Presidents: Richard Nixon* (Washington, D.C.: U.S. Government Printing Office, 1973), pp. 184-186; U.S., Congress, Senate, Committee on Governmental Operations and Committee on the Judiciary, *Hearings on Executive Privilege, Secrecy in Government, Freedom of Information,* Testimony of Attorney General Richard G. Kleindienst, 93rd Cong., 1st sess., Vol. I, pp. 18-52, especially pp. 45-46, 51.

17

An Approach to the Limits and Possibilities of Congress

Philip Brenner

Each day, in ever new ways, the U.S. Congress disappoints more people. This is not the fault of the Congress but of our expectations. There are profound limits to what Congress can do given the structure of our society. It is true that the Congress is only as good as the members we elect, and its rules and internal structures do affect what it does. But we should not expect that changing the personnel or the rules of Congress will enable Congress to do all the things we might want because all things are not possible. The important task for a student of Congress is to understand the limits and possibilities of Congress.

This undertaking is what a marxist approach to the study of Congress facilitates. Marxism is a systematic way of seeing the world and of asking questions about it. Without realizing it, many of us often take this approach when we discuss politics. Intuitively, we understand that modern politics relates to the way in which our society produces goods and services that are necessary for our survival.

I am grateful to the following people for their contributions to this essay: Gordon Adams, Lawrence Dodd, Paul Goldman, Richard Kohl, Lesley Valdes, Jean Woy, David Vogler, and editorial board members of *Politics & Society*.

And we often wonder why our political institutions operate in ways that seem consistent, inconsistent, or irrelevant to this basic purpose of producing goods and services. These are the starting points for a marxist study of Congress.

Such far-reaching economic questions may seem unrelated to a member's daily world. Members respond to immediate events, and they try to gain particular ends. They want to know who is for them, who is against them, and how they can make sure they have more for them than against them. They see other members constrained by constituent demands and pressured by interest groups that sometimes seem to have legislators on a string. These perceptions mold the behavior of members of Congress. Members may shift the focus of an issue to obscure its full import or try to redefine an issue in ways that win greater support.[1] For example, in the late 1970s those who sought to cut off foreign aid from countries that violated human rights gained support when they reframed the issue in terms of budget restraint.[2] Individually, Congress's actions appear to be dictated by a particular constellation of people and pressures at a given time, but the sum of its immediate decisions does create a pattern over time. The nature of the pattern is an indicator of the limits and possibilities of the Congress.

The pattern of congressional decisionmaking may be analyzed in several ways. Lawrence Dodd, for example, has focused on legislators' quest for power and the resulting cyclical changes in the organization of Congress.[3] To some extent the best approach is the one that makes the best sense to the reader. Any approach offers but a guide to interpreting immediate phenomena. Marx's explanation of the behavior of the French national legislature during the 1850s provides a succinct example of such interpretations. He focused on the conflicts between two powerful factions, the House of Bourbon and the House of Orleans. What divided them, according to his analysis, was "the material conditions of existence, two distinct sorts of property" that they represented. But, as he observed in describing the legislators:

> Who would deny that at the same time old memories, personal enmities, fears and hopes, prejudices and illusions ..., articles of faith and principles bound them to one or the other royal house.... The single individual who derives these feelings, etc. through tradition and upbringing, may well imagine that they form the real determinants and the starting point of his activity.... But one must make a ... distinction between the phrases and fantasies of the parties and their real organization and real interests, between their conception of themselves and what they really are.[4]

In this essay I will explore how a marxist approach helps us to appreciate the limits and possibilities of Congress.

THE SETTING: A CAPITALIST SYSTEM

Congress does not act in a vacuum. It is very much a part of the world around it. This is why we must start with the world outside Congress in order to understand Congress itself. The world to which the Congress relates is a messy place. It is neither static nor orderly, and that presents members of Congress with a daily problem. The problem is to figure out how to make some order of the confusion, how to get a handle on the constant changes so that they can be directed toward ends that the members of Congress seek. The legislators do not have a predetermined solution to the problem, nor are they prescient about the "correct" route to take. In effect, each decision is an experiment embedded in uncertainty as to whether it will work as intended.

In their search for order, members are rarely systematic. They operate from political intuition. They listen to a variety of voices — colleagues, staff, administration officials, constituents, the media, and technical experts — depending on the particular situation. Sometimes they seem captured and at other times independent.[5] Of course, members cannot be open to all points of view, so they try to get a handle on a situation by relying to some degree on ideology, that is, on a consistent perspective from which they can assess and respond to most events.[6] But traditional concepts of liberal and conservative have become blurred, making it difficult to adhere consistently to one ideology.[7]

Is the confusion that animates members' behavior random disorder, or is there a logic to it? In this section we will consider the possibility that the disorder confronting the Congress is rooted in the very structure of our society, that the changes result from ongoing conflicts generated by the way our society is organized.

The central fact about the United States is that it is a capitalist society. This means that our basic goods — food, clothes, houses, cars — and the raw materials that are necessary to make these goods, are produced, collected, and distributed by people who work for private companies. Many of the basic services also necessary for our daily survival, such as health care, are also private. Private firms thus produce the great wealth of the United States. They transform the raw materials into usable products that can be sold for sums much larger than the cost of the original materials. The workers who create the new value, however, receive only a small part of it in the form of wages. Part goes to pay for the materials, part is set aside to replace tools and machinery that wear out, and the remainder — or "profit" — is taken by the owners of the company to use as they wish.

With their profits, owners might buy yachts, support a symphony orchestra, or expand the company. This last use is critical. However much owners of a company may want to live like royalty, they must protect it from competitors. As the population grows, the company that does not grow will control an ever smaller percentage of the total market. This makes it vulnerable to expanding companies. From the perspective of the individual owner of wealth, then, the drive for greater profits is not mere avarice, but the very purpose of the enterprise, and it shapes the owner's decisions.

There is a tendency for companies to produce as much of a profitable commodity as they can, but this may lead to a surplus that drives the price down and makes production less profitable. In response, owners may stop production even if there is a demand for the commodity, though this is a viable solution only for companies that produce many different products. Because companies are private in our society, owners have the right to close down their factories or to withhold from the market the goods that their workers produce.

Viewed in this way, private property is more than a thing owned by someone. It is a relationship between those who have the right to determine how the property is developed and those who work on it — that is, who do the development.[8] This relationship sets up a context for struggle; it is not a natural law that owners control the conditions of production, the output of the production process, and the rewards. Such control must be asserted every day because every day workers also assert their right to control.

These assertions take many forms. At the point of production, workers may engage in a slowdown or protest a management decision. In collective bargaining they attempt to define the conditions of work and claim a larger portion of the profit through wage increases. Through the political process they may try to get regulations that constrain corporations.[9]

Owners may react to working class actions. They introduce "labor-saving" devices that can replace workers; they develop numerous job classifications that serve to undermine the unity of workers by differentiating between the jobs they do; and they establish new requirements for employment, often as pre-emptive attacks to divide workers and prevent their common action.[10] Employers must continually devise ways of getting labor from their workers because, in effect, they are buying workers' time, not necessarily their work. The struggle between owners and workers encourages owners to replace workers with machinery. Machines are more predictable than workers. They do not strike or demand higher wages and vacations with pay, and they have the potential to render the remaining workforce more manageable because it may be less skilled and easier to replace with new workers. An additional strategy is to raise prices of goods that workers purchase. Profit is the difference between the cost of materials, labor, and machinery, and the final price. If an owner can effectively control the market, as many of our major corporations do in their markets, it matters little to an owner whether he or she acquires the desired profit by holding down wages or by raising prices. What is lost at the bargaining table can be won back at the store.

The accumulation of profit is an uneven process. Victories by workers directly cut into profits. Moreover, they force owners to spend money on the search for cheaper materials, for new markets in order to sell more goods, and for alternative production processes that increase worker output. In turn, these actions impose a new set of constraints on the drive for accumulation. For example, owners may replace workers with machines because machinery is not as "ornery" as workers. But it is always there, in slow times as well as prosperous ones; while workers can be laid off in bad periods, loans incurred to buy the now idle machinery must still be repaid. While workers can be retrained, the skills of a machine are fixed. An owner is stuck with a machine until it is amortized, even if the owner's competitor has acquired a more productive model. To stay competitive, the owner may junk the first machine "before its time," but such decisions cut heavily into profits.

Though we live in an era of giant corporations that control vast resources and effectively manipulate their own markets, each corporation still operates relatively individualistically, looking out for its own profit and protecting its own property. Corporations' decisions are fairly uncoordinated. This has two important consequences.

First, the private companies, working separately, do not provide for all of the society's needs because they cannot make a profit doing so. The distribution of income in the United States is greatly unbalanced. Corporations tend to produce for the upper half of the population that can afford their services and products. In theory, under a private enterprise system there will always be a capitalist willing to produce and sell a product if there is a need for it. In reality, many products cannot be produced cheaply enough for poorer people to afford them and for capitalists also to make what they feel is a sufficient profit. For example, in many cities no private middle-income apartment houses have been built in more than 10 years because the return on investment would be too low. Yet we know there is a great demand for such housing.[11]

Second, the lack of coordination among private corporations makes it difficult for our society to respond in a collective way to problems that are commonly shared, such as the price increase by the Organization of Petroleum Exporting Countries (OPEC). Each company will seek the solution that serves its own needs best, and the sum of what is best for each company rarely equals what might be best for everyone. Even when private solutions work in the short run, individualization weakens our ability to plan in the long run for problems such as resource scarcity.[12]

In short, the disorder that confronts Congress seems to be inherent in the system of which the Congress is a part. Congress — along with capitalists, workers, and government — seeks to grapple with the problems engendered by private ownership of wealth. Like the others, it has no pat solutions, and like the others its agenda is framed by the very problems for which it seeks a solution.

AN ECONOMIC CRISIS AND CONGRESS'S RESPONSE

The accumulation of profit, with its ups and downs, is a risky business. This poses a major problem for our society, as well as for the capitalists, because the accumulation of profit is the stimulus for the private production of our basic goods and services. Without profit, private owners of wealth will not produce, and so the unevenness of accumulation affects what is produced, and where, and for whom. To see how this process affects the Congress, consider the changes in Congress during the economic crisis of the 1970s.

The Economic Crisis of the 1970s

The economic crisis of the 1970s affected our daily lives in many ways. Inflation meant that automobile prices more than doubled, and we got less car for twice the cost. Gasoline to drive the car — when it was available — tripled in price. Rent for our apartments soared, and housing prices — compounded by a doubling of the interest rates on mortgages — put the American dream of a house out of reach for many middle-class families. Real wages fell, and unemployment remained over the six-percent mark. The sense of possibility felt by students of the sixties is unknown to most college seniors today. Students must hustle hard to find "decent" jobs or any jobs. The prevailing mood of the 1970s was one of dislocation, uncertainty, and disquiet.

What we felt on a personal level reflected underlying problems in the economic system. Inflation and unemployment meant that private companies could not count on a steady or increasing profit, and so they were unwilling to risk their own capital for plant expansion or even inventory of parts and supplies. Corporations turned to banks for loans, and their debt passed the $1 trillion point early in the seventies. The failure in 1974 of the Franklin National Bank — the nation's twentieth largest — sent tremors through the business community.[13]

In this context of precarious investment possibilities, large corporations turned increasingly to other countries. They not only sought markets, cheap raw materials, and an inexpensive and pliable labor force, but investment opportunities. Capital regularly stayed abroad instead of flowing home, and in 1976 major business publications described a "liquidity crisis" in the United States.

The international solution to the search for profit was also hollow, however. In part it required a stable international currency for transactions.[14] By the turn of the seventies, currency manipulations by multinational corporations and banks — and often they were not distinguishable — had contributed to a significant weakening of the dollar, previously the common currency.[15] The fourfold rise in crude oil prices not only added to inflation in the United States, Europe, and Japan, but began to wreck the economies of less developed countries where banks had made large loans.

Congressional Response to the Crisis

The U.S. Congress was badly organized to grapple with the economic crisis. Its structure not only hindered coordinated planning, but also encouraged irrational responses to the crisis that may have made it even worse. Congressional reform seems to have been a partial response to this situation.

Through its structure, rules, and norms, the Congress is part of a system of subgovernments in Washington. Subgovernments are made up of a congressional committee or subcommittee, a corresponding executive branch agency, and the "client" served by the agency, such as a company, union, or manufacturing sector.[16] Each unit of the subgovernment tends to support the other, and staff revolve among units, as do key members. Members of the subgovernments interact at social functions in Washington and look to each other for "reliable" information in developing legislation and rules.

The norms of specialization and deference to congressional subcommittees or committees reinforce the operation of the subgovernments. Subgroups tend to focus on particular policy issue areas, rather than on the development of broad-based policy. During the 1970s, planning was further inhibited in Congress in cases where an issue did not fall neatly into the jurisdiction of one unit. As committees contended for control in a policy area, they sometimes worked to subvert the development of policy that they felt they could not yet control.

Subgovernment decisionmaking may have exacerbated the economic crisis by directing government money into areas that fueled inflation, such as military spending. As the crisis unfolded, workers demanded higher wages to avoid the further loss of real wages and worsened the profit crunch for corporations. In turn, corporations demanding government assistance also worked through the subgovernments.

Planning is also inhibited by the nature of congressional elections. Members are ultimately independent from each other because each runs independently in his or her district. Though the Congress is divided between two parties, party affiliation is not much more than a nominal designation. "There is no party," political scientist Andrew Martin observes, "through which the power to exercise democratic control can be deployed."[17] Party affiliation may still be the best predictor of how a member will vote on the floor, but the two parties do not develop and promote coherent policies on which individual members campaign in their districts.

During the early 1970s, congressional reforms reflected an initial misperception about the extent of the crisis. Members saw it in terms of particular groups having difficulty. Legislators sought to respond to these groups; thus they promoted the decentralization of the House and increased the influence of individual members — for example, by increasing staff support. Most notable in this regard was the so-called "subcommittee bill of rights" that ensured each House subcommittee funds, a staff, and a clear jurisdiction.[18] Democratic members were limited to one subcommittee chairmanship. By 1977 some second-term members were already chairpersons.

By the late 1970s, however, a tendency to provide the Congress with a planning capability emerged. Four reforms stand out in this regard. Party leadership was strengthened, coordination among committees was improved, committee jurisdictions were altered, and congressional staffs were increased. We shall consider each of these changes as they relate to planning.

Strengthened Party Leadership. In 1970 the autonomy of committees and their chairs was threatened when House Democrats sought to re-establish the party caucus as an instrument of policy. The Steering and Policy Committee, created by the leadership in 1973, effectively controls the agenda for the House Democratic party by setting priorities for action. The leadership under Speaker Thomas P. O'Neill, Jr. (D-Mass.) also brought under its authority the job of making Democratic committee assignments, previously the task of the Democratic members of the Ways and Means Committee. Formerly powerful Ways and Means was not the only House committee to lose some of its influence to the party leadership. Another locus of independent power, the House Rules Committee, went back to working as an arm of the Speaker. In the Senate, the leadership weakened the veto power available to an entrenched minority of senators through the filibuster in 1975, and in 1979 the filibuster was further eroded when Majority Leader Robert C. Byrd (D-W. Va.) moved quickly to close a loophole in the rule that permitted senators to filibuster by amendment.

By providing party leadership with the legitimate means to sanction deviant members, the Congress enhanced its planning capability. Through rules changes the leadership acquired the power to enforce the dictates of a policy plan that it was also involved in shaping. A concomitant to such increased control is coordination, and increased coordination characterized a second set of changes in Congress in the 1970s.

Increased Coordination. New forms of coordination emerged in the House and Senate that were intended to address the problem of committee competition. On key legislative matters such as a new charter for the Central Intelligence Agency, energy, and health care, several committees have been involved in drafting the bills through *sequential* consideration of relevant sections. This has permitted at least the effort to develop broad-based policy. In the House the leadership has shepherded the legislation carefully, and in 1979 it increased the staff size of the Steering and Policy Committee to facilitate such coordination.

The House also developed a new organizational form to bypass committees and allow planning to occur more easily: the ad hoc committee.[19] Ad hoc committees differ from select committees because their members are appointed directly by the Speaker. Thus they can become an arm of the leadership for creating policy and so reduce the points of access for groups. The leadership becomes the principal point of access. Although the use of ad hoc committees in the 95th Congress was limited to welfare and energy legislation, the leadership used this form as a potential threat against standing committees that might resist coordination in the future.

While these attempts to improve congressional coordination have been important, at best they are makeshift adjustments. As a staff report of the 1977 Senate committee created to re-evaluate the committee system stated, "different patterns of bill referral have become accepted and increasingly utilized mechanisms." But the heart of the matter, the committee report suggested, is the committee system itself, which "fails to address squarely the Nation's emerging policy problems." [20]

Committee Reorganization. Reform of the committee system focused on the number of committees and subcommittees, the jurisdiction of each, and the nature of the congressional budget process. The Senate Select Committee to Study the Committee System recognized the Senate's "wide overlap and competition in the historic jurisdiction of its committees,"[21] but it was able to get through Congress only a slight reduction in the number of committees. This change, however small, was clearly in the direction of coordination. In the House, committee reform was scuttled in 1974 because of jurisdictional fights. But in 1979, as a way of reducing the decentralizing effect of subcommittees, the leadership proposed that members be limited to service on no more than five subcommittees. Some representatives had served on as many as nine, and the limitation served to kill certain subcommittees by leaving them with no members.

At the heart of government involvement in the economy is the budget. Here the Congress acted with dispatch to facilitate planning and to reduce the number of access points that had made congressional budgeting "irrational." Prior to the Congressional Budget and Impoundment Control Act of 1974, the subcommittees of the House and Senate Appropriations Committees, and the Ways and Means and Finance Committees, were dominant. Budget-making resembled the process in the executive branch prior to the Budget and Accounting Act of 1921. At that time, it was said that:

> estimates of expenditure needs now submitted to Congress represent only the desires of the individual departments ... without making them, as a whole, conform to the needs of the Nation as represented by the Treasury and prospective revenues.[22]

The congressional budget committees formed in 1974 have not been able to take complete control of the budget, but each year they have managed to be more assertive, and their decisions have been reinforced by the House and Senate. Budget-making is still incremental, but the mechanism is in place to allow the Congress to address broad problems generated by the uneven process of accumulation that the previous decisionmaking pattern had difficulty confronting. The "larger" perspective is encouraged by the Congressional Budget Office, which the 1974 budget act also created. The CBO is a sort of rarity on Capitol Hill, an agency that is charged with developing broad-based policy and is not linked to a narrow issue area or subgovernment. Its early years have been marked by repeated criticism, and members accustomed to incremental planning have tried to use it for narrow ends. But it is also an instrument that could change the way Congress operates, as CBO professionals relentlessly pressure members to think big.

The New Congressional Bureaucracy. Congress itself is not a bureaucratic organization because it is not hierarchical. The enormous growth of staff, however, has created a phenomenon that is familiar to most people who deal with bureaucratic organizations. Layers of staff have come to buffer interaction between the public and the members. In the Senate many staffs are so large that third-level legislative assistants often complain that even they cannot obtain an audience with the senator for whom they work. The barrier allows legislators to disclaim responsibility for decisions by "blaming" staff, and it protects them from confronting groups directly. This decreases the access for smaller groups and directs a member's attention away from local problems.

Moreover, as the experts on Capitol Hill have become more professional, they have come increasingly to resemble their counterparts in the executive branch and in large national corporations. They are drawn from the same elite universities, reach conclusions by applying the same technical criteria, and often belong to the same social and professional circles. The ideas of the ruling class tend to become the ruling ideas not so much by coercion, but by a much less sinister process. The sorts of analyses that corporations use seem to be based on neutral, technical evaluations; they would appear to remove the Congress from parochial interests. Such analysis seems naturally appropriate — to the private holder of wealth [24] — for national planning and for problems associated with the accumulation of profit.

Summary

The dislocations and economic turmoil of the 1970s were a manifestation of the struggle we have described between owners and workers. In part, they reflected owners' efforts to reduce real wages by raising prices, but inflation also hurt corporate planning. This led to international manipulations that proved to be both a faulty solution and an impetus for further struggle as they contributed to unemployment and the impoverishment of particular regions and sectors of the United States. The Congress was thus called upon to buttress the declining real wage and stave off the unemployment with services and contracts.

Congress was a logical place to turn because it tended to be responsive to particular demands. The problems that led to group demands seem to have been exacerbated by "broker state" solutions, that is, by increasing aid to affected parties. Indeed, the incremental allocations satisfied few because they solved little. The resulting dissatisfaction was experienced by every member of Congress at the polls.[25] Since 1972, more members retired voluntarily than in any comparable period since World War II. In effect, the Congress itself had become discredited and had lost some legitimacy.

These newer members of Congress were ideologically diverse, but shared a vague commitment to modernize the legislature, to abolish some of the patterns that had made the old Congress the object of scorn. The old patterns, of course, were the very ones that had made Congress a weak planning instrument. Members may have had many personal reasons for the changes they helped to forge, but all were responding to the ongoing struggle outside of the Congress.

In turn, the internal changes have become a determinant of external struggle. The pattern of decisionmaking in Congress had acted like a harness on the efforts of some members to respond "rationally" to the crisis. The internal changes have not been always consistent, and they have reflected personal interests of the members and power grabs in the institution. Still, the orientation of change has been toward centralization, toward insulation from parochial demands, and toward an organizational structure that permits the Congress to plan and make broad policy decisions.

CONGRESS'S INSTINCT FOR SELF-PRESERVATION

By juxtaposing the congressional reforms of the 1970s with the economic crisis of that period, three lessons emerge. First, members of Congress respond to immediate concerns, and their most immediate concern is the personal need for job security — re-election. But voters' concerns do not materialize at random. They are structured by the ongoing crisis and also by elites other than senators and representatives. The second lesson, then, is that members of Congress respond in ways that other elites consider "reasonable." Third, the Congress cannot merely respond robot-like to these elites or it will appear to be biased, and so it tries to balance its response in a way that preserves its own legitimacy. In this section we will examine each of these three lessons and in so doing improve our understanding of the limits and possibilities of Congress.

First, Congress responds to immediate demands. Members do not come to understand an economic crisis in abstract terms. They experience it in the form of demands from constituents and interest groups who seek relief from the problems caused by the crisis. These demands then become the issues with which the Congress feels it must grapple.[26] In some cases a problem may involve a small company that is being squeezed by a large one, as the giant attempts to minimize its competition in order to raise prices more freely. In other cases it may involve a city or region of the country that has lost jobs when companies "ran away" looking for cheap or unorganized labor. The legislators may try to avoid meeting the demands by defining them in other terms or by creating obstacles — such as the new congressional bureaucracy — that discourage some groups and insulate the Congress from responsibility for a problem.

Similarly, in campaigns senators and representatives may avoid taking a stand that might anger some constituents or raise expectations of others.[27] But in any case, and certainly when they attempt to address problems directly, the legislators are facing problems generated by the process of accumulating profit. The accumulation process thus structures the congressional agenda.

As it responded to immediate problems in the 1970s, however, the Congress was confronted with a broader problem — the fiscal crisis of the state. During the 1970s the official unemployment rate surpassed nine percent, and the official inflation rate grew to between seven and ten percent, obscuring the even higher annual increase in the costs of four basic necessities: food, housing, energy, and health care. Increasingly, workers looked to the government for assistance to cover the cost of services they could not provide for themselves. Often the demand for assistance was indirect, though it was real nonetheless. Increased social security payments went to provide for retired people's needs that could not be covered by their families; middle-class families sent their children to public universities when they no longer could afford the costs of private higher education. Unemployment was partly relieved by state and local government employment, which in turn was facilitated by federal government revenue sharing. And corporations also demanded government assistance. In effect, these demands were a form of struggle that helped to generate what economist James O'Connor has called the fiscal crisis of the state.[28] Simply stated, government expenses increasingly outpaced revenues and did so for reasons rooted in the system. The government's response — a tax increase — was met in turn by strong worker resistance in the form of the so-called "tax revolt," as taxes became a source of further erosion of their real wages. This situation finally made clear to the Congress the need for planning.

Second, Congress responds in ways that other elites consider "reasonable." Members make decisions based on options as they perceive them. Their choices may be guided by personal motives such as ambition, power, or an easier work schedule that could give them more time with their families. Or members may be guided by a discomfort with combative situations. In part, their beliefs and decisions are the product of members' social backgrounds, including social class, education, ethnicity, previous occupation, race, sex, and religion. Social background can lead them to define what they believe are rational, acceptable, and desirable alternatives. Studies of legislators' social backgrounds can illuminate the sorts of options Congress will consider.

The recruitment process controls the types of members who will serve in Congress. In the bygone era of party machines, parties imposed some restraint on members and selected those who were within an "acceptable" range. As political parties continue to decline, the media become more important. The media define what kinds of behavior and attitudes of candidates are acceptable. To be sure, there is a broad spectrum of opinion in the various media, but there are also limits. These reflect, in part, the training and background of the reporters and editors, as well as the material constraint imposed by advertisers without whom private newspapers and radio and television stations cannot survive. The very fact that the media are private affects their orientation. Newspaper stories and editorials may not directly determine the fortunes of a particular candidate, but they affect our general perceptions.

In turn, our ideology affects the recruitment process. Candidates today must take on the character of entrepreneurs, rugged individuals who have one product to sell: themselves. Their ability to sell themselves depends on their ability to appear "responsible" to us. The sales process, of course, is a complex one. Increasingly, candidates must sell themselves first to political action committees and special interest groups. The candidate does not so much become a captive or tool of the groups, but rather there is a mutuality of interest, a common perspective, and they find each other.

The turmoil occasioned by the crisis of accumulation and the ongoing struggle provides fertile ground for these organizations. They offer structural solutions to problems, supply the resources for candidates to run independently, and help to define the campaign issues. They are the brokers of turmoil, parlaying popular anger into a new Congress that partly reflects their interests.

Third, Congress tries to preserve its legitimacy. If the Congress appeared to be no more than the craven pawn of special interests and the owners of wealth, we would deny it the right to make decisions that affect all of us. Fewer than a half million people effectively control major decisions about the use of most private property in the United States. We expect the Congress to act in everyone's interest, not only the interest of those few.[29] (Indeed, much of the recent decline in the respect for the Congress can be attributed to a popular belief that the Congress serves only narrow interests, and this distrust affects legislators at the polls when voters reject incumbents.) We thus expect the Congress to act at times *against* the immediate interests of corporations, and it does. For example, some environmental legislation can be seen as a restriction on the use of private property by its owners in order to benefit a large mass of people.

To be sure, Congress devotes much energy to symbolic actions with little material consequence in an effort to appear neutral. As David Truman explained 30 years ago, congressional hearings serve more to conform "to the procedural expectations of the community" than to gather information.[30] But some efforts that may appear to be only symbolic also have real impact, and these can create unforeseen possibilities for groups without wealth. Thus, the Congress may have been motivated to alter its own structure in part to make it seem less "captured" by special interests. In doing so, it created new relationships and new problems that alter the struggle in the world outside Congress.

CONCLUSION

The rapidity of change in the last third of this century — the breakdown of traditional values, the challenges to U.S. dominance abroad, the unprecedented coincidence of high inflation and high unemployment, the shifts in population, and the alteration of the labor force from production workers to service workers accompanied by the introduction of high technology in all spheres of our life — has created uncertainty for everyone. In this situation members of Congress became wary of the prescriptions of those to whom they once turned for answers: lobbyists, presidents, technocrats. Instead, Congress focused on internal reform and on asserting itself in new areas such as budget-making and foreign affairs.[31] Members have come to feel that they have as much political sense as traditional experts. Indeed, it might be argued that the distinctive feature of the twentieth century is indeterminacy, and that the greatest advances in science — from psychology to physics — have been preceded by an appreciation of the indeterminate nature of life. In the study of Congress we too must appreciate how important indeterminacy is, how it organizes the world of Congress and shapes what members do. Theirs is a battle against ambiguity, and for us to understand it we need to begin with the sources of indeterminacy. By focusing on the relations of production, a marxist approach facilitates that understanding.

The way in which our society produces goods and services defines the broad limits of congressional behavior. The accumulation of profit generates problems for which the Congress feels it must find solutions. Congress does not own or control the means of production, but must work through the owners of wealth. It must cajole or force owners of wealth to spend their profits or resources in ways that will provide food, clothing, housing, health care, transportation, and other basic necessities for everyone. In undertaking this task the Congress operates within the bounds of its own traditions and with constraints imposed by the structure of the Congress and the personal qualities of its members. But the members do not come to Congress like newborn infants. They arrive by way of a recruitment process that selects people whose ideology broadly conforms to the views of those who own wealth and whose interests increasingly coincide with theirs.

Paradoxically, this limit carries with it the seeds of possibility for congressional action because the owners of wealth do not all have the same interests. There are important divisions among them, rooted in conflicting ways that they accumulate profit. Some own companies that are labor intensive and tend to be hostile to unions, while others own capital intensive companies and often rely on unions to enforce worker compliance. Some corporations are principally domestic and become the victims of international trade when imported goods replace theirs, or dollar devaluations drive up the cost of supplies they purchase. Others are the owners of foreign factories and are the money market manipulators.[32] As Alan Ehrenhalt of Congressional Quarterly reports, the divisions manifest themselves openly in the political arena, where "younger conservatives increasingly see larger corporations as willing participants in an overregulated society. . . ." The split is captured in a speech by Senator Paul Laxalt (R-Nev.) before the Chamber of Commerce in 1978. " 'Thumb your nose at big business,' he told the audience, 'You can't count on this sector — at least right now — to represent the free enterprise section and the things you believe in.' "[33] As the Congress reflects the divided interests of new groups, it will thus affect the accumulation crisis and accompanying struggle in undetermined ways, but in ways that are certain to alter the struggle and bring on new pressures.

The second source of possibility, in addition to the conflicts among the owners of wealth, arises from the complexity of problems that confront the Congress. Solutions to problems of accumulation are not obvious, and so there are always several answers that seem plausible. Any one of them may unintentionally restrict the free use of property in ways that weaken the process of accumulation. Moreover, in cases where one company's greed — or even that of a whole sector such as the energy industries — creates problems that undermine the viability of accumulation by many other companies, the Congress may act to control the greedy ones as a means of protecting the system of private accumulation as a whole.

While it thus may restrict the use of property, the Congress leaves the control of property essentially untouched. Owners must find new techniques for accumulating profit, which in turn create new struggles. These struggles then generate further demands on the Congress. Similarly, when the legislature appears to act in everyone's interest, it raises people's expectations of what is possible and encourages them to press for more action.

Given the changing context of the private accumulation of wealth, the Congress continually performs a delicate balancing act. It precariously fashions solutions to problems caused by accumulation while it protects its own need for legitimacy. The changing context creates both the limits and possibilities of congressional action. A marxist approach thus offers a systematic way of exploring the changing context and a useful guide for investigating patterns of congressional behavior.

NOTES

1. E. E. Schattschneider, *The Semi-Sovereign People* (New York: Holt, Rinehart & Winston, 1960), chap. 2.
2. Philip Brenner, "Congress Watch: The Shifting Coalitions," *The Nation*, November 4, 1978, p. 2a.
3. Lawrence C. Dodd, *"Congress and the Quest for Power,"* in *Congress Reconsidered,* 1st ed., edited by Lawrence C. Dodd and Bruce I. Oppenheimer (New York: Praeger Publishers, 1977), p. 269.
4. Karl Marx, *Surveys from Exile,* ed. David Fernbach, (New York: Vintage Books, 1974), pp. 173-174.
5. Contrast, for example, the findings in Mark Green, *Who Runs Congress?* 3rd ed. (New York: Bantam Books, 1979), with those in Raymond Bauer et al., *American Business and Public Policy* (New York: Atherton, 1963).
6. Jerrold S. Schneider, *Ideological Coalitions in Congress* (Westport, Conn.: Greenwood Press, 1979).
7. Theodore J. Lowi, *The End of Liberalism,* 2nd ed. (New York: W. W. Norton & Co., 1979), chap. 3.
8. Bertell Ollman, *Alienation: Marx's Conception of Man in Capitalist Society* (New York: Cambridge University Press, 1971), chap. 1.
9. Gosta Esping-Anderson, Roger Friedland, and Erik Olin Wright, "Modes of Class Struggle and the Capitalist State," *Kapitalistate,* nos. 4-5 (Summer 1976): 190-192.
10. Harry Braverman, *Labor and Monopoly Capital* (New York: Monthly Review Press, 1974), Part I; Stephen A. Marglin, "What Do Bosses Do? The Origins and Functions of Hierarchy in Capitalist Production," *Review of Radical Political Economics,* vol. 6, no. 2 (Summer 1974); Katherine Stone, "The Origin of Job Structures in the Steel Industry," *Review of Radical Political Economics,* vol. 6, no. 2 (Summer 1974).
11. Michael Parenti, *Democracy for the Few,* 3rd ed. (New York: St. Martin's Press, 1980), pp. 103-104.
12. Richard J. Barnet, *The Lean Years* (New York: Simon & Shuster, 1980).
13. Editors, "Banks: Skating on Thin Ice," *Monthly Review,* February 1975. See also Bruce Steinberg et al., *U.S. Capitalism in Crisis* (New York: Union for Radical Political Economics, 1978).
14. Fred L. Block, *The Origins of International Economic Disorder* (Berkeley: University of California Press, 1977), chap. 2.
15. U.S. Tariff Commission, "Money Crises and the Operation of Multinational Firms," in *Exploring Contradictions,* ed. Philip Brenner, Robert Borosage, and Bethany Weidner (New York: David McKay Co., 1974); David M. Kotz, *Bank Control of Large Corporations in the United States* (Berkeley: University of California Press, 1978); U.S., Congress, Senate, Committee

on Governmental Affairs, *Voting Rights in Major Corporations: A Staff Study,* 95th Cong. 1st sess., January 1978.
16. David J. Vogler, *The Politics of Congress,* 3rd ed. (Boston: Allyn & Bacon, 1980), pp. 295-296; Douglass Cater, *Power in Washington* (New York: Random House, 1964); Gordon Adams, "Disarming the Military Subgovernment," *Harvard Journal on Legislation,* vol. 14, no. 3 (April 1977).
17. Andrew Martin, "Is Democratic Control of Capitalist Economies Possible?" *Stress and Contradiction in Modern Capitalism,* ed. Leon Lindberg et al. (Lexington: D.C. Heath & Co., 1975), p. 19.
18. Norman J. Ornstein, "Causes and Consequences of Congressional Change: Subcommittee Reforms in the House of Representatives, 1970-73," in *Congress in Change,* ed. Norman J. Ornstein (New York: Praeger Publishers, 1975), pp. 105-108.
19. David Vogler, "The Rise of Ad Hoc Committees in the House" (Paper delivered at the annual meeting of the American Political Science Association, New York, New York, August 31-September 3, 1978).
20. U.S., Congress, Senate, Temporary Select Committee to Study the Senate Committee System, *The Senate Committee System: First Staff Report,* 94th Cong., 2nd sess., July 1976, p. 8.
21. Ibid.
22. See also "Senate Panel Develops Plan to Cut Committees from 18 to Five," *National Journal,* August 21, 1976, p. 1189 and Philip Brenner, "Congressional Reform: Analyzing the Analysts," *Harvard Journal on Legislation,* vol. 14, no. 3 (April 1977): 664-670.
23. Quoted in Joseph Harris, *Congressional Control of Administration* (Garden City, N.Y.: Anchor Books, 1964), p. 66.
24. Bertram Gross, *Friendly Fascism: The New Face of Power in America* (New York: M. Evans & Co., 1980), chaps. 2, 12.
25. Thomas E. Mann, *Unsafe at Any Margin* (Washington, D.C.: American Enterprise Institute, 1978).
26. Erik Olin Wright, *Class, Crisis and the State* (London: New Left Books, 1978), pp. 15-19. The need to act is usually apparent to the Congress, despite its reputation for delay. Senator Jennings Randolph (D-W.Va.) tells a story about President Franklin Roosevelt in March 1933. FDR had called in a group of members to meet with him in the White House. "At one point another Congressman in the group had the temerity to suggest that the New Deal might be attempting too much, too soon. 'But gentlemen,' President Roosevelt retorted, 'do you realize that we must *act now*?' End of debate." As quoted in *Wall Street Journal,* August 30, 1978, p. 1.
27. Richard F. Fenno, Jr., *Home Style: House Members in Their Districts* (Boston: Little, Brown & Co., 1978), pp. 165-168.
28. James O'Connor, *The Fiscal Crisis of the State* (New York: St. Martin's Press, 1973), chap. 1.
29. Alan Wolfe, *The Limits of Legitimacy* (New York: The Free Press, 1977), chap. 10; O'Connor, *The Fiscal Crisis of the State,* chap. 2.
30. David B. Truman, *The Governmental Process* (New York: Alfred A. Knopf, 1951), pp. 372-377. See also Murray Edelman, *The Symbolic Uses of Politics* (Urbana: University of Illinois Press, 1964).
31. See, for example, Louis Fisher, *The Constitution Between Friends* (New York: St. Martin's Press, 1978), chap. 7; Thomas M. Franck and Edward Weisband, *Foreign Policy by Congress* (New York: Oxford University Press, 1979).

32. Richard J. Barnet and Ronald Muller, *Global Reach* (New York: Simon & Schuster, 1974). See also O'Connor, *The Fiscal Crisis of the State,* chap. 1; John Kenneth Galbraith, *Economics and the Public Purpose* (Boston: Houghton Mifflin Co., 1973), chaps. 2, 3.
33. "The Right in Congress: Seeking a Strategy," *Congressional Quarterly Weekly Report,* August 5, 1978, p. 2025.

18

Congress, the Constitution, and the Crisis of Legitimation

Lawrence C. Dodd

The American Constitution was constructed upon a theory of politics, a theory most evident in the essays by James Madison in the *Federalist Papers*. The theory assumed that a basic motive driving politicians is a quest for power to control the policy decisions that impose the authority of the state on the citizenry at large. As power seekers, politicians crystallize the factional divisions that undergird any society and fuel the political strife in which faction seeks to dominate faction in order to maximize particularized interest. In the heat of political battle and the impassioned aftermath of victory, the power quest can be so all-consuming that the victorious faction and factional leaders overlook the general interest and civil liberties of the public.[1]

Because the power quest can pose such a fundamental threat to political freedom and stability, Madison argued that the best way

For their useful comments on an earlier draft of this essay, the author would like to thank Bruce Buchanan, Gary Freeman, Bruce Oppenheimer, Terry Sullivan, and Al Watkins. In addition, he owes a continuing debt to the numerous graduate and undergraduate students who have shared with him their insights and questions regarding congressional politics.

to protect civil liberties and property was through a constitution that divides the power of the state among governmental institutions. With separation of powers, checks and balances, and federalism together dispersing power, little chance exists that one individual or faction can gain sufficient leverage to dominate the nation. Rather, governmental action will require cooperation among institutions that share power. In the act of cooperating, each institution should jealously guard its prerogatives.

Madison did not assume, however, that institutions would, in fact, jealously guard their prerogatives. After all, institutions have no autonomous being, but are only aggregations of individuals who act in the institution's name. Recognizing this problem, Madison concluded:

> In order to lay a due foundation for that separate and distinct exercise of the different powers of government, which to a certain extent is admitted on all hands to be essential to the preservation of liberty, it is evident that each department should have a will of its own. . . .[2]

The entire logic of the Constitution rests on this critical variable: *institutional will.* Should any one branch of government consistently fail to assert an institutional will, then the powers of that branch would be usurped by another branch, checks and balances would cease to operate, and "the preservation of liberty" would be jeopardized.

Because of the critical importance of institutional will, the founders were not content to hope blindly that each institution would be capable of developing and sustaining institutional cohesiveness. They saw the Constitution as an instrument that could structure institutions, nurture cohesiveness, and generate an institutional will. Madison stated this proposition quite clearly:

> . . . [T]he great security against a gradual concentration of the several powers in the same department consists in giving to those who administer each department the necessary constitutional means and personal motives to resist encroachment of the others. The provision for defense must in this, as in all other cases, be made commensurate with the danger of attack. Ambition must be made to counteract ambition. The interests of the man must be connected with the constitutional right of the place.[3]

Based on this proposition, the founders created a single executive and gave to the president the power to nominate department heads. Similarly, they created a single Supreme Court composed of justices with virtual lifetime tenure. These and other devices were expressly designed to nurture the cohesiveness of the presidency and the Supreme Court. The founders wanted to ensure that the executive and judicial branches of government could assert their institutional wills.

When the writers of the Constitution came to the legislative branch, however, they lost their fervor for constitutional provisions that would nurture institutional cohesion. The constitutional provisions for Congress, such as bicameralism and separate selection procedures for the House and Senate, seem to generate internal conflict and weakness. There are several reasons why the founders failed to undergird the institutional will of Congress as they did the presidency and the Supreme Court.

Madison believed that the way politicians approach political institutions and seek power through them strongly depends upon the nature of the extant society and on political realities within it. The Constitution was written for an agrarian society in which political service at the national level was physically and economically difficult. Moreover, because the role of the national government was quite limited in an agrarian society isolated by the Atlantic from European wars, and because the federal Constitution left considerable power to state and local governments, Madison believed that long-term service at the national level would not be very attractive to politicians. Power would be pursued more easily and perhaps more effectively in local or state politics. At the national level of government, there would be a high turnover of elected officials. The few politicians who stayed on for long-term congressional careers would acquire expertise and would be relied upon as power wielders.[4]

Madison's great fear was that the Congress, in the context of an agrarian and isolated society, would come to rely on too few leaders, particularly the presiding officer of the House, to exercise power. The experience of the colonial assemblies suggested that a legislature in control of the power of the purse and guided by a strong-willed leader could come to dominate governmental affairs. Similarly, Congress could be an overly cohesive, aggressive institution using its taxing and spending power to dominate the other branches. Hence, the best constitutional course was not to reinforce the natural cohesiveness that Congress would derive from high turnover and centralized organizational power in an agrarian age, but to constrain Congress in order to equalize the balance of power between Congress, the presidency, and the Court.[5]

The Madisonian theory of politics thus envisioned a constitutional system in which each branch of government would be sufficiently cohesive to have an institutional will, assert itself in its own area of governmental authority, cooperate in areas of shared authority, and respond effectively to aggrandizing efforts by other branches. As long as the underlying premises held, the Madisonian model worked to a large extent as Madison had expected. But Madison's assumptions did not hold indefinitely, not because politicians ceased to seek power or because the constitutional system of checks and balances or separation of powers was revised, but because the character and setting of the nation itself changed. As the environment changed, politics began to follow dynamic patterns unforeseen by Madison.

The general thesis of this essay is that the capacity of Congress to generate a cohesive institutional will and play a strong role in national politics is conditioned by the impact of external environmental factors on the ways in which politicians approach congressional service and organize institutional power. During the past two centuries, the United States has passed through three broad environmental eras in which distinct modes of electoral and organizational politics characterized Congress and influenced its power and role in American politics: the era of confrontation (1789-1860), the era of expansion (1876-1910), and the era of consolidation (1920-1965). Between these eras came periods of rapid and fundamental change in the nation's domestic and international life: the Civil War and Reconstruction (1860-1876) and the Progressive age and World War I (1910-1920).

Congress sustained its institutional cohesiveness and played a forceful role in national government during the eras of confrontation and expansion. Then, during the era of consolidation, as careerist legislators began to lobby for an ever more decentralized form of congressional organization, Congress experienced a long-term, cyclical decline in its capacity to generate authoritative leadership and institutional cohesion. As a consequence, the executive branch of government increasingly came to dominate Congress, although Congress was able to maintain a significant role in national policymaking.

During the past two decades domestic and international developments have been occurring that may further alter congressional behavior and cripple the capacity of Congress to act. The 1960s and 1970s were a great period of protest that saw transformations as fundamental in their significance as those of the Civil War and Reconstruction or the Progressive age and World War I. As a result, the nation may be entering a fourth era of American politics, an era of reassessment characterized by greater electoral vulnerability, a decline in members' policymaking competence, and a personalization of their struggles for organizational power. Institutionally, Congress will become more fragmented, more variable in its policy commitments, more dominated by a professionalized staff, and more immobilized in its independent capacity to make innovative policy decisions.

The tension between the motives of ambitious politicians seeking power through congressional service and a highly volatile, complex, and threatening environment should produce an institution virtually incapable of generating strong leadership, sustaining an institutional will, or protecting its constitutional prerogatives. As a consequence,

Congress and its members may lose public support. This essay concludes with a discussion of the conditions that could give rise to this crisis of congressional legitimation and suggests constitutional reforms designed to resolve the crisis. We turn first to a discussion of the historical dynamics that have generated the modern Congress.

THE CONGRESSIONAL ROLE IN NATIONAL POLITICS

The Era of Confrontation, 1789-1860

During the first 70 years of our history, the national government approximated the one foreseen by Madison. It was an era of confrontation. The nation struggled over the fundamental goals and values to which the new Republic would be committed — agrarian or industrial democracy; slavery or freedom; isolationism or a manifest destiny.[6] By and large, the economy remained agrarian, the citizenry was isolated from the immediacy of international affairs, local and state governments were strong, and the national government was out of sight and out of mind.[7]

Congress served as a great debating society, a forum for the far-reaching ethical and political struggles of the day. The leaders and careerists in Congress — the Websters, Clays, and Calhouns — were individuals gifted in debate, in identifying and articulating broad principles, and in compromise. Men such as these led elite caucuses that ran the House and Senate. Through positions of party and committee leadership (particularly on the revenue committees) and through informal personal influence, a few careerists dominated the organizational politics of Congress. Most members were content to serve for two to four years, follow the guidance of regional leaders, and return home to build state and local careers in business or politics.[8] With congressional power largely centralized in the hands of a small elite, Congress maintained relatively clear command of its role as legislative decisionmaker for the nation, but it was balanced by strong presidents such as Washington, Jefferson, Jackson, and Polk, and by an assertive Court.

The Era of Expansion, 1876-1910

Events of the 1860s and early 1870s altered the situation dramatically. The Civil War ended formal ambiguities about slavery and state supremacy and clearly established the hegemony of the national government in political affairs. The industrial revolution, the effect of which was exacerbated by the war, helped create an interdependent economy based on interstate commerce. It also provided America, as well as other nations, with the technical means to expand trade to far-off lands and gain international markets for domestically manufactured goods. America discovered the world, the world rediscovered America, and the national government discovered anew its constitutional responsibility for foreign policy and the regulation of American involvement in foreign commerce.

Congress became the center of the expanding activity of the national government because of its constitutional powers to regulate interstate and foreign commerce, to give advice and consent (on the part of the Senate) to treaties and ambassadorial nominations, to control defense authorizations and appropriations, and to declare war. Consequently, ambitious politicians focused more intently on Congress in the aftermath of the Civil War and Reconstruction. Voluntary turnover of members began to decline as more and more politicians were attracted to congressional service as a means of exercising real power over important policy decisions. Committee work was taken more seriously, and significant committee reforms and changes were instituted. The formal party leadership began to assert itself, with the leaders gaining considerable authority because they offered services — such as selection of committee members and chairs, policy development and guidance, mediation of parliamentary conflicts, scheduling of legislation — that were necessary to avoid the chaos implicit in the changing Congress.[9]

The late nineteenth and early twentieth centuries thus constitute a second great era of American politics — the era of expansion, during which the national government extended its control over the economy, its sovereignty over the states, and its involvement in international politics.[10] Congress, led by strong central leaders and in control of the power of appropriation, taxation, and the tariff, could dominate the judicial and executive branches.[11] But this dominance was short-lived.

During the early twentieth century, the nation experienced a new dramatic upheaval in the underpinnings of its political and social life, an upheaval fueled by the Progressive movement and World War I. This period in American politics was as significant in many ways as the period of transformation during the Civil War and Reconstruction. The national government accepted critical new roles as regulator of the economic and social life produced by industrialization, roles greatly expanded by the Depression and World War II. During this period, the nation became convinced of its unlimited power — not only power nationally to secure a good life for its citizens but power internationally both to remake the world order and to make it safe for democracy.

The Era of Consolidation, 1920–1965

The coming of the Progressive movement and World War I refocused American politics, and the nation entered a new era, the era of consolidation. In this era the national government consolidated its control over the economy, its supremacy over the states, and its dominant role in international affairs. These decades were characterized by cooperative federalism, by a distributive politics in which major interest groups (particularly labor and business) fought for the spoils of government through partisan control of government, and by strong international involvement. Major changes in the character and role of Congress also characterized this period.

CONGRESS DURING THE ERA OF CONSOLIDATION

In order to understand the changes in Congress during the era of consolidation, one must take into account the preceding congressional developments. During the era of national expansion, Congress experienced three internal trends. First, party leaders in both the House and Senate increased their power through control over committee appointments, selection of committee chairs, bill referral, parliamentary procedures, and other means. Second, with the expanding political responsibility of the national government, congressional committees grew in number and in influence. Third, more and more politicians were attracted to congressional service and ran successfully for election and re-election. With declining turnover, there emerged a growing number of career-oriented members seeking to sustain long-term congressional service in order to gain personal influence over national policymaking.[12]

As the nation moved to consolidate major roles for the national government in both domestic and international affairs, these three trends within Congress became increasingly incompatible with each other. In the words of Cooper and Brady, Congress faced an "adaptation crisis." [13] Career-oriented members found that a centralized system of congressional government denied them the personal autonomy and policy influence they wanted. Somehow new organizational procedures, structures, and rules had to be created that would serve the career aspirations of members while nurturing sufficient institutional cohesion to protect the capacity of Congress to generate authoritative decisions and assert an institutional will. To a large extent, however, the adaptation process became an effort by career-oriented members to create procedures and structures that would maximize their immediate career interests, unguided by an awareness of the consequences for Congress as an institution.

Personal Goals of Members

Among the many career interests characterizing the new, professional members of Congress, three were paramount.[14] First, members became *electoral entrepreneurs* who developed a range of image-building and constituent-service enterprises designed to enhance their electoral security. With the rise of electoral entrepreneurship, dramatic and measurable patterns in congressional elections emerged.[15] In particular, members came to benefit from the growth of an "incumbent advantage," that is, a vote advantage over their electoral challengers.

The second career goal that grew to fruition during the age of consolidation was a widespread desire to gain a reputation for policymaking competence. This goal required that a member specialize within committees in particular areas of public policy, become expert in those areas, and be able to speak with authority on them. Policy competence came to entail not only knowledge in a policy arena, but sensitivity to the formal and informal norms and procedures governing the policymaking process, skill at legislative draftsmanship, and facility at legislative maneuvering.[16] The concern for policymaking success led members to form supportive coalitions of policy allies in Congress and to seek association outside Congress with interest groups and bureaucratic agencies that could provide critical information and assistance in policy debates and maneuvers.[17] The era of consolidation thus witnessed the development of members as *policy entrepreneuers*.[18]

Third, members wanted control over the formal organizational and parliamentary prerogatives governing policymaking. This desire for significant power positions within Congress placed career-oriented members in direct conflict with the system of strong party leadership that had emerged during the era of expansion. Between 1905 and 1920, insurgent members of Congress stripped the Speakership of virtually all of its formal authority within the majority party and in the House rules, and they discarded the role of a powerful majority party leader in the Senate.[19] Increasing reliance on committee government during the era of consolidation meant that fundamental congressional policymaking responsibility was placed in a series of discrete and relatively autonomous committees and subcommittees, each having control over the decisions in a specified jurisdictional area. Members thus became *power entrepreneurs* who sought to obtain committee assignments early in their careers that would provide them with the broadest possible base for policy influence. Members also sought to nurture their seniority on those committees in order to gain personal control of the committees and key subcommittees.

These three goals — to enhance electoral security, to develop policy expertise, and to control positions of power in Congress —

formed a sort of goal hierarchy for careerists. Before members had the time and emotional freedom to seek policy competence, they needed a reasonably secure electoral base. And before obtaining sufficient seniority to reach key positions of committee leadership, members normally would develop their reputation at policy competence. Hidden within the orderliness of this sequential progression, however, was an underlying tension. As congressional service became increasingly attractive and as incumbents became skilled as electoral entrepreneurs, newer members of Congress generally proved able to move through the earlier stages of career progression faster than more senior members left the Congress. Newer members often found themselves ready to direct policymaking in key areas only to be constrained by senior members in positions of power. Because of the requirements of seniority, which seemed essential to avoiding the return of dominance by strong party leaders, members were prohibited from challenging a senior member for leadership of a committee. For this reason, unhappy members focused their attention less on removal of key occupants of the existing power structure and more on measures designed to reduce the authority of existing positions, to create new positions that would exercise this authority, and to spread the new positions among a wider number of members.

The Characteristics of Committee Government

The era of consolidation witnessed the spread of power from party to committee government and the proliferation of power positions within the committee system. For Congress and, ultimately, for the members of Congress, the costs of decentralized power were great. While committee government nurtured the development of legislative expertise and individualized policy creativity, it also undermined the ability of Congress to fulfill its constitutional responsibilities to make public policy and oversee executive implementation of that policy.

Four flaws of committee government were particularly critical. First, committee government lacked strong, central leadership. Second, committee government lacked fiscal coordination; the decisions of the authorization, appropriations, and revenue committees bore little relationship to one another. Third, committee government created problems of institutional responsiveness and democratic accountability; the decentralization of power within committees made it difficult for the public to hold any congressional majority accountable for policy decisions or nondecisions. Fourth, committee government led to a failure of objective, independent oversight of the executive branch; committees with oversight responsibility usually had close ties to lobby groups and bureaucratic agencies with a vested interest in the outcome of programs and policies.

Danger of Presidential Imperialism

All of these flaws, exacerbated by the continuing pressures for decentralization, created a tension between personal power and institutional power in Congress.[20] As Congress moved toward greater dispersion of organizational power within the institution, it became so immobilized on major policy questions that political activists turned to the presidency for policy leadership and for centralized control of the bureaucracy. As presidents became increasingly responsible for policy formulation and implementation, however, they sought power commensurate with their responsibility, often going beyond constitutional norms and usurping congressional power prerogatives.

Such presidential imperialism eventually provoked Congress into attempts to constrain the presidency and strengthen Congress. These efforts included congressional reforms to bolster centralized party leadership, improve budgetary and policy coordination, and strengthen congressional oversight of the executive.[21] Because the quest for personal power continued as the underlying motivation of individual members, the centralizing reforms became constrained by considerations of personal power prerogatives, building flaws into them that would provide openings through which the new procedures could be undermined as the crisis passed. Thus Congress was characterized by cyclical organizational dynamics; long periods of organizational decentralization were momentarily halted by short-lived periods of power centralization.

Conclusion

In essence, the era of consolidation was a period of American politics devoted to institutionalizing at a state, national, and international level American commitment to an industrial economic order. Government served to ensure proper functioning of the order by distributing special goods, regulations, and services to whichever of the two major groups within the economic order — business or labor — was momentarily capable of coalescing with other social and economic forces to capture Congress and the presidency and produce laws and regulations to nurture a productive industrial order. The security of the social order came through establishing minimal standards of governmental relief support to the poor, through economic regulation and defense preparedness, and through an activist involvement in international affairs and military conflicts.

The development of distributive policy commitments came largely through presidential leadership and the use of executive intervention to break policy deadlocks in Congress. In the process, the expectations and symbolic authority of the executive branch expanded dramatically. Simultaneously, much of the routine of government — marginal and incremental adjustments in national policy commitments — occurred in the interaction among the committees of Congress, the agencies of the national bureaucracy, and major interest groups.

Short-term attempts to centralize power during this period were eroded by renewed efforts at power dispersion. In the 1960s and early 1970s Congress began to institutionalize the most decentralized structure of subcommittee government in its history. Despite reforms that strengthened party leadership, budgetary coordination, and oversight capacity, subcommittee government appeared likely to become the dominant form of congressional organization, particularly in light of the environmental changes of the sixties and seventies.

THE AGE OF PROTEST, 1960s-1970s

Post-Industrial Economic Order

While politics during the era of consolidation was preoccupied with presidential power, congressional routine, and distributive policymaking, by the 1960s fundamental changes were occurring in the structural underpinnings of industrial democracy. Events were propelling the nation toward a post-industrial economic order. The economy remained one based on mass production and a strong agrarian base, but technological innovations of the postwar space age expanded both agrarian and industrial productive capacity while reducing reliance on a large domestic workforce.

The resulting vulnerability of the agrarian and industrial workforce focused greater attention on careers in education, technology, leisure industries, and public and private service delivery. It also created a growing body of citizens concerned with issues such as the fate of disadvantaged groups, health care, quality education, urban planning, mass transit, cultural affairs, and consumer and environmental protection.

While the dominant political forces remained fixated on struggles of industrial democracy — the classic partisan conflicts among business and labor and traditional efforts to generate tax breaks or jobs for the politically faithful — a growing segment of society was becoming concerned with issues of an interdependent, communal life in an increasingly urbanized, post-industrial world. The effective articulation of these policy concerns came to Congress largely through mass protest movements. The most important of these were the great civil rights movement, the consumer and environmental campaigns, and, above all, the protest against the Vietnam War.

As the new preoccupations of the sixties and seventies found legitimacy and increased salience, they altered the structure of political conflict. First, many of the new issues divided the traditional political groups internally. Questions of affirmative action created great factional strife within labor unions, for example. Second, the new programmatic concerns such as national health care were often so costly that their enactment would necessarily entail greater tax burdens on the affluent recipients of traditional distributive politics and necessitate a re-distribution of resources from traditional programs and groups to new programs. Third, many of the new groups and issues of the sixties and seventies raised cultural and lifestyle concerns — feminism, gay rights, abortion, racial equality — that conflicted with codes of morality and religious beliefs among many traditional groups in society. The centrality of these cultural and symbolic issues often overshadowed the substantive issues of post-industrial change and led groups that might have been potential supporters of redistributive politics to see all issues proposed by new social forces as threatening cherished social and cultural values.

Emergence of Conflicting Factional Groups

The new policy concerns of the 1960s and 1970s thus produced a complex set of cross-cutting domestic issues that divided the public into a vast array of conflicting factional groups. In particular, these cross-cutting issues broke down the simplicity of labor-business conflict that had emerged during the era of consolidation and made difficult the building and sustenance of a national majority coalition that could encompass new and old issues alike.

The arguments of many if not most of the groups reflected a major change in the standards applied to policy debate and evaluation. Politics in the era of consolidation was justified by the canons of procedural democracy. In the 1960s and 1970s, however, the new concern was less with procedural legalities than with substantive con-sequences. The underlying standard of evaluation became *substantive justice,* the assertion that policies be evaluated in terms of substantive consequences for individuals, groups, and society as a whole, often regardless of procedural formalities. For example, it was unjust for citizens of one state or locality to be deprived voting rights, a good education, efficient mass transit, or a clean environment because the state or locality with legal jurisdiction over the problem had few fiscal resources or a repressive political structure. The application of this argument across a wide array of policy concerns necessarily led to calls for action by the national government, the one level of government capable of ensuring equitable treatment of groups re-gardless of the region, state, or locality in which they lived.

The New Federal Activism

With the move toward the politics of post-industrialism, then, came a second major change. Not only did a broad array of conflicting factional groups spring up, but in addressing many of the issues raised by the new political forces, the national government during the Johnson and Nixon presidencies took an increasingly activist role in policy domains traditionally or constitutionally left to state and local government, most notably, issues of suffrage (procedures for securing the voting rights of all citizens and standards for legislative apportionment) as well as health, education, law enforcement, and consumer and environmental protection.

The end result of these policy innovations was a qualitative change in state-federal relations. The new federal activism of the 1960s and 1970s did not constitute short-term intervention by the national government in state and local affairs, but long-term penetration of state and local policy activity. Once state and local governments accepted federal programs and federal money, their residents came to expect certain services. Without continued acceptance of federal programs and money, local and state governments had difficulty meeting these expectations.

Along with federal programs and federal money, however, came federal regulations and review covering policy questions entirely apart from the policy domain that a specific program was designed to address. For example, a state university accepting federal money for research might face federal threats to freeze those funds if the university failed to comply with federal affirmative action standards in admission or hiring or failed to provide specific types of ramps for the handicapped. Similar types of rules, across a wide range of federal concerns, were applied to local and state entities accepting federal funds.

Thus, in the 1960s and 1970s the nation moved from a *cooperative federalism* in which the national government occasionally intervened in state and local affairs to a *cooptative federalism* in which national concerns for substantive justice served to justify national dictation of state and local policies. In less than 20 years, state and local governmental units became constrained and guided, in many if not most major policy decisions, by federal regulations and actions. The national government penetrated the units of state and local policymaking even in policy domains the Constitution clearly reserved to the states or the people. Yet precisely as the national government was expanding the scope of its programmatic and fiscal commitments, international developments undercut the nation's capacity to fulfill these responsibilities.

International Developments

On the international stage, the postwar years witnessed three significant developments: the end of overt colonialism and the rise of third world nationalism; the emergence of the United States as defender of the industrialized, noncommunist world; and the re-in-dustrialization of Europe, particularly Germany, and Japan. During these years, the United States experienced a decreasing ability to influence the underdeveloped nations and ensure cheap access to the resources, such as oil, that third world nations possessed. Si-multaneously, the United States became increasingly responsible for the defense of the western industrialized nations. This responsibility meant that a large portion of the national budget was devoted to defense and foreign policy commitments. Yet by accepting responsibility for the security of nations who then devoted less of their fiscal resources to military preparedness than they might have otherwise, the nation freed its allies to use their resources to nurture the development of their productive capacity.

With fewer defense constraints on their national budgets, many western nations developed extensive social services, such as national health care, while the United States continued to debate the economic feasibility of such programs. Simultaneously, the re-industrialization of Europe and Japan had serious economic consequences for the United States. In capturing a significant share of the market tra-ditionally controlled by American industry, these nations severely curtailed American industrial employment and profits.

During the the 1960s and 1970s, these three international trends coincided to constrain America's fiscal capacity to continue distributive policies while responding to new post-industrial policy demands. The Vietnam War, together with a series of events ranging from the Bay of Pigs fiasco to the hostage crisis in Iran, conveyed the clear message that the economic and military power of an industrial giant does not necessarily translate into power over nonindustrial nation states. The nation thus confronted its growing incapacity to control the direction of world affairs.

The 1973 Arab oil embargo and the consequent rise of OPEC and cartel economics weakened America's international economic po-sition by producing annual deficits in its balance of payments. Its domestic economy was also weakened by the greater relative capacity of other industrialized nations to sustain strong productive capacity despite the energy crisis. Thus the United States experienced runaway inflation and growing unemployment. These economic developments eroded the financial resource base on which the nation could draw to sustain economic productivity and generate the revenues to meet the growing programmatic and fiscal responsibility of the national government.

Simultaneously, the widespread deployment of American military forces at home and around the world, and the extensive responsibility of the United States for western defense, built into the national budget a large fiscal commitment that hindered the nation's flexible control of the revenues it could generate. This extensive and perhaps overzealous commitment to an international American military presence not only limited the flexible funds available for developing new and experimental forms of military hardware and defense capacity but also limited funds the United States had for its own re-industrialization, for the development of new energy sources, and for social programs that could respond to the new political forces and provide relief to the victims of inflation and unemployment.

The reverses that the United States experienced in the 1960s and 1970s on the international scene were intricately linked to the politics and policies that dominated the nation in the era of consolidation. Policies during this era had encouraged domestic energy entrepreneurs to "drain America first." These policies, which kept cheap foreign oil out of the country while American oil reserves were being exploited, built huge domestic fortunes and financed the careers of a generation of politicians who served the oil interests. Similarly, tax policies gave depreciation allowances and other incentives to industry under the assumption that such policies stimulated modernization. In actuality, however, such procedures allowed industries to divert huge sums of money into more immediately profitable endeavors or into salaries and fringe benefits, allowing American plants to deteriorate at the long-term expense of the nation's economic well-being. Analogously, the buildup of a permanent military force at home and abroad served the interests of domestic manufacturers of traditional military hardware, sustained local economies built around military installations, and supported the political careers of the politicians who fueled the preoccupation with unilateral American defense responsibility for the noncommunist world.

In all of these policy areas, the ethic of distributive politics, with its emphasis on short-term governmental rewards to those groups and factions that support victorious politicians and parties, diverted the nation from an assessment of its long-term needs and priorities.[22] Needless to say, the decisionmaking structure within Congress — with its emphasis on incremental, routinized decisionmaking rather than on innovative and comprehensive policy formulation and aggressive policy surveillance — reinforced the tendency to respond to short-term political pressures rather than long-term policy needs. The end result was a nation ill-prepared to face the challenges of a post-industrial world of scarcity and international volatility.

Conclusion

Upon reflection, it would appear that the transformations produced by this period are just as dramatic as those unleashed by the Civil War and Reconstruction or by the Progressive movement and World

War I. A nation that 20 years ago saw itself as dominant, autonomous, and secure in the world, possessed of virtually limitless resources, productive capacity, and military might, today finds itself increasingly dependent on the world community, painfully conscious of resource limits, questioning its economic capacities and governmental competence. We have a national government today that faces an expanding array of conflicting policy demands and has leverage over many of the state and local policymaking domains necessary to respond to these demands, yet is constrained by limited resources with which to meet the demands and support the programs for which the public holds it responsible.

Hard choices must be made about the relative weight to be given to the needs and demands of different groups and programs; about the type of policies to be undertaken to meet the challenge of the post-industrial era; about the means to be utilized to nurture and sustain our domestic economy and energy autonomy; and about the role and policies of the nation in the international community. These choices necessarily require a broad reassessment of domestic and international policy commitments and procedures. This reassessment should be made in a representative assembly with the capacity to make informed, authoritative decisions that are responsive to the American public. Unfortunately, today Congress may be far less capable of making such decisions than it was during the era of consolidation and committee government. This prospect exists because the emerging external and internal worlds of the contemporary Congress together create an environment that undermines the capability and incentives of career-minded members to unite in majority coalitions that can govern.

ERA OF REASSESSMENT: THE CONGRESSIONAL RESPONSE

As the nation moves into the era of reassessment, the external environment and internal organization of the contemporary Congress together create an exceedingly complex world for members. Externally, the nation is balkanized into special interest groups concerned not solely with the traditional broad issues of industrial democracy but with a myriad of general and particularized issues that suggest the coming of a post-industrial world of scarcity. Labor and business remain the two largest groups and thus define the general character of our electoral and partisan politics. Yet labor and business find themselves challenged by forces preoccupied with a wide range of new issues that do not fit neatly into their orthodox policy orientations. With cross-cutting issues thus splintering the public, parties and party leaders find it increasingly difficult to find a cohesive set of policy positions that can appeal to a majority of the public over an extensive time period.

Internally, congressional government is similarly fractured. Approximately 140 subcommittees in each house possess significant resources and decisionmaking autonomy independent of their parent committees. Yet subcommittee government does not exist in a vacuum. Significant formal authority also rests in central party leaders and, sporadically, in a central budget process. This bifurcated and balkanized congressional structure links up with the complex features of the external environment to create an extensive set of new pressures within Congress, pressures that undermine both its institutional integrity and the career aspirations of its members. In particular, the existence in the electorate of a wide range of narrow specialized interest groups creates strong external support for the institutionalized subcommittee government that has arisen.

In the new congressional world, the cross-cutting policy pressures on the individual members of Congress should be immense. They are pressured both by newly politicized special interest groups in their constituencies and by traditional economic groups that have long dominated local electoral politics. Simultaneously, members continue to face the paradoxical tension that exists between their immediate career aspirations and the long-term institutional interests of Congress. The decentralized system of subcommittee government provides a very real opportunity for individual members to gain a power position early in their careers and through it to seek personal influence over particular policy choices that fall within the jurisdiction of their subcommittees. Yet the decentralized subcommittee system makes difficult the broad-scale, comprehensive policy planning and program creation that seem required by the redistributive and corrective policy issues to which members increasingly must respond.

Thus the policy pressures from the external environment of Congress today, in combination with the continuing conflict between the career aspirations of members and organizational requisites of Congress as an institution, create serious new constraints on members of Congress that may well alter their patterned behavior and, as a result, the functioning of Congress. While it is admittedly difficult to forecast with any certainty the precise ways in which these various factors will interact, a useful beginning can be made by considering the impact that the new congressional world may have on members' capacity to realize their congressional career goals.

Electoral Vulnerability

First, consider the goal of re-election. During the period of committee government, both voluntary and involuntary turnover was low.

Local party organizations and strong partisan identification among the public helped secure the re-election of incumbent members of dominant state and regional parties. Incumbents were able to build powerful supporting coalitions through attachment to dominant interest groups. Porkbarrel and casework activity by members helped to offset the disruptive effects of an attractive challenger or an unpopular presidential candidate heading the party ticket.

In the new political world, all of these factors are becoming less influential in congressional elections. Political parties are disintegrating as objects of attachment and as mechanisms of organizational support. Likewise, labor and business are no longer the sole or primary interest groups in the electoral arena, but have been joined by groups that believe themselves left out of the mainstream of governmental life or unrepresented in policymaking. Congressional elections are one of the most visible and potentially significant electoral arenas in which protest groups can strike. In particular, state and local groups seeking to influence the national government's actions regarding state and local policy should focus increased attention on congressional elections.

Likewise, attempts by incumbents to defeat electoral challengers through emphasis on the member's power within the Washington establishment may not prove as great an asset as in the past. It is exclusion from that establishment and its services that alienate many constituents. And many are also alienated by the decisions of the establishment that do touch them, particularly those affecting lifestyle concerns. In addition, "historical memories" of individualized services delivered by specific members of Congress may have decreasing electoral utility as constituents become increasingly mobile.

Seen in this context, congressional primaries and general elections increasingly should be characterized by protest efforts against incumbents, with incumbents caught in a peculiar bind, particularly in the Senate. Even a homogeneous constituency contains groups that believe themselves unrepresented by their members in Congress. The more heterogeneous the constituency, the more likely the rise and success of countervailing radical and reactionary protest movements that hold members accountable for policy stands. Likewise, it should become more difficult for members to build durable electoral coalitions and to develop a "home style" that works effectively over time across a complex, changing, and diverse constituency. Thus involuntary as well as voluntary turnover may begin to occur at a higher level than during the era of consolidation. The changes in the electoral environment and member turnover should be reflected in significant increases in the number of marginal districts, a decreasing statistical advantage of party and incumbency factors, and increasing electoral volatility (i.e., upset defeats of powerful and "safe" incumbents).

Decline of Policymaking Competence

With members facing a more complex and volatile electorate and a more decentralized congressional structure, the level of their policymaking competence probably will decline. Electoral uncertainty will tempt members to emphasize re-election activity more than in the past; less time will be left for nurturing policymaking competence. Members will move to power positions earlier in their careers, reducing the time for apprenticeship and constraining their ability to gain policymaking expertise before entering leadership roles. In addition, the legion of autonomous subcommittees will give members the opportunity to move from subcommittee to subcommittee within a parent committee, changing policy specializations to increase electoral advantage or policy influence without giving up committee seniority. Such frequent movement could reduce the quality of legislators' policymaking expertise and increase reliance on a professionalized staff. It could also increase the chance for seasoned committee chairs on committees characterized by high turnover in subcommittee leadership to reassert power. We thus could expect significant power struggles between committee and subcommittee leaders within such committees.

The greater variability in policy specialization of individual members over time also could have a second, corollary result. It may become increasingly difficult for programs and bureaucratic agencies to be assured of congressional support — not because the policies or agencies have been found wanting through systematic investigative oversight or have lost their initial congressional majority, but because key supporters have moved to greener pastures (or have been defeated). And new subcommittee leaders and members are concerned with different "pet" programs. A rise in the variability of subcommittee leadership and membership thus could lead to a decrease in the continuity of congressional policy commitments, reducing the probability that national programs will be implemented in accordance with congressional intent and probably threatening their long-term viability.[23]

The decline in policymaking competence and the increased discontinuity in congressional policy commitments should be exacerbated by the changing nature of coalitional politics within Congress. The addition to the political spectrum of cross-cutting issues raised by post-industrial change and concern over public morality should splinter the traditional coalitions without producing new, viable, and cohesive ones capable of generating stable majorities.

In general, we can expect to see more policy entrepreneurs who rise to power positions earlier than did their counterparts during the era of consolidation. These policy entrepreneurs, as subcommittee chairs, will have fewer real resources, less expertise and skill, and will face more complex legislative and policy decisions than their predecessors. Thus they will need assistance from central party leaders who can coordinate the efforts of the disparate factions and sub-committees. Yet they will approach the party leaders with fears of power aggrandisement and suspicions about the real utility of party leaders in legislative efforts. These fears and suspicions will be influenced by, and will influence, the congressional power structure.

More Personalized Power Struggles

In the era of consolidation, the struggles over power positions in Congress centered largely on conflicts about the proper authority of particular power positions and reform efforts to disperse power among a greater number of positions and members. Because committee seniority dominated the selection of committee chairs and maintained the viability of the decentralized power structure, conflict was largely depersonalized. In the future, conflict should become more personalized, however. First, key congressional power positions — party leadership posts and subcommittee chairs — have not been filled historically by following well-established norms of seniority. Conflict over the occupants of these positions therefore would not threaten the seniority norm.

Second, with so many power positions and with subcommittee chairs having some incentives to move to new positions, every Congress should start with a significant number of open positions, particularly subcommittee chairs. In these conflicts over subcommittee chairs, seniority claims may be emphasized, with some members stressing their subcommittee seniority and others stressing their committee or House seniority as bases for justifying their selection. Over time some form of seniority criteria governing subcommittee chair selection may develop within committees. However, given the more complex factional nature of Congress and the less critical historical importance of protecting the seniority norm at a subcommittee level, seniority criteria will almost certainly be balanced by such considerations as a candidate's ideological and regional orientation, policymaking competence, and electoral needs and security. Thus we can expect more overt conflict over and variability in the possession of power positions within committees.

Likewise, we can expect more conflict over party leadership positions. In the past, the selection of party leaders was not characterized by extensive and continuing conflict, in part because the positions did not carry extensive formal power, and in part because compromise among persistent dominant factions produced leadership teams that reflected' party diversity. Today, however, party leadership positions carry significant formal authority, thus making them more attractive. Yet, with the greater factional complexity of the parties, it is less likely that stable leadership teams can be created that balance dominant factional interests and subdue conflict. Even the most skillful party leaders may face policy choices so complex and conflictual that viable policymaking majorities are impossible to produce or sustain. With party leadership positions thus potentially more valued, yet reliant on more complex and volatile intraparty coalitions, we may see greater conflict in the selection of party leaders and more rapid turnover in the occupants of leadership positions.

The problems faced by congressional leadership should be magnified by members' continuing quest for personal power, a quest that should produce even greater concern for personal autonomy. Greater electoral volatility will make members more attentive to constituent politics, more insistent on maintaining independence in roll call voting, and less willing to engage in compromises or to confront difficult policy choices. The greater pressures of particularized groups for attention to their special interests will reinforce members' own desires to have personal influence on policymaking, thus sustaining the existence of numerous specialized subcommittees attentive to an ever-widening range of policy concerns.

Conclusion

The picture of Congress that emerges from a consideration of the concerns of individual members to nurture and protect their electoral maneuverability, policy influence, and power position acquisition is a chaotic one. Within Congress, we can expect the nature of careerism to change. The ever growing importance of the national government in this era of cooptative federalism will continue to attract ambitious politicians to Congress. Yet precisely because of the increased importance of national policymaking to state and local affairs, congressional seats may become such focal points that the number and quality of serious challengers to incumbent officeholders will increase. As a result, we can expect more members to leave involuntarily owing to defeat or retire under the threatening cloud of defeat.

In addition, with less real personal power, more electoral uncertainty, and greater personal sacrifice characterizing congressional service, members will leave earlier in their careers than in the past in search of higher elective or appointive office or lucrative lobbying or legal consulting positions in the Washington establishment. Fourteen or more years in Congress, instead of 20 to 40, will constitute a realistic career expection. Members will envision more readily than in the last 60 years a "life after Congress."

Thus a key characteristic of Congress in the future will be volatility. Congressional elections probably will produce more serious and potentially successful challengers to incumbents. Partisan majorities and party control of the House and Senate may fluctuate considerably more than in the era of consolidation. Coalition politics within Congress should become far less stable, with the conservative coalition and northern liberals ceasing to be the dominant cohesive groups shaping roll call behavior. Coalitional politics will be made even more difficult both by the cross-cutting complexity of the issues and by an increased variability over time in subcommittee policy entrepreneurs and congressional party leaders.

What are the consequences for Congress of the rising turnover and increased organizational chaos? Will a flight from subcommittee government toward elite or party government result as occurred during the nineteenth century? Probably not. First, the level of turnover is not expected to rise to the nineteenth-century norm of 50 percent, but simply range above the postwar levels. Career-oriented politicians will continue to see congressional careers as electorally possible, if not as easy to secure as in past decades. Second, subcommittee government should persist because members will see subcommittee autonomy and dominance as critical to the realization of their personal career aspirations.

Politicians will continue their quest for personal power within Congress, with the quest simply occurring in a shorter time span and a more volatile environment. In this environment, the persistence of subcommittee government may be reinforced by the emergence of a professional staff at the subcommittee level. Professional staff members, who may become the real long-term congressional careerists, could provide continuity and expertise in Congress somewhat analogous to the continuity provided by the civil service bureaucrats in the executive branch. We may be moving into a new period of legislative professionalism at the national level, with the staff being a critical core of the professional Congress. Unfortunately, while a professional staff can sustain Congress as a functioning organization, it will not be able to replace the members as professional actors or nurture the institutional power of Congress.

THE DECLINE OF CONGRESS: A CRISIS OF LEGITIMATION

Ultimately, the power of Congress rests on the ability of its elected members to legislate; to respond effectively to policy needs, interests and demands; in short, to act. Congress must generate leadership that can unite a majority of its members and speak for them authoritatively if it is to be an effective representative institution. And it must be able to coordinate its policy processes and ensure that the executive executes its policy decisions.

The Congressional Dilemma

The coming of committee government undermined all of these requisites of congressional power. The increased dispersion of power in subcommittee government and the greater volatility of the new political environment together should multiply the problems of congressional leadership, coordination, and oversight. Subcommittee government will not produce the large number of elected careerists and the long-term, powerful elected congressional experts who existed in the period of committee government and who served somewhat to counterbalance officials of the executive branch. Congressional professionalism will rest on a staff whose personal interests (such as staff dominance of institutionalized subcommittees) may conflict ultimately with the interests both of individual members and of the institution itself.

The expanded role of party leaders and the creation of a new budget process provide some centralized congressional capacity for constraining, directing, and integrating the policy actions at the subcommittee level. However, the powers of the party leaders and budget committees derive from the members of Congress whom they seek to constrain and direct. In light of the immense career pressures members are likely to feel in this new era and their concomitant desire for freedom of action in pursuit of immediate career aspirations, particularly electoral security, the increased authority of the party and budgetary leadership will appear thin straws on which to hinge considerable hope for strong, authoritative, forceful, and sustained congressional leadership. This is true particularly in light of the complex policy choices facing members of Congress, choices that would make leadership of a collegial body difficult under the best organizational circumstances.

The Consequences

As a rule, autonomous congressional policymaking on major policy issues in this new era will be incremental at best, immobilized and incoherent as a norm. While on occasion we may see forceful congressional leadership and integrated policymaking, such actions probably will occur primarily in the direst of crises and probably will exhaust the willingness of members to cooperate with the leadership on future major policy questions. The inability of the central party and budgetary officials to sustain forceful leadership will critically undermine the ability of Congress to act.

In the face of an increasingly immobilized Congress, the pressures for action by other institutions will be immense. Such conditions particularly tempt presidents to establish their popularity and power by bold strokes of leadership and by forceful efforts to "save the Republic." Thus we can expect severe incursions of presidents into the constitutional powers of Congress, incursions more severe and coming at a faster pace than in the era of committee government. This faster pace will occur in part because (1) Congress will move toward decentralization more rapidly as a result of the greater pressures by members for personal autonomy; (2) subcommittee government will create greater problems of immobilism than did committee government; and (3) the complex policy problems of the new era will create greater demands for rapid government action.

As a result, and assuming that there are no unforeseen countervailing changes in the systemic setting of national or international politics, we shall surely witness the further decline of Congress, the rebirth of the imperial presidency, and a severe constitutional crisis surpassing any previous one.

The great fear is that a point will be reached in this cyclical decline of Congress beyond which the citizenry no longer looks to Congress as a necessary participant in national governance, a point at which the slow transformation away from representative democracy becomes an institutionalized and popularly accepted reality. Unfortunately, various national surveys indicate that the public is increasingly doubtful of the capacity of Congress as an institution to act, particularly on the major policy concerns of the day.[24] As Richard Fenno has so aptly noted, citizens may love their representatives in Congress, but they do not love Congress.[25] And while similar patterns characterize other institutions, both in America and the West generally,[26] the congressional survey results are particularly troubling because Congress is so clearly the touchstone of American democracy, and executive government is so clearly the probable long-term consequence of congressional decline.

Ironically, as we move into a post-industrial world of scarce resources and complex policy choices, members of Congress may become ultimate victims of Fenno's paradox, as well as its immediate perpetrators. In the emerging world, they stand to lose electoral security, policymaking competence, and long-term personal control over significant power positions. In spreading organizational power so widely that Congress cannot act, members undermine not only the legitimacy of the institution but also the popular belief in the viability of congressional policymaking. Given the severity of the policy problems raised by the coming of post-industrialism in contemporary America, it is doubtful that the citizenry will continue to "love" members of Congress simply because they cut bureaucratic red tape or deliver highways and dams. Congressional incapacity to act in the midst of severe crisis must ultimately delegitimate not only Congress but the individual members of Congress by challenging popular beliefs that they are effective, responsive representatives serving the fundamental needs of the people.

The Crisis of Legitimation

It would seem, then, that Congress has moved beyond a *crisis of adaptation* and now, in light of the probable characteristics of the new era into which we are moving, will face a serious and growing *crisis of legitimation,* a crisis that threatens the very foundations of American democracy.[27] Continued congressional immobilism on major policy problems in a post-industrial world of scarce resources necessarily will challenge popular belief in the viability and desirability of representative government that historically has served to legitimate Congress, to sustain popular support for its decisions, and to nurture popular insistence that its constitutional prerogatives be protected. This legitimation crisis flows from two interacting factors: *congressional organization* and *congressional environment.*

Organizationally, Congress has proven increasingly incapable of creating an internal structure that could produce decisive, innovative, independent, and authoritative policy decisions on major policy issues. Yet the severity of the legitimation crisis now descending on Congress, and more broadly on American politics, flows from more than the inability of Congress to resolve its adaptation crisis constructively and create a responsive organizational structure capable of providing sustained leadership, coordination, and oversight.

While the congressional incapacity to act would no doubt ultimately generate a crisis, it is augmented by the pell-mell rush of the nation into a new environmental setting. Congress today faces complex and seemingly intractable issues — redistributive politics amidst diminishing resources; national enforcement of substantive justice amidst growing unhappiness with a large national bureaucracy; sustenance of our international economic security amidst increasing dependence on expensive foreign resources and foreign goods; the solidification and modernization of our military defense capacity at a time when domestic social problems require considerable financial outlays. Organized to process incremental, routinized distributive policy choices, Congress now must confront a world in which most major policy decisions require comprehensive, innovative, and redistributive policy actions. Both in terms of its organizational structure and its environmental context, Congress's serious incapacity to act may lead to a widespread questioning of its legitimate role in national governance.

What we may be witnessing, then, is the self-destruction of the Madisonian system of government. This self-destruction is not necessarily the result of malevolence, evil motives, or evil people. The quest for power by members of Congress may derive from the genuine desire to serve humanity. The effort of members of society to seek a redress of personal grievances and protect personal interests is merely an articulation of their constitutional rights. Finally, presidential assertiveness and "imperialism" may derive from a very genuine presidential concern for economic stability or national security and from an accurate perception that Congress cannot act.

Nevertheless, the potential for self-destruction is real. Because of the cyclical nature of the power struggles and the occasional recentralization and resurgent periods within Congress, as in the 1970s, the long-term weakening of Congress is not as readily evident as it might be. Such short-term resurgence, however, simply diverts attention from the long-term momentum toward congressional impotence. In fact, when we examine the probable long-term characteristics that will emerge from the recent "reformed" Congress, in light of the concomitant changes in our national and international environment, what we foresee is greater congressional impotence and greater executive usurpation of congressional power.

The age of protest witnessed major transformations as significant in many ways as those that occurred during the Civil War and Reconstruction or the Progressive movement and World War I. Events of the 1960s and 1970s raised important questions of substantive justice and national purpose and unleashed new economic, social, political, and technological changes that are producing fundamental transformations in national life as great as those that arose with the emergence of industrial democracy in the late nineteenth century or its consolidation in the twentieth century. These transformations should produce a Congress of less secure incumbents and more immobilized policymaking.

Proposals for Constitutional Change

With these changes, a new era is upon us, an *era of reassessment.* As in the other eras of American politics, policy questions will center on the nation's social and economic order, on the desired form of federalism, and on our role in international affairs. Yet unlike the earlier eras, today even more fundamental questions must be faced: Is representative government a central value that we wish to nurture? If so, how can we reassert and sustain representative institutions as we move into a post-industrial world? Failure to address these questions could lead to the end of representative government. Willingness to face the potential severity of the emerging legitimation crisis and act constructively to resolve it could introduce a creative transformation and rebirth of representative democracy.

In acknowledging the crisis facing Congress and moving to address it, we must recognize that the root of the problem lies not in Congress per se but in the Constitution, in its failure to provide constitutional provisions that nurture the organizational integrity of Congress in ways comparable to the Supreme Court and the presidency. In retrospect, it is understandable why the founders failed to provide specific functions and organizational structures for Congress that would help ensure its institutional integrity and help it generate an institutional will. The founders were structuring a constitution for a very different world, a world in which Congress could be expected to maintain its organizational cohesion without constitutional assistance. But the rise of industrial America and the coming of the post-industrial era of scarcity have created conditions that undermine the ability of Congress to organize effectively, assert an institutional will, balance the other branches of government, and respond authoritatively to new policy challenges.

What is to be done? Clearly, it is time to reconsider the appropriateness of our constitutional structure to the problems and realities of our time. Perhaps a more effective representative government can be constructed by changes in the current constitutional structure. For example, constitutional amendments could give greater authority to the Speaker, Majority Leader, or other organizational leaders. Such authority might include significant responsibility to appoint committee members and/or leaders, greater procedural powers, and tightened control over congressional perquisites. Amendments of this kind would help redress problems of congressional leadership caused by committee and subcommittee government and give the congressional leaders "bargaining chips" they could use in coalition building analogous to the "chips" the president possesses, such as the veto power and the ability to make political appointments and nominate federal judges. Another constitutional amendment could create a Congressional Security Council that would help Congress regain constitutional control of war-making under specified emergency conditions. To bridge the legislative division created by bicameralism, the Constitution could authorize or require joint congressional committees in key areas such as national security, budgeting, and oversight. Finally, a revision of the presidential veto authority could enhance congressional control of policymaking by making overrides easier or vetoes harder.

All of these constitutional changes would be designed to mesh with the pre-existing system of separation of power and checks and balances. Their intent would be to strengthen the ability of Congress to know and express its will authoritatively, creating a constitutionally supported incentive structure conducive to the creation of majority coalitions. The problem with accepting the basic constitutional design of Madison, however, is that it reasserts a separation of powers, checks and balances system.

Political analysts often lament that in a separation of powers system majoritarian politics is slowed by the force of institutional pluralism.[28] This argument is a strong one and suggests that one might wish to enact concomitant constitutional changes designed to nurture the capacity of national majorities to bridge the branches of government. For example, hand in hand with strengthening Congress could go a variety of reforms designed to strengthen the one organizational device that historically has shown some capacity to unite the separate branches in a responsive, accountable fashion: the political parties. In addition, the construction of some form of parliamentary government could be considered. For example, Congress could be given the power to pass a vote of no confidence that could remove the president and activate selection of a new president either through a specific institutional process or through new elections. Presidents also could be required to draw cabinet members from Congress (with members retaining their seat in Congress). Obviously, such proposals constitute a significant move away from Madisonian government.

A final proposal stems from the recognition that representative government entails more than a strong Congress at the national level. Strong representative assemblies that are close to the people yet have sufficient authority, scope, and financial resources to influence public policy are also needed. The creation of subnational, multistate regional governments might provide one means of sustaining our commitment to a federal system of government in which popular control of policymaking would be invested in that governmental body closest to the problem yet possessed of sufficient jurisdictional authority to address it effectively. Similarly, new devices of representative decisionmaking could be envisioned at the local level.

New and revitalized forms of regional and urban government would not only nurture representative democracy at local and regional levels and constrain the rise of cooptative federalism, but also would help Congress to address creatively those questions that are truly national in scope. Relieved of policy issues better left to regional assemblies, Congress might be less compelled to rely on bureaucratic expertise and rulemaking as a substitute for congressional deliberation and decisionmaking on questions requiring national action.

In considering constitutional changes such as these, we must recognize, of course, that constitutional revision is a serious and difficult business. It requires a realistic and hard-headed assessment of human nature, of the implications of different institutional arrangements, of the social conditions within which politics is to be conducted, and of the consequences that will derive from the interaction of these elements of political life. In many ways Madison's performance in the *Federalist Papers* is still the best guide to this type of analysis. And certainly we must remember that the effects of large-scale constitutional change in any particular national environment are difficult to forecast.

Despite the problems of constitutional change, however, the nation cannot shy away from facing the legitimation crisis that confronts Congress and thus challenges the maintenance of representative government in America. A failure to face this crisis may result in the disintegration of our political order and the loss of meaningful democratic control over public policy. Facing the crisis squarely may not only revitalize Congress but liberate the nation to approach constructively the policy dilemmas and opportunities of the post-industrial world. If we successfully confront both the constitutional and policy dilemmas facing us, we may lay the foundations for a more equitable and democratic society. The era of reassessment could activate a great renewal and expansion of democratic government in America.

NOTES

1. James Madison, "Federalist #10," in Alexander Hamilton, James Madison, and John Jay, *The Federalist Papers,* ed. Clinton Rossiter (New York: New American Library, 1961), pp. 77-84. For interpretations of the Madisonian theory, see Robert Dahl, *A Preface to Democratic Theory* (Chicago: University of Chicago Press, 1963); and Vincent Ostrom, *The Theory of A Compound Republic* (Blacksburg, Va.: Public Choice, 1971).
2. Madison, "Federalist #51," pp. 321-323.
3. Ibid.
4. Madison, "Federalist #48," p. 309; and "Federalist #53," pp. 334-335.
5. Ibid. See also Robert Scigliano, *The Supreme Court and the Presidency* (New York: Free Press, 1971); and Gordon S. Wood, *The Creation of the American Republic, 1776-1787* (Chapel Hill: The University of North Carolina Press, 1969).
6. The historical interpretation of political eras developed in this paper has been particularly influenced by J. Zvi Namenwirth, "Wheels of Time and the Interdependence of Value Change in America," *Journal of Interdisciplinary History,* vol. 3, no. 4 (1973): 649-684.
7. James Sterling Young, *The Washington Community, 1800-1828* (New York: Harcourt, Brace & World, 1966), pp. 13-37.
8. For statistical and documentary evidence, see Nelson W. Polsby, "The Institutionalization of the U.S. House of Representatives," *American Political Science Review* 62 (1968): 144-168; Randall B. Ripley, *Power in the Senate* (New York: St. Martin's Press, 1969), p. 43; H. Douglas

Price, "Careers and Committees in the American Congress: The Problem of Structural Change," in *The History of Parliamentary Behavior,* ed. William O. Aydelotte (Princeton, N.J.: Princeton University Press, 1977), pp. 28-62; Morris P. Fiorina, David W. Rohde, and Peter Wissel, "Historical Change in House Turnover," in *Congress in Change,* ed. Norman J. Ornstein (New York: Praeger Publishers, 1975).

9. On the House, see George R. Brown, *The Leadership of Congress* (Indianapolis: Bobbs-Merrill Co., 1922); and Richard Bolling, *Power in the House* (New York: Capricorn, 1968). On the Senate, see David J. Rothman, *Politics and Power* (New York: Atheneum Publishers, 1969).

10. The major study of this era among contemporary political scientists is David W. Brady's *Congressional Voting in a Partisan Era* (Lawrence, Kansas: University of Kansas Press, 1973).

11. This was, in fact, the thesis of the classic study of the era: Woodrow Wilson, *Congressional Government* (Gloucester, Mass.: Peter Smith, 1885).

12. H. Douglas Price, "Careers and Committees in the American Congress: The Problem of Structural Change," in *The History of Parliamentary Behavior;* and Nelson W. Polsby, Miriam Gallagher, and Barry Rundquist, "The Growth of the Seniority System in the House of Representatives," *American Political Science Review,* 63 (1969): 787-807.

13. Joseph Cooper and David W. Brady, "Organization Theory and Congressional Structure" (Paper delivered at the annual meeting of the American Political Science Association, New Orleans, Louisiana, September 4-8, 1973), pp. 46-52. See also Samuel P. Huntington, Congressional Responses to the Twentieth Century," in *The Congress and America's Future,* ed. David B. Truman (Englewood Cliffs, N.J.: Prentice-Hall, 1965).

14. The approach taken here has been heavily influenced by Richard F. Fenno, Jr., *Congressmen in Committees* (Boston: Little, Brown & Co., 1973); and David R. Mayhew, *Congress: The Electoral Connection* (New Haven: Yale University Press, 1974).

15. On emerging patterns in congressional elections, see Milton C. Cummings, *Congressmen and the Electorate* (New York: Free Press, 1966); John Kingdon, *Candidates for Office* (New York: Random House, 1968); Robert S. Erikson, "The Advantage of Incumbency in Congressional Elections," *Polity* 3 (1971): 395-405; Charles Jones, *Every Second Year* (Washington, D.C.: Brookings Institution, 1967); Barbara Hinckley, "Incumbency and the Presidential Vote in Senate Elections," *American Political Science Review* 64 (1970); Thomas E. Mann, *Unsafe At Any Margin: Interpreting Congressional Elections* (Washington, D.C.: American Enterprise Institute, 1978); Charles S. Bullock, III, "House Careerists: Changing Patterns of Longevity and Attrition," *American Political Science Review* 66 (1972); David R. Mayhew, "Congressional Elections: The Case of the Vanishing Marginals," *Polity* 6 (1974): 295-317. For a discussion of how the economy affects election results, see Edward R. Tufte, *Political Control of the Economy* (Princeton, N.J.: Princeton University Press, 1978). On incumbents' approaches to district politics, see Richard F. Fenno, Jr., *Home Style* (Boston: Little, Brown & Co., 1978).

16. See, for example, the discussion in John F. Manley, "The House Committee on Ways and Means: Conflict Management in a Congressional Committee," *American Political Science Review* 59 (1965): 927-939.

17. Randall B. Ripley and Grace N. Franklin, *Congress, the Bureaucracy and Public Policy* (Homewood, Ill.: The Dorsey Press, 1976); R. Douglas

Arnold, *Congress and the Bureaucracy* (New Haven: Yale University Press, 1979); and Lawrence C. Dodd and Richard L. Schott, *Congress and the Administrative State* (New York: John Wiley & Sons, 1979).

18. For an earlier discussion of members of Congress as policy entrepreneurs, see Eric M. Uslaner, "Policy Entrepreneurs and Amateur Democrats in the House of Representatives," in *Legislative Reform: The Policy Impact,* ed. Leroy N. Rieselbach (Lexington, Mass.: Lexington Books, 1978).

19. See Kenneth W. Hechler, *Insurgency: Personalities and Politics in the Taft Era* (New York: Columbia University Press, 1940); and John D. Baker, "The Character of the Congressional Revolution of 1910," *Journal of American History* 60 (1973): 679-691.

20. For earlier and more extensive development of the ideas presented here, see Lawrence C. Dodd, "Congress and the Quest for Power," in *Congress Reconsidered,* 1st ed., edited by Lawrence C. Dodd and Bruce I. Oppenheimer (New York: Praeger Publishers, 1977); and Lawrence C. Dodd, "Congress, the Presidency and the Cycles of Power," in *The Post-Imperial Presidency,* ed. Vincent Davis (New Brunswick: Transaction, Inc., 1980).

21. For useful discussions of reform politics in the 1970s, see Roger H. Davidson and Walter J. Oleszek, *Congress Against Itself* (Bloomington, Ind.: Indiana University Press, 1977); and Leroy N. Rieselbach, *Congressional Reform in the Seventies* (Morristown, N.J.: General Learning Press, 1977).

22. On the politics of oil, see Bruce I. Oppenheimer, *Oil and the Congressional Process* (Lexington, Mass.: Lexington Books, 1974); see also John F. Manley, *The Politics of Finance* (Boston: Little, Brown & Co., 1970). On military politics, see Lewis Anthony Dexter, "Congressmen and the Making of Military Policy," in *New Perspectives on the House of Representatives,* ed. Robert L. Peabody and Nelson W. Polsby (Chicago: Rand McNally, 1969). For a broader interpretation, see Theodore Lowi, *The End of Liberalism* (New York: W. W. Norton, 1969, 1979).

23. For excellent discussions of the impact of policy formulation and the congressional environment on policy implementation, see Jeffrey Pressman and Aaron Wildavsky, *Implementation* (Berkeley: University of California Press, 1973); and Michael N. Green, *The Federal New Towns Program: Policy Making in a Subgovernment in Flux,* (Masters Report, University of Texas, 1978).

24. For a good summary, see Glenn R. Parker, "Some Themes in Congressional Unpopularity," *American Journal of Political Science* 21 (1977): 93-109.

25. Richard F. Fenno, Jr., "If, As Ralph Nader Says, Congress Is 'The Broken Branch,' How Come We Love Our Congressmen So Much?" in *Congress in Change.* See also Glenn R. Parker and Roger H. Davidson, "Why Do Americans Love Their Congressmen So Much More Than Their Congress?" *Legislative Studies Quarterly* 4 (1979): 53-61.

26. See, for example, Bruce Cain, John Ferejohn, and Morris P. Fiorina, "Legislators v. Legislatures: A Comparative Analysis of Fenno's Paradox" (Paper delivered at the Conference on Congressional Elections, Houston, Texas, January 10-12, 1980).

27. My interpretation has been influenced significantly by Jurgen Habermas, *Legitimation Crisis* (Boston: Beacon Press, 1973).

28. James MacGregor Burns, *The Deadlock of Democracy* (Englewood Cliffs, N.J.: Prentice-Hall, 1963).

The Contributors

DAVID W. BRADY is Professor of Political Science at the University of Houston. He received his Ph.D. from the University of Iowa in 1970. His publications include *Congressional Voting in a Partisan Era: A Study of McKinley Houses and a Comparison to the Modern House of Representatives* (1973), *Public Policy and Politics in America* (1978), and numerous articles in professional journals. He is presently working on a Project 87 grant concerning the effect of critical elections on the U.S. House of Representatives.

PHILIP BRENNER holds a Ph.D. in political science from The Johns Hopkins University and teaches political science at the University of Maryland, Baltimore County. The author of *Class Collaboration: The Limits and Possibilities of Congress* (forthcoming), he has served on the editorial board of *Politics and Society* and as a Congressional Fellow (1969-70).

CHARLES S. BULLOCK, III is Richard B. Russell Professor of Political Science and Research Fellow of the Institute for Behavioral Research at the University of Georgia. He received his Ph.D. from Washington University, St. Louis. He has done research on Congress, civil rights, and policy implementation and co-authored *Law and Social Change* (1972), *Racial Equality in America* (1975), *Coercion to Compliance* (1976), and *Public Policy and Politics in America* (1978).

JOSEPH COOPER is Dean of Social Sciences and Lena Gohlman Fox Professor of Political Science at Rice University. He has served as Staff Director of the U.S. House Commission on Administrative Review and as Secretary of the American Political Science Association. He is the author of a monograph on the development of the committee system and of numerous articles on congressional structures, processes, and politics.

ALBERT D. COVER is Assistant Professor of Political Science at the University of Michigan. He received his B.A. from Wesleyan University and his M. Phil. and Ph.D. from Yale University. He has received a Woodrow Wilson Fellowship, an NDEA Fellowship, and has served as a Congressional Fellow (1973-74). He is the author of several papers and articles on congressional elections.

ROGER H. DAVIDSON is Senior Specialist in American Government and Public Administration at the Congressional Research Service, U.S. Library of Congress. He is on leave from the University of California, Santa Barbara, where he has served as Professor of Political Science and Associate Dean of the College of Letters and Science. He received his Ph.D. from Columbia University. He has worked for committees of both the House and Senate and has served as consultant to the White House and several national study commissions. The author of numerous books and articles on national policymaking and Congress, he is working with Walter J. Oleszek on *Congress and Its Members,* an interpretive textbook to be published by CQ Press in 1981.

I. M. DESTLER is a Senior Associate at the Carnegie Endowment for International Peace, Washington, D.C., where he directs the Project on Executive-Congressional Relations in Foreign Policy. He received his Ph.D. from the Woodrow Wilson School of Public and International Affairs, Princeton University. He is the author of *Presidents, Bureaucrats, and Foreign Policy* (1972) and *Making Foreign Economic Policy* (1980), and co-author of two books on U.S.-Japanese Relations: *Managing an Alliance* (1976) and *The Textile Wrangle* (1979).

LAWRENCE C. DODD, Professor of Political Science at Indiana University, received his B.A. from Midwestern State University (Wichita Falls, Texas) and his Ph.D. from the University of Minnesota. He is the author of *Congress and Public Policy* (1975), *Coalitions in Parliamentary Government* (1976), and co-author of *Congress and the Administrative State* (1979). He has served as President of the Southwestern Political Science Association (1979-80) and as a Congressional Fellow (1974-75).

JOHN W. ELLWOOD holds a Ph.D. in political science from The Johns Hopkins University, has taught at the University of Virginia, and has served as a Congressional Fellow (1974-75). From 1977 to 1980 he served as Special Assistant to the Director of the Congressional Budget Office. He has returned to academia as research analyst in public policy at the Woodrow Wilson School of Public and International Affairs, Princeton University. Having written extensively on Congress and third party behavior, he is currently working on a study of the impact of technical and analytic experts on congressional decisionmaking.

MORRIS P. FIORINA is Professor of Political Science at the California Institute of Technology. He received his Ph.D. from the University of Rochester and has written extensively on the subject of American politics, especially in the areas of representation and electoral accountability. His books are *Representatives, Roll Calls, and Constituencies* (1974), *Congress: Keystone of the Washington Establishment* (1977), and *Retrospective Voting in American National Elections* (1981).

BURDETT A. LOOMIS is Assistant Professor of Political Science at the University of Kansas. He received his Ph.D. from the University of Wisconsin and served as a Congressional Fellow (1975-76). He has written articles on congressional careers and organization and has co-authored a text on U.S. politics.

DAVID R. MAYHEW is Professor of Political Science at Yale and Chairman of the Political Science Department. He received his Ph.D. from Harvard University and served as a Congressional Fellow (1967-68). His publications include *Party Loyalty Among Congressmen* (1966) and *Congress: The Electoral Connection* (1974).

MORRIS S. OGUL, Professor of Political Science and Chairman of the Department of Political Science at the University of Pittsburgh, received his Ph.D. from the University of Michigan. He is the author of *Congress Oversees the Bureaucracy* (1976), paperbound edition (1978), and is co-author with William J. Keefe of *The American Legislative Process,* 5th ed. (1981).

BRUCE I. OPPENHEIMER is an Associate Professor of Political Science at the University of Houston. He received his Ph.D. from the University of Wisconsin and has been both a Brookings Fellow (1970-71) and a Congressional Fellow (1974-75). His publications include *Oil and the Congressional Process: The Limits of Symbolic Politics* (1974), "Policy Effects of U.S. House Reform: Decentralization and the Capacity to Resolve Energy Issues" (1980), and articles on the House Rules Committee. He is currently continuing his research on the impact of congressional reform on the development of energy policy.

NORMAN J. ORNSTEIN teaches political science at The Catholic University of America and is Adjunct Scholar at the American Enterprise Institute. He was a Congressional Fellow (1969-70) and currently serves as a consultant on political coverage to the Public Broadcasting System. His books include *Congress in Change: Evolution and Reform* (1975); *Interest Groups, Lobbying and Policymaking* (1978); *Vital Statistics on Congress, 1980* (1980); and *The New Congress* (1981). His article is part of a broader study of the U.S. Senate that Ornstein, Peabody, and Rohde will publish through CQ Press.

ROBERT L. PEABODY is Professor of Political Science at The Johns Hopkins University. He has served as Associate Director of the American Political Science Association Study of Congress and as Staff Assistant to former House Speaker Carl Albert. He is the author of numerous books on Congress including *Leadership in Congress* (1976); editor of *Education of a Congressman* (1972); co-author of *To Enact a Law: Congress and Campaign Finance* (1972); co-author of *Congress: Two Decades of Analysis* (1969); and co-editor of *New Perspectives on the House of Representatives*, 3rd ed. (1977).

DAVID E. PRICE is Associate Professor of Political Science and Policy Sciences at Duke University. His doctorate is from Yale University, where he taught until 1973. His publications include *Who Makes the Laws?* (1972), *The Commerce Committees* (1975), and *Policy-making in Congressional Committees* (1979). He served as Legislative Aide to Senator E. L. Bartlett, on the campaign staff of Senator Albert Gore, and, most recently, as Executive Director of the Democratic Party of North Carolina.

DAVID W. ROHDE, Professor of Political Science at Michigan State University, received his B.S. from Canisius College and his Ph.D. from the University of Rochester. He has served as a Congressional Fellow (1972-73) and is co-author of *Supreme Court Decision Making* (1976).

BARBARA SINCLAIR is an Associate Professor of Political Science at the University of California, Riverside. Her writings on the U.S. Congress include articles in *The American Political Science Review, Journal of Politics, American Journal of Political Science,* and *Legislative Studies Quarterly.* She served as an APSA Congressional Fellow in the House Majority Leader's Office from 1978 to 1979.

JAMES L. SUNDQUIST, a senior fellow at the Brookings Institution, has worked in both the legislative branch (as a Senate administrative assistant) and the executive branch (in the Executive Office of the President). He is the author of several books including *Politics and Policy: The Eisenhower, Kennedy and Johnson Years* (1968) and *Dynamics of the Party System: Alignment and Realignment of the Political Parties in the United States* (1973). A work entitled "The Decline and Resurgence of Congress" is scheduled to appear in 1981. His essay in this volume is condensed from a chapter in *Setting National Priorities: Agenda for the 1980s*, published by The Brookings Institution.

JAMES A. THURBER is Director of Battelle Memorial Institute's Human Affairs Research Centers, Washington, D.C. Operations and is on leave from American University where he was Associate Professor of Government and Public Administration. His primary research areas are American public policymaking, congressional budgeting, and legislative reform. He has served on the staffs of U.S. Senator Hubert Humphrey, the House Commission on Administrative Review (the Obey Commission), and the Temporary Select Committee to Study the U.S. Senate Committee System. He holds his doctorate in political science from Indiana University.

WILLIAM WEST, Assistant Professor of Political Science at West Virginia University, recently received his doctorate from Rice University. The author of *The Politics of Administrative Rulemaking* (forthcoming), he is currently engaged in a study of the legislative veto.

Suggested Readings

Aberbach, Joel D. "Changes in Congressional Oversight." *American Behavioral Scientist* 22 (1979): 493-515.

Abramowitz, Alan J. "A Comparison of Voting for U.S. Senators and Representatives in 1978." *American Political Science Review* 74 (1980): 637-640.

Arnold, R. Douglas. *Congress and the Bureaucracy.* New Haven, Conn.: Yale University Press, 1979.

Asher, Herbert B. "The Learning of Legislative Norms." *American Political Science Review* 67 (1973): 499-513.

Asher, Herbert B., and Weisberg, Herbert F. "Voting Change in Congress: Some Dynamic Perspectives on an Evolutionary Process." *American Journal of Political Science* 22 (1978): 391-425.

Bacheller, J. M. "Lobbyists and the Legislative Process: The Impact of Environmental Constraints." *American Political Science Review* 71 (1977): 252-263.

Bauer, Raymond A.; de Sola Pool, Ithiel; and Dexter, Lewis A. *American Business and Public Policy.* New York: Atherton, 1963.

Bibby, John F., and Davidson, Roger H. *On Capitol Hill.* 2nd ed. Hinsdale, Ill.: Dryden, 1972.

Bolling, Richard. *House Out of Order.* New York: E. P. Dutton, 1965.

———. *Power in the House.* New York: E. P. Dutton, 1965.

Born, Richard. "Changes in the Competitiveness of House Primary Elections, 1956-1976." *American Politics Quarterly* 8 (1980): 495-506.

Brady, David W. *Congressional Voting in a Partisan Era.* Lawrence, Kansas: University of Kansas Press, 1973.

Brady, David W.; Cooper, Joseph; and Hurley, Patricia A. "The Decline of Party in the U.S. House of Representatives, 1887-1968." *Legislative Studies Quarterly* 4 (1979): 381-407.

Bullock, Charles S., III. "House Careerists: Changing Patterns of Longevity and Attrition." *American Political Science Review* 66 (1972): 1295-1305.

———. "House Committee Assignments." In *The Congressional System: Notes and Readings,* edited by Leroy N. Rieselbach. 2nd ed. North Scituate, Mass.: Duxbury Press, 1979.

———."Redistricting and Congressional Stability, 1962-1972." *Journal of Politics* 37 (1975): 569-575.

Burnham, Walter Dean. "Insulation and Responsiveness in Congressional Elections." *Political Science Quarterly* 90 (1975): 411-435.

Clausen, Aage R. *How Congressmen Decide.* New York: St. Martin's Press, 1973.

Clem, Alan L., ed. *The Making of Congressmen: Seven Campaigns of 1974.* North Scituate, Mass.: Duxbury Press, 1976.

Cooper, Joseph. "Strengthening the Congress: An Organizational Analysis." *Harvard Journal on Legislation* 2 (1975): 301-368.

_____. *The Origins of the Standing Committees and the Development of the Modern House.* Houston, Texas: William Marsh Rice University, 1971.

Cover, Albert D. "Contacting Congressional Constituents: Some Patterns of Perquisite Use." *American Journal of Political Science* 24 (1980): 125-134.

_____. "One Good Term Deserves Another: The Advantage of Incumbency in Congressional Elections." *American Journal of Political Science* 21 (1977): 523-541.

Crotty, William J., and Jacobson, Gary C. *American Parties in Decline.* Boston: Little, Brown & Co., 1980.

Davidson, Roger H. *The Role of the Congressman.* New York: Pegasus, 1969.

Davidson, Roger H.; Kovenock, David M.; and O'Leary, Michael K. *Congress in Crisis: Politics and Congressional Reform.* Belmont, Calif.: Wadsworth, 1966.

Davidson, Roger H., and Oleszek, Walter J. *Congress Against Itself.* Bloomington, Ind.: Indiana University Press, 1977.

Dexter, Lewis A. *How Organizations Are Represented in Washington.* Indianapolis: Bobbs-Merrill Co., 1969.

_____. *The Sociology and Politics of Congress.* Chicago: Rand McNally, 1969.

Dodd, Lawrence C. "Congress and the Quest for Power." In *Congress Reconsidered,* edited by Lawrence C. Dodd and Bruce I. Oppenheimer. 1st ed. New York: Praeger Publishers, 1977.

_____. "The Expanded Roles of the House Democratic Whip System." *Congressional Studies* 6 (1979).

Dodd, Lawrence C., and Schott, Richard L. *Congress and the Administrative State.* New York: John Wiley & Sons, 1979.

Eckhardt, Bob, and Black, Charles L., Jr. *The Titles of Power: Conversations on the American Constitution.* New Haven, Conn.: Yale University Press, 1976.

Edwards, George C., III. *Presidential Influence in Congress.* San Francisco: Freeman, 1980.

Erikson, Robert. "Is There Such a Thing As A Safe Seat?" *Polity* 8 (1976): 623-632.

_____. "The Advantage of Incumbency in Congressional Elections." *Polity* 3 (1971).

Eulau, Heinz, and Karps, Paul. "The Puzzle of Representation." *Legislative Studies Quarterly* 2 (1977): 233-254.

Fenno, Richard F., Jr. *Congressmen in Committees.* Boston: Little, Brown & Co., 1973.

_____. *Home Style.* Boston: Little, Brown & Co., 1978.

_____. "If, As Ralph Nader Says, Congress Is 'the Broken Branch,' How Come We Love Our Congressmen So Much?" In *Congress in Change,* edited by Norman J. Ornstein. New York: Praeger Publishers, 1975.

_____. *The Power of the Purse.* Boston: Little, Brown & Co., 1966.

Ferejohn, John A. *Pork Barrel Politics.* Stanford, Calif.: Stanford University Press, 1974.

Ferejohn, John A., and Fiorina, Morris P. "Purposive Models of Legislative Behavior." *American Economic Review: Papers and Proceedings* 65 (1975): 407-415.

Fiorina, Morris P. *Congress: Keystone of the Washington Establishment.* New Haven, Conn.: Yale University Press, 1977.

_____. *Representatives, Roll Calls and Constituencies.* Lexington, Mass.: Lexington Books, 1974.

Fiorina, Morris P.; Rohde, David W.; and Wissel, Peter. "Historical Change in House Turnover." In *Congress in Change,* edited by Norman J. Ornstein. New York: Praeger Publishers, 1975.

Fishel, Jeff. *Party and Opposition.* New York: David McKay Co., 1973.

Fowler, Linda. "Candidates' Perceptions of Electoral Coalitions." *American Politics Quarterly* 8 (1980): 483-494.

Fox, Harrison W., Jr., and Hammond, Susan Webb. *Congressional Staffs: The Invisible Force in American Lawmaking.* New York: Free Press, 1977.

Frantzich, Stephen E. "Computerized Information Technology in the U.S. House of Representatives." *Legislative Studies Quarterly* 4 (1979): 255-280.

Freeman, J. Leiper. *The Political Process.* New York: Random House, 1955.

Froman, Lewis A., Jr. *The Congressional Process: Strategies, Rules and Procedures.* Boston: Little, Brown & Co., 1967.

Goodwin, George, Jr. *The Little Legislatures.* Amherst: University of Massachusetts Press, 1970.

Harris, Joseph. *Congressional Control of Administration.* Washington, D.C.: Brookings Institution, 1964.

Hayes, Michael I. "Interest Groups and Congress: Toward a Transactional Theory." In *The Congressional System: Notes and Readings,* edited by Leroy N. Rieselbach, 2nd ed. North Scituate, Mass.: Duxbury Press, 1979.

Henry, Charles P. "Legitimizing Race in Congressional Politics." *American Politics Quarterly* 5 (1977): 149-176.

Hershey, Marjorie R. *The Making of Campaign Strategy.* Lexington, Mass.: Lexington Books, 1974.

Hinckley, Barbara. *Stability and Change in Congress.* New York: Harper & Row, 1971.

_____. "The American Voter in Congressional Elections." *American Political Science Review* 74 (1980): 641-650.

_____. *The Seniority System in Congress.* Bloomington, Ind.: Indiana University Press, 1971.

Hoadly, John F. "The Emergence of Political Parties in Congress, 1789-1803." *American Political Science Review* 74 (1980): 757-779.

Holtzman, Abraham. *Legislative Liaison.* Chicago: Rand McNally & Co., 1970.

Huitt, Ralph K., and Peabody, Robert L. *Congress: Two Decades of Analysis.* New York: Harper & Row, 1969.

Huntington, Samuel P. "Congressional Responses to the Twentieth Century." In *The Congress and America's Future,* edited by David B. Truman. 2nd ed. Englewood Cliffs, N.J.: Prentice-Hall, 1973.

Hurley, Patricia, and Hill, Kim Quarle. "The Prospects for Issue-Voting in Contemporary Congressional Elections." *American Politics Quarterly* 8 (1980): 425-448.

Jackson, John. *Constituencies and Leaders in Congress.* Cambridge, Mass: Harvard University Press, 1974.

Jacobson, Gary C. *Money In Congressional Elections.* New Haven, Conn.: Yale University Press, 1980.

Jewell, Malcolm E. *Senatorial Politics and Foreign Policy.* Lexington: University of Kentucky Press, 1962.

Jewell, Malcolm E., and Patterson, Samuel C. *The Legislative Process in the United States.* 3rd ed. New York: Random House, 1977.

Johannes, John R. *Policy Innovation in Congress.* Morristown, N. J.: General Learning Press, 1972.

Jones, Charles O. "Representation in Congress: The Case of the House Agricultural Committee." *American Political Science Review* 55 (1961): 358-367.

———. *The Minority Party in Congress.* Boston: Little, Brown & Co., 1970.

———. "The Role of the Congressional Subcommittee." *Midwest Journal of Political Science* 6 (1962): 327-344.

———. "Will Reform Change Congress?" In *Congress Reconsidered,* edited by Lawrence C. Dodd and Bruce I. Oppenheimer. 1st ed. New York: Praeger Publishers, 1977.

Keefe, William J. *Congress and the American People.* Englewood Cliffs, N. J.: Prentice-Hall, 1980.

Keefe, William J., and Ogul, Morris S. *The American Legislative Process.* 4th ed. Englewood Cliffs, New Jersey: Prentice-Hall, 1977.

Kingdon, John W. *Candidates for Office.* New York: Random House, 1968.

———. *Congressmen's Voting Decisions.* New York: Harper & Row, 1973.

Kuklinski, James H. "District Competitiveness and Legislative Roll Call Behavior: A Reassessment of the Marginality Hypothesis." *American Journal of Political Science* 21 (1977): 627-638.

LeLoup, Lance T. *Budgetary Politics.* Brunswick, Ohio: Kings Court Press, 1977.

LeLoup, Lance T., and Shull, Steven. "Congress Versus the Executive: The 'Two Presidencies' Reconsidered." *Social Science Quarterly* 59 (1979): 704-719.

Loewenberg, Gerhard, and Patterson, Samuel. *Comparing Legislatures.* Boston: Little, Brown & Co., 1979.

Lowi, Theodore J. *The End of Liberalism.* New York: W. W. Norton & Co., 1969, 1979.

McPherson, Harry. *A Political Education.* Boston: Little, Brown & Co., 1972.

Manley, John F. *The Politics of Finance.* Boston: Little, Brown & Co., 1970.

Mann, Thomas E. *Unsafe At Any Margin: Interpreting Congressional Elections.* Washington, D.C.: American Enterprise Institute, 1978.

Mann, Thomas E., and Wolfinger, Raymond E. "Candidates and Parties in Congressional Elections." *American Political Science Review* 74 (1980): 617-632.

Matthews, Donald R. *U.S. Senators and Their World.* New York: Vintage Books, 1960.

Mayhew, David R. *Congress: The Electoral Connection.* New Haven, Conn.: Yale University Press, 1974.

———. *Party Loyalty Among Congressmen.* Cambridge, Mass.: Harvard University Press, 1966.

Nelson, Garrison. "Partisan Patterns of House Leadership Change, 1789-1977." *American Political Science Review* 71 (1977): 918-939.

Norpoth, Helmut. "Explaining Party Cohesion in Congress: The Case of Shared Party Attributes." *American Political Science Review* 70 (1976): 1157-1171.

Ogul, Morris S. *Congress Oversees the Bureaucracy.* Pittsburgh: University of Pittsburgh Press, 1976.

Oleszek, Walter J. *Congressional Procedures and the Policy Process.* Washington, D.C.: Congressional Quarterly Press, 1978.

Oppenheimer, Bruce I. *Oil and the Congressional Process: The Limits of Symbolic Politics.* Lexington, Mass.: Lexington Books, 1974.

_____. "Policy Effects of U.S. House Reform: Decentralization and the Capacity to Resolve Energy Issues." *Legislative Studies Quarterly* 5 (1980): 5-30.

_____. "The Rules Committee: New Arm of Leadership in a Decentralized House." In *Congress Reconsidered,* edited by Lawrence C. Dodd and Bruce I. Oppenheimer. 1st ed. New York: Praeger Publishers, 1977.

Orfield, Gary. *Congressional Power: Congress and Social Change.* New York: Harcourt Brace Jovanovich, 1975.

Ornstein, Norman J. *Congress in Change: Evolution and Reform.* New York: Praeger Publishers, 1975.

Ornstein, Norman J., and Elder, Shirley. *Interest Groups, Lobbying and Policymaking.* Washington, D.C.: Congressional Quarterly Press, 1978.

Ornstein, Norman J., and Rohde, David W. "Shifting Forces, Changing Rules, and Political Outcomes: The Impact of Congressional Change on Four House Committees." In *New Perspectives on the House of Representatives,* edited by Robert L. Peabody and Nelson W. Polsby. Chicago: Rand McNally & Co., 1977.

Parker, Glenn R. "The Advantage of Incumbency in House Elections." *American Politics Quarterly* 8 (1980): 449-464.

_____. "Some Themes in Congressional Unpopularity." *American Journal of Political Science* 21 (1977): pp. 93-110.

Parker, Glenn R., and Parker, S. L. "Factions in Committees: The U.S. House of Representatives." *American Political Science Review* 73 (1979): 85-102.

Payne, James L. "The Personal Electoral Advantage of House Incumbents, 1936-1976." *American Politics Quarterly* 8 (1980): 465-482.

Peabody, Robert L. *Leadership in Congress: Stability, Succession and Change.* Boston: Little, Brown & Co., 1976.

Peabody, Robert L., and Polsby, Nelson W., eds. *New Perspectives on the House of Representatives.* 3rd ed. Chicago: Rand McNally, 1977.

Peters, John G., and Welch, Susan. "The Effects of Charges of Corruption on Voting Behavior in Congressional Elections." *American Political Science Review* 74 (1980): 697-708.

Pierce, John C., and Sullivan, John L. *The Electorate Reconsidered.* Beverly Hills, Calif.: Sage Publications, 1980.

Polsby, Nelson W. *Congress and the Presidency.* 3rd ed. Englewood Cliffs, N.J.: Prentice-Hall, 1976.

_____. "Institutionalization in the U.S. House of Representatives." *American Political Science Review* 62 (1968): 144-168.

Polsby, Nelson W.; Gallagher, Miriam; and Rundquist, Barry. "The Growth of the Seniority System in the House of Representatives." *American Political Science Review* 63 (1969): 787-807.

Price, David E. *Who Makes the Laws?* Cambridge, Mass.: Schenkman Publishing Co., 1972.

Price, H. Douglas. "Congress and the Evolution of Legislative Professionalism." In *Congress in Change,* edited by Norman J. Ornstein. New York: Praeger Publishers, 1975.

Ragsdale, Lyn. "The Fiction of Congressional Elections as Presidential Events." *American Politics Quarterly* 8 (1980): 395-398.

Reid, T. R. *Congressional Odyssey: The Saga of a Senate Bill.* San Francisco: W. H. Freeman, 1980.

Rieselbach, Leroy N. *Congressional Politics.* New York: McGraw-Hill, 1973.

———. *Congressional Reform in the Seventies.* Morristown, N. J.: General Learning Press, 1977.

———, ed. *Legislative Reform: The Policy Impact.* Lexington, Mass.: Lexington Books, 1978.

———. *The Roots of Isolationism.* Indianapolis: Bobbs-Merrill & Co., 1966.

Ripley, Randall B. *Majority Party Leadership in Congress.* Boston: Little, Brown & Co., 1969.

———. *Party Leaders in the House of Representatives.* Washington, D.C.: Brookings Institution, 1967.

———. *Power in the Senate.* New York: St. Martin's Press, 1969.

Ripley, Randall B., and Franklin, Grace N. *Congress, the Bureaucracy and Public Policy.* Homewood, Ill.: Dorsey Press, 1980.

Rohde, David W., and Shepsle, Kenneth A. "Democratic Committee Assignments in the U.S. House of Representatives." *American Political Science Review* 67 (1973): 889-905.

Rothman, David J. *Politics and Power.* New York: Atheneum, 1969.

Rudder, Catherine E. "Committee Reform and the Revenue Process." In *Congress Reconsidered,* edited by Lawrence C. Dodd and Bruce I. Oppenheimer. 1st ed. New York: Praeger Publishers, 1977.

Saloma, John S., III. *Congress and the New Politics.* Boston: Little, Brown & Co., 1969.

Schneider, Jerrold E. *Ideological Coalitions in Congress.* Greenwood, Conn.: Greenwood Press, 1979.

Schwarz, John E., and Shaw, L. Earl. *The United States Congress in Comparative Perspective.* Hinsdale, Ill.: Dryden Press, 1976.

Seidman, Harold. *Politics, Position, and Power.* 2nd ed. London: Oxford University Press, 1975.

Shepsle, Kenneth A. *The Giant Jigsaw Puzzle.* Chicago: University of Chicago Press, 1978.

Sinclair, Barbara Deckard. "Determinants of Aggregate Party Cohesion in the U.S. House of Representatives." *Legislative Studies Quarterly* 2 (1977): 155-175.

Stone, Walter J. "The Dynamics of Constituency: Electoral Control in the House." *American Politics Quarterly* 8 (1980): 399-424.

Sullivan, Terry. "Voters Paradox and Logrolling as an Initial Framework for Committee Behavior on Appropriations and Ways and Means." *Public Choice* 25 (1976).

Sundquist, James L. *Politics and Policy.* Washington, D.C.: Brookings Institution, 1968.

Truman, David B. *The Governmental Process.* New York: Alfred A. Knopf, 1951.

Turner, Julius. *Party and Constituency: Pressures on Congress.* Rev. ed. by Edward V. Schneier, Jr. Baltimore: Johns Hopkins Press, 1970.

Uslaner, Eric M. "Policy Entrepreneurs and Amateur Democrats in the House of Representatives." In *Legislative Reform: The Policy Impact,* edited by Leroy N. Rieselbach. Lexington, Mass.: Lexington Books, 1978.

Vogler, David J. *The Politics of Congress.* Boston: Allyn & Bacon, 1974.

———. *The Third House.* Evanston, Ill.: Northwestern University Press, 1971.

Wahlke, John C.; Eulau, Heinz H.; Buchanan, W.; and Ferguson, L.C. *The Legislative System: Explorations in Legislative Behavior.* New York: John Wiley & Sons, 1962.

Wayne, S. J. *The Legislative Presidency.* New York: Harper & Row, 1978.

Weisberg, Herbert F. "Evaluating Theories of Congressional Roll Call Voting." *American Journal of Political Science* 22 (1978): 554-577.

Westefield, L. P. "Majority Party Leadership and the Committee System in the House of Representatives." *American Political Science Review* 68 (1974): 1593-1604.

Wildavsky, Aaron. *The Politics of the Budgetary Process.* Boston: Little, Brown & Co., 1964.

Wilson, Woodrow. *Congressional Government.* Gloucester, Mass.: Peter Smith, 1885, 1973.

Wolfinger, Raymond E., and Hollinger, Joan Heifetz. "Safe Seats, Seniority, and Power in Congress." *American Political Science Review* 59 (1965): 337-349.

Young, James S. *The Washington Community, 1880-1828.* New York: Columbia University Press, 1966.

Index